BRITISH ANTISLAVERY 1833–1870

HOWARD TEMPERLEY

BRITISH
antislavery
1833-1870

UNIVERSITY OF SOUTH CAROLINA PRESS

Columbia, S.C.

First published 1972 in Great Britain by
LONGMAN GROUP LIMITED
London, England

This edition published 1972 in the United States of America by
UNIVERSITY OF SOUTH CAROLINA PRESS
Columbia, South Carolina

International Standard Book Number: 0-87249-268-0
Library of Congress Catalog Card Number: 72-2902

Suggested Library of Congress classification furnished by McKissick Memorial Library of the University of South Carolina:
HT1161.T

Manufactured in the United States of America

For Alison Lynn Temperley

Contents

Preface

This study deals with the activities of British abolitionists during the years following the Emancipation Act of 1833. It sets out to show the principles upon which they acted, the goals they pursued, the methods they adopted and the problems they faced. In particular it seeks to describe how these men, most of whom had played active parts in the struggles over slavery in the British Empire, sought to come to terms with a new situation in which the evils they wished to remedy were to be found chiefly in the territories of foreign powers.

A preliminary word of explanation should perhaps be given about these abolitionists. The term abolitionist is one that could be used to describe a host of individuals and groups—for example those British Ministers, government officials and naval personnel who gave their energies (and in the case of the latter sometimes their lives too) in the struggle against slavery. The great majority of Englishmen, certainly after 1833, can be seen as "abolitionists" in the sense that they disapproved of slavery and wished to see it abolished. But for present purposes the term is used, as it was by contemporaries both in Britain and the United States, to describe those activists who belonged to or supported antislavery organizations. To be an abolitionist in this sense usually entailed, besides an organizational affiliation, a commitment to attitudes and policies not shared by the majority of his fellow countrymen, sincerely opposed to slavery although they were.

Since British concern for the suppression of slavery continued well beyond the end of the century a terminal date has had to be set somewhat arbitrarily. The year 1870 was chosen because by that time most of the initial aims of the abolitionists had been achieved and their attention had not yet turned, as it was to do later, to the problems of Africa and the East.

The preparation of this study has spanned the better part of a decade. It began as a Yale doctoral dissertation, "The British and Foreign Anti-Slavery Society, 1839–1868". Whatever the merits of that original version it was plain that much more could be said about the British antislavery movement than had been possible given my need to focus, rather exclusively, on the work of a single body. Principally lacking, I was aware, was an adequate discussion of government policies and the activities of other groups, such as Buxton's African Civilization Society and the provincial

Garrisonian organizations, whose work touched on that of the BFASS only marginally. The present version represents a major revision. The beginning and terminal dates have been changed, new chapters have been added, and a good deal of superfluous material has been deleted. In addition, I have provided an epilogue which carries the story up to the present day. The principal focal point is still the British and Foreign Anti-Slavery Society, as with any account which aspires to describe the antislavery campaigns of these years it must necessarily be. The BFASS was the metropolitan organization and in humanitarian endeavour, as with so much else in British life, direction came from the centre. But I have sought to pay enough attention to the activities of the provincial bodies and to opinion outside of the capital to keep them in focus and fill out the picture.

I owe a debt of gratitude to many friends and colleagues for their assistance in this undertaking. My debt to the late David M. Potter, who supervised my Yale dissertation and who subsequently encouraged me in facing the task of revision, is simply immense. No one could have been more patient, understanding and painstaking. I should like also to thank David Brion Davis, C. Duncan Rice and Robin Winks of Yale, Louis Billington and John White of the University of Hull, George Shepperson of the University of Edinburgh, Roger Anstey of the University of Kent, Robert C. Reinders of the University of Nottingham, and Edward H. Milligan of Friends House Library, London, for their practical help in reading through my manuscript in its various intermediate versions and for correcting me on many points of detail and substance. Needless to say, such errors as remain are mine and not theirs. I am additionally indebted to Louis Billington and C. Duncan Rice for allowing me access to their unpublished dissertations, and to Dr G. C. Taylor for permitting me to make use of her excellent typescript compilation of British antislavery letters in the Boston Public Library collection. Miss June Lewis of the University of East Anglia typed the final version of the manuscript. Finally I would like to thank the Graduate Fellowship Committee, Yale University, and the American Council of Learned Societies for providing me with the leisure in which to undertake this study.

H.T.

University of East Anglia,
Norwich
August 1971

Introduction

When the British Government announced in the summer of 1833 its plans for abolishing slavery in the sugar colonies, it was at once evident that a major phase in the history of the British antislavery movement was ending. More than 800,000 slaves, the backbone of the economies of the West Indies and Mauritius and the largest body of slaves yet to have been emancipated in modern times, were, as from the first of August 1834, to be set free. They were not, it was true, to be immediately and unconditionally free in the sense of being allowed to do as they pleased. A period of apprenticeship varying in length from four years in the case of non-agricultural to six years in the case of agricultural slaves was to follow, during which it was intended that they should accustom themselves, under appropriate restraints, to the responsibilities of their new status. But there was no longer any doubt that slavery, as it had existed, was doomed and that after a short time emancipation would be complete.

The satisfaction which British abolitionists felt at this announcement was tempered with some misgivings. The Government's measures were not quite those they would have chosen had they been given a free hand. A few of the more radical among them objected vehemently to the clauses giving compensation to owners and most had strong reservations about the apprenticeship scheme. But as practical men they knew well enough that no Act passed by a Parliament representing many different views and interests would ever give them exactly what they wanted. The remarkable thing about the Emancipation Act was that it came so close to doing just that. So for the great majority the knowledge that the holding of chattel slaves by whites within the Empire, for long a major and in recent years virtually the sole object of their attention, was about to be abolished far outweighed any misgivings they had about the manner in which this was to be accomplished. After the years of struggle and frustration, their triumph seemed virtually complete.

Like many victories, the passage of the Emancipation Bill was followed by a period of hiatus. Because they had concentrated so much of their effort on securing the overthrow of colonial slavery, many abolitionists now found themselves at a loss as to what to do next. Disband? Some of the local societies did in fact begin winding up their affairs. But most anti-slavery leaders rejected this course. They had already had enough experience of government inaction and planter intransigence to recognize the need for keeping a watching brief on how the new Act was being applied. But this was not, or so it appeared in the aftermath of victory, a very ambitious undertaking. Was there not something more they could do?

The idea that they should turn their attention to solving the problems of slavery in other parts of the world did not originate with any particular individual or group. In a sense it was already implicit in the assumptions upon which they had been working. If slavery were morally wrong, as they and a large segment of the British public were now convinced it was, then the nationality of the slaveholder became a matter of secondary importance as compared with the obligation to act.

That their thoughts were turning in this direction became increasingly evident as the thirties wore on. The first positive indication that this was how their minds were working appeared in the spring of 1834 when the Agency Committee, formerly an offshoot of the Anti-Slavery Society and later an independent organization in its own right, formally changed its name to The Society for the Universal Abolition of Slavery and the Slave Trade. This first attempt to give the movement an international dimension proved shortlived. But by the end of the decade two new organizations, each with powerful backing, had been established with similar aims in view—Buxton's African Civilization Society and Joseph Sturge's British and Foreign Anti-Slavery Society.

The problems with which these bodies proposed to grapple were formidable ones. In the United States, the slave population at this time was estimated to be approximately 2,750,000, in Brazil 2,500,000, in the Spanish colonies 600,000, in the French colonies 265,000, in the Dutch colonies 70,000, in the Danish and Swedish colonies 30,000, and in Texas 25,000. This was in addition to those held in bondage in the British East Indies and by France, Holland and Portugal in various parts of Asia and Africa, amounting to several millions more; and exclusive also of those held in bondage by independent native powers in the East and in other parts of the world, of whose number it was impossible to form even a rough estimate.[1] Most disturbing of all was the fact that the slave trade, despite all Britain's efforts to have it suppressed, continued unabated. Between 1830 and 1840 upwards of 300,000 Negroes had been exported westward from Africa. Most contemporary estimates were a good deal higher.[2]

In seeking to deal with these aspects of slavery, the British movement

1. British and Foreign Anti-Slavery Society, *Proceedings of the General Anti-Slavery Convention of 1840* (London, 1841), p. 3.
2. Philip D. Curtin, *The Atlantic Slave Trade: A Census* (Madison, Wisconsin, 1969), 37–49, 234. See also Chapters 3 and 9 below.

entered a new phase, not merely in terms of its goals but also in the techniques it used. New methods needed to be adopted and new procedures worked out. The result was that the British abolitionists now found themselves grappling with a bewildering variety of novel and often unexpected problems.

Compared, for example, with their American counterparts, they had, up to this time, found their path remarkably easy, for the simple reason that the British political system, with its principle of parliamentary supremacy, had lent itself to the pursuit of a viable goal—namely statutory prohibition of slavery by the central government. By contrast the American political system, with its principle of federalism, offered no such means for direct action. Discounting the use of the President's discretionary powers in time of war—until the 1860s a purely theoretical consideration— slavery in the United States could be abolished on a national basis only by means of a constitutional amendment requiring the assent of three-quarters of the states.[3] Since roughly half of the states supported slavery (twelve out of twenty-four in 1830, fifteen out of thirty-three in 1860) such a measure was politically out of the question. Similar appeals to states' rights on the part of the West Indies had seldom been taken seriously.[4] When, for example, the Jamaican planters had claimed that Parliament had no right to interfere in the internal affairs of their island their protests were ignored; when they had threatened to secede from the Empire their statements were laughed at, and when they had resorted to coercive legislation their measures were overruled by the Privy Council. Whatever the theoretical status of the West Indian legislatures, Parliament had the power—in the last resort, the military power—to impose its will should it ever decide to do so. Thus so far as slavery in the British Empire was concerned, there had never been any doubt as to where, in the last analysis, authority lay or where abolitionists should apply for redress.

The availability of an appropriate constitutional channel for action had also ensured the support and moderating influence of politicians. This was not because British politicians were more enlightened than politicians elsewhere. (Whether they were or not is here irrelevant.) It was because, in the British Empire, emancipation had been a practical

3. For a more detailed discussion of this issue see Howard Temperley, "The British and American abolitionists compared" in Martin Duberman, ed., *The Antislavery Vanguard* (Princeton, 1965), pp. 343–61.
4. Although this had been a consideration in the 1780s when it strengthened the hand of those abolitionists who believed that the slave trade rather than slavery should be the principal object of attack. Thomas Clarkson, *The History of the Rise, Progress and Accomplishment of the Abolition of the African Slave-Trade by the British Parliament* (2 vols, London, 1808), *1*, 282–7.

proposition in a sense in which it was not in the United States. British
politicians, in short, had been able to attack slavery directly, without
resorting to the sort of devices used by the Americans and while at the
same time remaining well within their recognized sphere of responsibility.

Thus, up to the 1830s, the British movement had been preserved
from many of the difficulties and frustrations which beset the American.
After the 1830s, this was no longer the case. British abolitionists were
no longer primarily concerned with conditions existing within the Empire.
In this respect the Act of 1833 and its sequel, the abolition of apprenticeship, marked the end of an era. As in the United States, abolitionists
were now obliged to seek reforms in areas where their influence could
carry little weight and where there was absolutely no prospect of an early
victory. This was aptly revealed when the British and Foreign Anti-
Slavery Society itself became the recipient of dividends from a Brazilian
mining concern employing slaves, over whose affairs it found itself entirely
powerless.[5] British abolitionists, in fact, were in very much the same position
with respect to what happened to slavery in Brazil or Tunis as the Americans
were with respect to what happened in Mississippi or South Carolina.
They could attempt to exert pressure through the British government
in much the same way that the Americans sought to exert pressure through
the Federal Government; they could stir up public opinion in Britain
just as the Americans could stir up public opinion in the North; they could
send out emissaries, distribute pamphlets, dispatch formal addresses,
harangue visiting clergymen and write articles for newspapers. In short,
they could adopt any one of a number of techniques familiar to their
American counterparts, none of which held out much hope of altering
the basic situation.

One result of this was that the British movement became subject
to many of the same frustrations, and so to many of the same internal
stresses and conflicts, that characterized the American movement throughout: quarrels arose; factionalism spread; groups divided; old policies
were rejected as ineffective; new and equally ineffective policies were
adopted; practical politicians retired to the wings and extremists stepped
boldly forward into the centre of the stage. "Its first concern", observes
Gilbert H. Barnes, speaking of the American movement, "was not
the abolition of slavery; it was 'the duty of rebuke which every inhabitant of the Free States owes to every slaveholder.' Denunciation of

5. British and Foreign Anti-Slavery Society, Minute Books, 28 June, 31 Aug. 1844,
Bodleian Library, Oxford—referred to hereafter as BFASS Minute Books. These
dividends, which had been presented to the Society by conscience-stricken investors,
became such an embarrassment they were returned to the donors.

the evil came first; reform of the evil was incidental to that primary obligation."[6] The same might be said of the later British movement also, though it should be remembered that, in both cases, this choice of policy was not altogether a voluntary one. If the abolitionists did little more than denounce slavery, it was because there was little else that they could do.

A similar parallel is evident in the attitudes of political leaders in the two countries. There is, to cite only one example, a striking affinity between T. B. Macaulay's "My especial obligations in respect to negro slavery ceased when slavery itself ceased in that part of the world for the welfare of which I, as a member of this House, was accountable", and John Quincy Adams' "With the Slave and Abolition Whirligig I hope to have no concern".[7] Both were statements of men who felt, despite their deep-rooted hatred of slavery, that the antislavery movement was no place for practical politicians.

But the most bewildering aspect of the new situation—and here again the parallel with the American movement is evident—was the amount of dissension generated within the movement itself. For abolitionists to disagree over matters of general policy was no new phenomenon. In the past they had differed strongly in their opinions upon such questions as whether to attack slavery or the slave trade or whether to concentrate their efforts on influencing Parliament from within or by public pressure from without. But the dissensions which now arose were more serious. In part, they can be attributed to sheer frustration. Unable to come to grips with their real enemies, antislavery men expressed their combativeness in their relations with one another. This, however, was not the only reason for friction. Many of their difficulties, it is clear, stemmed from the very multiplicity of the means now at their disposal. In dealing with the slave trade, for example, there were three general courses to choose from: they could attempt to cut off the trade at its root by advocating intervention in Africa itself; they could support a policy of naval blockade; or they could attempt to bring pressure to bear upon the individual importing nations. Choosing one of these general courses meant, in turn, selecting from among a number of different and often sharply conflicting methods. Intervention in Africa could mean establishing colonies; setting up trading posts for the encouragement of legitimate commerce; teaching the natives new agricultural techniques; supporting Christian missions, or using

6. Gilbert H. Barnes, *The Anti-Slavery Impulse* (New York, 1933), p. 25.
7. *Hansard's Parliamentary Debates* 77 (26 Feb. 1845), 1300—referred to hereafter as *Hansard*. John Quincy Adams to Dr Benjamin Waterhouse, 15 Oct. 1835, in Samuel Flagg Bemis, *John Quincy Adams and the Union* (New York, 1956), p. 330, note 16.

military units to police the interior. Similarly, bringing pressure to bear
on importing nations could be done by issuing diplomatic protests;
offering to cancel debts; suggesting favourable trade agreements; applying
economic sanctions; fostering the growth of antislavery sentiment among
the inhabitants, or by outright military intervention. The range of alternatives was thus far broader than ever before and included a perplexing
variety of possibilities no one of which was promising enough to secure
unanimity of support.

Nor was it simply over tactics that disagreements now arose. Abolitionists also found themselves divided over matters not entirely connected
with the antislavery cause but pertaining to other public or ideological
questions. Previously the British movement had been remarkably free
from such complications. When it came to attacking slavery, Whigs and
Tories, free-traders and protectionists, Quakers and Baptists, however
differently they felt about other issues, had found relatively little difficulty
in sinking their differences. After 1833 this became more difficult. The
reasons are clear. Abolition had become, politically speaking, something
of a marginal issue, with the result that, even for dedicated abolitionists,
it did not necessarily take precedence over other issues with which they
were concerned. And since slavery could no longer be attacked by direct
means, they were compelled to adopt indirect ones, such as manipulating
tariffs, discouraging the consumption of certain products and attempting
to impose embargoes on goods from slaveholding nations. These methods
naturally bore on questions other than slavery, and when contingent
issues were thus raised antislavery men naturally found themselves at
odds. However firmly they might agree on the essential sinfulness of
slavery, there was no guarantee that they would also agree on, or attach
equal weight to, for example, free trade, pacifism, religion, temperance,
the welfare of the British working classes or the interests of British
merchants. The choice was no longer between slavery and freedom: it
was between such alternatives as benefiting the freedmen in the West
Indies or improving the lot of the workers in Manchester, discouraging
the slave trade abroad or encouraging the consumption of non-alcoholic
beverages at home. So we find the abolitionists struggling with a variety
of conflicting causes and strongly disagreeing with one another over
issues which, for the most part, had no direct bearing on slavery at
all.

Compared with the period which preceded it, this was a confusing
time in the history of the British movement. From the very outset,
abolitionists found themselves involved in a succession of perplexing
situations. Not only were they balked in their attempts to come to grips

with the problems with which they set out to deal, but they were continually being sniped at by other abolitionist groups, criticized in Parliament and in the press, and roundly condemned by large segments of the liberal-minded, antislavery, British population.

And yet, on the world scene, these were years of remarkable achievement. The Atlantic slave trade was ended and the slaves were freed in the United States and in the colonies of most of the European powers. British abolitionists felt justified in taking at least some of the credit for these developments. Thomas Clarkson, describing the earlier movement, once compared it to a river: beginning as a number of springs and rivulets—each, in his attached diagram, appropriately marked with the name of some early abolitionist or humanitarian—the waters combined to become streams which, in turn, became a river, growing ever wider and more majestic as it wound its way towards a sea marked "Universal Freedom".[8] In the minds of British abolitionists this river still flowed on as they saw their own movement growing and achieving a co-ordinated international expression. On the other hand, if one looks at their movement not in its international but in its domestic context quite a different picture emerges. It is the reverse of the one which Clarkson described. Instead of uniting, the waters divided. It was as if instead of flowing to the sea it had entered a delta where it was again transformed into a number of streams, some flowing strongly, some weakly, some turning into sluggish backwaters, some disappearing altogether.

Why this happened and what it meant to those abolitionists whose careers continued on into the forties, fifties and sixties is the burden of what follows.

8. Clarkson, *1*, 30–3, 259–64.

1

The antislavery
tradition

The abolition of slavery in England was the result of a judicial decision. In 1772, James Somerset, a Virginian Negro who had been brought to England by his master, escaped, was befriended by Granville Sharp, and, as a result of the ensuing action in the Court of King's Bench, was set at liberty along with some ten thousand other British Negro slaves. Sharp's subsequent attempts to have the ruling in this case extended to include the slaves in the colonies ended in failure. British Common Law, he learned, did not apply in those parts of the Empire where slavery was recognized by colonial law.[1]

Up to this time, antislavery activity in Britain had consisted largely of unco-ordinated individual efforts. During the 1780s, however, the first organized anti-slavery societies appeared. The first of these, established in 1783, were, significantly enough, the result of Quaker initiative. In August 1782 the Philadelphia Meeting for Sufferings, acting on behalf of the Quakers of that state, dispatched a letter to

1. F. J. Klingberg, *The Anti-Slavery Movement in England* (New Haven, 1926), pp. 40–1.

I

its London counterpart urging the British to use their influence to end the slave trade. A resolution was accordingly submitted to the London Yearly Meeting which in the summer of 1783 approved a petition calling on Parliament to declare the trade illegal.[2] To promote their object the London Quakers established two bodies, an official committee of the Meeting for Sufferings consisting of twenty-three members and an informal committee of six whose main task was to insert antislavery material in metropolitan and provincial newspapers. These were, in embryo at least, antislavery societies and during the next four years they were active in securing interviews with members of government, circulating petitions and distributing such tracts as Joseph Woods's *Thoughts on the Slavery of Negroes*, Anthony Benezet's *Caution and Warning*, and the Meeting for Sufferings' own *The Cause of our Fellow Creatures the Oppressed Africans*.[3] From the first, these committees relied heavily on the already existing hierarchy of Quaker meetings. In the seventeenth century the Meeting for Sufferings, as its name suggests, had been concerned mainly with defending Quakers from persecution. To this end it had established a network of correspondents through whom it had direct access to county quarterly meetings and through them with the area monthly meetings which conducted business for neighbouring Quaker groups. This had proved a highly effective way of mobilizing resistance against persecutors and in the 1730s had been developed further as a means of parliamentary lobbying against successive Affirmation and Tithe Bills. Now the rapid and efficient machinery built up for their own protection proved equally effective in working for others. If the Meeting for Sufferings wanted pamphlets distributed or MPs approached in their constituency areas it had the means to hand. As we shall see, this network of Quaker cells remained the backbone of organized antislavery effort in Britain up to the time of the American Civil War and even beyond.

Quakers were not, of course, the only people who opposed slavery at this time. Granville Sharp was still active, and younger men such as Thomas Clarkson and William Wilberforce were also beginning to turn their attention to the moral dilemmas which it raised. A broadening of the base of antislavery effort occurred in May 1787 with the formation

---

2. Meeting for Sufferings, Philadelphia, to Meeting for Sufferings, London, 15 Aug. 1782 in Letters to and from Philadelphia, *1*, pp. 198–9, and Minutes of the London Meeting for Sufferings, 1780–83, pp. 316 ff, MSS, Friends House, London.
3. Minute Books of the Meeting for Sufferings Committee on the Slave Trade, 1783–92, and Thompson-Clarkson MSS 2/9, Friends House, London. The steps by which this propaganda campaign was mounted are admirably summarized in Patrick C. Lipscomb III, "William Pitt and the abolition of the slave trade" (unpublished Ph.D dissertation, University of Texas, 1960), pp. 72–127.

of the Society for the Abolition of the Slave Trade, which brought together the Quaker and non-Quaker elements in the movement. The committee of this new organization consisted of five of the six members of the unofficial Quaker committee, three other Quakers, and three non-Quakers, among them Granville Sharp, who, as doyen of the British movement, became the Society's first chairman.

Up to this time no clear distinction had been made between slavery and the slave trade as objects of attack. The new society, however, resolved to limit its attention to the trade. Sharp himself appears to have had some doubts on this score but was overruled by his colleagues.[4] In other respects, however, its aims and methods were much the same as those of the original Quaker bodies. But the scale of its operations was much wider. One of its first tasks was to draw up a list of correspondents, including non-Quakers, although according to Clarkson who shared in this undertaking, members of the Society of Friends continued to account for as much as nine-tenths of its support.[5] This assistance was now more important since the new society could no longer rely entirely on the financial backing of the London Quaker bodies. A drive was therefore begun to establish active auxiliary organizations in the main towns throughout the country. Much of this work was done by Thomas Clarkson during a series of tours in 1787–88. The provincial auxiliaries which he established were given the dual roles of circulating antislavery material supplied by London and collecting gifts and subscriptions on behalf of the central committee.

This method of organization proved so successful that in 1789–91 the Society was able to mount the first large-scale campaign in British history to mobilize public opinion in favour of a benevolent cause. It also showed remarkable ingenuity in the methods it employed. These included many of the techniques of popular agitation later adopted by abolitionists in the United States and by radical reformers in Britain—the circulation of petitions, the boycotting of slave produce, the holding of mass gatherings, the insertion of propaganda material in newspapers and the distribution of literature to MPs and other influential citizens. One technique, more reminiscent of modern than of eighteenth- or nineteenth-century methods of agitation, was the widespread currency given to the Society's plaque, designed by Josiah Wedgwood, showing a Negro holding up his manacled hands in supplication over the motto 'AM I NOT A MAN AND A BROTHER', which was henceforward to be the traditional emblem of the movement. Meanwhile the committee was active in presenting its views through

4. Lipscomb, pp. 98–9; Prince Hoare, *Memoirs of Granville Sharp* (London, 1820), pp. 400–1.
5. Clarkson, *1*, 445.

spokesmen in Parliament, among whom Wilberforce quickly distinguished himself as the most influential and eloquent. In short, although some of these techniques were later improved and a number of new ones added, there remains surprisingly little in the methods of later abolitionists which cannot be traced back to this first campaign.[6]

Another notable feature of the movement during these early years was its international-mindedness. Informal links between British, American and French abolitionists had existed for some time and among the Society's first acts was to send letters to the two leading American antislavery groups in Philadelphia and New York, telling them of its existence and aims.[7] It also lost no time in establishing contact with liberal elements in Paris and was gratified, early in 1788, to learn of the establishment of a sister organization there, the Amis des Noirs. An extensive correspondence was carried on between these bodies. It was characteristic that on hearing that Brissot, the founder of the Amis des Noirs, was to visit the United States the London organization should have written to Philadelphia and New York warmly commending him to the hospitality of the Americans.[8] In part this was merely the traditional internationalism of the eighteenth-century intelligentsia, but it also reflected the nature of the problem with which they were obliged to grapple.[9] The slave trade, as their critics were continually pointing out, was a form of international commerce; for one nation to withdraw unilaterally, morally desirable though that might be, would merely leave the field open to its competitors. From the British point of view, the rivals most to be feared were the United States and France—particularly France whose rapidly developing sugar plantations in Santo Domingo were, as a result of massive importations of slaves from Africa, beginning to threaten the position of Britain's own sugar colonies in the West Indies. For Britain to withdraw from the trade would mean not only giving up a profitable form of com-

6. E. M. Hunt, "The North of England agitation for the abolition of the slave trade, 1780–1800" (unpublished MA thesis, University of Manchester, 1959).
7. Thomas E. Drake, *Quakers and Slavery in America* (New Haven, 1950), pp. 85–113; John Woods, "The correspondence of Benjamin Rush and Granville Sharp, 1773–1809", *Journal of American Studies* 1 (1967), 1–38; Hoare, p. 417; Society for the Abolition of the Slave Trade, Minute Books, 5, 17 July 1787, British Museum—referred to hereafter as SAST Minute Books.
8. SAST Minute Books, 8 April 1788.
9. This applied less to the Americans who were at this time more immediately concerned with the emancipation of slaves than with the abolition of the trade. It is significant that in writing to New York and Philadelphia the London organization should have noted that it had been established "With a more particular view to the discouragement of the Slave Trade", *ibid*, 17 July 1787. On the need for international action see Chevalier de Ternant to Granville Sharp, 28 Feb. 1788 quoted in Hoare, p. 421, n. 2.

merce but also sacrificing her position as the world's leading sugar producer. Deprived of their supplies of labour, West Indian planters would be in no position to meet the French challenge. Even those Englishmen who were aware of the horrors of the trade found this course difficult to accept. If anything were to be achieved, most agreed, it would have to be done either by general international agreement or, failing that, by joint action between Britain and France.

Informal talks between the British and French governments were accordingly begun in the autumn of 1787. De Montmorin, the French Foreign Minister, professed himself sympathetic to the British proposals but others, among them Louis XVI, expressed reservations. They pointed out that the policies of other nations and the likely effects on the economy of Santo Domingo would first have to be considered. All this would take time. As it became clear that no immediate results were to be expected from these negotiations, abolitionists increasingly pinned their hopes on the efforts of political pressure groups working within France itself. In August 1789 Clarkson went to Paris to give his personal assistance to the Amis des Noirs in presenting its case to the French Assembly. Initially, hopes were high. His arrival coincided with the storming of the Bastille and he was much encouraged by the ferment of liberal thought he encountered. But, like the British, the French were unwilling to act on their own and for want of any positive British commitment the Assembly voted the proposals down. Disappointed, Clarkson returned to England at the end of six months. All hopes of joint action were subsequently wiped out by the advent of war.[10]

The immediate effect of this conflict and of the increasing radicalism of the French revolutionaries was to weaken the cause. By diverting energies elsewhere and by making reforms of all kinds seem evidence of Jacobin influence, a climate of opinion was created hostile to innovation. When the slaves in Santo Domingo rose in rebellion in August 1791 their action was widely attributed to the subversive activities of abolitionists. British planters prophesied similar uprisings in their own communities unless agitation was promptly stopped. During the next decade the abolition question was almost forgotten. Between 1797 and 1804 the London Abolition Committee did not hold a single meeting.[11]

Nevertheless, the events of these years helped to prepare the way for victory. The Santo Domingo rebellion, alarming though it was to British planters, removed for the time being the threat of foreign competition.

10. Lipscomb, pp. 166–80; Earl Leslie Griggs, *Thomas Clarkson, Friend of the Slaves* (London, 1936), pp. 51–9.
11. SAST Minute Books, 1797–1804.

Meanwhile, within the Empire itself, a new challenge to their interests was appearing. The acquisition of Trinidad by the Treaty of Amiens in 1802, the conquest in 1803 of Berbice, Essequibo, Demerara, St Lucia and Tobago, and the likelihood that before the war was over yet other territories would fall into British hands, constituted a threat to the old-established sugar interests. As British possessions these colonies enjoyed equal access to British markets. Their new lands were fertile. Providing they could get the labour they needed there was little doubt that they would soon be able to out-produce and undersell the older colonies. Already many planters were producing at a loss. The only solution was to prevent their rivals obtaining labour. This led West Indians to reconsider their attitude towards the trade and some of them to come out openly in support of abolition. Capitalizing on this change of front and on the recent entry into Parliament of the new liberal Irish members, the abolitionists in 1804 renewed their campaign. In 1805 an abolition Bill was narrowly defeated in the Commons. The following year, thanks to the support of the new Fox–Grenville Ministry and a clever exploitation of the "national interest" case by the abolitionists, a Bill providing for the abolition of the trade to the conquered colonies triumphantly passed both Houses. In 1807 this was superseded by a stronger measure which forbade the carrying of slaves in British vessels and their importation into any British colony.[12]

In choosing to concentrate their energies on the slave trade rather than on slavery, British abolitionists had been swayed by a variety of considerations. To have attacked both simultaneously would have meant demanding more than public opinion could be expected to accept.[13] Of the two, the trade was patently the more vulnerable. Even the unsentimental British public had been shocked by disclosures such as those in the *Zong* case in 1781, in which it was shown that a slaver captain, in order to collect on his insurance, had had 132 ailing slaves thrown overboard. Whatever the horrors of slavery, they could scarcely compare with these. Contemporary opinion, moreover, was highly sensitive on questions involving private property and established institutions to which categories slavery clearly belonged, whereas regulating trade had long been recognized as a function of Parliament.

So conscious were the abolitionists at this stage that they might be thought to be asking too much that the Society had felt obliged in 1788

12. Lipscomb, pp. 346–51, 445–503; L. J. Ragatz, *The Fall of the Planter Class in the British Caribbean, 1763–1833: A Study in Social and Economic History* (New York, 1928), pp. 204–307; Eric Williams, *Capitalism and Slavery* (Chapel Hill, 1944), pp. 149–50.
13. Hoare, pp. 415, 427–8; Clarkson, *1*, 286–8.

to issue a public disclaimer stating that "however acceptable a temperate and gradual abolition of slavery might be to the wishes of Individuals it never formed any part of the Plan of this Society".[14] This was true, although it was also perfectly clear that the arguments being used to discredit the one could also be used (as they later were) to discredit the other. To this extent the position from which the second stage of the assault would be launched was already being prepared. Nevertheless, the fact remains that so long as the struggle over the trade continued, little thought was given to the practical problems of coping with slavery itself. This would not seem to have caused the abolitionists much uneasiness. When occasionally their minds did turn in the direction of slavery, they readily found arguments to support the course they had chosen. If the slave trade were abolished, so they told themselves, the price of slaves would increase and planters, no longer able to regard their Negroes as expendable, would be obliged to treat them more humanely. Some carried the argument a stage further by pointing out that since free labour was cheaper and more efficient than slave labour, piecemeal and ultimately complete emancipation would result. "By aiming at the abolition of the slave-trade" Clarkson asserted, "they were laying the axe at the very root."[15]

The failure of the West Indian planters to modify their practices in accordance with these benign economic laws only gradually became apparent. The abolitionists' attention had meanwhile turned elsewhere. In 1807 the Society for the Abolition of the Slave Trade, its work completed, was replaced by a new organization, the African Institution.[16] The aims of this body were threefold: to see that the new laws against the slave trade were properly enforced; to encourage legitimate commerce with Africa, and to persuade other countries to follow Britain's example by giving up the trade. The first of these objects was soon achieved, for there was never any doubt of Britain's determination to make the new legislation effective. The other two proved more elusive. During its early years, the Institution was much concerned with the new British crown colony of Sierra Leone. Humanitarians first became interested in this colony in 1789 when it was made a refuge for freed Negroes taken to Nova Scotia after the American Revolution. The settlement was later expanded as a private commercial venture. In neither capacity had it lived up to expectations. In 1808 it was taken over by the British government more out of reluctance to leave it any longer in the hands of incompe-

14. SAST Minute Books, 12 Aug. 1788.
15. Clarkson, *I*, 286.
16. There is still no adequate modern study of the work of this organization. Accounts of its many activities will, however, be found in its *Reports* (27 vols, London, 1807–27).

tent private individuals than with any expectation of profit. But despite
this dubious record, the African Institution had high hopes of turning
it into a progressive, well run colony to serve as a model to African nations
nearby. In this it was disappointed. The Institution's limited resources—
its annual income was seldom more than £1,000, scarcely enough to
cover its domestic activities—and a succession of scandals involving the
colony's administration brought discredit to the Institution and disillusionment to its members. As a result, interest in Africa declined, and from 1814
onwards the Institution's attention focused increasingly on the third objective, the suppression of the slave trade through international agreement.[17]

The full magnitude of this task was only just becoming apparent.
While the Napoleonic wars continued, the world's mercantile powers
had been too preoccupied with other matters to give much thought to the
traffic, although by 1814 four of them besides Britain—Denmark, the
United States, Sweden and Holland—had withdrawn from it. With the
advent of peace, however, there opened up the prospect of making these
laws general and perhaps even of making the trade, like piracy, a matter
for international action. The African Institution threw its full weight into
the struggle. In 1814 eight hundred petitions bearing almost a million
signatures were submitted to Parliament, urging the government to do
everything in its power to have the trade outlawed.[18] These exhortations
were largely superfluous. Ever since 1807 suppression had been not
merely an official aim but an active policy. The real problem, as became
evident at the Congresses of Paris and Vienna, was not getting Britain
to act but persuading other countries to respond. France, in particular,
was eager to reopen the traffic. She joined with Spain and Portugal in
pointing out that while the British had seen that their colonies were kept
well stocked with slaves during the war, other nations had not. It was only
just that they should be allowed a period in which to make up for lost
time before they too withdrew from the trade. The British rejected this
argument and backed up their demands with generous offers of territorial
concessions (France was offered Trinidad) and financial subsidies (Spain
was promised £800,000) in return for their cooperation. These efforts
were of no avail and although a general declaration of the powers gathered
at Vienna was obtained which described suppression as a "great and noble
cause" all attempts to reach specific agreement failed. The results of
the Aix la Chapelle Congress in 1818 were equally unsatisfactory. By 1820

17. Christopher Fyfe, *A History of Sierra Leone* (London, 1962), pp. 105–12,
122–3; Philip D. Curtin, *Image of Africa: British Ideas and Action, 1780–1850*
(Madison, Wisconsin, 1964), pp. 142–3.
18. Sir George Stephen, *Anti-Slavery Recollections: in a series of letters addressed
to Mrs Beecher Stowe* (London, 1854), p. 55.

it was clear that while Britain remained firmly committed to suppression, her success would depend on her ability to negotiate effective suppression treaties with each individual power. Until this network of treaties was complete the slave trade, under whatever flags traders chose to sail, seemed destined to continue.[19]

The failure of their policies on the coast of Africa and the inability of Britain to sway foreign powers were not the only disappointments the abolitionists met at this time. Evidence had gradually been accumulating that the improvement in the treatment of slaves which had been expected to follow the cutting off of the trade to the colonies was not occurring. Conditions on the plantations had apparently changed little since 1807. Planters still clung obstinately to their old ways. Accounts of particular cases of mistreatment which filtered back to England showed only too clearly that colonial courts were as reluctant as ever to interfere between masters and slaves and, when they did so, to impose effective punishments upon the former. Comparisons with United States census records revealed that West Indian Negroes died earlier and produced fewer offspring, proof, so it was claimed, that the British slave system was harsher and that planters were still practising their old technique of working their charges to death. All this was disquieting and led the leaders of the movement to wonder if more direct action might not be needed. If the planters continued to pursue policies contrary both to humanity and their own interests was it not time someone acted for them?[20]

These ideas gave a new impetus and direction to the antislavery movement and led, in the spring of 1823, to the establishment of a new body, the Anti-Slavery Society. In membership this organization and the African Institution were not very different. Some of the aristocratic trimmings were swept away—two dukes, two marquises, eleven earls—and replaced by an approximately equal number of commoners. But the

19. For more detailed accounts of Britain's early efforts to secure suppression by international agreement, see W. L. Mathieson, *Great Britain and the Slave Trade, 1839–1865* (London, 1929), pp. 1–27; Sir Reginald Coupland, *The British Anti-Slavery Movement* (London, 1933), pp. 151 ff; Christopher Lloyd, *The Navy and the Slave Trade: the suppression of the African slave trade in the nineteenth century* (London, 1949), pp. 39–78; Klingberg, pp. 135–70; Griggs, pp. 112–21.
20. Thomas Clarkson, *Thoughts on the Necessity of Improving the Conditions of the Slaves in the British Colonies* (London, 1823), pp. 1 ff; Anon, *Negro Slavery, or, a view of some of the more prominent features of that state of society as it exists in the United States of America and in the colonies of the West Indies, especially in Jamaica* (London, 1823), p. 39. Demographic comparisons between American and West Indian slavery involved more problems than the abolitionists realized. See *Correspondence between John Gladstone, Esq., M.P. and James Cropper Esq., on the present state of slavery in the British West Indies and in the United States of America* (Liverpool, 1824), pp. 44–7.

executive committees contained a similar core of Quakers and other hardworking humanitarians, among them Clarkson, Wilberforce, Zachary Macaulay, William Allen, James Stephen and Samuel Hoare, all veterans of earlier struggles. There were also some newcomers: Samuel Gurney, George Stacey, James Cropper, T. B. Macaulay and, most notable of all, Thomas Fowell Buxton, who in 1824 took over from Wilberforce the role of leader and parliamentary spokesman.[21] The African Institution, although it remained in being until 1827, declined in influence as attention turned from the old issues of the slave trade and African civilization to the new issue of colonial slavery.

The aims of the Anti-Slavery Society, or, to give it its full title, the Society for the Mitigation and Gradual Abolition of Slavery throughout the British Dominions, were modest. At least they seem modest by later standards although, needless to say, many contemporaries regarded them as dangerously radical. It did not demand the immediate overthrow of slavery, merely the adoption of measures to protect slaves from wanton mistreatment, together with a plan for gradual emancipation leading ultimately to complete freedom. By limiting itself to such proposals it sought to enlist the support not only of radicals but of conservatives and even of the planters themselves.

That there was already a good deal of sympathy in the country at large was immediately evident. In late years interest in antislavery had flagged. The African Institution, because it preferred to work quietly through recognized government channels, had never sought, and had certainly never succeeded, in arousing much popular enthusiasm. But Clarkson, stumping the country once again, was able to report that a general sense of goodwill towards the cause still existed and could easily be made into an effective political force. He was especially encouraged by the readiness of people to establish local auxiliaries. By 1826 there were seventy-one such bodies contributing to the Society's funds. Once again Quaker participation was much in evidence, although by no means all the auxiliaries were Quaker run and relatively few were entirely Quaker in membership. The metropolitan Quaker organization also came to the Society's assistance with regular annual donations of between £300 and £1,000.[22]

21. Twenty-four of the fifty-five original vice-presidents and committee members of the Anti-Slavery Society were also vice-presidents or directors of the African Institution. The Duke of Gloucester was president of both organizations. Anti-Slavery Society, *First Annual Report* (London, 1824), pp. ii–iii; African Institution, *Eighteenth Report of the Directors* (London, 1824), pp. i–ii.
22. Thomas Clarkson, "Diary, 1823–24", MSS, National Library of Wales, Aberystwyth; Anti-Slavery Society, *Accounts of Receipts and Disbursements 1823–6, 1827–8, 1829–30, 1831* (London, 1826–31). The actual grants received from the London Society of Friends were, 1824: £300; 1825: £400; 1826–1830: £500 per annum; 1831: £1,000.

As the new leader of the cause, Buxton lost no time in presenting the Society's views to Parliament. On 15 May 1823, he submitted a proposal to the House calling for the emancipation at birth of all children born after an agreed date, and at the same time for legislation to protect those who remained in bondage from the more flagrant abuses of the existing system. By adopting such a plan the Government would not be depriving the slave holders of their existing human property but merely of the increase on that property. The amelioration of conditions would, in the long run, benefit the owner as much as the slave.[23]

Although it sympathized with some aspects of this scheme, the Liverpool Ministry felt that it was altogether too radical. Replying on behalf of the Government, George Canning submitted an alternative set of resolutions. With the Negroes in their existing state he pointed out, it was still too early to consider emancipation as a practical measure. But, in view of some recent reports from the West Indies it was obvious that something needed to be done at once to improve their condition and to prepare them for eventual freedom. The problem was who should be responsible? It was the Government's view that the formulation and execution of appropriate measures should rightly be left to the colonists themselves.[24]

The adoption of these somewhat vague proposals, which were to constitute the basis of official policy for the next decade, did little to placate the abolitionists. It was plain that in delegating responsibility to the colonies the Government was evading the issue. Nevertheless, it was now committed to taking some action. On 28 May Lord Bathurst, Secretary for War and Colonies, wrote to colonial governors telling them about Parliament's resolutions and enclosing a copy of Canning's speech. Six weeks later, on 9 July, he sent a circular outlining in more detail the kind of measures the Government had in mind. It was particularly anxious, the circular explained, that slaves be given more opportunity for religious instruction, that obstacles to manumission be removed, that slave families not be broken up, that the flogging of women be discontinued entirely and that in general the use of the lash be more carefully regulated. It ended with a request that these proposals be given the sanction of law at the earliest possible opportunity.[25]

Had the planters chosen to follow these instructions, as they could well have done, secure in the knowledge that any laws they made and were responsible for enforcing could always be evaded, emancipation would almost certainly have come much later than it did. Instead, they adopted a defiant stance. In Jamaica, where resistance was especially pronounced,

23. *Hansard*, 9 (15 May 1823), 257–75.   24. *Ibid*, 275–87.
25. Copies of Bathurst's letter and circular are reprinted in Klingberg, Appendix B.

a committee of the Assembly accused the Government of having embraced the "principles laid down by the enemies of the colonies" and some members even went so far as to call for immediate secession from the Empire. In Barbados a mob of settlers, believing that one of the missionaries sympathized with Bathurst's views, attacked and wrecked his chapel. In Demerara events took an even nastier turn. The excitement among the whites was communicated to the Negroes, and resulted in an insurrection which was duly crushed with extreme and largely gratuitous brutality.

The lines were now clearly drawn. In the years that followed the pattern became only too familiar: Government instructions; opposition by the Assemblies; irresponsible acts of violence; strenuous denunciation on the part of the Anti-Slavery Society leading to more Government instructions and more opposition. Had it not been for the unsettled state of national politics at this time the cycle might have been broken sooner. As it was the process was allowed to continue, each episode adding to the accumulated backlog of impatience and frustration.[26]

Thus by 1830 few, and least of all the supporters of the antislavery party, had any illusions about the effects of the Government's policy. So far the Anti-Slavery Committee, supported by its network of provincial auxiliaries, had concentrated its efforts on working through Parliament. Now lack of progress made it turn to other methods. For some time its younger and more radical elements had been pressing for a more aggressive approach and, specifically, for an appeal to the people themselves rather than to their elected representatives. The success of this type of campaign, they claimed, had already been proved, though on a limited scale, in London itself. A similar appeal should now be made to the country at large through the agency of salaried lecturers. Buxton and the conservative wing of the Society were not averse to this proposal and in the early summer of 1831 a subcommittee was established to put the new plan into effect.[27]

The Agency Committee, as this new body was called, consisted originally of eighteen members. It was supposed to meet daily but in practice this proved too demanding, with the result that most of the administration work devolved upon an inner caucus of three members, George Stephen, son of the abolitionist James Stephen, and two Quakers, Joseph

26. Accounts of this phase of the antislavery struggle will be found in Klingberg, pp. 182–272; Coupland, pp. 118–34; Mathieson, pp. 115–95, and W. L. Burn, *Emancipation and Apprenticeship in the British West Indies* (London, 1937), pp. 80–96.

27. Agency Committee, *Report of the Agency Committee of the Anti-Slavery Society Established in June 1831 for the Purpose of Disseminating Information by Lectures on Colonial Slavery* (London, 1832).

and Emmanuel Cooper. They engaged five lecturers, each at a salary of £200 a year, and assigned them to specific districts with the responsibility of arousing public opinion there. Two of these lecturers played prominent roles in the later movement, John Scoble as Secretary of the British and Foreign Anti-Slavery Society and George Thompson as the leader of the Garrisonian faction. The Committee also received the gratuitous services of a number of others, including those of that fervid but somewhat eccentric abolitionist, Captain Charles Stuart, recently returned from the United States where he had been assisting in the revivalist efforts of Charles Finney and his holy band.[28]

The methods used by the Committee had, in fact, much in common with those used by religious revivalists. In adapting them to the needs of the antislavery cause, it established a new and highly effective technique later used with even greater effect in the United States.[29] Committee lecturers went from town to town, speaking in public halls and meeting houses and urging their audiences to circulate petitions, thus paving the way for the formation of local auxiliaries. By the end of 1832, Stephen later claimed, there were 1,200 such organizations scattered through the country.[30]

From the beginning, the Committee had many of the characteristics of an independent organization, although it did not officially separate from the Anti-Slavery Society until the summer of 1832. The reasons for this separation were partly administrative and partly ideological. The agency system had proved so successful, not least financially—total receipts during its first six months amounted to well over a £1,000[31]— that it was now well able to stand on its own feet. The older body, although pleased to see public opinion being aroused, had continued to think mainly in terms of working through Parliament and was suspicious and possibly a little jealous at the growing influence of a group over which it found it had little control. The Agency Committee, in turn, resented the interference of the Anti-Slavery Society and distrusted the conservatism

28. Stuart is an interesting case of someone who played a part in the antislavery movements on both sides of the Atlantic. In 1825, as Principal of Utica High School, he had become friendly with Theodore Dwight Weld and had actually helped to support him for a time. He was later instrumental in converting Weld to the antislavery cause. After working with the Agency Committee, he returned to the United States. See below, p. 195.

29. See Chapter 10 below.

30. Stephen, p. 161. See also p. 192 below.

31. In addition to the sums collected by its agents, the Committee had received a number of large contributions, mainly from Quakers—James Cropper gave £500, Joseph Sturge £250. On at least one occasion during the intensive campaign of 1832 the Committee was bailed out by the Society of Friends. Agency Committee, *Report*, p. 22; Stephen, pp. 158, 186-7.

of its members.[32] It was the contention of these younger abolitionists that the Society had erred in two ways: it had limited its emotional appeal to what they regarded as a select group of "pious sentimentalists"— namely the Clapham Sect—which was not only detached from the people but actually distrusted by them, and, at the same time, by thinking too much in terms of what Parliament would or would not accept, had confused the moral issue of slavery with questions of political and economic expediency. "It was evident," Stephen later recalled, "that if the religious world could be induced to enter upon the subject, severing it from all its political relations and viewing it simply as a question between God and man, the battle was won."[33] Not that the Committee was averse to making political and economic capital out of the question when this could be done without compromising its moral views. In its instructions to lecturers it stressed the benefits which would accrue to Britain as a result of emancipation. Commercially, slavery was mischievous. Colonies which simply produced raw materials were of less value to the mother country than those which absorbed manufactured goods as well. By freeing the slaves, Britain would be raising up a population of consumers. Adam Smith could be quoted as an authority on this point. Lecturers were also urged to relate British slavery to the forms of slavery which had existed in the ancient world and to point out that, mild though these had been, they had always involved those who embraced them in ruin.[34] But, fundamentally, the argument must always rest on the doctrine that slavery was a crime in the eyes of God and as such should be immediately and unconditionally abolished. Only by making slaveholding a "sin" and so distinguishing it from other forms of social evil could an effective appeal be made to the "sober, honest, well meaning and consistent Christians" in the community.[35] In the Committee's view, the antislavery struggle was:

a question essentially of a religious character and though in some degree mixed up on the one hand with matters of political economy and on the other with the liberty of the subject it is important not to abandon the high ground of Christian duty for the sake of gaining the support of a party, or exacting the applause of a popular assembly.[36]

While the notion of the essential sinfulness of slavery was one which people found little difficulty in accepting, its corollary, that slavery should

32. David B. Davis, "James Cropper and the British Anti-Slavery Movement, 1823–1833", *Journal of Negro History*, 46 (1961), 166–8.
33. Stephen, p. 160.
34. "The private instructions to the Lecturers employed by the Agency Anti-slavery Society", in *ibid*, pp. 253–8.
35. *Ibid*, p. 160.
36. "Letter of Instructions", June 1831, in *ibid*, p. 138.

be immediately and unconditionally abolished, met with more resistance. Naturally, many wondered about the practical implications of such a policy. Did it mean, as the West Indians claimed, "emancipation from all control, at once unlimited in its character and instant in its execution"? This, Stephen told his agents, never had been contemplated. What had been meant was simply "the immediate substitution of *judicial* for *private and irresponsible authority* involving the simultaneous establishment of equality with the free born subject in the enjoyment of civil rights".[37] After all, laws already existed to protect society from the irresponsible or malicious actions of individuals and there was no reason for supposing that these would prove inadequate in the present instance.

Thus there were now two national societies, one seeking to influence Parliament mainly from within by introducing motions and lobbying members, and the other attempting to bring pressure from without by appealing directly to the public conscience. In practice, however, there appears to have been a good deal of overlapping. Despite internal wrangling and some personal bitterness, of which the public remained largely unaware, the two organizations continued to have much in common.[38] Both were heavily dependent on Quaker financial support. In the course of the 1832 campaign the Meeting for Sufferings' Standing Committee on Slavery

37. *Ibid*, p. 137. Immediacy became the official doctrine of abolitionists on the two sides of the Atlantic at more or less the same time, reflecting in both cases the failure of gradualist policies. David B. Davis, "The emergence of immediatism in British and American antislavery thought," *Mississippi Valley Historical Review,* 49 (1962–3), pp. 219–22; Howard Temperley, "British and American abolitionists compared", in *The Antislavery Vanguard: New Essays on the Abolitionists,* ed. M. M. Duberman (Princeton, 1965), pp. 352–54.

38. Stephen's *Anti-Slavery Recollections,* written more than twenty years after the event, contain many inaccuracies and contradictions and are particularly biased in their treatment of the Anti-Slavery Committee. They are, however, the fullest account we have of the Agency Committee's activities. The Committee's own minute books have now disappeared, having been taken, so it was later asserted, by Stephen to Australia when he emigrated there in 1855. The minute books of the Anti-Slavery Society, which have been preserved (they are in Rhodes House, Oxford) are not always very revealing so far as the Agency Committee is concerned. They do, however, show that Stephen's memory was playing him false when he claimed that the Committee was, from the first, an independent organization. This is borne out by the Committee's first *Report* . . . (London, 1832) in which it describes itself simply as "The Agency department of the Anti-Slavery Society". Stephen is also wrong in his claim that the Anti-Slavery Society objected to its policy of arousing public opinion. The Society had, in fact, endorsed this policy. The break, when it did finally occur, on 4 July 1832, was over the general issue of its supervisory powers and specifically over the question of its right to inspect materials prior to publication. See Davis, *Mississippi Valley Historical Review, 49,* 222. Although correct in drawing attention to Stephen's errors, Davis tends to gloss over the very real antagonisms which existed between these two organizations, and to which others besides Stephen bear witness. See pp. 26, 33–4 below.

granted £2,500 to the Anti-Slavery Society and £1,800 to the Agency Committee.[39] This was in addition to the substantial sums given by individual Quakers, many of whom contributed to both bodies. The Agency Committee, of course, had taken the lead in popularizing the notion of immediatism, but the Anti-Slavery Society, too, was moving away from its earlier policies of amelioration and gradualism. Both were further agreed that emancipation could be achieved only through the intervention of the British government. Their differences, in short, related to emphasis and method rather than basic doctrine or policy and so constituted no bar to cooperation. Thus they continued working together, directing their respective affairs from adjacent offices at 18 Aldermanbury Street, up to the eve of the Emancipation Act itself.

The antislavery campaign of 1832 was helped by the simultaneous struggle over the reform of Parliament. The excitement over this issue, the passage of the Reform Bill in June, the subsequent dissolution of Parliament, and the preparations for a general election, led to a general feeling of exhilaration. Reform was in the air and for the moment there was no clear idea of where it would end. Inspired by the mood of the country, the Agency Committee redoubled its efforts, focusing attention on winning the support of the new electors. Special boards of correspondence were established in London, Edinburgh and Dublin to coordinate local efforts. A nationwide poster campaign was organized—a step which, according to Stephen, the older society regarded with its customary suspicion. Sympathizers were further urged to obtain pledges of support from candidates, and when candidates disagreed with one another, to concentrate on "the two or three respectable voters who could, often, decide a candidate's fate".[40]

The election was held in December, and when Parliament reassembled in January 1833 it was clear that the agitation had had its effect. Buxton expressed himself delighted at the temper of the new House. The Ministry, however, still appeared reluctant to act. There was no allusion to slavery in the King's speech and when Buxton, alarmed at this omission, gave notice of his intention to introduce a motion, efforts were made to dissuade him. The Agency Committee reacted promptly by launching a new campaign. "Sin will lie at our door," one abolitionist declared, "if we do not agitate, agitate, agitate.... The people must emancipate the slaves for the Government never will."[41] A protest meeting was held in Exeter

39. Minute and Account Books of the Standing Committee of the Meeting for Sufferings Appointed to Aid in Promoting the Total Abolition of Slavery and the Slave Trade, 1820–1833, MSS, 115–17, Friends House, London.
40. Stephen, pp. 167–9, 184–7.
41. Henry Richard, *Memoirs of Joseph Sturge* (London, 1864), pp. 99–102.

Hall, in the Strand, from where a huge crowd marched in procession through Whitehall to Downing Street to present its resolutions to the Prime Minister.

In fact, the cabinet was more ready to accept emancipation than was supposed. As early as 14 January, it had resolved on "entire emancipation of the slaves to take effect from 1 January 1835 or January 1837, probably the former".[42] Its delay was less the result of reluctance than of the difficulty it found in framing a Bill which would put its decision into effect and, at the same time, cause the least possible dislocation to production, for it was generally assumed that, once freed, the Negroes would refuse to work.[43] It was around this question rather than the general desirability of emancipation that the discussion in the cabinet and the later debates in Parliament largely revolved.

The ministerial plan, drawn up by Sir James Stephen and presented to Parliament by Lord Stanley on 14 May, was vigorously debated. In its original form it provided that, as from 1 August 1834, slavery, as a legal status, would cease to exist throughout the British colonies. Children under the age of six at the time the Act came into force, or born subsequently, would be immediately freed. All others were to be registered as apprenticed labourers for a period of eleven years in the case of field hands and six years in that of domestics. As apprentices they would be required to devote threequarters of their time to the service of their masters in return for food and clothing, the remaining quarter being free for them to use as they chose. In return, the planters would receive a loan of fifteen million pounds.[44]

Abolitionists found two features of the plan particularly obnoxious— the prolonged and, as they regarded it, wholly unnecessary period of apprenticeship and the compensatory loan. On the first of these issues the Government was prepared to compromise, and after some debate the length of apprenticeship was reduced to four years in the case of domestics and six in the case of field hands. But on the question of compensation it remained obdurate, actually substituting for the proposed loan an outright gift of £20 million, a step justified, so it claimed, by the shortening of apprenticeship. This new plan placed the abolitionists in a difficult position and for the first time there appeared the possibility of an open breach between the two organizations.[45] Buxton and the Anti-Slavery Society, although opposed to compensation, were prepared to accept it rather than see the measure defeated, in which event they foresaw serious

42. Burn, p. 103.   43. *Ibid*, p. 105.   44. *Ibid*, p. 116–17.
45. Charles Buxton, *Memoirs of Sir Thomas Fowell Buxton, Baronet, with Selections from his Correspondence* (London, 1848), p. 327.

disturbances in the West Indies. The Agency Committee, on the other hand, viewing the issue from a moral standpoint, could see no justification whatever for compensation. The doctrine of the essential sinfulness of slavery, Sir George Stephen later wrote, "disowned compensation: it did more; it reprobated it as an indirect participation in the crime". Compensating the slaveholder for the loss of his slaves was like compensating the criminal for the loss of his stolen property.[46] The supporters of the Committee therefore urged determined opposition, pointing out that the Ministry, given the state of popular excitement, would have no alternative but to bring in a new and more satisfactory measure. In later years and in deference to their American allies, who held similar views on compensation, these abolitionists were to set great store by the stand they took at this time.[47] In fact, they exercised little influence since the struggle was now in Parliament where the antislavery cause was represented by Buxton and his colleagues. Nevertheless, the two leading spokesmen of the radical wing of the movement, Daniel O'Connell and Joseph Pease, were among the minority who voted against the Ministry on this issue.[48]

The Bill which finally passed into law on 29 August 1833, although not entirely to the liking of the British antislavery leaders, represented as complete a victory as could reasonably be expected in the circumstances. Viewed from any but their own perfectionist standpoint it was an amazing achievement, the more so because it had been accomplished in so short a time. After the false starts and failures of the years after 1807, the antislavery body had in 1823 succeeded in drawing together and launching a crusade which in ten years had given them almost complete victory. Or so it seemed, though much still depended upon how the new Act was applied and how the West Indians responded to it.

46. Stephen, p. 191.
47. British and Foreign Anti-Slavery Society, *Proceedings of the General Anti-Slavery Convention of 1840*, pp. 459–60, 533.
48. *Hansard, 20* (31 July 1833), 206.

2

Emancipation and after

Between the passage of the Emancipation Bill and 1 August 1834, when it took effect, a period of eleven months elapsed. Although to outside observers this seemed a long time to wait it gave those actually responsible for administering the measure little enough time to come to terms with the problems involved. The Act itself was not intended to be comprehensive but merely laid down general guidelines. It was left to the colonial assemblies, acting in conjunction with the Colonial Office and the colonial governors, to decide such matters as the hours during which apprentices would work, the punishments to be imposed for failures to meet the new requirements and the duties of the special magistrates provided for in the Act. These last were individuals appointed by the Colonial Office to see that the measure was fairly and impartially administered. All this naturally involved a great deal of preparation, much more, certainly, than would have been involved if the Government had followed the abolitionists' advice and opted for immediate emancipation. Instead, it was now faced with having to define an entirely new category of person, the apprentice, who would be neither a slave nor a freeman but who would have some of the characteristics of both.

While the Colonial Office and the colonial assemblies struggled with these problems, the two antislavery societies continued to meet. So far as the Anti-Slavery Society was concerned, there seemed little to do but to await the issue of events. But among the younger and more radical elements associated with the Agency Committee significant developments were occurring. In part these followed naturally from the assumptions upon which they were already working. In committing themselves to the view that slavery was a "sin" and giving the struggle against it many of the attributes of a religious crusade they had, unconsciously, prepared themselves for new undertakings. Slavery, after all, was a sin wherever it occurred, irrespective of the nationality of the sinner, or, for that matter, of his victim. "Benevolence, true Christian benevolence", *The Abolitionist* declared "is not bounded by latitudes, or limited to soil."[1] To this extent the final phases of the British struggle had prepared the way for a widening of the enterprise. To explain the developments which actually occurred, however, allowance must also be made for individual circumstances, and, in particular, for the presence in Britain at this juncture of a young and still relatively unknown American abolitionist, William Lloyd Garrison.

Since the early days of the struggle against the slave trade, the British had paid little attention to antislavery developments in the United States. Slavery there, because it was a more integral part of the economy and because Negroes constituted a social challenge of a kind which the British did not have to face, presented a rather different problem. In any case, abolitionists had lately been kept fully occupied by the West Indian issue. Americans, on the other hand, had remained very much concerned with what was happening in Britain. This was borne home to British abolitionists by the arrival of Garrison in May 1833. Even before coming to England he had formed a notion, possibly inspired by his old Quaker mentor Benjamin Lundy, that the different national antislavery movements were in some sense parts of a single enterprise. At the masthead of each number of *The Liberator*, the weekly which he edited and published jointly with Isaac Knapp, appeared the slogan 'OUR COUNTRY IS THE WORLD— OUR COUNTRYMEN ARE MANKIND'. His reason for coming to England, however, was not to convert the British to this view—although this may

1. Referring to the Anti-Slavery Society, *The Abolitionist*, which became the official journal of the radicals, observed, "Success, though partial, seems to have produced its usual effect of languid torpor, and, as if exhausted, our abolitionists have resigned themselves to rest bordering on apathy", *The Abolitionist*, Aug. 1834.

conceivably have been in the back of his mind[2]—but to collect funds for a Negro college and to discredit the allegedly proslavery American Colonization Society whose emissary, Elliot Cresson, was then in the country on a fund-raising mission. This was an old feud and one with which the British had already been made familiar by Charles Stuart and by Garrison's own *Thoughts on African Colonization* (Boston, 1832).[3] In a letter to Lord Brougham the previous August he had described his aim in writing this pamphlet as being to expose "the scheme which is now in operation in this country for carrying to the pestilent shores of Africa—nobody can tell when but some time between now and the last day—our whole coloured population—a scheme which, for folly, imbecility, violence and presumption, exceeds the wildest ever attempted by men of sane minds in any age— a scheme which directly tends to increase the value of slaves, to degrade and persecute the free people of colour, to quiet the consciences of slaveholders and to perpetuate the system of slavery."[4]

This was a point of view which the British, who knew little about the American Colonization Society, readily accepted.[5] Of much more immediate interest were the tidings which he brought of recent developments in the United States, where, he was happy to tell them, their own doctrine of immediate emancipation was gaining support and where preparations were already afoot to launch a national antislavery society on the British model.[6] This was agreeable news and as its bearer he at once found himself welcomed into the inner circles of the British movement. These were days when Americans still looked to the British as the leaders of the antislavery struggle and thus men whose approval was very much worth having. Garrison lost no opportunity to learn what he could from them about techniques of agitation and to exploit his own role—for which it must be admitted he had no official sanction—as the visiting representative

2. As was indicated by a speech which he gave in Exeter Hall. W. P. Garrison and F. J. Garrison, *William Lloyd Garrison, the Story of His Life Told by His Children* (4 vols., New York, 1885–89), *1*, 369–76.
3. Charles Stuart, *Liberia: Or the American Colonization Scheme Examined and Exposed* (Glasgow, 1833). To what extent the American Colonization Society actually *was* proslavery is debatable although there is no doubt that its policies appealed to some proslavery elements as a means of getting rid of free Negroes. Perhaps its chief failure, like that of the movement to bring about the mitigation and gradual abolition of slavery in the British colonies, was its inability to produce practical results. By 1830, after thirteen years of effort, only 1,420 Negroes had been actually colonized, E. L. Fox, *The American Colonization Society, 1817–1840* (Baltimore, 1919), p. 89.
4. Garrison to Brougham, 1 Aug. 1832. Brougham Papers, University College, London—referred to hereafter as Brougham Papers.
5. Barnes, *Antislavery Impulse*, pp. 36–7, 53 n. 36.
6. W. P. and F. J. Garrison, *1*, 437–8.

of American abolitionism. He visited Clarkson and Wilberforce at their homes and eagerly cultivated the acquaintance of the younger generation of abolitionists. He was particularly impressed by George Thompson. The two were much of an age and type. According to one account what first brought them together was a bitter personal attack which Thompson made on Buxton for having supported compensation and apprenticeship.[7] This story, which may or may not be factually accurate, is certainly in character and aptly illustrates the angularity of temper and propensity for uncompromising moral stands shared by both. The friendship that sprang up between them was to last for life—probably the only friendship in the case of either that did not end in recriminations and bitterness.

Since his arrival in Britain, Garrison had been casting around for some practical way of showing his fellow countrymen that American abolitionists enjoyed the support of the British.[8] Inviting Thompson to America seemed an obvious solution. It is easy to see why the idea appealed to him. Not only would he have the services of an experienced platform orator who could instruct Americans in the latest British techniques of agitation, but his mere presence would proclaim to Garrison's countrymen at large that the mantle of Wilberforce and Buxton was now passing to the Americans. Buxton, to whom Garrison confided his plans, was sceptical and expressed reservations about the wisdom of an Englishman campaigning in the United States. These doubts Garrison brushed aside with an assurance that, foreigner or not, he was certain of a good hearing. Thompson declared himself ready to go.[9] The only problems remaining were financial. Garrison had had to borrow money to come to England and the New England Anti-Slavery Society, which became the official sponsor of Thompson's visit, was too poor to pay his expenses. Would it be possible, Garrison asked, for his British colleagues not only to spare Thompson for three years but also to put up the money necessary to support him in the United States for that period?[10]

How much of an impression Garrison himself made on British abolitionists at this time is not revealed. Probably not much. He was still a young man and the peculiar brand of antislavery extremism which he later came to represent—and which, as we shall see, was to have a con-

7. William Farmer, "Sketch of the life of George Thompson", *Liberator*, 26 Feb. 1864. It should be borne in mind that this account appeared long after the event by which time an elaborate Garrisonian legend had developed.
8. See, for example, W. L. Garrison, *Slavery in the United States of America: An Appeal to the Friends of Negro Emancipation throughout Great Britain* (London, 1833).
9. W. P. and F. J. Garrison, *1*, 437–38.
10. Glasgow Emancipation Society, *First Annual Report* (Glasgow, 1835), p. 10.

siderable impact in Britain as well as in America—was as yet unformulated. But his proposal regarding Thompson's mission had far reaching effects to the extent that it introduced many British abolitionists for the first time to the wider implications of the antislavery struggle.

The first evidence of this was the formation in the latter months of 1833, largely it would appear at Thompson's instigation,[11] of two new antislavery organizations, one in Edinburgh and the other in Glasgow.[12] In each case the immediate object was to obtain financial backing for his American mission. But the general aims of the two bodies went far beyond this. As the Glasgow Emancipation Society explained in its public declaration of principles, the ultimate object was nothing less than "the Abolition of Slavery Throughout the World".[13] How it proposed to set about this it explained in a series of letters to antislavery leaders in Britain and abroad. Writing to Buxton and Lord Suffield, the joint heroes of the late debates in Parliament, John Murray, Secretary of the Glasgow organization, expressed pride in having "set an example to you in the Southern Metropolis". For the Scots to take the lead would, he admitted, be regarded by some as turning things upside down. He went on to say, however, that they themselves were keenly aware of how little they could achieve on their own.

However useful these societies may be, either by their correspondence or their agents . . . it would be of essential importance to get our Government to take up the Question not so much as one in which her interference was a matter of right but as one in which her influence used amicably and judiciously would . . . be of great avail with the other powers whose subjects still hold slaves.

This policy, he shrewdly pointed out, would involve no change of principle since Britain was already committed to interfering in the affairs of other nations in seeking to put down the slave trade. So far she had met with little success. Widening the scope of her efforts and attacking slavery itself need involve no great expenditure of funds and might, in the long run, produce more results. Regarding Britain's right to interfere, he felt that "it might be prudent to insist upon it but delicately", although he doubted if it would "be much if at all disputed" since "Great Britain has herself set such a noble example".[14]

11. *Abolitionist*, Aug. 1834, pp. 34–7.
12. The Edinburgh society was formed on 25 October, the Glasgow society on 12 December. In each case these new bodies were created out of the elements of pre-existing organizations.
13. Glasgow Emancipation Society, Minute Books, 12 Dec. 1833, Mitchell Library, Glasgow—referred to hereafter as GES Minute Books.
14. Letters from John Murray to T. F. Buxton and Lord Suffield, 19 Feb. 1834, *ibid*. See also letter to General Lafayette, 6 Feb. 1834.

Buxton and Suffield were unimpressed. Buxton's comment was that
if the object were to get rid of American slavery it would be possible to
make out a much stronger case after West Indian emancipation had been
carried through.[15] This answer was not to the liking of Glasgow which
had been looking for a call to action, not a plea for delay.[16] Suffield's
response was even less encouraging. In his view, the proposals were not
only premature but positively harmful. "I am led", he observed, "by some
knowledge of the vehement jealousy of all interference on the part of this
country that exists in America to believe that every effort made by us to
expedite the downfall of slavery in that part of the world would have the
effect of retarding it." The best way for the British to influence America
was to give "exclusive attention to the extinction of slavery in our own
Colonies". He emphasized the point already made by Buxton, that making
a showpiece of the West Indies would do more to put an end to slavery
in other parts of the world than could be done by any other means.[17]

These reactions were disappointing. Buxton and Suffield were not
only prominent figures in the antislavery struggle but leading members of
the London Society on whose behalf they could be presumed to speak.
More encouraging news, however, had already begun to reach the Scots
from another quarter. The Young England abolitionists associated with
the Agency Committee, with whom Thompson had retained contact and
of whose doings he had been keeping his Scots supporters informed,
had for some time been thinking along lines similar to their own. Who
among the English abolitionists was responsible for this is not known.
It is clear that Thompson had some hand in it although his later boast
that he had "succeeded in establishing a London Society" was probably
not justified.[18] He was neither rich nor influential enough to achieve
anything without extensive backing. That Joseph Sturge, later to become
the founder of the British and Foreign Anti-Slavery Society, had also
played an active part is suggested by a letter he wrote to his old friend and
fellow abolitionist William Forster in the autumn of 1833. Begging
Forster not to dismiss out of hand what might at first appear a utopian
scheme, he urged him to consider seriously the possibility of mounting
a "general crusade" against slavery "throughout the civilized world".[19]
This was also the notion that Garrison had been stressing since his arrival

15. Buxton to Murray, 24 Feb. 1834, *ibid.*
16. Glasgow Emancipation Society, *First Annual Report* (Glasgow, 1834), p. 14.
17. Suffield to Murray, Feb. 25 1834, GES Minute Books.
18. "I have succeeded in *establishing* a London Society, which, but for my presence
in London and the effect of my lecturing in different parts of England, would not,
I am confident, have been in existence", Thompson to Murray, 17 April, 1834, *ibid.*
19. Henry Richard, *Memoirs of Joseph Sturge*, pp. 204–5.

the previous spring. In short, such ideas were in the air, and although they did not appeal to the more conservative Anti-Slavery Society they fitted exactly the needs of its Agency offshoot. The Scots were thus delighted but scarcely surprised when Thompson wrote informing them that at a meeting held on 17 February the Agency Society had formally agreed to make worldwide emancipation its official goal and to adopt as its new title 'The British and Foreign Society for the Universal Abolition of Negro Slavery and the Slave Trade'.[20]

Of all the organizations which over the years attempted to direct British antislavery efforts this was the shortest lived. As an active body it lasted only eighteen months and during this time it achieved little of significance. It is of interest, therefore, principally for the evidence it gives of the way in which British antislavery thought was now developing. Perhaps the most remarkable thing about it is its resemblance to the British and Foreign Anti-Slavery Society founded six years later. In this respect it is worth noting that of its twenty-eight members, eight were to serve on the committee of the later organization, including John Scoble, who acted as secretary to both.[21] Most striking of all, however, is the similarity in the aims of the two bodies. In an editorial in the first number of its new periodical *The Abolitionist* which appeared, appropriately enough, on 4 August 1834, three days after the Emancipation Act had taken effect, it observed:

The people of England stand on a proud eminence. . . .They have purged themselves from the imputation of a crime, than which no greater can be perpetrated against human nature or the great moral Legislator of the universe. They can now consistently bring the moral influence with which they are invested, to bear on those nations which may still persist in perpetrating a similar crime, and demand in the name of . . . outraged humanity, the universal recognition of the rights of man.

Its immediate aim was to coordinate the efforts of all those abolitionists in the country who wished to see the objectives of the antislavery movement broadened. At the time of its inception, the Society received pledges amounting to £600. With this money, and the contributions of the provincial auxiliaries, it proposed to sponsor a succession of missions by British abolitionists to the United States. Thompson's was to be the first.

20. Thompson to the Glasgow Emancipation Society, 18 Feb. 1834, GES Minute Books.
21. These were Stafford Allen, Richard Barrett, James Carlile, Joseph Cooper, J. S. Elliott, Thomas Price, Henry Sterry and John Scoble. *Report of the British and Foreign Society for the Universal Abolition of Slavery and the Slave Trade* (London, 1835); British and Foreign Anti-Slavery Society, *Annual Reports*, 1840–50—referred to hereafter as BFASS *Annual Reports*.

Depending on the success of that, others would follow. All told, it was to be an ambitious programme.[22]

One result of the launching of this enterprise was to make it more difficult than ever to conceal the differences dividing the two wings of the movement. So far these had been kept not only from the general public but from most of the movement's provincial supporters as well. This had not been difficult so long as both were concentrating on the same issue. But now that the radicals were turning to other matters altogether, explanations could no longer be avoided. Replying to a puzzled letter from the Glasgow Emancipation Society enquiring why more of the "distinguished veterans of the Anti-Slavery Cause" were not on its committee, the Universal Abolition Society stated that these individuals had for some years past been failing to pull their weight. In the final struggles over West Indian slavery,

The old Anti-Slavery Society was timid, inactive and destitute of a well defined anti-slavery principle. It was therefore a matter of extreme difficulty to stir up the country to energetic exertion or to simultaneous action. It was too often the case that the Agency Committee had to carry on a domestic and therefore painful warfare at the same time that all their exertion and all their time were peremptorily required to conduct their Controversy with the public. . . . For these reasons, it could hardly be expected that the Agency Committee would embarrass their future operations by courting a renewal of their alliance. They preferred confining their number to those individuals who, though less known to the public, had proved themselves to be the most useful Allies and the most constant to Anti-Slavery principles.[23]

This, of course, was unfair to the Anti-Slavery Society which, cautious though it had been, had borne the burden of presenting the abolition case in Parliament. That these services should now be overlooked showed only too clearly how divided the movement had become.

Another consequence of the launching of the Universal Abolition Society was to take the initiative from the Scots. The programme it proposed went well beyond anything they had envisaged. Thompson explained the situation to them as tactfully as he could, stressing the importance of centralized control and coordinated planning. As the first British antislavery societies to have embraced the cause of abolition in America they had earned a special place in the movement, and for this reason he would always consider himself peculiarly their representative. But they

22. George Thompson to the Glasgow Emancipation Society, 18 Feb. 1834, GES Minute Books.
23. John Crisp, Secretary pro. tem. of the UAS to the GES 29 March 1834, GES Minute Books, April 1834.

could now most effectively advance the cause by assisting the London body in its efforts and by remitting to it the funds they had so far collected on his behalf. This they agreed to do, forwarding to London £100 as their initial contribution.[24]

Everything now hinged on the success of Thompson's mission. Armed with gifts from British abolitionists to their American colleagues he set sail from Liverpool on 15 August 1834. From the first, Suffield's predictions were borne out. At the New York hotel where he had intended to stay the boarders joined together in passing resolutions which obliged the management to ask him to find accommodation elsewhere. In Lowell he was pelted with bricks. In Boston mobs marched down the streets with placards denouncing him as a racial amalgamationist. The press deliberately fermented the popular anger by branding him a foreign incendiary brought over to subvert American institutions. Much of this was to be expected. Unfortunately for Thompson, the newspapers also succeeded in dredging up an incident in his past involving the embezzlement of funds belonging to an employer. Although the matter had been settled amicably and generous restitution made, the story was damaging. In such circumstances it was remarkable that the tour lasted as long as it did. His last major mission was in May 1835, when he visited New York for the annual meeting of the American Anti-Slavery Society. Thereafter he remained in Boston under the protection of his American hosts making occasional expeditions to neighbouring towns. Finally, in November, finding even Boston too hot, he was smuggled out of the city and placed on board the New Brunswick packet bound for Halifax.[25]

The effect of Thompson's visit was to polarize opinion in the United States on the antislavery question. Whether in the long run this and the general atmosphere of violence and excitement it created did more to advance or hinder the cause was a question on which even the antislavery leaders were undecided. Moderates were alienated by Thompson's extremism, as they were by Garrison's own. Garrison, of course, proclaimed the tour a triumph and it was soon enshrined in Garrisonian

24. Thompson to William Smeal, 18 Feb. 1834; GES Minute Books, 20 Feb., 20 March 1834. This would appear to have been the only sum paid by the GES to Thompson through the UAS. Later sums were apparently paid to him direct. The generosity of the Glasgow society was remarkable. According to its *Annual Reports* it paid £642 to him between 1834 and 1838. GES *Annual Reports*, 1835–39.
25. C. Duncan Rice, "The anti-slavery mission of George Thompson to the United States, 1834–1835", *Journal of American Studies*, 2, (1968), 13–31.

legend.[26] But few agreed with him.[27] The taunt of "foreign emissary",
taken up by President Jackson in his annual message to Congress in December 1835,[28] cut deep, as even the Garrisonians themselves were ultimately
to admit.[29] Oddly enough, the tour probably had its greatest impact in
Britain where people were only beginning to become aware of the magnitude of the struggle developing across the Atlantic. The lectures which
Thompson delivered on his return and the pamphlets and clippings which
he brought with him, which were eagerly read, presented a new image of
the United States.[30] Here was a country where a small but courageous
band of reformers was struggling for expression in the face of ruthless
opposition. People had, of course, been familiar for long enough from
newspapers and travellers' accounts with the discrepancy between Americans' protestations of liberty and their holding of several millions of their
populace in bondage, but the image which Thompson now presented was
essentially novel. The United States was a nation in turmoil, where not
only Negroes but decent white people went in fear of their lives, where
Northern proslavery mobs roamed the streets burning churches while
the agents of law and order stood passively by. This image, which Thompson was the first to present to the British public but which was to achieve
its most forceful expression two years later in Harriet Martineau's *Martyr
Age of the United States*, became a potent force in British antislavery
thinking. The American abolitionists were shown as men engaged in a
struggle of epic proportions, overshadowing anything the British had
experienced or were likely to experience. "It is a totally different thing",
declared Harriet Martineau, "to be an abolitionist on a soil actually

26. W. P. and F. J. Garrison, *1*, 438–9; *2*, 58–9.
27. Both Gilbert H. Barnes and John L. Thomas take the view that the tour was
a mistake. Barnes even goes so far as to say that "all" abolitionists admitted this.
Barnes, ch. 5, n. 10; J. L. Thomas, *The Liberator: William Lloyd Garrison* (Boston,
1963), p. 194.
28. James D. Richardson, ed., *Messages and Papers of the Presidents, 1789–1897*
(10 vols., Washington D.C., 1896 ff), *3*, 175.
29. In 1853, when a third American visit by George Thompson was proposed
(he had made a second visit in 1850–51) even a staunch Garrisonian like Lucretia
Mott could write: "No—as a parallel, the English should raise the cry of 'down with
the aristocracy'—when it might be a question of expediency whether their money
should be used in employing an American Republican as an agent, or one of their
own countrymen equally well qualified." Lucretia Mott to A. W. Weston, 18 Nov.
1853, Weston Papers, Boston Public Library.
30. George Thompson, *A Voice to the United States of America from the Metropolis
of Scotland, being an account of various meetings held in Edinburgh on the subject of
American slavery upon the return of Mr. G. Thompson from his mission to that country*
(Edinburgh, 1836); C. C. Burleigh, ed., *The Reception of George Thompson in
Great Britain* (Boston, 1836); Glasgow Emancipation Society, *Report of the Discussion in Dr. Wardlaw's Chapel, between Mr. George Thompson and the Rev. R. J.
Breckinridge . . . June, 1836* (Glasgow and Boston, 1836).

trodden by slaves, and in a far off country, where opinion is already on the side of emancipation."[31] Few British abolitionists had had to face angry mobs and fewer still had gone in fear of their lives; but to Americans, so it seemed, these were everyday experiences. They were now the "real" abolitionists and it was in America that the "real" struggle was taking place. This glorification of the American movement, the beginnings of which are discernible in the 1830s,[32] was to reach its height in the 1840s and 1850s when, as we shall see, it became the principal concern of one section of the British movement.

But in the mid-1830s Britain's own problems were proving real enough. While Thompson was ducking proslavery brickbats in Lowell and Andover, abolitionists in Britain had been studying reports of the progress of emancipation in the colonies. Early accounts could hardly have been more satisfactory. Despite all that had been said about the inevitability of riot and bloodshed there had been no serious disturbances of any kind. On the island of St Christopher some apprentices, believing that they had been given full freedom, had put up a show of refusing to work with the result that five of the ringleaders had been removed and six others flogged. Impressed by this show of force the remainder had settled down with alacrity.[33] A similar incident in St Ann's parish, Jamaica, had been settled with equal promptitude.[34] Everywhere else, the Negroes had accepted their new status with equanimity. This was no less true, observers were pleased to note, in those two colonies, Antigua and Bermuda, which had exercised their discretion, as they were empowered to do under the Act, by embarking on emancipation immediately. Antigua, in particular, was regarded as a test case since it resembled the other colonies more closely than did Bermuda, where most of the slaves were engaged in maritime occupations and where apprenticeship was obviously inappropriate.[35] The report of the Governor of Antigua that everything was quiet and that most of the Negroes had continued working on the plantations

31. Harriet Martineau, *The Martyr Age of the United States of America* (Newcastle, 1840), p. 1. This first appeared as an article in the *Westminster Review* in December 1838, and was later widely distributed in pamphlet form.
32. A new monthly periodical, *Slavery in America with Notices of the Present State of Slavery and the Slave Trade throughout the World*, edited by the Rev. Thomas Price, began appearing in July 1836 and continued publication until August 1837. It was concerned mainly, although not entirely, with American developments. Price belonged to the Universal Abolition Society and later became a prominent member of the British and Foreign Anti-Slavery Society.
33. W. L. Mathieson, *British Slavery and its Abolition, 1823–38* (London, 1926), p. 250.   34. W. L. Burn, *Emancipation and Apprenticeship*, p. 175.
35. *Ibid*, p. 169.

was considered especially gratifying.[36] Everywhere tranquillity prevailed. "It is quite amazing", wrote Buxton in March 1835, "it is contrary to reason, it cannot be accounted for, but so it is".[37]

As the months passed and more reports accumulated a less roseate picture began to emerge. To some extent this was foreseeable. Any scheme as novel as the gradual transition from slavery to freedom of some 800,000 people and which required the cooperation of numerous government agencies and colonial committees was bound to have its troubles. Yet even when allowances were made, the accounts which were now coming in were disquieting. For one thing, few people had realized up to this point the extent to which, despite the provisions of the Act and the appointment of the special magistrates, power would remain in the hands of the old ruling class. That the planters would, during this period of apprenticeship, continue to exert an authority over their workers which was not very different in kind to that which they had wielded during the days of slavery had, of course, been understood and had been one of the principal reasons why abolitionists had objected to the Act. What had not been foreseen, or not fully, was the degree to which the colonial assemblies would control its application. There was something more than a little ironical in the fact that those very bodies which had proved most resistant to change in the past should now have so powerful a voice in determining how it was to be carried out. Yet short of making revolutionary changes in the structure of government and society there was no way in which this could be avoided. In each colony, it became evident, the success or failure of apprenticeship depended largely on a proper understanding being reached between the governors and the special magistrates on the one hand and the assemblies and the planters on the other. In some instances this was achieved, the governors agreeing to respect the privileges of the assemblies and they, in turn, agreeing not to exert their power to the point where relations with the executive or with the apprentices might be jeopardized. In these cases apprenticeship operated smoothly. But in a number of colonies, the most notable being Jamaica, no such understanding was achieved and there apprenticeship worked badly.[38]

It was from Jamaica that the most disquieting stories now came. As early as February 1835 William Knibb, a Baptist missionary in Trelawny parish and an abolitionist sympathizer, was writing that apprentices

36. Mathieson, *British Slavery and its Abolition*, pp. 245–7.
37. T. F. Buxton to his sister, 16 March 1835, in Charles Buxton, *Memoirs of Sir Thomas Fowell Buxton*, p. 374.
38. For details about how the apprenticeship system worked in individual colonies see the Burn and Mathieson volumes cited above; also P. D. Curtin, *Two Jamaicas; the Role of Ideas in a Tropical Colony, 1830–65* (Cambridge, Mass., 1955).

in his area were still being brutally flogged. Throughout the island, he reported, there was a growing dissatisfaction with the whole system and he urged that a member of the Anti-Slavery Society be sent out to observe what was happening.[39] Simultaneously reports from other sources were reaching Britain that planters in Jamaica had used emancipation as an excuse to withdraw from the Negroes many of the privileges they had enjoyed under slavery, including the right of pregnant women to be exempted from heavy field work and of field gangs to be attended by water carriers. Disagreements over hours of work were also reported, in particular over whether apprentices should be allowed part of Friday afternoons free to cultivate their own provision grounds in preparation for Saturday's market. With even a modicum of goodwill it should have been possible to settle these questions amicably and the failure to do so was put down to sheer spite on the part of the planters. Substantial evidence for this came not only from the private reports reaching British abolitionists but from official communications as well.[40] Among the abolitionists' correspondents Knibb was the most informative. Every morning, he wrote, a gang of some forty women was to be seen passing his door in chains. Children too young to work were being turned off the plantations. But the most damaging story of all was his report in the summer of 1835 that work was already in progress all over the island to erect treadmills.[41] On investigation this proved to be no exaggeration. The idea, it turned out, had originated, not as might have been expected, with the Jamaica Assembly, but with the newly appointed British Governor, the Marquis of Sligo. On his arrival in Jamaica, Sligo had been faced with the problem of what to do with apprentices who defied regulations. He had responded by recommending the treadmill as "a salutary mode of punishment". This turned out to be an egregious blunder. Previously, treadmills had been unknown on the island, although a few were apparently in use in the neighbouring colony of Trinidad. Being unfamiliar with these machines, and lacking a mechanical turn of mind, Jamaicans had little idea of how to build them. In consequence many of those which appeared were so ramshackle in construction and badly weighted that they resembled instruments of torture rather than of punishment. Nevertheless, work went ahead and before long fearful tales were reaching Britain of apprentices left hanging by their wrists while their shins were mashed by these murderous contraptions.[42]

39. John Howard Hinton, *Memoir of William Knibb, Missionary in Jamaica* (London, 1847), p. 228.   40. Burn, pp. 175–8.   41. Hinton, pp. 228–9.
42. Burn, pp. 149, 282–4; Mathieson, *British Slavery and its Abolition*, pp. 287–8. An eye-witness account of what such punishment involved will be found in Joseph Sturge and Thomas Harvey, *The West Indies in 1837* (London, 1838), p. 339.

All this, of course, bore out Buxton and Suffield's assertion that the extinction of slavery in Britain's own colonies would continue to demand the abolitionists' close attention. The Universal Abolition Society had never dissented from this view although it had seen no reason why such attention should not be combined with other activities. So alarming, however, were the stories now emanating from the West Indies that the two organizations agreed on the need for joint action. In April 1835 they issued an invitation to abolitionists all over the country to attend a general convention in Exeter Hall on 15 May to consider what should be done. The principal speakers on this occasion were Buxton and Lord Brougham, until recently Lord Chancellor in Grey's cabinet and an abolitionist of long standing. They reviewed at length the reports from the colonies, from which they concluded that the Negroes had acquitted themselves creditably in the most trying circumstances and despite continual provocation. The same could not be said of their white masters.[43] It was agreed, therefore, that Buxton should call on the Government for a committee of enquiry to look into the whole matter.[44] On 19 June he moved in the House for the appointment of a select committee to determine specifically whether the planters had met the conditions under which it had been agreed that compensation would be granted. Sir George Grey, replying on behalf of the Government, said that although abuses existed they should be regarded as temporary and were due, in the first instance, to the lack of administrative personnnel on the spot. The Government was keeping in touch with what was happening and had already taken steps to see that things were remedied. In retrospect, it is clear that Grey was being less than frank, an impression shared by many of his audience at the time. Nevertheless, apparently satisfied with the explanation given, Buxton withdrew his motion.[45]

Most abolitionists found this puzzling. Why raise the issue at all if he intended to back down immediately? In private correspondence he did his best to defend himself. Writing to Zachary Macaulay he denied that there was any foundation for the view that he had been overawed by the ministers of the Crown. His real reason for withdrawing his motion was that, however much might be wrong with apprenticeship, he saw no point in harrying the Government at that time. Abolitionists should hold their protests in reserve until the planters attempted, as sooner or later he believed they would, to reintroduce slavery on a permanent

43. *Anti-Slavery Reporter*, July 1836, pp. 352–3.
44. Anti-Slavery Society Minute Books, 15 May 1835, British Empire Manuscripts, E 2/4, Rhodes House, Oxford—referred to hereafter as ASS Minute Books.
45. Burn, p. 334.

basis through the imposition of vagrancy laws and other regulations.[46] Although there was something to be said for this view the fact remains that he was remarkably negligent in failing to take his supporters into his confidence many of whom, as a result, believed him guilty of a betrayal of trust.[47]

As might be expected, the reaction of the members of the Universal Abolition Society was particularly hostile. To their minds there was now little doubt that he had abandoned the cause. Additional evidence for this was seen in his attitude towards the old question of compensation, which again became an issue in the latter months of 1835. The problem this time concerned the island of Mauritius. In allocating to the planters their share of the £20 million the Government had run into unexpected difficulties. Because of its proximity to Africa, slave smuggling had continued well into the 1820s. Naturally, there were no records to show which of the slaves had been introduced illegally or even, because of the wholesale falsification of documents, how many there were altogether.[48] At a joint meeting of the two antislavery committees, held on 14 August, Buxton inquired whether he would be representing the views of British abolitionists correctly if he were to state in the House that they would agree to support Mauritian claims on condition that the planters, in return, would promise to give up the apprenticeship system. He made this inquiry casually in the course of conversation and, at least according to his account, no objections were raised.[49] When, however, he laid this plan before the House, representing it as having come from both organizations, the Universal Abolition Committee not only protested, but published a strongly worded resolution in *The Times* dissociating itself from the proposal.[50] To accept the right of compensation, it claimed, implied a right to hold slaves.[51] "I have anxiously desired," Sturge wrote to Buxton, "that in any steps which Christians might take for the poor oppressed African race, they might not sacrifice principle to worldly expediency, and it has been my belief that the Divine blessing has hitherto not crowned their

46. Charles Buxton, *Memoirs of Sir Thomas Fowell Buxton*, pp. 377–8.
47. See the resolutions of the "Special Meeting of the London Anti-Slavery Committees" held at 18 Aldermanbury on 23 June 1835, ASS Minute Books.
48. W. L. Mathieson, *British Slave Emancipation, 1838–1849* (London, 1932), pp. 208–11, 223–5. According to Sir John Jeremie, Governor of the island, the Mauritian planters received compensation for some 30,000 Negroes who had never, legally speaking, been slaves. BFASS, *Proceedings of the General Anti-Slavery Convention of 1840*, p. 257.
49. Robert Stokes, Secretary of the Anti-Slavery Society, to Buxton, 7 Dec. 1835, in ASS Minute Books, 16 Dec. 1835.
50. *The Times*, 28 Nov., 14 Dec. 1835. See also an article on the subject in the *Christian Advocate*, 30 Nov. 1835.
51. Stephen to Buxton, 15 Dec. 1835, ASS Minute Books, 23 Dec. 1835.

efforts because this has not been kept sufficiently in view."[52] Buxton replied that he fully agreed with those who regarded the Mauritians as undeserving, but since Parliament had voted the money and the question was now merely one of allocation, he felt justified in advocating the course most likely to be of immediate practical benefit to the Negroes. "One that seeth, not as men seeth; who is not severe against frailties and infirmities, who fathoms the real purposes and intentions of the heart . . . will . . . perceive that my motives have not been impure."[53] Sturge, who held stricter views on such matters, replied that although he had no intention of withdrawing from the cause, he felt he could "no longer satisfactorily cooperate with those who appear to me to act upon the principle that the end sanctifies the means".[54]

While the abolitionists were thus quarrelling among themselves, reports had continued to come in from the West Indies which suggested that conditions far from improving were actually growing worse. The planters, it seemed, were using all the resources at their disposal to circumvent the Act; the supervision provided by the special magistrates was inadequate because of their lack of numbers and because those who were there had chosen to identify themselves with the interests of the employers rather than with those of the apprentices; the flogging of both sexes continued, as did other forms of physical coercion, including, of course, punishment on the notorious treadmills. One missionary even went so far as to say that he had seen more cruelty since emancipation than during all the years of slavery. Instead of being free, even in a conditional sense, the apprentices remained "emancipated prisoners" liable to similar punishments and labouring under much the same incapacities as before.[55]

This was a highly biased picture. As we now know, apprenticeship was working about as well as could reasonably be expected given the obstacles to be overcome.[56] That there were cases of maltreatment was, however, plain enough even to the most unbiased observer. As always, conditions in Jamaica were particularly worrying. Relations there between the administration and the planters had deteriorated to such an extent that Lord Sligo was reduced to the extraordinary expedient of writing to Lord Suffield requesting antislavery demonstrations in England to use as a lever in his dealings with the planters.[57] Obviously some action on the part of the antislavery body was needed. The problem was deciding what to do.

52. Sturge to Buxton, 30 Nov. 1835, in *ibid*, 16 Dec. 1835.
53. Buxton to Sturge, 4 Dec. 1835, *ibid*, 16 Dec. 1835.
54. Sturge to Buxton, 28 Dec. 1835, *ibid*, Jan. 1836.
55. Richard, pp. 120–4.   56. Burn, *passim*.   57. *Ibid*, p. 335.

As at the time of the struggles over the 1833 Bill, abolitionists were faced with a choice between two possible courses of action. Either they could work quietly through Parliament in the expectation that sooner or later it would see fit to do something about the situation, or they could launch a general appeal to the country with a view to bringing pressure to bear externally and provoking the Government to action in that way. As might be expected, Buxton and the supporters of the Anti-Slavery Society generally chose the first course while the radicals leaned towards the second. The situation was thus very similar to that which had existed in 1832–33, although there were differences. During the controversy over the Emancipation Bill both metropolitan bodies sought to mobilize all the support they could muster. In the struggle over apprenticeship this was not the case. For long periods the Anti-Slavery Society did nothing at all.[58] Whether this was, as the radicals charged, simple inertia, or whether it was a deliberate policy based on Buxton's contention that abolitionists not in Parliament should hold their protests in reserve and leave the day to day conduct of affairs to parliamentarians like himself, remains unclear. Even more puzzling was the disappearance, in the autumn of 1835, of the radicals' own metropolitan organization, the Universal Abolition Society. The last recorded meeting of this body was on 19 August, when it met jointly with the Anti-Slavery Society.[59] What happened thereafter, whether it formally dissolved or simply stopped meeting, is unclear and until new sources are found is likely to remain so. It was later claimed that Sir George Stephen, who had been the leading spirit of the Agency Society, was opposed to agitation on the apprenticeship issue, and this may well have been a factor.[60] A partial explanation may be found, however, simply by examining the predicament in which the radicals now found themselves. Nothing they had touched so far had gone quite right, including Thompson's mission which, for reasons they had not foreseen, was proving less than the popular triumph that had been anticipated. In particular, developments in the West Indies had shown their programme to be, if not ill-conceived, at least premature. In short, the time had come for a rethinking of policy. Traditionally, this was the task of a metropolitan committee and a sufficiently flexible and energetic body might well have succeeded in performing it, perhaps, as in 1834, changing its name

58. There is no record of any meetings having been held between 20 June 1836 and 7 June 1837. Thereafter the committee met roughly fortnightly. ASS Minute Books. The last number of the *Anti-Slavery Reporter* appeared in July 1836.

59. ASS Minute Books, 19 Aug. 1835. The last issue of *The Abolitionist* had appeared the previous May.

60. William Farmer, "Sketch of the life of George Thompson", *Liberator*, 5 March 1864, p. 37.

in the process. In this instance, however, the tattered metropolitan organization, for reasons which remain obscure but which were no doubt connected with the prevailing disillusionment of its members over what they had done so far, failed to respond. Instead it was a provincial organization that stepped into the lead.

The emergence at this juncture of the Birmingham Anti-Slavery Society as the leading radical body in the country was principally the work of its secretary, Joseph Sturge. Sturge was a familiar Quaker type, solid, honest, a poor orator but an effective committeeman. His main assets so far as the antislavery cause was concerned were his wealth, his energy and, as we have already seen, his unshakeable commitment to moral principle. He was the son of a prosperous Gloucestershire farmer and, like many in his social position in England at that time, had had only a short formal education. In his late teens he had gone into business as a corn merchant, and by 1830 was so well established that he was able to hand over his affairs to his brother and devote himself entirely to benevolent causes. During the 1820s, as a protégé of James Cropper—whose daughter he subsequently married—he had supported the Anti-Slavery Society and later played an active role in setting up the Agency and Universal Abolition Committees of which he was one of the principal benefactors. The tales emanating from the West Indies convinced him that emancipation was largely a fraud and that further action was needed. Finding the Anti-Slavery Society apathetic and failing to get the leadership he wanted from the Universal Abolition Committee he determined to act on his own, using the Birmingham society as his instrument.[61]

It was thus around Sturge and the Birmingham committee that the new agitation revolved. He began in the autumn of 1835 by organizing a series of demonstrations against apprenticeship, beginning with a mass meeting in Birmingham Town Hall on 14 October.[62] Although this unquestionably helped draw attention to the issue it did nothing to solve the main problem which at that stage was lack of information. There were, of course, letters from missionaries and other sympathizers on the spot, but the material in these was not always of the type required and even when it was, there was a general fear of using it in case informants might be victimized.[63]

61. Richard, pp. 22–58.
62. *Ibid*, pp. 125–6; Birmingham Anti-Slavery Society, *Report of the Proceedings of the Great Anti-Slavery meeting at the Town Hall, Birmingham,* ... *With an Appendix Containing Notes of the Condition of Apprenticed Labourers in the West Indies* (Birmingham, 1835).
63. There was some justification for this fear. In 1823, William Shrewsbury, a Methodist minister, had been driven from Barbados on suspicion that he had been sending derogatory reports to England. Coupland, *The British Anti-Slavery Movement*, p. 127. Correspondents in the West Indies continually urged the British

Official reports from the governors and other functionaries were also of some help but these were usually so full of special pleadings that it was impossible to get any clear overall notion of what was happening.

Buxton, too, was aware of this problem. In March 1836 he somewhat redeemed himself in the eyes of the Sturgites by moving, this time successfully, for a committee of enquiry. The hearings began in April and continued throughout the early part of the summer. Some witnesses, among them R. R. Madden, who had recently returned from Jamaica where he had been acting as a special magistrate, were highly critical of what was being done. In Madden's opinion there was little improvement in the Negro's position and such new privileges as he enjoyed were highly precarious. Other witnesses took the opposite line, arguing that cases of maltreatment were far from typical and much less widespread than was claimed. The committee's report, when it appeared in August, inclined towards the latter view. There were, it conceded, faults in the system but these would be remedied in time, given the willingness of the planters to cooperate. What grounds it had for supposing the planters would want to cooperate it did not explain.[64] Unimpressed by these bland assurances, Sturge decided that there was no alternative but to visit the West Indies to see things for himself.

The expedition which left Falmouth for Barbados on 17 October consisted of four members, Sturge, two other Birmingham Quakers, Thomas Harvey and William Lloyd, and the former Secretary of the Universal Abolition Society, John Scoble. In Barbados the party split up, Lloyd and Scoble going to British Guiana while Sturge and Harvey went first to Antigua to evaluate the effects of full emancipation there, later continuing by way of the more southerly Windward Islands, to Jamaica.

The experiences of these investigators in the main confirmed the views they had already formed before leaving England. Of the four works which the expedition produced, Sturge and Harvey's *The West Indies in 1837*, published in January 1838, although by no means impartial, was probably the fairest in its assessment. In Antigua, the authors claimed, all classes agreed that emancipation was a success. Production and profits were up

to be cautious in the use they made of their material. One wrote: "It is necessary to warn our friends against giving publicity to any correspondence with persons here. You will be plied by many insidious persons from hence; who, under the pretence of friendliness to the cause, will seek to know the sources of your information, to destroy those who correspond with you. Let me request of you, therefore, to be watchful, and never to show your letters. Copy out the information if you will, but let them know nothing of names and persons." Birmingham Anti-Slavery Society, *Report of the Proceedings of the Great Anti-Slavery Meeting at the Town Hall, Birmingham*, p. 1.
64. Burn, pp. 336–9.

and a happy atmosphere characterized relations between the races.[65] Jamaica, by contrast, presented a much darker picture. The authors were, of course, opposed to apprenticeship on principle, as "a system of coerced and unrequited labour".[66] But even admitting, for the sake of argument, that the provisions of the Act might be consistent with humanity, they concluded that the system as it was actually being administered was quite the opposite. At every point the Act was being violated by the planters in their efforts to get as much work as possible out of the apprentices with a minimum of remuneration. A particularly shocking example of the sort of tyranny against which they were protesting had been brought to public attention shortly before the appearance of their book with the publication of *The Narrative of James Williams*.[67] Williams was a Negro apprentice whom Sturge had redeemed and brought back to England. Largely it would seem because of his "insolence of manner" Williams had fallen foul of the special magistrates in St Ann's parish, with the result that he had been seven times flogged, thrice thrown into the estate dungeon and four times consigned to the treadmill, all within the space of thirty months. His account of these experiences, the accuracy of which was later attested by Governor Smith, was presented as "the tale of near eight hundred thousand of our fellow-subjects". This was an exaggeration, but it showed only too clearly how easily the apprenticeship system could be abused when administered by unscrupulous men. That such incidents were not confined to Jamaica was shown by the accounts of the other two members of the expedition, Scoble and Lloyd.[68] According to them, conditions in British Guiana were every bit as bad as those witnessed by Sturge and Harvey. All four writers agreed that the so-called abuses were not incidental occurrences but sufficiently general to warrant their being regarded as integral parts of the system and that the only way to get rid of them was by getting rid of the system itself.

Sturge's return in May 1837 coincided with the appointment of a second parliamentary committee to enquire into the application of the 1833 Act, and he spent some time outlining his impressions before that body. He had little hope, however, that Parliament would see fit to take action unless aroused by popular agitation.[69] The Anti-Slavery Society,

65. Sturge and Harvey, pp. 63–72.   66. *Ibid*, p. 319.
67. *Narrative of Events since the First of August, 1834, by James Williams, an Apprenticed Labourer* (London, 1837).
68. John Scoble, *British Guiana* (London, 1838); William Lloyd, *Letters from the West Indies* (Birmingham, 1839).
69. In fact the committee's report, which appeared in June 1837, went no further than to recommend "a strict and searching enquiry into the state of the Workhouses in the West Indian Colonies, and especially into the construction and use of Treadmills" PP, 1837, 7, 745.

although still in existence, had not met for almost a year. Nevertheless, with a general election in the offing and a growing public concern over apprenticeship it was able to muster enough energy to summon a meeting at Exeter Hall. Adopting a technique learned from the Agency Committee it issued an *Address to the Electors of Great Britain* calling on them to use their influence at the hustings to demand pledges from candidates on behalf of their "coloured fellow subjects".[70] That these efforts had little influence on the outcome of the election is suggested by the fact that Buxton himself lost his seat in the Commons. This was a grave blow to the Society, although it made no difference to the Sturgites who distrusted Buxton's principles and placed little reliance on his support.

The problem of establishing a base from which to launch a campaign against apprenticeship was solved by the formation of a new organization. Acting in his capacity as Secretary of the Birmingham Anti-Slavery Society, Sturge sent a circular to sympathizers around the country inviting them to a conference in London to discuss what was happening in the colonies. The Exeter Hall convention, held in November 1837, led to the formation of the Central Emancipation Committee and the establishment of a new periodical, *The British Emancipator*. The Anti-Slavery Society, which was not approached until a few days before the meeting, agreed to send a delegation. But after hearing the delegation's report and examining the convention's resolutions, which confirmed its suspicions about the new body's radical tendencies, it resolved to continue acting independently.[71] In fact, little more was heard from it.

The campaign which now developed was essentially a repeat performance of that of 1832-33. Even the performers were the same. George Thompson, putting aside for the moment his American concerns, toured Scotland addressing meetings and organizing societies, while Sturge, Scoble and their associates did the same in England.[72] Once again petitions and remonstrances poured into Parliament. At the centre of these operations was the Emancipation Committee, coordinating efforts much as the old Agency Committee had done. From the first there was no shortage of funds. Its budget for the first nine months amounted to £4,466, which shows it to have been wealthier than either the Anti-Slavery Society or the British and Foreign Anti-Slavery Society or, indeed, any other antislavery organization of which there are records. The larger donors were all Quakers as were also, apparently, most of the members of

70. ASS Minute Books, 13 July 1837.
71. *Ibid*, 13–16 Nov. 1837.
72. Henry B. Stanton, *Sketches of Reforms and Reformers of Great Britain and Ireland* (New York, 1849), p. 208; William Farmer, "Sketch of the Life of George Thompson", *Liberator*, 5 March 1864, p. 37.

the thirty-eight auxiliary societies which contributed to its coffers.[73] It is clear from the names of these bodies that the old Quaker connections still provided the structural basis of the movement. Probably as much as ninety per cent of the money spent in the campaign against apprenticeship came from Quaker sources, despite the fact that the Central Emancipation Committee never came to rely, as the Anti-Slavery Society had done, on direct grants from the Society of Friends.

Thus the Government once again found itself in the familiar position of having to defend a well-intentioned but obviously ineffectual policy in the face of organized public pressure. Nevertheless, it showed no signs of wishing to retreat. In February 1838 a motion by Lord Brougham in the House of Lords, calling for the immediate abolition of apprenticeship, was overwhelmingly defeated.[74] A month later, however, a similar motion in the Commons, proposed by Sir George Strickland and supported by Daniel O'Connell, Joseph Pease and Dr Lushington, gained 215 of the 484 votes cast.[75] Petitions meanwhile continued to pour in from constituencies and there were excited gatherings in Exeter Hall. England, as a writer in the *Spectator* put it, was "in convulsions" over the apprenticeship issue.[76] On 22 May a snap division in a thinly attended House resulted in a resolution by Sir Eardly Wilmot favouring the ending of apprenticeship on 1 August being approved by a small majority, although action was later stayed by Government intervention.[77]

But it was the colonial assemblies and not Parliament which ultimately brought apprenticeship to an end. The implications of what had been happening in London had not been lost on them. How long the Government would be willing to resist the increasing opposition both within and outside Parliament was problematical. The planters did not relish the prospect of having their legislatures overruled yet again. Besides, they were now facing the problem of what to do on 1 August when those apprentices not engaged in field work would automatically become free. Many planters, weary of the whole system and the irritating supervision it involved, had begun to wonder if it were worth while hanging on to the bitter end. Three colonies, Antigua, Bermuda and Montserrat, had already dispensed with apprenticeship. The remainder now decided to follow suit: Nevis in March; the Virgin Islands in April; Grenada, St Vincent, St Kitts

73. This may be inferred from their titles: e.g. The Anti-Slavery Friends Society, Aberdeen. In all, the provincial societies contributed just over £1,000, the largest single contribution being £100 from the Anti-Slavery Friends Society, Birmingham. *British Emancipator*, 14 Nov. 1838, p. 176.
74. Richard, p. 167.
75. *British Emancipator*, 7 April 1838, p. 52.   76. *Spectator*, 30 March 1838.
77. Burn, p. 356.

and Barbados in May; British Guiana and Tobago in June; the Bahamas, Dominica, Jamaica, and finally Trinidad, in July.[78]

The news that the last vestige of West Indian slavery, their principal target of attack for so long, had ceased to exist, was greeted with jubilation by British abolitionists. Buxton, who had at last come around to Sturge's point of view, sent him a warm letter of congratulation. "I bless God", he wrote, "that He, who has always raised up agents such as the crisis requires, sent you to the West Indies." Like many others, however, who wrote or spoke in celebration of the occasion, he could not forbear adding that this was by no means the end of the struggle. Slavery still existed in other parts of the globe, while the slave trade, "of all evils the monster evil", continued to expand.[79]

These were matters about which Sturge scarcely needed reminding. In recent months he, like Buxton, had been giving them much thought. In fact, unknown to one another, both had been pondering the movement's future in the hope of finding some way of coming to grips with those wider issues which, now that West Indian slavery was ending, stood out more intractably than ever. Both, as we shall see, had ideas on the subject. But it was Buxton, the conservative, who emerged as the true visionary.

78. *Ibid*, pp. 357–9; Richard, p. 172.
79. Buxton to Sturge, n.d. (July ? August ? 1838) in Charles Buxton, *Memoirs of Sir Thomas Fowell Buxton*, p. 428.

3

Buxton's solution

Following his defeat in the general election
of 1837 Buxton had devoted himself to
reviewing the position of the antislavery
cause and to devising plans for its future
development. Few could claim better qualifi-
cations. Now in his mid-fifties, he had
behind him more than twenty years' experience of antislavery effort, including thirteen
years as leader and spokesman for the anti-
slavery group in Parliament. There were
thus few aspects of the struggle with which
he was not already thoroughly familiar.
He also knew, better than most, how
governments worked and how they could be
influenced. Among his friends he counted
many of the leading political figures of the
day, and he could rely on their lending a
sympathetic ear to any proposal he cared
to make. In the country at large his prestige
had never been higher. His reluctance to
champion the campaign against apprenticeship and his electoral defeat had in no way
prejudiced his standing in the eyes of the
public. As Wilberforce's successor he was
still the recognized spokesman of the anti-
slavery movement in Britain. Others might
champion particular causes, but in the
country at large his was still the authoritative
voice of the movement.

By far the most disquieting development

of the 1830s, in Buxton's view, was the increased activity of the Atlantic slave trade. To contemporaries it seemed as if, since Britain's withdrawal in 1808, this traffic had steadily grown. "Will you believe it", he wrote to his old friend J. J. Gurney, "the Slave Trade, though England has relinquished it, is now double what it was when Wilberforce began."[1] It is clear that this was an exaggeration. But in the 1830s information on the trade was lacking and it was only too easy, extrapolating from such fragmentary figures as were available, to reach the conclusion that the traffic was indeed reaching alarming proportions. Buxton himself put the number of Africans carried annually from West Africa to the Americas at 150,000. Most people regarded this as a little on the high side but other contemporary estimates were not significantly less. In 1848, when the Foreign Office finally came out with comprehensive statistics on the subject, they showed that the numbers involved had grown from 100,000 in 1788 to 135,000 in the 1830s.[2] In fact these estimates were all wildly exaggerated. It now seems probable that the trade, having reached a plateau in the early eighteenth century, had remained at around the same level ever since. But regardless of whether the number was 150,000, 135,000, or, as now seems more likely, 50,000,[3] it was plain that, so far as the abolitionists' programme was concerned, something had gone seriously wrong.

What had happened, of course, was precisely what their opponents had said would happen: Britain's withdrawal had left a vacuum which other nations, eager for trade and less hampered by scruples, had hastened to fill. This is not to say that the Act of 1807 had been entirely a dead letter. To the extent that it had cut off the trade to Britain's own possessions, it had undoubtedly had some influence in diminishing total numbers. More important in this respect was the corresponding United States legislation which, though less strictly enforced, had largely closed that

1. Buxton to Gurney, 18 Aug. 1838, in Charles Buxton, *Memoirs of Sir Thomas Fowell Buxton*, p. 435.
2. Thomas Fowell Buxton, *The African Slave Trade and its Remedy* (2nd edn, London, 1840), p. 15; PP, 1847/8, 22 (623), 8. Another notable authority was James Bandinel, who ran the Foreign Office department responsible for collecting statistics on the trade and who put the figures for 1838 and 1839 at 122,000 and 70,000 respectively. James Bandinel, *Some Account of the Trade in Slaves from Africa* (London, 1842), pp. 285–7.
3. Curtin, *The Atlantic Slave Trade*, pp. 37–49, 266. Curtin performs a valuable service in drawing attention to the unreliability of the 1848 figures and to the uncritical way in which they have been used by historians. He fails to note, however, that they merely confirmed what most contemporaries already believed and corresponded to the figures cited in Parliament over the preceding years. See, for example, *Hansard*, 7 (16 July 1844), 924, 931, 950.

country to the traders.[4] What the loss of these markets meant in quantitative terms it is impossible to say. In any case, such diminution as it had brought about was offset by the growing demand for slaves elsewhere. Latin Americans, particularly Cubans and Brazilians, now showed the same desire for slaves that had previously characterized the British and Americans. The reasons were the same. Labour was short and importing Negroes from Africa was the easiest way of obtaining it. The difference was that instead of being carried in British vessels they were now carried in vessels belonging to Spain or Portugal or any other country offering immunity from capture.

Thus the fact that the trade had expanded can be explained in simple economic terms. It was, as it had always been, a profitable form of enterprise. Much more remarkable was the persistence with which, year in and year out, Britain had sought to have it suppressed. Historians are rightly sceptical of those who claim, as the supporters of this policy did, to be acting from disinterested motives. In practice those who make such claims too often turn out to have other less selfless objectives in mind. This at least was the view of suppression taken by Britain's foreign critics.[5] In their eyes there were three principal explanations for her policy. First, there was her need for additional labourers to use on her West Indian plantations. But while it is true that some of the slaves liberated from foreign vessels were used in this way it is also clear that this was, at most, a side effect and not a cause of suppression. There were, after all, many easier ways of obtaining Africans than by liberating them from other people's ships. The Sierra Leone indentures scheme, the principal means by which liberated Africans were taken to the West Indies, operated for only a short time, involved relatively few Negroes—less than 10,000 all told—and was universally regarded an economic failure.[6] More immediately plausible is the claim that Britain's object was not so much to obtain labourers for herself as to deny them to her competitors. Eric Williams and others have pointed out that the West Indies supported suppression for precisely this reason.[7] The trouble with this explanation is that it

---

4. Curtin, as a "shot in the dark", accepts the figure of 1,000 a year for slave imports into the United States. In view of the abolitionists' failure to exploit what would, from every point of view, have been an explosive issue, it seems likely that even this estimate may be on the high side. *Ibid*, 74–5.

5. Warren S. Howard. *American Slaves and the Federal Law, 1837–1862* (Berkeley, 1963), pp. 1–13. All the points made by Howard were stressed by contemporary critics.

6. See pp. 129–30 below.

7. Eric Williams, *Capitalism and Slavery*, p. 175. A general account of the West Indian's view on suppression will be found in The Kingston Committee, *The Jamaica Movement for Promoting the Enforcement of the Slave Trade Treaties*

scarcely accounts for *Britain's* policy and actually weakens the case of the economic determinists who—like Williams himself—argue that the primary aim of British policy at this time was to benefit home rather than colonial interests. For if humanitarianism were a charade and the true objective was "the destruction of the West Indian monopoly" what was she doing policing the seas on the West Indians' behalf?[8] This paradox, however, need not detain us, for even the briefest examination of British attitudes towards her sugar colonies at this time shows that the notion is absurd.[9]

Finally, it has been argued that Britain's real motive was not her wish to have the slave trade suppressed but her desire to establish, under the guise of suppression, a trading monopoly with the west coast of Africa.[10] In other words, claiming the right to police the coast was a good excuse for keeping foreign ships out and allowing British ships in. It is, of course, true that many of those who supported suppression had, like Palmerston, wider objectives in view and that these included the expansion of legitimate trade. This was something which the abolitionists themselves frequently stressed. And undoubtedly there were cases where foreign vessels were discriminated against unfairly. It is difficult, however, to draw general conclusions from such actions. Foreign vessels, after all, were more likely to be engaged in slaving than British ones. And abolitionists who pointed to commercial advantages to be gained usually did so as an afterthought, and on occasion even had to remind one another that there was nothing intrinsically dishonourable about a financial motive.[11] But the chief weakness of the "national interest" argument is that, economically, suppression did not make sense. The cost of maintaining the African Squadron far exceeded the value of Britain's annual trade with Africa.[12] This was a point on which the opponents of suppression laid great

and the Suppression of the Slave-Trade, with Statements of Fact, Convention and Law: Prepared at the Request of the Kingston Committee (London, 1850).

8. Williams himself is, understandably, confused on this issue. He observes that home commercial interests opposed the blockade policy and that West Indian interests supported it. He fails to note, however, that the efforts to have the African Squadron withdrawn failed. Since the aim of his book is to show that home interests triumphed over colonial interests this fact would have been hard to reconcile with his general argument. Williams, pp. 169–77. For a general critique of Williams's views see Appendix C below.

9. See J. H. Parry and P. M. Sherlock, *A Short History of the West Indies* (2nd edn. London, 1963), pp. 198–215. Palmerston, in an exchange with Cobden, specifically denied that this was an important consideration. PP, 1847/8, *22* (272), 19.

10. Howard, pp. 5–8.

11. See, for example, Sir George Stephen, *A Third Letter to the Right Hon. Lord John Russell on the Plans of the Society for the Civilization of Africa* (London, 1840), pp. 5–14, and *The Niger Trade Considered in Connexion with the African Blockade* (London, 1849).

12. Williams, p. 171.

stress. Nothing reveals the weakness of the "economic interest" argument more clearly than the fact that the "commercial part of the nation"— those who inside and outside Parliament were regarded as the keepers of the nation's business conscience—when in the 1840s it woke up to what was happening, threw all its weight into *opposing* the policy precisely on the grounds that it was an unwarranted drain on the national exchequer.[13]

Thus one is left with the explanations which Englishmen themselves gave for their actions. Among them it was universally agreed, by those who opposed the policy no less than by those who supported it, that the fundamental motive was moral. Whether the policy was wisely conceived and even whether its effects were, from a moral standpoint, desirable, were, as will be shown in a later chapter, matters for debate. But that those who supported it—except, of course, the West Indians and possibly a handful of African merchants—*believed* they were acting altruistically there can be no doubt. The evidence overwhelmingly supports the view that since the days when Britain herself had been the leading carrier of slaves she had undergone a crisis of conscience. Parliamentary speeches on the subject continually alluded to her past guilt. Some speakers conjured up images of a divine judgment and a coming Day of Wrath, others of a future age of peace on earth where all peoples would bask under Britain's benevolent protection. Perhaps these millennialist and millennarian allusions should not be taken too seriously. Often, no doubt, they were mere figures of speech. But their frequent recurrence reveals the nature of Britain's commitment. Whether they believed in the reality of a divine judgment or not, large numbers of British people were convinced that it was their destiny to redress a past wrong and that the suppression of the slave trade was in some way connected with their own moral redemption.[14]

More important in the present context than the question of motivation is the way in which this policy had developed. There were, broadly speaking, three possible areas where the trade might be attacked: in Africa where the slaves originated; on the Atlantic, across which they travelled; and within the importing nations where they were put to work. At various times efforts were made in all three. The Sierra Leone Company and later the African Institution were both very much concerned with the possibility of encouraging African civilization as a means of cutting off the trade at its root. These policies, as we have seen, came to nothing and by 1815 had been largely abandoned. The government had meanwhile con-

13. See Chapter 9 below.
14. See, for example, Lord Palmerston's comments, *Hansard*, 76 (16 July 1844), pp. 922–48.

centrated its efforts in the other two areas. By negotiating a series of agreements with the principal importing nations, using where necessary diplomatic pressure and economic concessions, it had attempted to obtain their
active cooperation in putting down the trade. Such agreements were
concluded with Spain and Portugal in 1817 and with Brazil in 1826.[15]
Had these countries honoured their treaty obligations there is no doubt
that the trade would have been drastically reduced and perhaps actually
eliminated in a very short time. In fact the treaties had little effect. The
authorities in both Cuba and Brazil, despite repeated British protests,
not only failed to take action against the trade but most of the time actively
encouraged it. In Cuba, for example, Spanish officials shared between
them a tax levied on every slave landed. Two barracoons for the accommodation of newly imported Negroes stood just outside the gates of the
Captain-General's residence.[16]

Having thus failed to achieve her object either in Africa or Latin
America, Britain had increasingly fallen back on the only remaining
alternative—hounding the traders off the high seas. Here her superior
naval strength stood her in good stead. Even so, many problems remained.
Legally she had no right to interfere even with the most blatant slavers
except where she was licensed to do so. These agreements were difficult
to negotiate and even harder to enforce. What they amounted to was a
series of bilateral arrangements allowing a mutual right to search vessels,
usually within specified geographical limits, along with provisions for
arresting offenders and trying them before joint tribunals. Since these
were *mutual* right of search treaties, other nations were as entitled to
search and seize British ships as Britain was to search and seize theirs.
In practice, however, since British ships were no longer engaged in the
traffic and other nations showed little interest in suppressing it, they meant
simply that Britain could act as policeman of the seas, intercepting slavers
where the law permitted and arraigning them before international courts.

Even for a country with Britain's resources, this was a formidable
undertaking. It required, in the first place, the maintenance of effective
naval patrols along the coasts of Africa and Latin America. Sending only
the oldest and slowest craft to these stations was useless since the slavers
often had the latest and fastest types of vessel available, some of them
heavily armed. By the late 1830s the normal complement of the Cape and

15. Mathieson, *Great Britain and the Slave Trade*, pp. 12–13, 20–21.
16. *Ibid*, pp. 17–18. In both Cuba and Brazil the authorities were intimidated by
the political and economic power of the planters. The planters, for their part,
could see no reason why their labour supply should be cut off and their profits
diminished to satisfy the whim of Great Britain. Arthur F. Corwin, *Spain and the
Abolition of Slavery in Cuba, 1817–1886* (Austin, Texas, 1967), pp. 47–67.

West Africa Squadron, on which the main responsibility for combating the trade devolved, had risen to seventeen vessels and some eight hundred men.[17] The cost of all this, although less than some of the opponents of suppression later claimed, was plainly considerable. Nor could it be measured in financial terms alone; the death rate, principally from disease but also because of armed encounters with slavers, was significantly higher among personnel engaged in this type of work than in the navy as a whole.[18]

Keeping these forces up to strength and properly supplied was only one of Britain's problems and the least intractable. Much more difficult was the task of providing them with the authority needed to carry out their duties effectively. For example, the first right of search treaties proved in practice almost impossible to enforce because they allowed for the seizure of vessels only when slaves were on board. It therefore became the practice for slavers to take on their cargoes after nightfall or to hang about until the coast was clear, knowing that once on the open sea the chances of interception were small. Some actually threw their slaves overboard to avoid capture. These difficulties were eventually overcome by negotiating new treaties allowing for the detention of vessels on suspicion of being equipped for carrying slaves.

But the principal obstacle in Britain's way was not making individual treaties effective but making the system as a whole complete. As experience showed, no sooner were the slavers denied the use of one flag than they turned to another. By the 1830s, juggling with flags and alternative sets of papers had become a standard technique in the trade. Often a vessel would sail empty to Africa under one flag and having loaded return under another, the choice depending on the current state of the treaty system. Here, of course, Britain had to contend with the pride and jealousy of other nations. Even those which had declared the trade illegal were reluctant to give her the right to interfere with their vessels. The outstanding example was the United States. Americans remembered only too clearly the way in which Britain flouted their maritime rights during the years before the War of 1812, and they were not disposed to make any concessions now. Overcoming such opposition was a slow and intricate business, requiring skill and patience. Nevertheless some progress was made. In 1830 four major maritime nations, France, Spain, Portugal and the United States, were still outside the treaty system. By 1838 the field had been narrowed to two, Portugal and the United States.[19]

17. Lloyd, pp. 129–30, 279–89.   18. *Ibid*, pp. 130–8, 288–9.
19. A detailed description of Britain's treaty system at this time will be found in J. Bandinel. For fuller accounts of Britain's efforts to suppress the trade see the Mathieson and Lloyd volumes cited above; also, H. G. Soulsby, *The Right of Search and the Slave Trade in Anglo-American Relations, 1814–1862* (Baltimore, 1933).

It was thus on the completion of the treaty system that the champions of suppression pinned their hopes. They did so, not because they expected an easy or rapid victory but because the other methods that had been tried had proved even less workable. By process of elimination rather than conscious planning the struggle against the slave trade had become, in effect, the blockade policy.

It was against this background that Buxton during the months following his parliamentary defeat began taking stock of what had so far been achieved. He was, of course, already roughly familiar with the way in which policy had been shaping. As a member of Parliament he had sat through many debates on the subject and in 1835 had put forward a suggestion of his own that the slave trade be considered a form of piracy.[20] Nevertheless, the surprise and consternation expressed in his letter to Gurney, and later in his writings, suggest a man who had suddenly woken up to what had been happening around him. In fact this was very much what had occurred. Emotionally if not intellectually he was becoming aware of the slave trade for the first time.

This may seem surprising for a man who for thirteen years had been regarded as the leader of the antislavery cause in Britain. But, in common with most other abolitionists, he had taken remarkably little interest in what had been going on. This indifference may be traced back to the 1820s when, as we have seen, colonial slavery supplanted the trade as the principal concern of the movement. The old African Institution, already tottering, had been overshadowed by the new Anti-Slavery Society and in 1827 had ceased operations altogether. The Anti-Slavery Society had limited its activities strictly to the West Indian issue. In its minute books the trade is seldom mentioned. Articles had continued to appear from time to time in the *Anti-Slavery Reporter* giving details about new treaties, the capture of slavers, the numbers of slaves being landed and similar matters. But most of these were reprinted from elsewhere and were inserted in a way that suggests they were there more for the record than because readers were expected to form specific views, still less take positive action. Thus, by the 1830s, when abolitionists once again began taking an interest in other aspects of the slavery issue, the suppression policy was already regarded as a government affair, which was essentially what it had become.

Buxton, indeed, was the first abolitionist for more than two decades to attempt a broad view of the situation. He was at once struck by three things. One was the way in which the trade seemed to have grown; the

20. Charles Buxton, *Memoirs of Sir Thomas Fowell Buxton*, p. 373.

second was the extent to which its general features had remained unchanged over the years; the third was how ineffectual the official policy
of suppression had so far proved. This last was the most disturbing.
He had long ceased to feel any personal commitment to this policy,
but like others he had continued to support the government on the supposi-
tion that if the trade were not actually being diminished it was at least
being held in check. With a growing sense of disillusionment he began
to realize that the figures showed quite the opposite. Despite all the treaties,
naval patrols, joint courts of arbitration, and other arrangements,
it was still the law of supply and demand and not the laws of Britain or of
any other country that determined how many slaves crossed the Atlantic
annually. The evidence was overwhelming and he hastened to set it
forth in *The Slave Trade*, written in 1838 and published early the following year. His aim was to show, using the government's own reports and
figures, how the trade operated and why, in spite of all that had been
done, it continued to grow. *The Slave Trade* was, in effect as well as in
intention, a scourging attack on the whole suppression system. The picture
it gave was of a situation steadily worsening. Year by year more wars
were being fought in Africa, more slaves dying on their way down to the
coast, more succumbing to fever and dysentery on their journey across
the Atlantic. All told, allowing for the dead as well as the captives, the
Atlantic slave trade was depriving Africa of something like 400,000 inhabitants a year as compared with approximately half that figure fifty
years earlier. If one also allowed for the Mohammedan slave trade the
total fell not much short of half a million. Most of these figures were
simply conjecture, but his general thesis, that since Britain had begun her
operations thirty years earlier the situation had failed to improve, seemed
only too well established. Nor did he hold out any better hope for the
future. Agreements might be made with this country or that but the day
when every country would be bound by them was so remote that it might
never come. Meanwhile the trade would continue unabated. "It will
avail us little", he concluded, "that ninety-nine doors are closed, if one
remains open. To that outlet the whole Slave Trade of Africa will rush."[21]

Taken on its own, *The Slave Trade* could be regarded as a council of
despair, and this indeed was how many readers took it. Buxton's intention,
however, was quite different. In *The Remedy*, a lengthy supplement to
The Slave Trade, completed in 1838 and included in the later editions
of the work, he showed that he regarded the position as still far from hope-
less. Britain had not met with success so far mainly because her efforts
had been misdirected. Her error had lain in putting too much emphasis

21. Buxton, *The Slave Trade and its Remedy*, p. 209.

upon the use of her naval strength and not enough on other methods. In particular, she had failed to appreciate how much could be done by mobilizing Africa's own resources against the trade. Potentially, Africa was one of the richest continents. In her fertile soils, teeming wild life and rich mineral deposits, and in the native craftsmanship of her peoples, there was enormous wealth to be tapped. The trouble was that so long as the trade continued, all these remained virtually unexploited. The aim must be to break the cycle. If once the trade were stopped, perhaps only in a limited area, and proper encouragement given to agriculture and legitimate commerce, the potentialities of the country would soon be realized. A flourishing society would grow up which, although limited in area initially, would have the potential to extend outwards to include the whole continent. "It may sound visionary at the present time", he observed, "but I expect that at some future, and not very distant day, it will appear, that for every pound she now receives from the export of her people, a hundred pounds worth of produce, either for home consumption or foreign commerce, will be raised from the fertility of her soil."[22] He was careful not to disclaim the possibility that blockading might play a useful role. Indeed, he wished to see the African Squadron reinforced. But the main effort should be directed towards educating and encouraging the Africans themselves, and, above all, to driving out the trade by means of legitimate commerce. It was on this rather than on naval intervention that success ultimately depended.

There was little that was genuinely new in these suggestions. The idea of establishing a model society in Africa had been common currency since the 1780s, although less had been heard of it since the failure of Britain's one serious attempt to put it into practice, the Sierra Leone colony, had proved such a disappointment. The recurrent misfortunes of that settlement and the appalling mortality among those who went there had firmly impressed on the minds of Englishmen the notion of West Africa as the white man's grave.[23] Nothing would have been more damaging to Buxton's arguments than the belief that what he was advocating was simply another Sierra Leone. He was careful therefore to point out that what had happened there had been altogether so exceptional as to rule out general comparisons. The site chosen had been one of the worst possible, even on that inhospitable stretch of coast. The soil was infertile and so had prevented agricultural development. Access to the interior was cut off by dense jungle. And, being on the coast, it was subject to all the fevers which the surrounding mangrove swamps were known to generate. For his own project he favoured an inland location, far away from

22. *Ibid*, p. 281.   23. Curtin, *Image of Africa*, pp. 88–9, 179, 285–6.

the fevers of the coast. It would have rich soils and would be connected
to the sea and to other parts of the interior by good natural waterways.
Where exactly such a location was to be found he did not say but where he
expected to find it was plainly somewhere along the upper reaches of
the Niger.[24]

He was also somewhat embarrassed by the tendency to identify his aims
with those of the American Colonization Society. That such a confusion
should have arisen was understandable, for they had much in common.
The American Colonization Society itself added to the confusion by pro-
claiming him a convert and sending its secretary, the Rev. R. R. Gurley,
to England with proposals for joint action. As an abolitionist and one of
the first in England to have spoken out against colonization Buxton was
alive to the danger of having his plans linked with what had now come to
be regarded as a discredited project.[25] Addressing the World Anti-Slavery
Convention in 1840 he was at pains to assure the American delegation
that he was "an utter enemy to the Colonization Society".[26] In response
to Gurley's approaches he at first limited himself to saying that, while he
had no quarrel with what the colonizationists were doing in Liberia,
he regarded their activities in the United States as injurious. When Gurley
had the temerity to say that so far as he could see the main features of
Buxton's plan were "identical with the scheme and uniform policy which,
at all times, had been pursued . . . by the American Colonization Society"
he took a firmer line. The main object of his plan, he explained, was to
civilize Africa, while that of the Colonization Society was to provide a
means of disposing of America's surplus black population. "Our professed
objects", he concluded, "although akin are not the same; the field of
your operation is primarily America, that of ours Africa." It was unfortunate that he failed to note that one of the principal reasons for the Colonization Society's decline from favour was that, as with so many other projects,
the African side of its operations had sadly failed to live up to expectations![27]

24. Buxton, *The Slave Trade and its Remedy*, pp. 344–61.
25. As a result of Elliott Cresson's visit to England in 1832 a British subsidiary
of the American Colonization Society, the British African Colonization Society,
had been established. By 1839 this body had a nominal existence only, although
a few of its members now spoke up on Gurley's behalf. The aims of this organization
had been almost identical to those now proclaimed by Buxton, being "to promote
the establishment of Christianity and civilization among the natives of Africa,
chiefly by the employment of persons of African birth or descent and to secure
the entire abolition of the slave trade". R. R. Gurley, *A Mission to England on
Behalf of the American Colonization Society* (Washington, 1841), pp. 34–5.
26. BFASS, *Proceedings of the General Anti-Slavery Convention of 1840*, p. 245.
27. Gurley, pp. 1, 8–9, 18, 63–7. For general accounts of this society's operations
see E. L. Fox, *The American Colonization Society* and Philip J. Staudenraus,
The African Colonization Movement, 1816–1865 (New York, 1961).

How Buxton's own scheme might fare in practice was a question which was meanwhile exercising a good many minds. A preliminary printing of *The Remedy* had been run off in August 1838. He presented copies to the leading members of the Melbourne Cabinet, urging them to look into his proposals and to let him know whether they seemed viable. Their attention was directed especially to the final chapters in which he set out in summarized form the immediate practical steps to be taken.[28] Although these were intended to be merely the first exploratory probings, from which in time a wider policy would develop, they could hardly be described as modest. Indeed, by previous standards, they were grandiose. To begin with, there was to be a stepping up of British cruiser operations as a means of harassing traders. More ships were to be added to the African Squadron, including a number of steamers, preferably manned by coloured seamen, to explore the mouths of rivers. The commanders of these steamers would conclude treaties with the local chiefs, who would be persuaded to give up slaving and engage in other forms of commerce. In Buxton's view, too much should not be expected from the coastal tribes who had been in contact with slave traders long enough to become hardened cases. But better results were to be anticipated from those in the interior. They would be particularly amenable if they could be shown, as he believed they could, that legitimate commerce would in the long run be a great deal more profitable. To do this, however, would require a considerable outlay of funds. Trading posts would need to be established at appropriate points and vessels sent out to deliver and pick up goods. Even this would not be enough. Assistance would have to be given in keeping the peace while these arrangements were being made; model farms would need to be established to experiment with different types of cultivation; the Africans themselves would have to be taught how to apply the lessons learned from these experiments; and, initially at least, they would need to be supplied with seeds and implements. Under British tutelage—but not, he was careful to add, under British dominion—the Africans would be raised from their existing state of poverty and barbarism to one of prosperity and enlightenment.[29]

What Buxton was proposing, in short, was a massive pump-priming operation undertaken mainly at government expense. Private individuals would help. It was they who would build the trading posts, stock them with goods, establish experimental farms, collect geographical information and in general "use all the means that experience may point out, for a

28. Buxton, *The Slave Trade and its Remedy*, Preface to *The Remedy*, p. ii.
29. Buxton, *The Slave Trade and its Remedy*; a summary of his proposals will be found on pp. 518–22.

profitable and successful employment of British skill and capital in the African continent".[30] But this would mostly be at a later stage. Initially, the main task would be the government's for on it would devolve the responsibility for preserving the peace, keeping the slave traders at bay and sending out embassies to negotiate treaties with the African chiefs.

Had these suggestions come from a less distinguished source, or simply at another time, they would have been dismissed out of hand. Every detail could be traced back to proposals which had been made before, often many times over.[31] Lord Melbourne was highly sceptical of their achieving anything at all. Palmerston, who was as committed as anyone to African civilization and the suppression of the slave trade, thought them "a wild and crude idea. In order to extirpate the Slave Trade by commercial settlements, you must begird with them the whole circumference of Africa; for this plan is peculiarly open to the objection which Buxton makes to our Slave Treaties, that nothing is done till all is done".[32] They also ran counter to the general trend of British African policy which, since the 1780s and 90s had been towards retrenchment. While her commitment to seeing the slave trade suppressed had grown, her concern with Africa as a whole had declined. This had shown itself in many ways but most notably in a refusal to sponsor further schemes of exploration or settlement. As a field for colonial venture, Africa had been abandoned.[33]

And yet Buxton's plan was not easily shrugged off. His reputation was high. The defects of the treaty system and the inability of the cruisers to capture more than a small proportion of slavers were matters of genuine concern. More important, the Government's own position was perilous. In the spring of 1839 the defection of a group of radicals had temporarily put the Whigs out of office. A similar defection by the humanitarians would probably put them out for longer. Buxton, therefore, had to be humoured. In December 1838 he was told that the Ministry had decided to go along with the substance of his plan but that the details would require closer examination.[34] What the Government had in mind was to make a parade of accepting his programme but to amend it in such a way as to make it innocuous.

This was clear from the proposals which it announced on 1 February 1839. These provided for the exploration of the coastal regions around the mouth of the Niger and the conclusion of treaties with the local chiefs.

30. *Ibid*, pp. 520–1.
31. Curtin, *Image of Africa*, p. 302.
32. Palmerston to Glenelg, 24 Sept. 1838, in J. Gallagher. "Fowell Buxton and the New African Policy, 1838–1842", *Cambridge Historical Journal*, *10* (1950–52), 44.
33. Curtin, pp. 142, 289–96.
34. Buxton, *The African Slave Trade and its Remedy*, Preface to *The Remedy*, p. ii.

But there was to be no penetration into the interior and no establishment of trading posts along the Niger itself.[35] Buxton rightly interpreted this as an attempt to undercut his plan and responded with countermeasures. So successful were these that it quickly became clear that in its attempts to side-track him the Government had considerably underestimated the support he could command. In April he made preliminary arrangements with the leaders of the humanitarian group in Parliament for the establishment of a private body to help sponsor his programme and in June this organization was officially launched.[36] The following month Buxton himself received the seal of royal approval with the conferral of a baronetcy.

The African Civilization Society was the most aristocratic of all British antislavery bodies. It was presided over by no less a figure than Prince Albert. Among its Vice-Presidents were four archbishops, five dukes, eight marquises, fifteen earls and eighteen bishops. These were, of course, honorary positions but the executive committee, of which Buxton was chairman, was scarcely less imposing. It included thirteen peers, twenty MPs, among them such notables as Stephen Lushington, R. H. Inglis and T. B. Macaulay, as well as several leading Quakers, among whom were Samuel Gurney and William Allen.[37] If the social standing of its members were all that was needed for the success of a benevolent organization, the African Civilization Society would have been successful indeed. Its formation certainly impressed the Government. Within a matter of days the Colonial Secretary announced that the Ministry was setting aside its earlier plans and would back Buxton's proposals to the extent of sending a frigate and two steamers to explore the Niger.[38]

From this point on, the success or failure of Buxton's programme hinged on what happened to the Niger expedition. Initially, he had hoped that it would be ready to depart by November 1839, but various events conspired to delay preparations. Among these was the discovery that there were no government vessels with the shallow draught necessary for river navigation. After a fruitless search for suitable private vessels, a contract was signed with John Laird's of Birkenhead to build three iron paddle steamers specially for the expedition. The two larger vessels, the *Albert* and the *Wilberforce*, were to be identical, weighing just over 460 tons, and each equipped to carry about a hundred passengers and crew. The

35. Gallagher, *Cambridge Historical Journal*, *10*, (1950–52), 64.
36. *Friend of Africa*, 1 Jan. 1841.
37. *Prospectus of the Society for the Extinction of the Slave Trade and for the Civilization of Africa* (London, 1840).
38. Charles Buxton, p. 450.

smaller vessel, the *Soudan*, was to weigh 250 tons and would carry a total ship's complement of around fifty. Its purpose would be to explore along the narrower creeks and tributaries which the larger vessels, because of their greater width and draught, could not penetrate. All three were to be flat-bottomed but equipped with sliding keels which could be raised or lowered for use at sea. Internally they were to be divided into watertight compartments to ensure against sinking should they run aground.

One problem which received particular attention was the effect which the notorious African "climate" might have on the crews. According to the accepted medical opinion of the time the many continuous and inter- mittent fevers associated with the region[39] were produced by miasmas arising out of the mangrove swamps along the coast. The principal noxious element in these gases was believed to be sulphuretted hydrogen, produced by the action of salt water on decaying vegetable matter. Samples of water taken from the Niger delta and analysed in London showed significant traces of this substance, while those taken from the upper reaches proved relatively free. It thus appeared that once it had got above the coastal swamps the expedition would be safe. The main problem was to provide protection during the early stages.[40] To overcome this, elaborate air circulation systems were provided for each of the vessels. A series of fans, driven by the engines when in operation or by the river current when moored, was supposed to draw air in through enormous iron tanks containing chloride of lime and distribute it through tubes to the holds and cabins. In practice, these ventilation systems proved so ill-designed as to be unusable, although the "purificators" continued to take up valuable deck space. When, after descending the Niger, the *Wilberforce* jettisoned its "purificator", the great tank was said to have looked from the distance "like a floating omnibus".[41]

---

39. It was still customary to classify fevers by their symptoms, hence such terms as "continuous" and "intermittent". The two principal fevers, as we now know, were yellow fever, which manifested itself in the form of occasional but often devastating epidemics, and malaria, which was endemic throughout the region. Not until 1881 was it shown that in both cases infection was produced by the mosquito bite. The fever from which the members of the Niger Expedition suffered was presumably malaria.
40. It cannot be said that Buxton and his colleagues were neglectful of the need to protect the health of the expedition. Tremendous efforts were made, as the numerous articles appearing in *The Friend of Africa* testify, to determine the causes of fever and to provide means for combating it, not only by means of the "purificators" but also by providing a generous complement of ships' doctors, see *Friend of Africa*, Jan.–Feb. 1841.
41. William Allen and T. R. H. Thomson. *A Narrative of The Expedition sent by Her Majesty's Government to the River Niger in 1841* (2 vols, London, 1848), *1*, 26–30, 461; *2*, 70–2.

While the vessels were being built and equipped, the task of mobilizing private support continued. The African Civilization Society organized a mass meeting in Exeter Hall with Prince Albert in the chair; auxiliary organizations were established around the country; a new periodical, *The Friend of Africa*, appeared carrying highly optimistic accounts of what the expedition would achieve; eminent authorities on tropical medicine were consulted; help was solicited and obtained from the nation's leading missionary organizations;[42] a special agricultural society, an offshoot of the African Civilization Society, began drawing up plans for the model farm.[43] Never before had African affairs attracted so much attention. After a generation of neglect, Africa had suddenly become a subject of intense national interest.[44]

The Niger Expedition finally set sail, under the command of Captain Trotter, on 12 May 1841. Besides their crews the three vessels carried with them two botanists, a geologist, a mineralogist and a zoologist, all recruited and employed by the African Society. Also with the expedition was a party of West Indians led by Alfred Carr, described as 'a West Indian gentleman of colour', whose responsibility it would be to establish the model farm with the assistance of coloured workers recruited in Sierra Leone. The plan was for the three ships, once they had reached the mouth of the Niger, to pass through the dangerous delta region as quickly as possible, trusting to their speed and the "purificators" to save them from the fever-producing miasmas. Thereafter, they would make their way in a leisurely fashion upstream, pausing to make scientific observations and negotiate treaties with the local chiefs. At the confluence of the Niger and Benue, a tract of land would be purchased and arrangements made for Carr and his associates to begin cultivation. The three vessels would then continue their ascent of the river, making more treaties, exploring tributaries and generally collecting such data as might be useful to later and possibly more ambitious expeditions.

At first all went well. The ships reached Sierra Leone without mishap. There their crews were made up to full complement with native seamen. Workers were hired for the model farm project and a small brigantine, a former slaver, purchased to carry them. Two Church of England missionaries, Schon and his assistant, Crowther, also joined the expedition.

The first cases of fever occurred off the Gold Coast, three weeks after

42. Gallagher, *Cambridge Historical Journal*, *10* (1950–52), 49.
43. Charles Buxton, pp. 441–2.
44. Curtin, *Image of Africa*, pp. 302–3.

leaving Sierra Leone, and on 23 July produced the first fatality, Henry Halbert, a mulatto seaman from Falmouth. This caused some astonishment, as did the fact that the fever was most widespread among the West Indians, it having been assumed that Negroes would have a natural resistance to the disease.[45] But the officers were not unduly worried by this development since some fever was always to be expected on the Coast and the expedition pressed ahead without delay. By the time it entered the Niger on 15 August, only one other death, that of John W. Bach, the mathematical instrument maker, had been reported.[46] The vessels were now embarked on what was considered the most dangerous part of the voyage. Nevertheless, spirits remained high and there were no further signs of deterioration in the expedition's health. It was not until 4 September, by which time the ships were already some three hundred miles from the sea and well beyond what Buxton had considered the fever zone, that malaria began its serious ravages. There was one death on 7 September, another on 9 September and two on 11 September. So many members of the *Soudan* were prostrated by fever that that vessel had to be taken in tow.[47]

The expedition was now approaching the confluence of the Niger and Benue where the model farm was to be established. After surveying the land on either side a promising-looking tract was sighted about sixteen miles in length and four in width on the west bank of the river directly opposite the entrance to the Benue. On 14 September a treaty was concluded with the representatives of the local chief who agreed to cede this tract to the British Crown in return for a total payment of £45 to be paid in instalments. Carr and his assistants were put ashore together with one of the botanists, one of the ship's doctors and a junior officer from the *Soudan*.

By the time these arrangements were completed half the members of the expedition were laid low with fever and others were coming down with it hourly. On 16 September Captain Trotter proposed dividing the expedition into two groups, one to ascend the Niger and the other the Benue. By the 18th, however, it was evident that the sickness was still spreading and that plans would have to be changed. After a hasty consultation with the other commanders he determined to load as many of the sick as possible onto the *Soudan* and send them at once to the sea. On the 19th the *Soudan*

45. Allen and Thomson, *1*, 130–1.
46. *Ibid*, 161, 465. Although Bach died of fever, it was claimed that it was of a non-endemical kind. It was also noted that he had been "previously debilitated by irregular habits". These must have been rather a liability for anyone in his profession. *Friend of Africa*, Dec. 1841.
47. Allen and Thomson, *1*, 331, 337.

with its cargo of invalids departed and the two remaining vessels began getting up steam, the *Albert* to explore the upper reaches of the Niger, the *Wilberforce* to attempt the Benue. Even in this short interval, however, the number of cases of fever increased. On the *Wilberforce* thirty-two men were now sick, leaving only fourteen fit for duty, while the *Albert* was in little better condition. After further consultation it was decided that the *Wilberforce* should at once follow the *Soudan* to Fernando Po, taking as many of the sick as possible with her.[48]

It was now left to the *Albert* with a scratch crew to attempt the further ascent of the river. For the first three days reasonable progress was made but illness increasingly slowed down operations. On 28 September Egga was reached, the largest town so far visited, with a population estimated at about 10,000. It was now clear that it was beyond the physical capabilities of Captain Trotter and his men to go any further. Only six white members of the expedition were capable of duty and much of their time was taken up attending to the sick. Also the river was falling and there was a very real danger that if the vessel once went aground it would not be refloated until the following year. On 5 October orders were reluctantly given for the *Albert* to turn and begin the 320 mile run back to the coast. The voyage was a nightmare. Two members of the crew delirious with fever leaped overboard. At the model farm it was discovered that Carr and the two white men left to assist him were prostrated with fever. They were accordingly taken on board and command given to an American Negro emigrant, Ralph Moore, whom the expedition had picked up in Liberia. Apart from the Krumen recruited in Sierra Leone, the only fit members of the expedition were the geologist and the ship's doctor, the former tending the boilers while the latter supervised the navigation and attended the sick. On 13 October, when still over a hundred miles from the coast, the *Albert* was met by the *Ethiope*, a relief vessel sent out from Fernando Po, and with its assistance succeeded in reaching the sea on 16 October.[49] Observers seeing her emerging from the Nun estuary noted that she moved "like a plague-ship, filled with its dead and dying". They also glimpsed an emaciated figure being raised up. The figure was that of Captain Trotter.[50]

Buxton was heartbroken at the news of the expedition's failure and the growing list of casualties.[51] By the end of the year, forty-one of those who

48. *Ibid, 1*, 366–9.
49. "Notes of Proceedings on board Her Majesty's steamship vessel *Albert*, after departure of the *Wilberforce* by Dr McWilliam", *ibid, 2*, 79–141.
50. *Ibid, 2*, 78. The *Soudan* had been sent out as a second relief vessel and met the *Albert* and the *Ethiope* as they emerged from the Nun.
51. Charles Buxton, pp. 469–70.

had set out had died as a result of river fever and six others from miscellaneous causes.[52] Of those who had contracted the disease, many remained severely debilitated. The one remaining chance of saving the
scheme from ruin and turning what looked like an unmitigated disaster
into a success rested on the fate of the model farm. Early in March the
leaders of the African Civilization Society hopefully petitioned the new
Tory Government for a resumption of exploratory efforts and protection
for the agricultural project.[53] The Tories were in a much stronger position
than their predecessors and feeling that more than enough lives had been
sacrificed already were anxious to see the whole enterprise wound up as
speedily as possible. But since the model farm was in existence instructions
were sent to Fernando Po ordering a single vessel, manned as far as possible
by local Negroes, to ascend the river as far as the confluence. The commander of the vessel was then to decide whether or not the model farm
should be broken up. In either event, he was to explain to the settlers that
Britain had determined not to accept sovereignty over the land on which
the farm was situated, and that if they wished to remain they would have
to make their own arrangements with the local chief.[54] The Government,
clearly, had decided to wash its hands of the whole affair.

The vessel selected was the *Wilberforce*, now under the command of
Lieutenant Webb. The ascent of the river was not unlike the experience
of the previous year, except that the natives now appeared less friendly.
There were unmistakable signs that despite the treaties they had entered
into they were still engaged in slaving. At the model farm, a further disappointment awaited the expedition. Carr, the superintendent, who had
set out from Fernando Po the previous November intending to ascend
the river by canoe, had failed to appear and evidence suggested that he had
been murdered somewhere along the way. Discipline on the farm had
meanwhile broken down. Moore, the acting superintendent, had been
faced with continual insubordination and had only with difficulty prevented
the settlers preying on the surrounding natives, who, so far as could be
gathered, had behaved with remarkable generosity and forbearance.
The practice had grown up of using hired native labour for agricultural
work and Lieutenant Webb was disconcerted to find two coloured settlers
supervising this work armed with whips "apparently for the purpose of
urging those under them to greater exertion". All this persuaded him
that the farm would have to be abandoned, a decision in which the settlers

52. Allen and Thomson, *1*, 461–71.
53. Charles Buxton, p. 555.
54. Capt. W. Allen to Lt Webb, Fernando Po, 29 June 1842, in Allen and Thomson, *2*, 335–8.

themselves concurred. On 23 July, having loaded them and their possessions on board, and with fever already beginning to spread among the crew, the *Wilberforce* began its descent of the river.[55]

The failure of the Niger Expedition spelt the end of the African Civilization Society and of Buxton's plans for ending the slave trade by attacking it at source. Recriminations inevitably followed. According to the press, gifted now with the wisdom of hindsight, the undertaking had been ill-conceived from the start. This was a view which the subsequent parliamentary enquiry and the accounts of the survivors straggling back to England did little to dispel. The only argument advanced in its defence was that in every respect save one—the effect of the "climate" on the expedition's health—it had gone very much according to plan. Even this was open to question after Lieutenant Webb's discoveries on his return ascent of the river. Buxton was a discredited man. The deaths, particularly that of his friend, Captain Bird Allen, commander of the *Soudan*, preyed on his mind and friends noted "his wan pale face, the abstraction of his manner, and the intense fervour of his supplications". In January 1843 he went to London to play his part in winding up the affairs of the African Society. "I feel", he wrote to its secretary, "as if I were going to attend the funeral of an old friend." Death was now very much on his mind and his own health was failing. He had retired from London and was living on his estate in East Anglia. It was there that he died on 19 February 1845.

One thing at least the Niger Expedition had established: if the slave trade were to be suppressed it would have to be either by blockading or by action within the importing countries. There was no longer a third possibility.

55. *Ibid*, 149–50, 359–66, 376–7. All eight white members of Lt Webb's party suffered more or less severely from fever and two died of it.
56. "Papers relative to the expedition to the River Niger", PP, 1843, *48*.

4

Sturge's solution

While Buxton had been laying his plans
for the civilization of Africa, the Sturgites
had been considering what course they
should pursue. Five years earlier, finding
themselves, so they believed, in a similar
position, they had responded by forming
the Universal Abolition Society. Events
had shown their action to have been premature and they had again quickly become
embroiled in West Indian disputes. But
these earlier plans, although put aside, were
by no means forgotten. It was natural that
as the summer of 1838 progressed and
agreeable tidings continued to arrive from
the colonies, their thoughts should once
more have begun turning towards wider
issues.

Such notions were certainly very much
on the minds of those antislavery leaders
who on 1 August attended Sturge's grand
rally in Birmingham to celebrate the ending
of apprenticeship. Daniel O'Connell, in
his reply to Sturge's invitation, caught the
note precisely:

Make one of your professed objects *to consider
the propriety of forming a society to aid in the
universal abolition of slavery*. If you do *that*,
come what will, I am with you at Birmingham on the 1st August. I could not promise

unless I had an object of that importance in view. . . . Use what terms you think most expedient, so that you show an intention to *take into consideration* slavery in other nations. Specify America if you choose, or leave the name out of your plan. But frame your argument in such a way as to enable us to begin the work with the vile and sanguinary slaveholders of Republican America. I want to be *directly* at them. No more side-wind attacks; firing directly at the hull, as the seamen say, is my plan.[1]

This proved to be the prevailing theme of the Birmingham meeting. No one suggested, or not publicly at any rate, that now that British slavery was at an end the best thing that they could do would be to disband and turn their attention to other matters. Those who took this view, as some did,[2] either stayed at home or remained silent. Their voices were not heard at Birmingham.

Elaborate preparations were made for the occasion. The day began with hymn singing by a massed assembly of 3,000 children on the square in front of the Town Hall. This was followed by a procession through the city to Henenge Street where, in the presence of an estimated 13,000 spectators, Sturge laid the cornerstone of some new school buildings to be known as the Negro Emancipation Schools. More hymns were sung and short addresses on the subject of abolition given by the dignitaries present.

In the evening a large gathering assembled in the Town Hall. Many well-known figures were present, including Sturge, Dr Stephen Lushington, Daniel O'Connell and other notables, most of whom had travelled up from London for the occasion. In his opening address, Sturge reviewed the achievements of the antislavery movement so far and then went on to describe what still remained to be done both in the West Indies and elsewhere. The truth was that in the world as a whole, very little had been achieved. In the West Indies a careful watch would need to be kept on the treatment afforded the freedmen. In the world at large the slave trade now flourished on a broader scale than ever before. The only effective way of dealing with this was by the universal destruction of slavery itself.[3] Other speakers followed using much the same arguments and emphasizing the need for a general crusade against slavery. That antislavery stalwart, Stephen Lushington, MP for Tower Hamlets, referred specifically to the American practice of slaveholding. It was the duty of Britain, having

---

1. O'Connell to Sturge, 7 July 1838, in Richard, *Memoirs of Joseph Sturge*, pp. 175–6.
2. See Macaulay's remark quoted on p. xv above. A good many Englishmen may have agreed with Macaulay, but if they did, they saw no reason for making an issue of the matter and, possibly, exposing themselves to charges of moral unreliability.
3. Report of Sturge's speech in *British Emancipator*, 27 Sept. 1838.

already set the Americans an example, to keep that example before them
in all its force. As the final speaker, Daniel O'Connell, whose appearance
earlier in the evening had been greeted with tumultuous applause, made
a scourging attack on the United States. Like most British radicals of
this period he was an avowed admirer of American ideals and institutions
and for this reason found the American practice of slaveholding peculiarly
abhorrent. His views coincided with those of his audience which roared
its approval at each new sally. The United States, he informed them, was a
nation of hypocrites as exemplified by its first president, George Washington, who had exploited his slaves while he was alive and allowed them to
be emancipated only after his death. He believed that their very ambassador was a slave breeder. Was it possible that America would send such
a man? He hoped not but he believed that it was right to speak out. He
went on to quote from the slave laws of various Southern states and concluded by proposing a resolution, tumultuously carried by the assembly,
condemning slavery in professedly Christian nations and expressing
admiration for the courage of the American abolitionists.[4]

These proceedings received a good deal of attention in the press, particularly when it became known that Andrew Stevenson, the unfortunate
American minister to whom O'Connell had referred, had written to him
demanding an explanation. This was the accepted first step to issuing
a challenge to a duel. O'Connell, who had once killed a man in an affray,
was now strongly opposed to duelling. Nevertheless, he was delighted
to have his remarks acknowledged in this way. There followed a lengthy
and much publicized exchange of letters in the British and American
press about what O'Connell had actually said (which he professed to
have forgotten) and what Stevenson ought to have done in response.
On the whole the affair probably caused less of a flurry in Britain than in
the United States, where John Quincy Adams made an issue of it, in a
Congress already exercised over the issues of slavery and duelling, by
demanding the minister's recall and the establishment of a committee
of enquiry. The episode was perhaps best summed up by the *Boston
Courier*, which observed that if the American minister had not "made
himself a fool", he had "made himself look most admirably like one".[5]

While this curious affair was causing reverberations on both sides of the
Atlantic, Sturge was drawing up plans for the future. In January 1839

4. *The Testimony of Daniel O'Connell*, broadside, n.d., Library of Congress. Other
accounts of this speech will be found in *The Spectator*, 4 Aug. 1838; *British Emancipator*, 22 Aug. 1838, and the New York *Emancipator*, 27 Sept. 1838.
5. For a fuller account of this incident see Howard Temperley, "The O'Connell-
Stevenson contretemps: a reflection of the Anglo-American slavery issue", *Journal
of Negro History*, 47 (1962), 217–33.

he outlined his conclusions in a letter to the Editor of *The British Emancipator*. It was at once evident that his views were at odds with those of both Buxton and the Government. With a profit of 180 per cent on each slaving voyage, he pointed out, it was futile to look to a naval blockade as a means of suppression. Such a margin of profit meant that traders would always find ways of getting through, regardless of how many ships they had to sacrifice in the process. The only solution was "laying the axe to the root" and abolishing slavery itself. This was, it will be recalled, the same phrase that Clarkson had used more than thirty years earlier in connection with the attack on the trade. Sturge was now using it to justify precisely the opposite policy. Slavery, not the trade, was the root to which the axe must be laid. To achieve this, abolitionists would have to rely primarily on their moral and religious influence.

We have seen the effects of this influence in the abolition of our own colonial slavery, and both France and America are already feeling the powerful effects of our example. During the last two or three months I have endeavoured to ascertain the opinion of many of the friends of the cause in different parts of the Kingdom, and it has been gratifying to find a great unanimity of sentiment and a readiness to act in accordance with these views; but as there is a larger number of friends whose sentiments are as yet to be ascertained, I would earnestly invite them to a close examination of the subject and venture to express a hope that they will be prepared to suggest, or to adopt, measures which will promote in other countries the destruction of the accursed system which has happily almost ceased to disgrace the British Empire. The first step to be taken would probably be an efficient organization of a society. For this purpose a meeting of a few of our friends should be held to discuss the basis on which it should be founded, to be followed in a few weeks by one of a more general character, when the measures proposed might be considered and determined on, and a public meeting might afterwards be held to give them sanction and due notoriety.

No time was lost in putting this plan into effect. On 27 February, in the Guildhall Coffee House, twenty leading abolitionists sympathetic to Sturge's views met and approved a draft constitution which he had drawn up.[6] In the course of the following month further meetings were held at which it was agreed that copies of the draft constitution, together with invitations to a general antislavery convention to be held in Exeter Hall on 17 April, be sent to both the existing metropolitan societies and to all individuals who since 1833 had come to London as delegates of provincial organizations.[7]

The Exeter Hall convention, which lasted for two days, attracted a

6. British and Foreign Anti-Slavery Society, Minute Books, 27 Feb. 1839, Bodleian Library, Oxford—referred to hereafter as BFASS Minute Books.
7. *Ibid*, 13, 15 March 1839.

good number of abolitionists both from London and the provinces. Sturge explained to them the aims and structure of his proposed organization. The audience was sympathetic and it was agreed that a new body, to be known as the British and Foreign Anti-Slavery Society, should be established. A sub-committee was nominated to prepare a final draft of the constitution and to draw up a list of nominees for the executive committee. The following day it reported and a constitution and list of committee members was approved.[8]

Some provincial abolitionists who attended the Exeter Hall meeting expressed doubts as to the wisdom of founding a new national organization when there were already two such bodies in existence, the old Anti-Slavery Society and the Central Negro Emancipation Committee. (Buxton's African Civilization Society was yet to make its appearance.) This, however, caused Sturge no uneasiness for as he saw it the new body would quickly take the place of the other two. His prediction proved correct. As will be shown presently, the British and Foreign Anti-Slavery Society was in many ways a re-embodiment of the Emancipation Committee[9], which accordingly began its own gradual dissolution. Meanwhile the Anti-Slavery Society, having contributed little to the late struggle over apprenticeship, and, now that Buxton had turned his attention to Africa, sadly in need of both leadership and funds, was a spent force. On 26 April, exactly eight days after the establishment of Sturge's new organization, its committee resolved to suspend operations *sine die*.[10]

The British and Foreign Anti-Slavery Society was to prove the most enduring of all British antislavery organizations.[11] It was also, during the next thirty years, the only one with a consistent claim to national stature. This was partly because for most of this period, it was the only one with a firm metropolitan base. In a country as highly centralized as Britain, this had important advantages. From the practical point of view it meant

8. A full account of these proceedings will be found in *British Emancipator*, 1 May 1839.
9. "The elements of virtue and strength which have been embodied in the now expiring Emancipation Committee have already organized themselves anew in the British and Foreign Anti-Slavery Society, which, although it will do much more than the former could have done, will not leave undone that which it would have continued to do." *British Emancipator*, 10 July 1839, p. 266.
10. ASS Minute Books, 2 April 1839.
11. These are listed in Appendix A below. The British and Foreign Anti-Slavery Society, now known simply as The Anti-Slavery Society, is still active. At the time of writing its offices are in Denison House, Vauxhall Bridge Road, London SW1; for an account of its recent policies see Epilogue; also C. W. W. Greenidge, *Slavery* (London, 1958).

easy access to Parliament, to government departments and to the national press. London was also the place where visiting foreigners, whatever the reason for their presence in Britain, tended to congregate, and where, of course, foreign embassies were located. For an organization with aspirations to becoming an international force, these were important factors. But besides these practical advantages the mere fact of having London offices made a Society *look* like a national society in a way in which organizations whose headquarters were in Glasgow or Bristol, or even Edinburgh and Dublin, could not—a fact which was to cause abolitionists in those cities intense annoyance during the years ahead.

There was nothing particularly novel about the structure of this new body. It consisted essentially of a central office, a secretary and one or two assistants responsible for routine matters, a committee which met from time to time to consider issues of general policy, and a network of provincial auxiliaries which performed the dual function of keeping the parent society informed and making its views known to the country at large as well as, of course, collecting funds. The possibility of employing paid agents in the manner of the Agency Committee was considered but rejected on the grounds that this kind of approach was unsuited to the protracted type of campaign anticipated. Whatever lecturing had to be done, it was decided, could safely be left to the Secretary and the members of the Committee.

In theory, ultimate authority for the Society's actions lay with its members. These were individuals who made donations of £5 or more or who subscribed not less than ten shillings annually to its funds. Membership carried with it the privilege of attending a General Meeting held in London once a year at which a report of the preceding year's activities and a financial statement were presented and a Committee and Officers elected.[12] The lists of subscriptions and donations reveal that in July 1840 the Society had 236 members, in May 1841, 461, and in May 1847, approximately 850.[13] In practice, however, Annual General Meetings were so well stage-managed, members being told beforehand what resolutions to propose and whom to elect, that these gatherings became largely a formality. Thus for all practical purposes the Committee was a self-perpetuating body. On the one occasion when a General Meeting refused to endorse a Committee policy its recommendations were ignored. Thus,

12. "Constitution and objects of the British and Foreign Anti-Slavery Society," copies of which will be found appended to the Society's *Annual Reports*, 1840–70.
13. Lists of subscriptions and donations, *Annual Reports*, 1840, 1841, 1847. These figures do not include those who supported the Society indirectly through auxiliary bodies since they did not officially qualify for membership.

short of sacking the Committee—in which case the Society, like the American Anti-Slavery Society in 1840, would probably have split—the members could do little except offer suggestions or, as sometimes happened, register their disapproval by withdrawing their financial support.

The responsibility for formulating and implementing policies, therefore, rested with the London Committee. During the first year, because of the pressure of work, Committee meetings were held on an average once a week, though they subsequently became less frequent. Meetings were usually held on Friday afternoons and appear to have been conducted with a minimum of formality. Refreshments were provided and guests were often invited to join in the proceedings.

Among the thirty original members there were only five who had not served on one or more of the earlier national committees—twelve having belonged to the Anti-Slavery Committee, five to the Agency and Universal Abolition Committees and twenty to the Central Negro Emancipation Committee.[14] In later years it was often claimed by those who were opposed to the Committee's policies that this body had no connection with those earlier and—now that they had ceased to exist—universally respected organizations. Convenient though this argument was, it had little justification. In this as in many other respects what was most striking was the degree of continuity.

The Committee was conspicuously lacking in the type of aristocratic support that characterized the African Civilization Society and which, to a lesser extent, had also been a feature of the old Anti-Slavery Society. Like the Agency, Universal Abolition and Central Negro Emancipation Committees, with which it had more in common, it was composed exclusively of members of the middle class, of whom the great majority were nonconformists. As always, there was a strong contingent of Quakers. Among the sixty-seven individuals who held seats on the Committee between 1839 and 1870, thirty-two or just under half belonged to the Society of Friends.[15] Among the hard core the proportion was even higher.

14. In compiling lists of committee members of these organizations, the following sources were used: for the Anti-Slavery Society, ASS Minute Books, 1836–39; for the Universal Abolition Society, *Report of the British and Foreign Society for the Universal Abolition of Slavery and the Slave Trade* (London, May, 1835); for the Central Emancipation Committee, *The British Emancipator*, 2 April, 13 June 1838; for the British and Foreign Anti-Slavery Society, *Annual Reports* (London, 1840–70).

15. This was nothing unusual so far as the British antislavery movement was concerned. As we have seen, of the twelve original members of the Committee for the Suppression of the Slave Trade, founded in 1787, all save three were Quakers. It is interesting, for the purposes of comparison, to note that Quakers played a

It has been said of the American abolitionists that they represented a socially declining group, the New England intelligentsia, whose position was being challenged by rising mercantile and industrial interests, and who therefore turned to slavery as a means of bolstering their social positions.[16] Whatever the truth of this in the case of the Americans no such claims could be made about the British most of whom represented precisely those interests which, in the United States, are said to have been threatening the traditional order. Sturge's own career, that of a farmer's son who entered commerce and through hard work rose to be a wealthy merchant, contained elements common to the careers of most of his colleagues. William Allen, the oldest member of the Committee's inner caucus and in public life the most prominent, was the son of a silk weaver. Like Sturge, he had begun to work for his father at an early age, but finding little scope for his talents had left the family business to become an apprentice in a pharmaceutical establishment. There he had quickly risen to a responsible position, becoming the proprietor at the age of twenty-five. He was subsequently appointed a lecturer in chemistry at Guy's Hospital, and in 1807, at the age of thirty-seven, became a Fellow of the Royal Society.[17] Josiah Forster, another hard core member, was the son of a land surveyor. After attending a Quaker day school he became an assistant teacher in a school run by his uncle, which he left a few years later to open an establishment of his own. In 1826, at the age of forty-four, he had been able to retire on what was described as a "modest competence".[18]

These examples, which could easily be multiplied, illustrate a common social pattern. Coming from modest backgrounds, usually members of large families, they worked hard during their early lives, showed irreproachable business integrity, and retired at a comparatively early age. There were, however, some exceptions. G. W. Alexander, the Society's

much less prominent role in the American movement at this time. For example in 1851, the Executive Committee of the American and Foreign Anti-Slavery Society consisted of: 10 Congregationalists, 3 Presbyterians, 2 Baptists, 1 Wesleyan Methodist, 1 Episcopalian and 1 Quaker: Lewis Tappan, *Reply to Charges brought against the American and Foreign Anti-Slavery Society* (London, 1852), p. 13.
16. David Donald, "Toward a reconsideration of the abolitionists" in *Lincoln Reconsidered: Essays on the Civil War Era* (New York, 1956), pp. 18–36. Two recent studies have thrown doubt on Donald's analysis, see Bertram Wyatt-Brown, *Lewis Tappan and the Evangelical War Against Slavery* (Cleveland, Ohio, 1969), p. 3 and footnote, and Leonard L. Richards *'Gentlemen of Property and Standing': Anti-Abolition Mobs in Jacksonian America* (New York, 1970), pp. 131–55. In the case of the British it would make more sense to say that antislavery activity was a means of *achieving* social respectability. Not that this would explain much since in both countries there were many easier routes to social advancement.
17. London Friends' Institute, *Biographical Catalogue* (London, 1888), pp. 7–14.
18. *Ibid*, pp. 211–19.

Treasurer, was a partner in his family's bill-broking firm, and William
Ball was fortunate enough to marry an heiress, which spared him the
necessity of having to work at all. Samuel Gurney the elder, the Society's
most generous benefactor, is perhaps worthy of particular mention.
The Gurneys were one of the leading Quaker families in England. Samuel,
the second son, a brother of Elizabeth Fry and brother-in-law to Thomas
Fowell Buxton, was an outstanding financier, later described by Richard
Cobden as having shared with the elder Rothschild "the most comprehensive and sagacious views on money matters of any man of our times".[19]
With the help of his family connections and a large inherited fortune
he succeeded in building up a gigantic bill-broking business which for
more than twenty years was the largest of its kind in the world. He was
particularly successful in persuading small private banks to deposit their
surplus capital with his firm instead of with the Bank of England, so
becoming widely known as a banker's banker. On his death his personal
property was valued at £800,000 and the investments he controlled at
more than ten times that sum.[20] Among the other banking families
represented on the Committee were the Buxtons, Barclays and Lucases,
who were among those which later combined with the Gurneys to form
Barclays Bank Limited.[21]

The motives which led such men into antislavery work were mixed.
Benevolence is seldom disinterested and on close examination is usually
found in combination with other elements less highly regarded. It would
have been surprising if they had not enjoyed their sense of *richesse oblige*
and the social status which indulging it brought them. Plainly many of
them did. Nor does one have to look far to find traces of another element
often associated with conspicuous generosity—guilt. As Christians they
set themselves the loftiest conceivable standards of behaviour, so lofty
that not even the most devoted and self-abnegating could come close to
meeting them. The feelings of failure and frustration which this produced,
and which they acknowledged, often with surprising frankness, was a
powerful goad to action. The religious conscience is a formidable engine
and its workings are abundantly evident to anyone who dips into the personal diaries and reminiscences of these individuals.[22] Opponents, espe-

19. Richard Cobden to Joseph Sturge, 21 June 1856, Sturge Papers, British Museum,
Add MSS 43723/131.
20. Paul H. Emden, *Quakers in Commerce: A record of business achievement* (London,
1940), pp. 107–13. A bill-broker acted as an agent in the buying and selling of
promissory notes.
21. *Ibid*, p. 147. Barclays Bank was established in 1896.
22. See, for example, Josiah Forster, *Extracts from my Note Book: from 1831 to 1854*
(Tottenham, 1865). This was an exercise in self-laceration remarkable even by
nineteenth-century standards. Less extreme examples are to be seen in the short

cially in the United States, singled out this trait as evidence of a diseased mentality.[23] Such elements, however, were present in the make-up of many, probably most, middle-class nineteenth-century reformers, an outstanding example being Gladstone, whose belief in his own unworthiness, based on equally slender evidence, fully matched that of any abolitionist.[24] It is very doubtful whether in this respect, or with respect to the pleasure which they derived from their good works, abolitionists can be distinguished from other benevolently motivated individuals of the time.

The specific charge most frequently made against them by contemporaries was that their concern for the welfare of the Negroes betrayed an indifference to, or even a wish to divert attention from, the sufferings of other groups nearer home. Anyone who has read Dickens's *Bleak House* will recall his satirical portrayal of the philanthropic Mrs Jellyby, the female version of this type of reformer, who was so busy promoting the welfare of "the natives of Borrioboola-Gha, on the left bank of the Niger" that she neglected her own family.[25] This line of attack naturally appealed to slaveholders. A sustained Southern indictment of such "telescopic philanthropy" is the pseudonymous Dr Pleasant Jones's *The Slaveholder Abroad or Billy Buck's Visit to England* (Philadelphia, 1860) in which an American slave who accompanies his master to England comments on what he finds there. On one occasion he attends a meeting of the British and Foreign Anti-Slavery Society and is hugely amused to find so much concern for Negroes and so little for white men who needed it much more. This work may have been partly inspired by George Fitzhugh's *Cannibals All! or Slaves without Masters* (Richmond, Virginia, 1857) in which these arguments received their classic statement, although they had appeared in so many other versions over the years that they must be regarded as part of the standard defence of slavery.[26] What all these accounts had in

biographies of individual members of the British and Foreign Anti-Slavery Society in London Friends' Institute, *Annual Monitor, or, Obituary to the Members of the Society in Great Britain and Ireland* (London, 1803–1920).

23. e.g. "The basis of Northern Hostility to the South", *De Bow's Review*, 28 January 1860, 9–14, in David M. Potter and Thomas G. Manning, eds, *Nationalism and Sectionalism in America, 1775–1877: select problems in historical interpretation* (New York, 1949) pp. 136–7.

24. M. R. D. Foot, ed., *The Gladstone Diaries* (2 vols. so far, Oxford, 1968), especially *I*, 334, 401.

25. Dickens weights his case by making a dead issue, Niger settlement, Mrs Jellyby's field of interest. The cause most likely to arouse such philanthropic ladies in the 1850s was American slavery: see Chapter 11 below.

26. For an earlier version see St. George L. Sioussat, ed., "Duff Green's 'England and the United States' with an Introductory Study of American Opposition to the Quintuple Treaty of 1841," *Proceedings of the American Antiquarian Society*, *40*, (1930), 175–276.

common was the view that there must be something wrongheaded if not positively hypocritical in so marked a preoccupation with other people's problems.

While it is undoubtedly true that much more could have been done than was being done to alleviate suffering in Britain at this time, a closer look at the careers of the individuals against whom such charges were most commonly levelled shows that they had little foundation. Indeed, *had* Sturge and his colleagues felt that waging an antislavery struggle was in itself a sufficiently taxing occupation and so chosen to leave other issues aside, their attitudes would have been understandable. In fact this was not the case. Sturge himself came close to being the Compleat Reformer. As early as 1816, long before he turned his attention to slavery, he had become a supporter of the peace movement, and even during his later years this continued to claim much of his time and energy. In 1850 he visited Denmark and Schleswig Holstein in a last minute attempt to avert hostilities between those countries, and in 1854, on the eve of the Crimean War, he travelled to Russia on a similar mission. He was also a leading advocate of political and economic reform. In 1831 he became an active member of Thomas Attwood's Birmingham Political Union, and argued strenuously for the abolition of taxes on all necessities, universal free trade, the disestablishment of the Church of England, vote by ballot, and the abolition of capital punishment. Ten years later, he shocked middle-class conservatives by becoming a Chartist and campaigning for universal manhood suffrage. When, in 1841, the Chartists were torn between following the advocates of 'moral force' and 'physical force', it was he who conceived the idea of reorganizing the 'moral force' faction and of uniting it with the main body of middle-class reformers by launching the Complete Suffrage Movement. He was also one of the original members of the Anti-Corn Law League, though, as we will see, he afterwards broke with it over the sugar duties question. At the time of his death in 1859 he was actively involved in sponsoring adult education, building playgrounds for poor Birmingham children and maintaining out of his own pocket an institution for the reform of delinquent boys.[27]

Other members of the Committee showed a similar diversity of interests. William Allen was associated in one way or another with almost every philanthropical endeavour of the day. G. W. Alexander, besides being

27. Richard, *Memoirs of Joseph Sturge*; Stephen Hobhouse, *Joseph Sturge, his Life and Work* (London, 1919); William R. Hughes, *Sophia Sturge: a Memoir* (London, 1940); see also the chapter on Sturge in G. D. H. Cole, *Chartist Portraits* (London, 1941).

Treasurer of the British and Foreign Anti-Slavery Society, was Treasurer of the Aborigines Protection Society and a leading figure in the temperance movement. Samuel Gurney the younger, who in 1864 became President of the Society (though he was never very active in that capacity), held seats on the executive committees of no less than eleven philanthropical organizations and was closely associated with a number of others.[28] The list could be extended almost indefinitely. Not only were the Committee members themselves engaged in almost every type of benevolent enterprise, but so were their wives, sisters, brothers, uncles, aunts, and business colleagues. In short, the British and Foreign Anti-Slavery Society was part of a great complex of organizations, many of them with interlocking committees, devoted to education, peace, temperance, universal suffrage, women's rights, free trade, prison reform, religious conversion, famine relief and innumerable other worthy causes.

There was one charge, however, to which these reformers were vulnerable. Although they believed in helping the poor, the underprivileged and the handicapped, they drew the line at any indiscriminate mixing of the social classes. Abolitionists who were happy to shake hands with visiting American Negroes and wished to see slavery immediately overthrown, did not wish to see the immediate abolition of class distinctions in Britain itself, though they would probably have been less horrified by such a development than would most of their middle-class contemporaries. The antislavery appeal, however, was essentially an appeal by the middle-classes to the middle-classes. The lower orders of society, in so far as they intruded at all, generally featured as rowdies and hecklers who tried to break up meetings. Not until the 1850s was any attempt made, and then only a half-hearted one, to mobilize working-class support.

The world of these mid-nineteenth-century philanthropists was in many ways a narrow one. It was a world composed mainly of Quakers, Baptists, Methodists and other religious dissenters. Above all, it was a middle-class world. Its leaders were corn merchants like Sturge, bankers like Gurney, Alexander and Barclay, schoolmasters like Josiah and Robert Forster, scientists like William and Stafford Allen, manufacturers like Robert Charleton and Samuel Fox, or publishers like Charles Gilpin and Richard Barrett. These were the benevolent élite who controlled and to a large extent financed this astonishing array of organizations aimed at benefiting the human race. As individuals they were often associated in their business activities and in many cases were related by marriage. These interconnections were especially marked in the case of the Quakers

28. London Friends' Institute, *Biographical Catalogue*, pp. 319–25.

who were traditionally a close-knit group, but were by no means confined to them.[29]

What distinguished these philanthropists most of all, perhaps, was their peculiar sensitivity to conscience. To the modern mind this often seemed to manifest itself in puzzling ways, as may be illustrated by citing two examples. Shortly before his death Sturge happened to revisit the village of Kingley, where he had lived as a child. Walking through the streets he came to an inn which had formerly belonged to an old woman, long since dead. The sight of the building reminded him of an occasion when, as a small boy, he had knowingly allowed this woman to give him change in copper for a counterfeit sixpence. This memory so troubled him that he began making discreet enquiries and finding that a grand-daughter of the old lady still lived nearby, he arranged that she should be given a five pound note, taking care that this should be done anonymously, to avoid embarrassment and so that there would be no suspicion of im-proper motives.[30] The second example concerns the stand he took in 1835 over the question of Mauritian compensation. Even outside the antislavery camp it was generally agreed that the Mauritian planters were an undeserving lot, but since the money had already been voted and the question was merely one of allocation, Buxton's argument that the right course to follow was that most likely to be of practical benefit to the Negroes would seem a perfectly reasonable one. Yet Sturge, as we have seen, was not prepared to countenance giving support to the Mauritians on any account and actually broke with Buxton over this issue. Clearly what influenced him on both these occasions was not just benevolence. In the first case there is nothing to suggest that he felt any particular concern for the welfare of the granddaughter, and in the second the con-dition of the Negroes was made a matter of secondary importance. What seems to have motivated him in each instance was an overriding conviction that moral laws should not be broken and that those who had been guilty of doing so—in the one instance, himself, in the other, the Mauritian planters—should not be allowed to profit from their actions.

What one senses here, as elsewhere in the careers of these abolitionists, is a dedication to moral principle so unwavering as to take precedence over every other consideration, including sometimes the achievement of the object sought. A hostile critic might be tempted to deduce from this that principle and principle alone was what concerned them. This would be unfair, for there can be little doubt, from the nature of the causes they

29. Many examples of these family connections are given in Emden's *Quakers in Commerce*.
30. Richard, pp. 11–13.

embraced and the energy they devoted to them, as well as from their writings, that they were very much concerned with human suffering as a factor to be overcome. Nevertheless the terms in which they expressed their concern often had about them an abstract quality. What was morally wrong, Sturge was continually reminding his followers—and for him this included many things which, even to his contemporaries, appeared quite harmless—could never be politically right. This was, of course, very much in the nonconformist tradition. To such men the type of reasoning appropriate to secular matters differed little, if at all, from that appropriate to religious ones. The two spheres were virtually identical, as indicated by Samuel Gurney's characteristic remark that "the Worship of God is not, in my view, to be found in a state of indolence", and the advice given to Sturge by his old mentor, James Cropper, at the time of the formation of the British and Foreign Anti-Slavery Society: "I hope [your meeting] will be well attended; but do not fear if your numbers be small. *Keep to right principles and do what you are able*; and trust with all your hearts to God".[31] This was the nonconformist conscience in operation. When religious and secular life thus blended conscience became the ultimate touchstone. This explains their continued self-questioning as well as the inflexibility they sometimes displayed when confronted by situations of a new or complex character. Forever suspicious of being led astray, they were capable, when a moral principle was seen to be at stake, of being utterly implacable. The same mentality has been noted in the case of American abolitionists and has been attributed to America's peculiar social structure, or lack of structure.[32] Its existence in Britain suggests a simpler explanation, namely that religious idealism operated in a similar fashion on both sides of the Atlantic. So far as the antislavery cause was concerned the leadership of such men was a mixed blessing, for while it gave the movement a pertinacity which it would otherwise have lacked it alienated those of more subtle and pragmatic intelligence who felt, often with justification, that the issues were more complicated than abolitionists were prepared to admit.

It is interesting to reflect that although it would have been feasible to construct an antislavery case out of strictly Utilitarian or Benthamite principles no serious attempt was made to do so. This was not because the Society rejected such arguments. Like the Young England abolitionists of ten years before, whose ideas they continued to propound, they were

31. *Annual Monitor*, 1857, p. 76; Cropper to Sturge, 25 June 1839, in "Extracts from the letters of James Cropper", MSS, Friends House, London.
32. Stanley Elkins, *Slavery: A Problem in American Institutional and Intellectual Life* (Chicago, 1959), pp. 27 ff.

not above appealing to economic interest when it suited their˙purpose to do so. Slavery was not only wicked; it was also expensive. Only stupidity and the love of unbridled power prevented slaveholders from realizing that free labour would prove in the long run cheaper and more efficient. This was the standard reply to those who argued for the economic necessity of slavery. But much more central to their own way of thinking, and more frequently stressed in their public pronouncements, were the arguments based on natural law. Since there was no essential difference between the white man and the black, slavery was contrary to nature. It was tyranny of a peculiarly crude, shocking and unambiguous kind, the consequence of which was to degrade not only the slaves, by turning them into marketable commodities, but their masters also, who, being accustomed to the exercise of irresponsible power, became corrupt, cruel and, from the point of view of society, dangerous. The so-called "happiness" of the plantation Negro was no more than "the happiness of the stalled ox". The abolitionists' ultimate argument against slavery, however, was quite simply that it was a sin. Christ had instructed his disciples to love their neighbours. To reduce one's neighbour—who, Negro or white, was made in God's image—to the status of a chattel, steal his children, deny him the benefits of marriage, deprive him of the fruits of his labour, refuse him even the rudiments of education, and then, should he protest, subject him to brutal punishments, was a flagrant violation of God's law. On this ground, if on no other, slavery should be immediately and unconditionally abolished "without restriction and without price".[33]

The Sturgites also laid great stress on the moral character of the means they intended to employ. It was not their aim to meet violence with violence. Whatever was done, whether with regard to the suppression of the slave trade or the emancipation of slaves, should involve no use of physical force. Since no deviation from this principle was permitted, Committee members sometimes found themselves in embarrassing positions. At the World Anti-Slavery Convention, John Scoble happened to remark with seeming approval that Santo Domingo had "emancipated itself". Another delegate immediately demanded whether this self-emancipation had not involved violence and bloodshed. Realizing the implications of his statement, Scoble at once contradicted himself by saying that this was not so, for

33. BFASS, *First Annual Report* (1840), p. 17; also BFASS, *On the Duty of Promoting the Immediate and Complete Abolition of Slavery* (London, 1840); Rev. Benjamin Godwin, "On the essential sinfulness of slavery and its direct opposition to the precepts and spirit of Christianity", *Proceedings of the General Anti-Slavery Convention of 1840*, pp. 47–55; Thomas Clarkson, *A Letter to the Clergy of the Various Denominations, and to the Slaveholding Planters, in the Southern Parts of the United States of America* (London, 1841).

emancipation had, in the first instance been accorded Santo Domingo by the French Republic. It was only when Napoleon had attempted to reintroduce slavery that the Negroes had felt obliged to resort to arms. "Let it not be supposed", he concluded, "that I am the advocate or the apologist for physical force. I am persuaded that men can achieve their liberties without the sword, and I am satisfied that pacific principles, whenever brought to bear in passive resistance against oppression, will be found all powerful and all conquering."[34] The Haitian delegate at the Convention fortunately refrained from comment. Pacifism, as the Society was to discover, is seldom a popular course. By insisting on pacifist principles—for which Sturge and the other Quakers on the Committee must be held responsible—the Society, in the long run, lost much support.

As was to be expected, the members of the Committee[35] differed greatly in the amount of time and energy which they devoted to its affairs. Roughly speaking, they can be divided into four groups: the hard core members—about a third of the total number—who were regular in their attendance at meetings; the semi-active members, who attended only when there were matters of particular importance to be discussed or when other commitments left them free; the parliamentary members, who represented the Society's interests in the House, but who, as it happened, rarely attended meetings; and the inactive members who did little except provide the sanction of their names. The hard core members, among whom the Quakers were generally in the majority, naturally enough, tended to dominate the Society's affairs. Taking them as a group, however, there is nothing one can point to, at least in so far as their backgrounds and other interests are concerned, that would distinguish them from the semi-active members.

The original Committee contained only one MP, Dr Stephen Lushington. The son of a Director of the East India Company, Lushington had entered Parliament in 1806 where he had soon become recognized as one of the leaders of the antislavery party, being responsible, among other things, for the measure ending the intercolonial slave trade.[36] He rarely attended meetings of the Committee, but was often consulted on questions of policy, and, until he retired from Parliament in 1841, was its acknowledged spokesman in the House. Thereafter the connection between the Society and Parliament was less direct, for although other

34. BFASS, *Proceedings of the General Anti-Slavery Convention of 1840*, pp. 177–9.
35. For a list of these and for information about their professions, religious affiliations, etc., see Howard Temperley, "The British and Foreign Anti-Slavery Society, 1839–68" (Yale PhD thesis, 1961), appendices I and II.
36. T. F. Buxton to George Stephen, 19 Dec 1835, ASS Minute Books, 23 Dec. 1835.

members did, from time to time, hold seats in the Commons, the Committee usually chose more prominent individuals, such as Lord Brougham and William Evans, to represent its views.

The presence of Sir Thomas Fowell Buxton's name on the list of original Committee members may at first appear anomalous since, as we have seen, he was at this time advocating an altogether different approach to the slavery problem. Buxton, however, was a member in name only. He never attended a Committee meeting and was never, so far as the records show, called upon for advice. In fact he was the classic example of the inactive member. Others in this category included Samuel Gurney Jr, who became President in 1864—in his case an honorary position— and Stephen Lushington after he left Parliament. So far as most Committee members were concerned, annual re-election depended upon some degree of activity, but in such cases as these this requirement was waived, either because the person was wealthy—as was Gurney—in which case it was hoped that membership might induce generosity—or because his name was considered a particular asset. Thomas Clarkson, now in his eighties, was in some respects an inactive member, though he does not altogether fall into this category on account of his valuable work as a pamphleteer. He was first referred to as President of the Society in 1842, though there is no record of his having been formally elected to that position. From that time until his death in 1846 important documents were often sent to him for signature before being transmitted. After 1846 this office remained vacant until the election of Samuel Gurney Jr, in 1864.

In 1843 the Society began publishing a list of Honorary Corresponding Members. These were usually foreigners or prominent sympathizers who lived outside of London, though sometimes former members of the Committee who wished to be relieved of the obligation of attending meetings regularly were included. Joseph Sturge, for reasons best known to himself, remained one until his death, although for all practical purposes he might just as well have been a member.

The Committee acquired a set of rooms at 27 New Broad Street near Bishopsgate, which henceforward was its headquarters. Here a reference library was established consisting of works on slavery—including a number donated by the American Anti-Slavery Society—together with files of British, American and colonial newspapers.[37] It was here also that the Committee held its meetings and that the Secretary and his assistants

---

37. Among the publications ordered were the New Orleans *Bee*, the Charleston *Mercury*, the *Liberator*, the New York *Emancipator*, the Jamaica *Colonial Reformer* and the Barbados *Liberal*. BFASS Minute Books, 31 April, 31 Dec. 1839, 13 March 1840.

had their offices. Being Secretary was a full-time job. It involved, among other things, maintaining a correspondence with the Society's sympathizers at home and abroad, calling Committee meetings in times of emergency, making lecture tours around the country, preparing *Annual Reports* and generally acting as a link between the Society and its auxiliaries. Little is known about the first Secretary, the Rev. J. H. Tredgold, except that he was of a retiring nature, had been an active member of the old Central Emancipation Committee and evidently possessed private means since his services were performed gratuitously. John Scoble, his successor, was an abolitionist by profession who, as we have seen, had been one of the salaried lecturers employed by the Agency Committee, and had later risen to be Secretary of the Universal Abolition Society. He had twice visited the West Indies: once in 1837, in company with Sturge and once in 1839 on behalf of the Central Negro Emancipation Committee. He retired in 1851 to become Director of the Dawn Institute, an agency in Upper Canada responsible for looking after fugitive slaves from the United States.[38] His successor was L. A. Chamerovzow, an aspiring literary figure and a former Secretary of the Aborigines Protection Society, who retained the office until 1869.

In the spring of 1839 there were still several local antislavery societies in existence, most of them relics of earlier national organizations. The Glasgow Emancipation Society, for example, was one of the oldest, having originated in 1823 as a result of one of Thomas Clarkson's tours of the north. At first a subsidiary of Buxton's Anti-Slavery Society it was, as we have seen, reorganized in 1833 and in 1834 became an auxiliary of the Universal Emancipation Society with which it cooperated in sponsoring Thompson's visit to America. Since the demise of that organization it had continued operating on an independent basis.[39] Others, such as the Belfast Anti-Slavery Society, had been founded during the Agency Committee's campaigns of 1831 and 1832.[40] Of the forty-odd organizations which had supported the Central Negro Emancipation Committee the majority were still in existence, though few of them showed much sign of activity.

Sturge and his associates were fully aware that their influence, both in England and abroad, would depend to a considerable extent upon the amount of provincial support they received. Circulars were dispatched

38. Robin W. Winks, *The Blacks in Canada: A History* (New Haven, 1971), pp. 201–4.
39. William Smeal to L. A. Chamerovzow, Glasgow, 16 April 1853. Anti-Slavery Papers. Rhodes House, Oxford—referred to hereafter as BFASS Papers.
40. British and Foreign Anti-Slavery Society, *Anti-Slavery Reporter*, 1 July 1853, pp. 164–5—referred to hereafter as BFASS *Reporter*.

to friends in various parts of the country and a series of lecture tours by members of the Committee arranged.[41] The response was on the whole encouraging though some correspondents were sceptical about how much popular activity could be expected. T. J. Brewin, Secretary of the Cirencester Anti-Slavery Society, wrote that:

When abolitionists directed the attention of the benevolent public even to our own colonies, we were constantly met with 'Charity begins at home— there is no occasion to go 3 thousand miles from home to relieve misery.' If such was the public feeling when the slavery to be abolished was the crime of our own country, what great efforts can we expect when the evil to be abolished is the slavery of foreign and distant nations?[42]

Even so, he concluded, the London Committee could rely on the Cirencester organization which, though somewhat depleted, would do its best to live up to the principles contained in the Committee's circular. By the end of 1839 virtually all the existing societies with the exception of those in Glasgow, Edinburgh and Dublin, which, for the time being, preferred to remain independent, had become auxiliaries, in addition to which a number of new ones had been created.

Altogether between 1839 and 1868 there were about a hundred such auxiliaries, not all, of course, active at the same time.[43] A map of England showing their locations would reveal a fairly even distribution in relation to the general population. Ireland, Scotland and Wales were less well represented. In some cases these provincial organizations amounted to little more than groups of friends or parishioners who were willing, when asked, to assist the Broad Street Committee but who otherwise paid little attention to slavery. Others, especially in the larger cities such as Birmingham, Liverpool and Bristol, had an independent life of their own, published reports and pamphlets and swayed and were swayed by opinion in their localities. All auxiliaries were expected to support the policies of the London Committee and, with the exception of the female auxiliaries which constituted about one third of the total, had the right to appoint delegates to attend and vote at its meetings. It was also hoped, though this was not obligatory, that they would contribute to the Society's funds. Some were generous in this respect and made donations every year, others only occasionally and a few not at all. The largest number of donations received from auxiliary societies in any single year was thirty-three, although it is clear that at that time (1843–44) there were at least

41. For example, during December 1839 Sturge, Scoble and Alexander between them lectured in no less than twenty-nine towns around the country. BFASS Minute Books, 27 Dec. 1839.
42. Brewin to Tredgold, 27 July 1839, BFASS Papers.
43. BFASS *Annual Reports*, 1840–70.

seventy such organizations in existence. The situation was always in a state of flux, new auxiliaries being created and old ones dying out. These changes are almost impossible to trace except in terms of the contributions received by the London office. It is clear, however, that the number of auxiliaries declined significantly during the 1850s and 60s. Auxiliaries could, if they wished, secede from the parent body and in some instances, about which more will be said in due course, this occurred, though such cases were few and exceptional. There was nothing exceptional, however, about their disagreeing with the course which the London Committee was pursuing and refusing to contribute funds, as frequently happened.

The Society's income came almost entirely from voluntary contributions, the only significant exceptions being a grant of £800 in 1842 from the Society of Friends, a gift of £100 in 1860 from the Haitian Government, the sums it received from the sale of publications (which, incidentally, were almost invariably run at a loss) and, after 1855, rent from the subletting of property.[44] Voluntary contributions were of two kinds: subscriptions, usually of between 10 shillings and £5, which were given annually, and donations. During the 1840s its gross annual income ranged from £4,000 in 1841–42 to £800 in 1847–48, the average being about £2,000.[45] During the 1850s and 60s the average was approximately half this amount. The sources of income and the relative amounts which it received from each varied little during the period. Eighteen sixty, therefore, may be taken as a typical year. The Society's gross income in that year was £1,350 of which £160 came from rent, £66 from the sale of publications, £177 from subscriptions (180 in number) and £947 from donations. The donations may be subdivided as follows:

	NUMBER	AMOUNT
Donations from organizations and groups	12	£192
Private donations of £25 and over	13	£535
Private donations of £10 to £24	12	£203
Private donations of £5 to £9	2	£10
Private donations of less than £5	9	£7
TOTALS	48	£947[46]

From this it will be seen that the Society received almost half its income from a relatively small number of large donations. In most cases these were not

44. Hitherto the Society had been paying £70 per annum in rent for its offices at 27 New Broad Street. In 1855, when this property was acquired by the City of London, the Committee began, as an economical measure, to rent the whole building, subletting floors to legal and commercial firms.
45. BFASS, *Annual Reports*, 1840–70.
46. BFASS, *Annual Report*, 1860.

solitary contributions but sums which were given regularly, year after year, almost in the form of annual subscriptions. These large donors included several Committee members, of whom Samuel Gurney, Joseph Sturge, and G. W. Alexander were the most consistently generous. Between 1839 and 1848 these three alone were responsible for roughly one tenth of the Society's total income.[47] That all three belonged to the Society of Friends was no coincidence. The Quaker concept of wealth, not as an end in itself or as a means of acquiring material comforts but as an instrument for social and moral improvement, encouraged generosity. In commerce, as we have seen, many of them had been extremely successful and, since personal extravagance was frowned upon, philanthropy was one of the few respectable means which could be used to dispose of these large—in some cases embarrassingly large—fortunes.[48] Taking into account the sums received from auxiliary societies, many of which, like the parent organization, were Quaker controlled, it would seem that between two-thirds and three-quarters of the Society's income came from members of the Society of Friends.[49]

Apart from the two World Anti-Slavery Conventions of 1840 and 1843, both of which absorbed a good deal of money, the Society's main items of expense varied little from year to year, the principal ones being the salaries of the Secretary and his staff—Scoble and Chamerovzow both received £300 per annum—rent of offices and meeting halls, printing and publishing, the purchase of stationery, books and newspapers and travelling expenses.[50] The Treasurer, G. W. Alexander, who was also the Society's banker, allowed it an overdraft of up to £500 (sometimes stretched to £600) free of interest. This helped to tide it over bad years but resulted in its being seldom out of debt.

During its early months the Society made use of the *British Emancipator*

47. Samuel Gurney contributed £750, Joseph Sturge £650 and G. W. Alexander £625. "List of Subscriptions and Donations", in BFASS *Annual Report for 1848*. The American Anti-Slavery Society, during its early years, was similarly dependent on a few large donors. They were not, however, Quakers. Wyatt-Brown, p. 113.
48. Another was to give it to relatives. A much less efficient method was to reinvest it. Hudson Gurney once complained: "John Gurney in 1670 was a thriving merchant of Norwich with £20,000. John Gurney, his grandson, died in 1770 with £100,000, and I, the grandson of the last, wind up in 1850 with £500,000." This is a classic example of how those Quaker dynasties, by successive generations of thrift and hard work, built up their fortunes, see Emden, pp. 13–25.
49. A list of leading benefactors would include, besides Gurney, Sturge and Alexander, Jonathan Backhouse, John Bell, Edward Cropper, John Cropper, Abraham Darby, W. D. Crewdson, J. J. Gurney, Edward Pease, William Peckover, Joseph Sharples and Samuel Tuke, BFASS *Annual Reports*.
50. *Ibid*; with regard to the Secretary's salary see BFASS Minute Books, 28 Oct. 1842. At this time the salaries of the Secretary's two assistants amounted to £3.10s. a week, *ibid*, 25 Nov. 1842.

—officially the organ of the Central Negro Emancipation Committee and at that time the only antislavery periodical in England. Since membership of the two organizations overlapped to a large degree this caused no difficulty. It was felt appropriate, however, that the Society should establish a new periodical rather than adopt an existing one, although this was virtually what happened.[51] The last number of the *British Emancipator* appeared on 10 January 1840 and was followed on 15 January by the first issue of the *British and Foreign Anti-Slavery Reporter*.[52] The editing of the new paper was entrusted to an editorial committee, but in practice most of the work was done by the sub-editor, the Rev. J. H. Hinton, an influential Baptist who had previously edited the *British Emancipator*.[53] *The Reporter* consisted of sixteen quarto pages, was published twice monthly and originally cost threepence a copy.[54] Like most such publications it was run at a loss. Its paid circulation in 1841–42 was approximately 1,200 copies, an additional 700 being distributed free of charge, mainly to members.[55]

Considering its grandiose ambitions, the British and Foreign Anti-Slavery Society would at first sight appear a surprisingly makeshift organization. Its annual budget of £1,000 or £2,000, even taking into account the value of money at that time, was absurdly small. Compared with the sums expended annually by Britain in her attempts to suppress the slave trade, the financial resources of the Society were insignificant. The fitting out of the Niger Expedition alone cost more than all the Society's activities over a period of thirty years. Yet, placed alongside its predecessors, the Society compares remarkably well. Its average annual income between 1839 and 1848 was roughly the same as that of the old Anti-Slavery Society during the period 1823 and 1831,[56] and during its best year (1840–41) its budget was only slightly less than that of the Central Negro

51. *Ibid*, 17, 28 June 1839. The title originally suggested was *The Emancipator and British and Foreign Anti-Slavery Reporter*.
52. Copies of the first number were forwarded free to all *Emancipator* subscribers. *British Emancipator*, 24 Dec. 1839.
53. BFASS Minute Books, 27 Dec. 1839. There is a short description of Hinton in the *Dictionary of National Biography*. He remained sub-editor until 1841 when his place was taken by John Scoble, the new Secretary.
54. In 1842 the price was increased to 4d. and in 1845 to 5d., *ibid*, 26 Oct. 1841; 31 Oct. 1845.
55. BFASS *Annual Report for 1842*. The Society reported that during the preceding year returns from sales amounted to £268 as compared with publication costs of £631.
56. The income of the Anti-Slavery Society during these years was as follows: 1823—£1,093; 1824—£2,847; 1825—£2,639; 1826—£2,933; 1827—£1,797; 1828—£1,447; 1829—£2,134; 1830—£2,846; 1831—£3,399: Anti-Slavery Society, *Account of Receipts and Disbursements* (London, 1826–31).

Emancipation Committee.[57] As regards support from auxiliaries, the
seventy-odd societies of the mid-forties cannot, of course, compare with
the twelve hundred which according to Sir George Stephen—although
we have only his word that this was the number—supported the Agency
Committee in 1832.[58] In this respect, the Society would appear to have
been in about the same class as the Anti-Slavery Society and the Central
Negro Emancipation Committee.[59]

It would be a mistake therefore to underrate Sturge's new society
merely on account of the smallness of its central organization. The middle
class, to which it angled its appeal, was not large. And as has already
been shown, the influence which agencies of this kind could exert was,
in practice, out of all proportion to the size of their budgets or the number
of their members. The essential factor was their ability to communi-
cate.

In this respect, the Society was well provided. Information was collected
from correspondents in the West Indies, the United States, Canada,
France, Holland, Spain, Germany and the South American countries,
as well as from its auxiliaries at home. If a particular matter concerned
Great Britain and was important enough it could be drawn to the attention
of the appropriate government department, questions could be asked
in the House, articles published in the *Reporter*, a conference summoned,
deputations appointed to wait on the Prime Minister and members of his
Cabinet, advertisements might be inserted in newspapers, protest meetings
arranged and petitions circulated. More effective on occasion than this
public type of appeal was the personal influence which could be exerted
by members of the Committee. Once a particular course of action had
been adopted it was a relatively simple matter to make it known to the
British philanthropical community generally. Here the religious organizations could help. The Society of Friends, the Baptist Union and the
World Evangelical Alliance—to mention only three of those in which
Committee members held prominent positions—each had their own
methods of disseminating information, all of which, as we will see, were
used to promote the Society's policies. There were also informal channels
through which members could gain audiences with statesmen and politicians. So while it was impossible for the Society to *force* its views on
anyone there existed a variety of ways in which they could be made
known.

57. £4,031 as against £4,466. See *British Emancipator*, 31 Oct. 1838, p. 172.
58. Stephen, *Anti-Slavery Recollections*, p. 161.
59. Anti-Slavery Society, *Accounts of Receipts and Disbursements: British Emancipator*, 14 Nov. 1838, p. 176.

The outstanding achievement of the Society in its early years, and the one which attracted most public attention, was the holding of a World Anti-Slavery Convention. The idea originated with an American, Joshua Leavitt, editor of the New York *Emancipator*. Like other American abolitionists, Leavitt had been following British developments with keen interest. So long as the prime concern of the British was slavery in their own territories, these had only a limited relevance as far as the United States was concerned. But Sturge's letter to the *British Emancipator* seemed to Leavitt to open the way for more extensive cooperation. Commenting on it in an editorial on 21 March 1839, he observed that

as a means of concentrating our energies and harmonizing our movements, we venture to suggest to our British fellow laborers the expediency of calling together, from all civilized nations, a general anti-slavery conference to be held in London in the months of May or June, 1840. We can have delegates or communications from philanthropists in the United States, France, Denmark, Sweden, Holland, Jamaica, Haiti, Columbia, Mexico, India, Cape of Good Hope, Sandwich Islands, etc. O how contemptible seem the machinations of paltry demagogues for the preservation or acquisition of office in comparison with the deliberation of so august an assembly.

Sturge and his colleagues thoroughly approved of this suggestion, not only because it seemed a good way of inaugurating a new era in international cooperation in the struggle against slavery but also because it promised to make their own organization the dominant force in the enterprise. Early in June invitations were sent out to some thirty-five different countries. The response, particularly that of the Americans, was gratifying. Henry B. Stanton, President of the American Anti-Slavery Society, congratulated the Committee on its "active measures" and predicted a large delegation from the United States.[60] John Greenleaf Whittier, the Quaker poet, composed a poem in honour of the occasion, beginning with the lines:

> Yes, let them gather!—Summon forth
> The pledged philanthropy of Earth,
> From every land, whose hills have heard
> The bugle-blast of Freedom waking.[62]

Preparations for the Convention were begun well in advance. The Committee spent much time collecting information about the problems to be discussed. Since it was intended that the Convention should take into account *all* aspects of the slavery question, this was a formidable

60. BFASS Minute Books, 31 May, 3, 14 June, 26 July, 27 Sept., 25 Oct. 1839.
61. BFASS *Reporter*, 25 March 1840. A thousand copies were printed and distributed by the Committee. BFASS Minute Books, 13 March 1840.

undertaking and involved enquiring into many fields which the British had so far neglected. What, for example, was the status of slaves in Mohammedan countries and how did it differ from that in, say, the United States or Brazil? Where were slaves obtained; how did they reach their various destinations; to what extent were people in European countries implicated in this traffic; what proportion of the total population in different areas consisted of slaves; what were the attitudes of the governments concerned and—underlying all these questions—what could antislavery groups in general and the British in particular, do about it? The method adopted—a highly successful one as it turned out—was to send questionnaires to correspondents, mostly members of foreign antislavery organizations, missionaries and consular officials, requesting precise and detailed information.[62] In further preparation, a series of visits by members of the Committee to Continental countries was arranged and an intensive publicity campaign organized in Britain to awaken public interest and ensure a good attendance.[63]

The Convention commenced its sittings in Freemasons' Hall, Great Queen Street, on Friday, 12 June 1840.[64] Delegates and visitors began to assemble before ten o'clock and by eleven, when Clarkson, then in his eighty-first year, was supported onto the rostrum to deliver the opening address, the enormous hall was filled. A painting of this scene, by Benjamin Robert Haydon, which now hangs in the National Portrait Gallery, shows Clarkson, one hand upraised, surrounded by a sea of faces among which can be distinguished those of Daniel O'Connell, James G. Birney, Joseph Sturge, Henry B. Stanton, Wendell Phillips and Thomas Fowell Buxton.[65]

62. Questionnaires were sent to the following places: France, Denmark, the United States, Brazil, Mexico, Texas, Cuba, Puerto Rico, Canada, British West Indies, Cape of Good Hope and Mauritius: BFASS Minute Books, 26 July 1839. The replies received from the American Anti-Slavery Society were later published under the title, *Slavery and the Internal Slave Trade in the United States* (London, 1841).
63. Richard, pp. 208–14. BFASS Minute Books, June 1839–June 1840; Glasgow *Argus*, 16 Jan. 1840.
64. A verbatim account of the Convention's proceedings will be found in BFASS, *Proceedings of the General Anti-Slavery Convention Called by the Committee of the British and Foreign Anti-Slavery Society, June 12 to June 23, 1840* (London, 1841). See also Richard, pp. 214–19; W. P. and F. J. Garrison, *William Lloyd Garrison*, 2, 366–85; F. B. Tolles, ed., *Slavery and "The Woman Question": Lucretia Mott's Diary of her Visit to Great Britain to Attend the World's Anti-Slavery Convention of 1840* (Haverford, Penn., 1952); and James Mott, *Three Months in Gt. Britain* (Philadelphia, 1841).
65. This painting, which had been commissioned by the Society, was shown at the Royal Academy Exhibition in May 1841. It is a large canvas measuring thirteen feet by ten, and includes some 130 portraits. One contemporary described it as "a waggon load of heads, poor as a work of art but interesting from the number of portraits; these, though most may be recognized, are none of them faithful; they

It was a remarkable gathering. Virtually all of the leading British abolitionists were present, as were many of those from the colonies, including William Knibb and Henry Beckford from Jamaica, Robert Anderson from Trinidad, Joseph Ketley from Demerara, Giles Forward and H. S. Seaborn from Berbice, Donald McGregor from the Bahamas, Richard Musgrave and J. F. Walter from Antigua, R. H. Schombergh from British Guiana, A. V. Hittie from Mauritius, Governor Campbell from Sierra Leone and Thomas Rolph from Canada. Of the foreign delegations, that from the United States was the largest, consisting of fifty-three members.[66] The French delegation, led by M. Isambert and Hippolite de St Anthoine, was the next largest with six members. There were also present delegates from Spain, Switzerland and Haiti. The remainder of the seats in the front part of the hall—about two hundred and fifty—were taken up by delegates from provincial antislavery societies, various benevolent organizations and some thirty church groups.[67] Five thousand visitors packed the rear of the hall and the galleries.

The Convention remained in session for two weeks. The first day's proceedings were marred by a bitter debate over the question of admitting women delegates. In its original invitation, issued in June 1839, the Committee, unconscious of the divisions of opinion among Americans over the role of women in their movement, had failed to specify the sex of delegates assuming, mistakenly as it turned out, that all would be male.[68] Had the members of the Committee taken more interest in American developments they would have known that Garrison and the New England radicals had, ever since 1837, been pressing for the complete equality of women in antislavery work.[69] In May 1839 he and his followers had come close to taking over the American Anti-Slavery Society after a disagreement over just this issue. It may well have been the news of this incident that led the London Committee to issue a second summons, in February 1840, limiting the invitation strictly to "gentlemen".[70] The Committee's

may be said to be Haydonized". It was presented to the National Portrait Gallery by the Society in 1880: *National Portrait Gallery Catalogue* (5 vols, London, 1888) 2, 514.
66. Not including the women delegates whose credentials were not accepted— see below.
67. For example, the Congregational Union of England and Wales, the Congregational Union of Scotland, the United Associate Synod of Scotland, the Midland Association of Baptist Churches, and various other Baptist Associations. It is significant that these were all nonconformist bodies.
68. BFASS Minute Books, 24 April, 15 May, 27 May, 9 June 1840.
69. Russell B. Nye, *William Lloyd Garrison and the Humanitarian Reformers* (Boston, 1955), p. 107.
70. Minute Books, 9 June 1840. BFASS *Proceedings of the General Anti-Slavery Convention*, p. 25. The Garrisonians later asserted that this second invitation had

own view was that while it heartily supported the participation of women in antislavery work, and was active in sponsoring female auxiliaries, it did not believe that women should be allowed to interfere in the work of male organizations. This second invitation was ignored by the Garrisonians who, on 24 April, wrote to Tredgold that they were appointing a number of women. By the time this letter reached the Committee, it was too late to reply or indeed do anything except appoint a sub-committee to meet the ladies, apologize for the misunderstanding and state that the Society felt unable to alter its stand.[71] Meanwhile, in New York, Garrison had finally succeeded in packing the annual meeting of the American Anti-Slavery Society with his supporters—many of them women—whom he had brought down from New England in boatloads for the occasion. Once again the immediate point at issue had been the "woman question"— this time whether or not Abby Kelley, a female abolitionist from Massachusetts, should be allowed a seat on the executive committee. Finding themselves outnumbered, Lewis Tappan and all save one of the Committee members had resigned with the intention of founding a new society, free of Garrisonianism, and from which women would be definitely excluded,[72] so leaving the way open for Garrison to take control of the old organization. Abby Kelley and three other women, Lucretia Mott, Lydia Child and Maria Chapman, were among those elected to take their places.[73]

When therefore the American delegates began to arrive, the London Committee found itself in an embarrassing position. Not only were their visitors divided among themselves but they were accompanied by a group of indignant women, led by Lucretia Mott and Sarah Pugh, ready to make the most of any affront to their feminine dignity.[74] To make matters worse, Josiah Forster, who had been Clerk to the London Friends Yearly Meeting at the time of the Hicksite separations in America and was well known for his Quaker orthodoxy, took it upon himself to remind Lucretia Mott—who was a Hicksite—that she was a heretic and could not, therefore, expect to be treated as a Quaker while in England.[75] Other members of the Committee hastened to repair the damage but

been issued on the advice of the "New Organizationers"—i.e., those who seceded from the American Anti-Slavery Society in May 1840. W. P. and F. J. Garrison, 2, 353. This may have been so, although documentary evidence is lacking.

71. BFASS Minute Books, 9 June 1840. The sub-committee consisted of W. D. Crewdson, Rev. Thomas Scales, William Ball and J. H. Tredgold.

72. This was the origin of the American and Foreign Anti-Slavery Society.

73. W. P. and F. J. Garrison, 2, 348–9.

74. See, for example, the protest of the American women delegates from Pennsylvania, in Tolles, p. 28.

75. James Mott, pp. 15–16.

could not altogether dispel the unfortunate impression that had been made.

The debate in the Convention over the woman question centred around a motion by Wendell Phillips calling for the appointment of a committee to prepare an official list of delegates, with instructions to include the names of "all persons bearing credentials from any Anti-Slavery body".[76] In his own state of Massachusetts, he observed, abolitionists had for many years acted on the principle that women should be allowed an equal voice in determining antislavery policy and he urged the present gathering to follow this example. Several British delegates replied by pointing out that, regardless of what happened in Massachusetts, such a practice was altogether contrary to English custom, and, since the Convention happened to be meeting in England and not in Massachusetts, delegates should respect this fact. They also implied, although never actually stated—no doubt out of deference to the ladies concerned, who were present in the gallery—that any departure from normal practice would detract from the serious purpose of the Convention and would expose its proceedings to ridicule. At the same time they paid high tribute to women, both in England and the United States, for the part they played in promoting the cause, stressing in particular the work done by female branch organizations. Opposing the admission of the ladies, they argued, was no sign of disrespect, merely a practical expedient made necessary by public opinion and the circumstances of the occasion. In support of their British colleagues, two American abolitionists, Rev. Nathaniel Colver and James G. Birney, both anti-Garrisonians, described the recent differences between the antislavery parties in the United States over this issue and roundly denounced what Birney termed "the friends of promiscuous female representation".[77] George Bradburn of Massachusetts, a Garrisonian, rose to reply but was silenced by the Chairman on a point of order. At this point several of the English delegates, realizing that the debate was turning into a feud between rival American factions, got up to say that the topic was not a proper one for discussion, since it had nothing whatsoever to do with the general purpose of the Convention.

This question [complained one] however it may have been discussed in America, is totally new to me. I never heard a word of it before. I certainly never studied what is called the rights of women. . . . I appeal to you on all sides of the question, whether what you are pursuing is the great object for

76. BFASS, *Proceedings of the General Anti-Slavery Convention*, p. 23. A verbatim account of the ensuing debate will be found in *ibid*, pp. 23–46.
77. *Ibid*, pp. 41–2. Birney was one of the vice-presidents of the London Convention. The other vice-presidents were Joseph Sturge, W. T. Blair and R. K. Greville. John Scoble, Henry B. Stanton, Thomas Scales, William Bevan, Wendell Phillips and William Morgan were Secretaries.

which we are met. . . . We ought not to be compelled to discuss this question, or to decide upon it now. If it tears your Societies to pieces in the United States why would you tear in pieces our Convention?

Another delegate, Samuel Prescod from Barbados, stated that the ladies had not, as was claimed, come with any certain expectation of being received, and that the issue had been "most improperly forced" on the assembly. This was strongly denied by Wendell Phillips.

When finally the question was put to the vote, the Garrisonians were defeated by an overwhelming majority. This could scarcely have come as a surprise for, as they themselves must have realized, they were hopelessly outnumbered. That they had chosen to raise the matter at all may be ascribed, not to any hope of success, but to a conviction that any agitation of the issue was likely in the long run to do good.[78] When Garrison himself, whose departure from the United States had been delayed by unfavourable winds, arrived four days later and was informed of the Convention's decision, he refused to present his credentials or to take a seat, preferring to sit with the women in the gallery, thus causing, according to Birney, "a good deal of merriment" among the British delegates.[79] On the whole, however, the Garrisonians appeared to take their defeat with good grace and during the remainder of the Convention showed themselves willing and even eager to cooperate.

The papers presented to the Convention covered a wide variety of subjects, ranging from one by the Rev. Herbert Beaver, recently returned from Western Canada, on Red Indian slavery under the Hudson's Bay Company, to one by the Rev. John Bowring on Egyptian slave hunts. For the most part, however, they dealt with already familiar topics such as the essential sinfulness of slavery, the importance of boycotting slave produce, the attitude of the American churches towards slaveholding, British West Indian emancipation, and the Atlantic slave trade. In this connection, Buxton described the aims of the African Civilization Society and his hopes for the Niger expedition, and urged that these efforts receive the support of all present. Each paper was followed by a general discussion after which the matter was referred to a sub-committee to draw up a resolution, later to be approved by the Convention as a whole.

The foreign delegates agreed in stressing the importance of the links

78. "It is, perhaps, quite probable that we shall be foiled in our purpose, but the subject cannot be agitated without doing good, and you and the dear friends of human rights may be assured that we shall not easily allow ourselves to be intimidated or put down", W. L. Garrison to George Bourne, New York, 19 May 1840: W. P. and F. J. Garrison, 2, 357. It would appear, from this, that Prescod's statement was justified.
79. Nye, p. 128.

between the British antislavery movement and the movements in their own countries. Whatever happened in Britain, they pointed out, would sooner or later affect the rest of the world. Birney, Stanton and other American delegates explained that America still depended on England for its culture. If Britain were to take a firm stand in condemning slavery, her influence would be ten times that of all the American abolitionists combined.

Some of the American delegates took a radical line. George Bradburn of Massachusetts stated that the term "republic" had become meaningless in America, since the equality promised in the Constitution was denied to the Negroes, and freedom of the press to those who supported them. In this sense, Russia was more of a Republic than America. It was the duty of the people of Great Britain as outsiders to point out to the people of the United States the essential contradictions in their beliefs.[80] Others emphasized the influence of British literature in the United States. Their own voices, Wendell Phillips declared, were "only a whisper, which was drowned by the discussion of parties",[81] but things which would not be believed coming from them, would be accepted readily enough if found in the pages of the *Edinburgh Review*. They urged their British colleagues "individually as well as collectively, to make systematic efforts to secure a frequent, clear and full expression of the sentiments of the nation through its leading religious, political and literary periodicals on the subject of slavery and the anti-slavery enterprise in the United States". In particular, they called upon them to "fix the attention of the world on the successful results of West Indian emancipation"[82] about which, despite their own efforts,[83] there was still a lamentable ignorance, even among those sympathetic to the cause.

The Convention closed with a series of resolutions thanking the British and Foreign Anti-Slavery Society for having called the delegates together and entrusting to it the task of summoning another meeting within a few years. The Society was also made responsible for printing and publishing the records of the Convention and for promoting its general objects. Thus, it became, in a sense, the Convention's executor. This was a point of technical importance for it later became the basis for its often repeated claim to speak on behalf of the world antislavery movement as a whole.

80. BFASS, *Proceedings of the General Anti-Slavery Convention of 1840*, pp. 129–33.
81. *Ibid*, p. 127.   82. *Ibid*, p. 121.
83. The American Anti-Slavery Society had sent two observers, J. A. Thome and J. H. Kimball, to the West Indies to report upon the British experiment. Their account, *Emancipation in the West Indies: a six months' tour in Antigua, Barbadoes, and Jamaica in 1837* (New York, 1838), became an antislavery best-seller in the United States. It was also directly responsible for the national society's discarding of the old doctrine of "immediate emancipation gradually accomplished". Barnes, *The Anti-Slavery Impulse*, pp. 138–9.

Today the World Convention of 1840 is remembered chiefly for its resolution not to seat the American women delegates and the consequent refusal of Garrison to take his place with the other convention members. These events were certainly significant in that they gave abolitionists in Britain their first experience of issues which had already wreaked havoc in the American antislavery ranks and which would soon be causing similar havoc within their own. But to remember the Convention for this alone is to overlook much else that was important. It represented a drawing together of antislavery talent unique in the history of the movement. The published version of the proceedings, which runs to six hundred closely printed pages, gives a remarkably precise and detailed account of the state of the antislavery cause in the world at that date. For the first time in history, a gathering of abolitionists drawn from many countries had succeeded in viewing the antislavery struggle as a single conflict of world-wide dimensions. This was no mean achievement although what fruit it would bear was a matter which, when the Convention closed, still remained very much in doubt.

5

The abolition of legalized slavery in British India and Ceylon

Among the issues discussed at the World Convention was the question of slavery in the British East Indies. This was a problem which, although it had never assumed the same importance as slavery in the West Indies, had been troubling abolitionists for some time.

Contrary to common belief the Act of 1833 had not abolished slavery throughout the British Empire. The origin of this misunderstanding can be traced back to statements by abolitionists who boasted of "the abolition of slavery" when what they really meant was the holding of Negroes in chattel slavery by Europeans. The 1833 Act had, in fact, applied to four areas only, the West Indies, Mauritius, Canada (where slavery had already virtually disappeared thanks to local legislation), and the Cape of Good Hope. Elsewhere in Britain's possessions, and most notably in India and Ceylon, slavery in various forms continued to flourish on a scale so vast that only the roughest guess could be made as to how many slaves there actually were. According to the Rev. James Peggs, whose *Slavery in India* (London, 1839) was the standard work on the topic, the total slave population of India and Ceylon, including the independent native states, which at that time still comprised the greater part of the area, was just under one million. On the other hand, Professor William Adam of Harvard, an Englishman who had spent many years in India as a missionary and who was also considered an expert on the subject, told the World Convention that in his view the number of slaves within the East India Company's territories alone "did not fall short of one million and probably greatly exceeded that estimate".[1] For want of anything better to go on, this figure was the one generally quoted by Broad Street.[2] Like all contemporary estimates, however, it greatly underrated the extent of the problem. In fact, to judge from subsequent investigations, the servile population of British India at this time was closer to eight million and that of India as a whole rather more than double that figure.[3] It would appear, therefore, that within the territories of the East India Company there were three times as many slaves as in the United States and more than in all the countries of the New World combined.[4]

That a problem of these dimensions had not received more attention may seem puzzling. It must be remembered, however, that slavery in the East was a very different issue from slavery in the West. It was, for one thing, a problem which European settlers and administrators had inherited—in many cases recently and reluctantly—and not, as in the West, one which they themselves had created. There was, moreover, little question, at least so far as slavery was concerned, of one race exploiting another, or of white settlers reducing indigenous people to servitude or importing labourers of different stock from overseas, as had happened in the New World. It was a native growth of immemorial antiquity and, except for the relatively minor differences arising out of caste, masters and slaves were of the same colour and racial origin. Above all, what had daunted both abolitionists and colonial administrators hitherto was the utterly different economic and social structure upon which it rested.

In a sense, the two systems were the products of diametrically opposite circumstances: in the West there was an abundance of resources and a shortage of population; in the East there was an abundance of population and a shortage of resources. In other words, slavery in the New World had arisen in a situation characterized by a lack of labour, and a superfluity

1. BFASS, *Proceedings of the General Anti-Slavery Convention of 1840*, p. 77.
2. BFASS, *Slavery and the Slave Trade in British India* (London, 1841), pp. 1–6.
3. D. R. Banaji, *Slavery in British India* (Bombay, 1933), pp. 195–203.
4. Variously estimated at between six and eight millions, see BFASS, *Proceedings of the General Anti-Slavery Convention of 1840*, p. 3.

of land, combined with a growing demand in Europe for New World products. Economically speaking, the slave was part of his master's stock in trade, acquired and maintained largely for the financial profit he yielded. The slave systems of the Americas had all the familiar features of capitalist enterprise except that, being unable to find adequate supplies of free labour such as were available to entrepreneurs in Europe—mainly because what free labourers there were preferred to work for themselves— they had turned instead to obtaining labour by means of coercion backed up by the law. Thus, the initial motive for becoming a slaveholder was the expectation of becoming rich by developing the continent's resources, while there was no motive at all for becoming a slave and little incentive for working as one except the fear of punishment. Slaves in the West, generally speaking, had few privileges and those they had by no means compensated for the lack of those they might have expected to enjoy as freemen. Whatever else may be said of the system, it is clear that almost all of the benefits from it went to the master and virtually none to the slave.

In India, by contrast, slavery lacked these capitalistic features. Most slaves were kept for purposes which had no immediate connection with pecuniary profit. Those who held slaves did so mainly because having a large retinue of hereditary domestics and dependants made life easier and was a sign of affluence and station. Their primary object appears to have been to support themselves, their families and their slaves by the produce of the land and not, as was commonly the case in the West, to accumulate a fortune out of the surplus—for which, it should be added, the country's economic system offered little scope. Much Indian slavery was relatively benign. C. H. Cameron who investigated the matter in 1839 concluded that most slavery in the East was not, as in the West, "a system of mere violence and oppression" but seemed to be "held together by the mutual interests of master and slave, and by the force of habit". It required no great exercise of the imagination, he argued, to see the whole system as mutually beneficial.

The perpetual and hereditary service of their domestics is what the upper classes in India particularly desire as conducive to that privacy which belongs to their households. On the other hand the lower classes are glad to bind themselves and their posterity to such perpetual service, in order to be secure of subsistance in sickness and in old age . . . and in periods of scarcity.[5]

So far as he could tell, there was no conscious desire for freedom on the part of the slaves, who were well aware of the advantages of their condition as compared with that of the landless freemen. Whatever the validity of these observations, there was something to be said in a country where

5. "Papers respecting slavery in the East Indies", PP, 1841, *28* (328), 35-9.

population pressed so heavily on resources for having a master who, whatever else he might do, could at least be relied upon to act as a provider in time of famine.

This helps to explain the voluntary or quasivoluntary origin of certain types of Indian slavery. A freeman might become a slave in any one of a number of ways. The sale or gift of children by their parents was by no means always or even usually the act of gross inhumanity which to many Westerners it appeared. In times of general starvation which periodically afflicted most parts of India, parents were often compelled to choose between allowing their children to die or entrusting them to someone else's care. During the great Bengal famine of 1833 the streets of Calcutta are said to have been thronged with half-starved women offering to sell their children in return for a few measures of rice.[6] When the Indian Law Commissioners investigated this practice in 1840, there was a strong feeling that since "it would not be possible in this country to set up any tolerably safe and economical machinery for the distribution of public charity" it would be as well to allow such sales to continue. One Commissioner even went so far as to describe slavery as "the Indian Poor Law".[7] The sale of wives by husbands and the self sale of adults generally had a similar origin.

But perhaps the most striking thing about Indian slavery and what more than anything else distinguished it from slavery in the West was its diversity. This was amply borne out by the famous *Law Commission Reports* of 1841 which remain the best historical source on the subject.[8] After reading these accounts one is left with the impression that there can have been no variant on a slave system, however unlikely or bizarre, that was not represented on the Indian subcontinent. There were, for example, tribes living in the mountains of Behar which were considered slave tribes and whose members became the legal property of whoever could capture them.[9] There were also individuals who were considered free in some situations and servile in others as was commonly the case with freemen who married slaves. As in the West, children generally followed the condition of the mother, though in this, as in almost everything else, much depended on local custom and the whim of the master.

Even among slaves engaged in agricultural work the extent and type of service required varied enormously. Some, like slaves in the West, spent their entire lives in their owner's service, working under close supervision and urged on to further efforts by the threat of punishment. Others were permitted in the course of time to attain virtual independence.

6. Banaji, p. 48.   7. PP, 1841, *28* (238), 38.   8. PP, 1841, *28*, *passim*.
9. "Report from the Select Committee of the House of Lords on the India Charter Act", PP, 1852/3, *30*, 207.

Much of what passed for slavery might be more accurately described as serfdom or peonage. Slaves belonging to wealthy landowners mostly had lands given to them at a reduced rent or at no rent at all from which they were able to supply most of their needs. In return, they were required to render specified services such as performing menial duties about the estate or attending their masters on ceremonial occasions. Since their entire livelihood depended on their master's patronage, there was little chance of their running away. In theory they could be sold, but in practice this rarely happened except when the land itself changed hands. In parts of Southern India such as Malabar, Kanara and the Tamil country generally, the greater part of the labouring force consisted of persons of this type.[10]

Domestic slavery was even more varied. Besides cooks, housekeepers, maids and personal servants, all of whom were commonly slaves, it was the general practice among men of wealth to keep a number of concubines. The trade in these women was extensive. In Kashmir, according to one traveller, it was common for small girls of eight or nine to be sent to India to be sold for this purpose. Young girls were also in great demand by the owners of sets of dancing women who trained them for public display. In some of the larger private establishments the discipline of female slaves was entrusted to Negro eunuchs, illegally imported from Africa, but these were considered luxuries which only the rich could afford. The Newab of Moorshedabad is said to have had sixty-three such individuals in his household.[11]

But although the system was in general less harsh than that existing in the West, there were certain aspects of it that were specially shocking to English sensibilities. The flourishing trade in women and young girls was particularly distasteful. The existence of slavery also led to practices of a type which any government would have found difficult to tolerate. The *Calcutta Journal* reported, for example, that of two hundred boys emasculated at Jeddah preparatory to being shipped to India, only five survived the operation.[12] Within India itself, roving bands of Thugs haunted highways, murdering parents and selling the children, who were either too young or too terrified to give evidence against their captors. This seems to have been a lucrative business and was carried on with such skill that those engaged in it were rarely caught. Nor was it uncommon for owners to subject slaves to extreme forms of punishment, sometimes

10. L. S. S. O'Malley, ed., *Modern India and the West* (Oxford, 1941), p. 71.
11. William Adam, *The Law and Custom of Slavery in British India: In a Series of Letters to T. F. Buxton, Esq.* (London, 1840), pp. 74–102.
12. BFASS, *Slavery and the Slave Trade in British India* (London, 1841), p. 33.

involving mutilation or even death. Masters who indulged in practices of this kind, like those who imported slaves from Africa, were liable to severe penalties, but since only a small proportion of such cases reached the attention of the authorities, this was not much of a deterrent.[13]

The problem of dealing with these forms of slavery was made even more difficult by the lack of an effective legal system. Judges and other British functionaries found themselves contending not only with the vague and often conflicting injunctions of Muslim and Hindu law but also with a bewildering variety of local practices which differed from province to province and even from village to village. Even when the issues involved were quite minor, the arguments presented were apt to be of impenetrable complexity. As a result, there was often no alternative but to rely on the advice of local pundits or mufties, though this was generally admitted to be an unsatisfactory arrangement and apt to produce contradictory decisions. As a last resort, judges could always consult their private feelings, but as T. B. Macaulay explained to the House in 1833, the results obtained in this way were also likely to be conflicting.

I asked a most distinguished Civil Servant of the Company whether, at present, if a dancing girl ran away from her master, the Judge would force her to go back. "Some Judges," he said, "send a girl back, others set her at liberty. The whole is a mere matter of chance. Everything depends upon the temper of the individual Judge."[14]

This was not the sort of situation administrators like. If only for the sake of efficiency some general ruling was needed.

It seems to have been this consideration as much as a desire to remedy India's social ills that led Earl Grey's Government in the summer of 1833 to attempt a solution. The old East India Charter was shortly to expire and a new one needed to be approved. This happened to occur at the very time that the Emancipation Bill was under consideration. In fact, the new East India Company Charter Bill received its first reading in the Commons on 28 June, exactly a week before the Emancipation Bill was introduced, so that both were passing through Parliament simultaneously. Of the two, the Charter Bill, at least in its original form, was the more radical in its treatment of slavery. Whereas the Emancipation Bill provided for compensation and complete freedom in twelve years (later reduced to six), the Charter Bill made no allowance whatever for compensation and stated categorically that slavery should be abolished throughout the East India Company's territories by 12 April 1837.[15]

13. "Report from the Indian Law Commissioners relating to slavery in the East Indies", PP, 1841, *28*, 205–8—referred to hereafter as *Law Commissioners Report*.
14. *Hansard, 19* (10 July 1833), 532.
15. BFASS, *Slavery and the Slave Trade in British India*, p. 46.

It was unfortunate from the point of view of the success of this measure that Buxton and the other abolitionists in Parliament were at this stage so preoccupied with the issue of West Indian slavery. Had this not been the case, its fate might well have been different. As it was, it came under heavy fire, first from the Court of Directors, who claimed that insufficient latitude was being allowed to the Indian Government, and secondly from the two Houses where it was pointed out that given the state of Indian society at the time it was unnecessarily drastic and might well have dangerous consequences. The Duke of Wellington, recalling his Indian experiences, observed: "I know that in the hut of every Musselman soldier in the Indian army, there is a female slave who accompanies him in all his marches; and I would remind your Lordships to deal lightly with this matter if you wish to retain your sovereignty in India."[16] Although a few members supported the original draft, the majority agreed with Wellington that Indian slavery was a delicate matter and certainly not one to be tackled hastily. The Bill was therefore whittled down in the course of successive readings—first by the removal of the date specifying when slavery should be abolished, then by the insertion of provisions giving wide discretionary powers to the Indian authorities, and finally by the addition of a clause which delegated virtually all responsibility to the Indian Government. It was in this emasculated form that, on 28 August 1833, it received the Royal Assent.[17]

The history of the next nine years is essentially one of bureaucratic muddle, aggravated, on the one hand, by the indifference of the home authorities, and on the other, by the evident reluctance of the Indian Government to make use of the powers which it had been granted. The situation was in many ways reminiscent of that in the 1820s with respect to West Indian slavery, although in this instance the resistance came not from the slaveholders (who had not been consulted and therefore had no say in the matter) but from colonial functionaries. The general tenor of the new Act was, in fact, similar to that of Canning's "Resolutions" of 1823. Immediate steps were to be taken for "ameliorating the condition of the slaves" and "extinguishing slavery throughout the said territories so soon as such extinction shall be practicable and safe". As with Negro slavery a decade earlier, mitigation was to come first, abolition later.

On paper, the steps by which this was to be accomplished looked straightforward enough. The Indian Government in Delhi, consisting of the Governor General and a council of three, would draw up a draft

16. *Ibid*, p. 49.
17. Slavery was not, of course, the only matter dealt with by the Charter Act. In other respects the Act was a courageous measure.

Act and submit it to the Court of Directors in London. Once they had approved it, a copy of the Act together with any suggested amendments would be sent to Delhi where steps would at once be taken to see that it was implemented. Meanwhile the Court of Directors would see that Parliament was kept informed as to what was happening. In theory, the whole process could hardly have been simpler; in practice it turned out to be very complicated indeed.

The Indian Government was informed of Parliament's intentions in a letter of instruction from the Court of Directors of 10 December 1834,[18] which also urged it to use "the utmost discretion" in this matter. In their reply, the Delhi authorities expressed "cordial agreement" with the Court's views and went on to add that as a first step they intended referring the whole question to the newly appointed Indian Law Commissioners.[19] This was a sensible plan. The Law Commission, with T. B. Macaulay at its head, had only just begun its enquiry into Indian legal practices with a view to drawing up a single, comprehensive criminal code for the whole of India. It seemed a singular stroke of good fortune that the advice of so uniquely qualified a body should be available at this time. The news that the issue of Indian slavery was being placed in the hands of the Law Commission was duly passed on to Parliament, though not, it may be noted, until Buxton had made a point of asking for it.[20]

Three years now elapsed without further news from India. On 29 August 1838 the Court of Directors, having again been reminded that Parliament was awaiting information, wrote to the Indian Government stating that it was a matter of the utmost importance that "the attention of the Law Commissioners be immediately recalled to the question", and that a "clear and complete" statement be prepared for submission to Parliament at the earliest opportunity.[21]

This dispatch must have caused the Indian Government some embarrassment, for, in spite of its earlier assurances, it had so far failed to give the Law Commissioners any instructions at all. Whether this was through obstructiveness or, as would seem more likely, incompetence, is unclear. However, it was not until a copy of the Directors' latest dispatch was forwarded to them in November 1838, that the Commissioners became aware, for the first time, that they were expected to make any enquiry into slavery beyond that necessary to complete the penal code.[22] To make

---

18. PP, 1838, *51* (697), 22. The delay in sending these instructions was probably due to the India Board's need to acquaint itself with the subject first. A brief and not very informative collection of documents was got together and published in March 1834. PP, 1834, *44* (128), 171–214.

19. PP, 1838, *51* (697), 22.   20. *Hansard*, *35* (29 July 1836), 668–9.

21. PP, 184, *28* (238), 1.   22. *Ibid*, p. 10.

matters worse, the Indian Government now refused to give the Commissioners permission to conduct local enquiries on the grounds that a report was required at the earliest possible date. Fortunately, the Commissioners had already collected a considerable amount of material during their earlier researches and it was from this that they began, in December 1838, compiling a new report.[23]

Meanwhile, the first draft of their new penal code had arrived in England. Among its recommendations was one which stated that "no act which would be an offense if done against a free person be exempted from punishment because it is done against a slave". This was just the sort of thing that Parliament had been wanting, so without waiting for a reply to their earlier dispatch, the Court of Directors approved the proposal and on 28 September 1838 wrote to Governor General Auckland instructing him to "lose no time in passing appropriate legislation".[24] But if it looked to observers in Britain that at last something was going to be done, they were again disappointed. Auckland was sceptical about the Commissioners' suggestion. In any case, he pointed out—quite erroneously, as it happened—the penal law as already administered fully recognized the principle that master and slave should be placed on an equal footing. There ensued a bureaucratic wrangle in the course of which the question was referred back, first to the Law Commissioners and finally to the provincial administrations in Bombay and Madras. The result was that by the end of 1840 nothing further had been accomplished.

Understandably enough, abolitionists were now becoming impatient. Besides the moral issue involved in the continuance of slavery in British territories it was the view of many that the cultivation of tropical produce in India by means of free labour was one of the most promising ways of combating slavery in the West. James Cropper of Liverpool, a founding member of the Anti-Slavery Society, who happened to be a prominent East Indian merchant, had put forward this notion as early as 1821.[25] In the later 1830s it was taken up and developed by the Quaker abolitionists Joseph and Elisabeth Pease, and by George Thompson, who embraced it with the same passionate enthusiasm with which he had already embraced American abolition. It was this group which in 1839 (a bumper

---

23. The Commissioners, it should be noted, regarded this material as inadequate and actually stated at the time that "a much more searching and minute enquiry is necessary before the commission can venture to recommend positive measures for the mitigation and ultimate abolition of slavery," *ibid*, pp. 10–11.
24. *Ibid*, p. 4.
25. David B. Davis, "James Cropper and the British anti-slavery movement, 1821–1823", *Journal of Negro History*, 45 (1960), 245.

year for the establishment of new organizations) formed the British India Society.[26] The structure of this body closely resembled that of the British and Foreign Anti-Slavery Society. It consisted of a central committee, a number of provincial auxiliaries (of which the Glasgow Emancipation Society, thanks to Thompson's influence, became one[27]) and a periodical, *The British-Indian Advocate*, which began appearing in January 1841.[28] Its aims, however, extended well beyond the immediate issue of emancipation to East Indian reform in general. Among its prime objects of attack were the land tax and the inequitable system of land tenure which had hitherto prevented India from achieving its full potential as a supplier of tropical products. Once these were removed, India would quickly come into its own, so undercutting the slave economies of the West. A simple calculation, according to Pease, showed that the cost of maintaining a slave in Brazil or Cuba was five times that of supporting a free labourer in India. Allowing also for the vast physical resources of the East there was every reason to suppose that it could out-produce and undersell the New World in cotton and sugar as it had already succeeded in doing in indigo.[29]

Not all abolitionists shared Pease's optimism, and some had doubts about Pease himself. The American abolitionist, John A. Collins, described him to Maria W. Chapman as "literally a man of one idea. British India is his hobby. It is with him the universal panacea for all the ails [sic] the flesh is heir to."[30] Yet his theories were unquestionably influential, as was shown by the fact that the World Convention spent a whole day discussing them. "Perfect with proper legislation your system . . . of free labour, in the raising of cotton, on your East Indian possession," Stanton adjured the assembly. "Thus British philanthropy and British policy may stretch out its arms like Samson, and take hold of the two main pillars of American Slavery—conscience and the pocket—and with one mighty impulse, bring the whole fabric, with all its abominations tumbling to the ground."[31] Wendell Phillips was an early convert and Garrison, while in England, became an enthusiastic advocate. For a while the *Liberator* bristled with references to India. In varying degrees such

---

26. See British India Society, *Speeches delivered at a Public Meeting for the Foundation of a British India Society, held in the Freemasons Hall . . . July 6, 1839*, (London, 1839).
27. GES Minute Books, 1 Aug. 1839.
28. *British India Advocate* (nos. 1–15, London, 1 Jan. 1841 to 1 Jan. 1842).
29. John Hyslop Bell, *British Folks and British India Fifty Years Ago: Joseph Pease and his contemporaries* (London, 1891), pp. 32–42, 50–60, 72–82, 86, 105–11.
30. Collins to Chapman, London, 3 Dec. 1840, Weston Papers.
31. BFASS, *Proceedings of the General Anti-Slavery Convention of 1840*, p. 424.

notions played a part in the thinking of most British and not a few American abolitionists of the period.[32]

Meanwhile, attempts had been continuing to prod the government into activity. In 1836, Buxton had renewed his enquiries and had been told by Sir John Hobhouse, President of the India Board,[33] that action would soon be forthcoming. In 1839, replying to further questions by William Ewart, Hobhouse told Parliament that the matter was still being investigated but that a report could be expected shortly.[34] These assurances, although vague, created the impression that something was being done. When by the spring of 1840 no report had been received, the abolitionists determined that further action was needed. The London Committee on 30 March appointed a delegation to ask Stephen Lushington to raise the question again in Parliament. But Lushington was reluctant to do anything until the Law Commissioners' report had arrived, which, he had been given to understand, would be very soon. He urged the Anti-Slavery Society to remain patient, assuring it that he would make all necessary enquiries immediately the report was produced.[35]

This report, as we have already seen, had been delayed thanks to the Indian Government so that it was not until April the following year, 1841, that it reached Parliament. During the intervening twelve months public interest had been aroused by the appearance of a number of books and magazine articles on the question, the most notable being James Pegg's *Slavery in India*, George Thompson's *Lectures on British India*, and William Adam's *The Law and Custom of Slavery in British India*. At the same time, Broad Street had been pressing for immediate action. Auxiliary societies had been alerted and special meetings held.[36] Lushington, after further badgering by the Society, finally agreed to raise the issue in Parliament and on 9 February received a promise from Sir John Hobhouse that all correspondence on the subject would be published.[37]

Despite these efforts Parliament was dissolved on 22 June without any detailed consideration having been given to the issue. The Sturgites now

32. Bell, pp. 108–11; Garrison to Pease, 3 Aug. 1840, Garrison Papers, Boston Public Library—referred to hereafter as Garrison Papers; see also Sturge to Brougham, 29 Sept. 1841, Brougham Papers.
33. The India Board, or Board of Control, had been established by the India Act of 1784, and was empowered to override the Court of Directors. This body was directly responsible to the Government and Parliament for the direction of Indian affairs. The Board consisted of six members appointed by the Prime Minister and, after 1812, its President was always a member of the Cabinet.
34. BFASS, *Slavery and the Slave Trade in British India*, p. 55.
35. BFASS Minute Books, 30 March, 15 May, 2, 26 June, 3, 17 July 1840.
36. BFASS Minute Books, 15, 29 Jan. 1841.
37. *Hansard*, 56 (Feb 9 1841), 456.

determined to do what the Agency Committee had done in similar circumstances nine years before and to make a general appeal to the country. In its "Address to the Electors", copies of which were inserted in all the leading newspapers, the British people were urged to rise into action:

Your voice has been once heard, saying, "Africa be free"; let it once more be heard from the oppressed children of the East. In the British Senate must your demands be proffered and the sentence be pronounced. In the approaching appeal for your votes, give them to no candidate who will not pledge himself to the steady, uncompromising support of a measure for the total and unqualified abolition of slavery—abolition as great and perfect as that which has been effected in the West.[38]

Besides the "Address", two thousand placards explaining Britain's obligation to end Indian slavery were put on display. The campaign was aided by the appearance, early in May, of the Committee's own pamphlet, *Slavery and the Slave Trade in British India*. This work, which had been compiled by John Scoble, was too bulky for general distribution (it contained 72 pages) but an abridged version was soon brought out under the title *A Brief View of Slavery in India*, and copies of this were dispatched to some four thousand candidates and electors.[39] Help was also solicited from auxiliary societies, each being urged to appoint "suitable persons in their respective localities to lecture or assist in holding public meetings on the Subject of East Indian Slavery in the Towns of their vicinity, especially in those which return Members to Parliament, or, if practicable, throughout the Counties in which they are situated."[40]

The elections, which were held in late June and early July, resulted in a victory for Peel and the Tories. The Committee lost no time in preparing a petition for presentation to the new House and in appointing deputations to wait on the Prime Minister and the new President of the India Board, Lord Ellenborough.[41] What passed at these interviews is not known, but that these efforts were not wasted, is suggested by the subsequent course of events.

38. BFASS *Reporter*, 30 June 1841, p. 137. Replies to this address are also printed. See also BFASS Minute Books, 22 June 1841.
39. BFASS Minute Books, 30 April, 2 July 1841. Since the Committee was at this time approximately £1,000 in debt—largely as a result of the World Convention of the previous year—a special appeal for funds had to be issued to meet these campaign expenses. *Ibid*, 22 June 1841.
40. *Ibid*, 22 June 1841. To what extent the provincial societies responded to this appeal is not revealed, though that some supported the Committee's efforts is shown by letters received from the Edinburgh, Leeds and Dublin organizations; BFASS Papers, C 6/96, C 6/99, C 7/103, C 12/92.
41. BFASS Minute Books, 16 July, 3 Sept., 1 Oct. 1841. The interview with Peel, at which a memorial was presented (for text see BFASS *Reporter*, 22 Sept. 1841, pp. 198–9), was held on 22 Sept. and that with Lord Ellenborough on 28 Sept.

The Law Commissioners' Report, as presented to Parliament in April, contained thirty-three recommendations for future legislation regarding slavery. Their aim, as the Commissioners themselves admitted, was not to effect sweeping changes of the kind advocated by abolitionists but to ameliorate the system as a whole by removing some of its harsher features. This, they argued, was not only the safer course but also the one most likely in the long run to benefit slaves themselves.[42] While these recommendations were being studied, a dispatch arrived from Delhi stating that the Indian Government was still undecided over what course to take and would therefore be grateful if the whole subject could be regarded as still under consideration. To this the Court of Directors assented.[43] On 19 September however, Lord Ellenborough, acting on behalf of the new Government, sent a secret despatch to Auckland saying that the country was impatient and that further delays would be embarrassing. "There will", he added, "be an attempt on the part of the Anti-Slavery Society to get up agitation during the next three months. I have vainly cautioned them against the dangers of creating agitation in India, which would be fatal to the success of their own object."[44] The implication was that unless action was forthcoming soon it might be equally fatal to the plans of the Indian Government. Three weeks later, on 13 October, an official dispatch to Delhi from the Court of Directors put the matter even more bluntly.

... We cannot conceal from you our apprehension that any delay in complying with the intention of Parliament and the people of this country, might lead to some act of hurried and imperfect legislation, which adopted under feelings of excitement and without the local knowledge and information you possess, might have consequences injurious to the public peace and tending to defeat the benevolent design of its promoters.[45]

These dispatches evidently had the desired effect for in December 1841, the Indian Government finally got down to drafting regulations. By mid-January, however, progress was once again brought to a standstill, this time because of a difference of opinion in the Governor General's Council over whether masters should be allowed the right to administer moderate corporal punishment. Auckland himself was against allowing them any latitude in this respect on the grounds that such a right, however circumscribed by law, would be abused. Andrew Amos, on the other

---

42. *Law Commissioners' Report*, pp. 188–222.
43. Auckland to Court of Directors, 10 May 1841, PP, 1841, Sess 2, *3* (54), 109.
44. Ellenborough to Auckland, 19 Sept. 1841, in Sir Algernon Law, ed., *India Under Lord Ellenborough: a selection from the hitherto unpublished papers and secret dispatches of Edward, Earl of Ellenborough* (London, 1926), p. 18.
45. Extract of legislative dispatch to India, in Banaji, p. 355.

hand, believed that depriving masters of this right was tantamount to denying them any authority whatsoever. William Wilberforce Bird, the most radical of the Council members, was not only against recognizing a right to administer chastisement but was against recognizing slavery in any form at all. Unable to reach agreement it was decided to refer the matter back to the Court of Directors.[46]

In the meantime, Broad Street had also run into difficulties. Disheartened by the Indian Government's procrastinations, it had decided that the only hope of getting slavery abolished was to persuade Parliament to ignore the Charter Act of 1833 and, without reference to Delhi or the Court of Directors, to pass an emancipation measure of its own. This was what Ellenborough and the Court of Directors had been afraid would happen. To implement its policy, however, the Committee needed to obtain the backing of an active nucleus in Parliament. In this it had been unsuccessful. Lushington had retired at the end of the previous session, and although there were plenty of members who were prepared to lend a sympathetic ear and even to promise their support, no one was prepared to take the initiative.[47] Sir Eardley Wilmot, an abolitionist of long standing, who had already indicated his willingness to take Lushington's place, advised delay adding, somewhat irrelevantly, that it might be a bad thing at that time to draw American attention to Britain's shortcomings.[48] Neither Brougham nor Macaulay—now back in England—were prepared to commit themselves. Benjamin Hawes, after weighing the Committee's proposal, reluctantly declined, but suggested C. P. Villiers as a possibility. Villiers promised to look into the question and in the meantime undertook to present to the House any petitions the Committee cared to draw up.[49] This was the most hopeful response so far. After further prodding he made a brief speech in the Commons, outlining the provisions of the Charter Act for the abolition of slavery and demanding to know what practical measures, if any, had been taken. The Government's spokesman, Major H. B. Baring, replied that whatever legislation was adopted would have to originate in India. He was able to tell the House, however, that specific instructions had already been sent to India and that information about these would be made available shortly.[50]

The instructions which Baring mentioned had, in fact, been sent only

46. *Ibid*, pp. 389–98.
47. BFASS Minute Books, 2 Jan., 7 Feb. 1842.
48. Wilmot to Tredgold, 23 Sept. 1841, BFASS Papers, C 10/182; also Wilmot to Tredgold, n.d., C 10/184 and Wilmot to Morgan, 20 Jan. 1841, C 9/20.
49. BFASS Minute Books, 7, 28 Feb., 18, 29 April, 13, 30 May 1842. One such petition was presented on 13 May 1842, BFASS *Reporter*, 1 June 1842.
50. *Hansard*, 65 (Aug. 5 1842), 1074–75.

the previous week and took the form of a reply from the Court of Directors to the Indian Government's request for guidance on the matter of corporal punishment. The Directors, who had sided completely with Bird, advised the adoption of liberal measures the most sweeping of which would remove the legal basis of slavery by forbidding courts to give it any form of recognition.[51] Lord Ellenborough, who had just arrived in India as Auckland's successor, lost no time in making the Directors' injunctions effective. On 11 February he gave his official assent to Act V of 1843, according to which: (1) public officers were forbidden to sell persons in execution of judical decrees; (2) courts were forbidden to recognize slavery; (3) so-called slaves were not to be deprived of their property; and (4) acts which would be an offence if done to a freeman would be equally an offence if done to anyone on the pretext of his being a slave.[52]

Broad Street had been on the point of issuing another appeal to the country when it learned of the Indian Government's action. This news was broken to it in the course of an interview with Lord Fitzgerald, Ellenborough's replacement at the India Board. The Committee's first response was to express scepticism but after a further interview and an examination of Act V, it was sufficiently satisfied to send an address of congratulation to the Queen.[53] Correspondence was begun with sympathizers in India to find out how the Act was being administered and there was even some talk of setting up antislavery societies there.[54]

As might have been expected, Act V of 1843 had little immediate effect upon Indian slavery and certainly did not result in the "virtual extinction" which Lord Fitzgerald had prophesied in his talks with antislavery deputations. In practice, Indian slavery had never depended to any great extent on judicial sanctions, being largely the product of customs arising out of the existing system of land tenure. It is hardly surprising, therefore, to find C. H. Cameron, one of the former Law Commissioners, reporting to a Parliamentary Committee in 1852 that there was still a "great mass of slavery existing *de facto*", although he went on to add that this was, generally speaking, of a quite unobjectionable type and was considered advantageous by all parties concerned.[55] From the point of view of the Indian administrator, the new Act had much to commend it, for being essentially negative it required virtually no enforcement and actually relieved him of some responsibility. The British and Foreign Anti-

51. Court of Directors to the Government of India, 27 July 1842 in Banaji, p. 399.
52. PP, 1843, *58* (525), 13. The Act went into effect on 7 April 1843.
53. BFASS Minute Books, 13, 31 March, 1 Sept., 11 Oct. 1843. For the text of the address and the Queen's reply see BFASS *Reporter*, 29 Nov. 1843, p. 217.
54. BFASS Minute Books, 4 Aug., 29 Sept., 8 Dec. 1843.
55. PP, 1852/3, *30*, 206.

Slavery Society was also satisfied, although from time to time it felt obliged to remind the Indian authorities of their duty to inform slaves, especially those in newly acquired territories, of their right to freedom. For example, in January, 1847, a Broad Street deputation obtained a promise from Sir J. C. Hobhouse, President of the India Board, that further measures would be taken to acquaint slaves with their legal position and also that efforts would be made to persuade native rulers to abolish slavery within their territories.[56] By this time the Society was more interested in India as a source of free labour produce than in Indian slavery. The idea that India would undercut the slave economies of the West continued to intrigue abolitionists but the results, so far as sugar was concerned, could scarcely have been more disappointing and not until the American Civil War temporarily cut off supplies from the United States did India emerge as a major cotton producer.[57] In 1862, slave-holding was made a criminal offence, but there is nothing to suggest that British antislavery societies were responsible for this measure or even particularly interested in it.

In practice, the eradication of slavery in India was a gradual process which depended more on economic expansion than on legislation or judicial decrees. As railways were built and urban trades and industries established, alternative means of livelihood became available with the result that some slaves began asserting their independence.[58] But although Act V did not bring freedom to India it did remove the legal obstacles which might have hampered it. To this extent it prepared the way for the freedom that came once the structure of Indian society began to change.

Although it was well known that slavery existed in Britain's other eastern possessions, abolitionists had, until 1843, paid it little attention. This was sound policy for whatever was decided in India would determine Britain's policy towards her eastern possessions as a whole. This proved to be the case. In March 1843, at the same interview in which he announced the "virtual extinction" of slavery in India, Lord Fitzgerald told the Broad Street deputation that orders had already been issued for abolition in Malacca, Singapore and Penang and that similar orders would be issued shortly with respect to Province Wellesley.[59]

56. BFASS Minute Books, 28 Jan. 1847; also "Memorial to Sir J. C. Hobhouse", in BFASS *Reporter*, 1 March 1847, pp. 35–6.
57. See pp. 166–7 below.
58. O'Malley, pp. 267–8.
59. BFASS Minute Books, 31 March 1843. Here, as in India, abolition meant simply legal abolition. When slavery actually disappeared from these areas it is impossible to say. Certain practices analogous to slavery, such as debt-bondage, continued until very recently: Greenidge, *Slavery*, pp. 66–9.

The only colony that still remained to be accounted for was Ceylon. The situation there was particularly confusing since in theory most of the slaves—numbering between thirty and forty thousand—were already free because of the failure of the masters to observe registration laws. This fact, however, had had no effect either on the position of the slaves or the attitudes of their masters. In May 1841, Lord John Russell as Secretary for War and Colonies had sent instructions to the Governor of Ceylon, Sir Colin Campbell, to abolish slavery at the first opportunity. Campbell took more than a year to reply and when he did so it was at once evident that he had misunderstood Russell's instructions. Instead of drafting an emancipation act he had merely made provisions for further registration. In a sharply worded note, dated 8 December 1842, Russell's successor, Lord Stanley, told Campbell that his new measures were not only uncalled for but that they actually destroyed the government's case by giving slaveholders a second opportunity for registration. As it turned out, the situation was not quite as Stanley had supposed, for in his reply, dated 17 March 1843, Campbell was able to report that thanks to the influence of European residents not a single slave had been registered and that slavery in Ceylon was, therefore, virtually at an end.[60]

Broad Street, which had been following these developments closely, celebrated the arrival of the Governor's dispatch in a lengthy article in the *Reporter*.[61] Nevertheless there remained a handful of slaves in the mountainous Kandian province, which for administrative reasons had not been included in the areas subject to the registration ordinance, whose legal status had not been affected. The existence of these slaves caused abolitionists uneasiness, not because of their numbers—there were less than four hundred—or their condition, which was unlikely to be affected whatever changes were made in the law, but because as long as they remained slaves it could not truthfully be claimed that slavery had been abolished throughout the Empire. For propagandistic reasons, if for no other, it was necessary that the anomaly be removed. They were gratified, therefore, when in November 1845 it was reported that this had been done.[62]

Neither the British and Foreign Anti-Slavery Society nor any other abolitionist organization could claim responsibility for the ending of slavery in Britain's eastern dominions. It came about—almost incidentally one might say—as a result of the Charter Act of 1833. From that time on

60. This correspondence will be found in PP, 1843, *58* (568), 3–10.
61. BFASS *Reporter*, 14 June, 23 Aug. 1843.
62. *Ibid*, 26 Nov. 1845, pp. 213, 216. An ordinance abolishing slavery throughout Ceylon had gone into effect in December 1844.

slavery in India and, by extension, throughout her eastern possessions was doomed, at least in a legal sense. All the abolitionists needed to do was to bring pressure to bear on the government at a time when fulfilment was being delayed, and but for them would no doubt have gone on being delayed, owing to bureaucratic incompetence and the inertia of the colonial authorities.

6

The abolitionists and the sugar colonies 1838–1850

The broadening of the abolitionists' programme after 1838 meant that they could no longer give their undivided attention to the sugar colonies. They were agreed, however, that developments there would need careful watching. Few had been wholly satisfied with the arrangements made for safeguarding the freedom of the Negroes and past experience had given them ample opportunity for observing the ingenuity of the planters in circumventing even the most stringent regulations. Thus, from the outset, they were on their guard. The speeches that heralded the ending of apprenticeship contained many warnings about the need for continued vigilance. Only four years earlier, audiences were reminded, Britain had celebrated what appeared to be the most sweeping victory over slavery in modern times only to discover that the condition of the Negroes had not changed for the better and in some respects had actually worsened. "We speak not ignorantly or inadvisedly", the *British Emancipator* said in June 1838, "when we state our belief that those who have hitherto monopolized rule and authority and freedom in the colonies will make a general and determined effort to retain their dominion and to fix on the negro a yoke as heavy as that from which he is about to be delivered". What they feared was precisely what the Republican radicals after the abolition of slavery in the United States feared: that local authorities would impose regulations, supposedly for the maintenance of law and order or the encouragement of industry, which would have the effect of reducing the freedmen to the condition of serfs. The public was warned to be especially on the lookout for acts for the suppression of vagrancy, local police regulations, labour contract laws, regulations affecting the suffrage and restrictions upon the sale and transfer of lands.[1]

These warnings were echoed by the West Indian missionaries whose observations confirmed that the planters were bent on denying the Negro his rights and that unless the British public remained watchful there was a good chance that they would have their way. Far better, they pointed out, to act immediately to forestall such attempts than to wait until the mischief had been done. "The British Government", wrote the Rev. J. Phillippo from Jamaica,

must be urged to vigilant watchfulness over every law that may emanate from the local legislatures; and in order to do this be not in haste to disband the Anti-Slavery Society. The precipitancy in this respect was a source of vast mischief in 1834—a sad and fatal error. It should be kept disciplined for at least two years longer. Their existence will at least act as a salutary restraint, as on a battle field a good deal depends on making good a victory.[2]

Making good the victory was, in fact, the Central Emancipation Committee's main practical concern during the remaining eighteen months of its existence, and on its dissolution this responsibility passed to the British and Foreign Anti-Slavery Society.[3] As before, much of the abolitionists' information came from missionaries. Knibb, in particular, kept in close touch with Broad Street and when in England often sat in on its meetings. (His biography was later written by the Rev. J. H. Hinton, Editor of the *Anti-Slavery Reporter*.[4]) Among the others who corresponded regularly with the Society were John Clarke of Kingston, Jamaica, and

1. *British Emancipator*, 27 June 1838, p. 124.
2. Phillippo to Sturge [June ?] 1838. This letter was quoted by Sturge in his Birmingham address on 1 August 1838. *British Emancipator*, 22 Aug. 1838, p. 145. Philippo, of course, was mistaken in supposing that the antislavery societies were disbanded in 1834.
3. "Fundamental Principles of the British and Foreign Anti-Slavery Society", in *Annual Reports*, 1840–1870.
4. John Howard Hinton, *Memoir of William Knibb, Missionary in Jamaica* (London, 1847).

T. F. Abbot of Berbice. It was largely as a result of the efforts of these and other sympathizers, that fifteen auxiliary societies were established in the West Indies between 1839 and 1843—eleven in Jamaica and one each in Trinidad, Demerara, Barbados and Berbice. Up to 1843 these societies had contributed £260 to the support of the London organization. Thereafter contributions declined but small sums were still being received as late as the 1860s.[5] There was no corresponding decline in the concern of active abolitionists in Britain for the welfare of the West Indian Negroes.

This was natural enough. Abolitionists continued to feel responsible both for the freedman's present condition and for his future prospects. But wishing him well was not the only factor which influenced their thinking. From a very early stage it had been brought home to them— for on this score the letters they received from abroad could leave them in no doubt—that their international standing depended in large part on what happened in the West Indies. If emancipation went well their influence and reputations would be enhanced, but if it went badly both would be jeopardized. Their efforts to make the antislavery cause a truly international one were predicated, therefore, on making West Indian emancipation a success. This was all the more important because the only previous experience of large-scale emancipation in modern times, the freeing of the Negroes in Santo Domingo in the 1790s, had ended in unmitigated disaster, if not for the Negroes at least for their masters, an episode the planters elsewhere continued to cite as objective proof that emancipation would never work.[6] West Indian emancipation, then, was a new test case, almost a laboratory experiment one might say, which would prove to the world not only that peaceful emancipation was possible but that it could be advantageous to all concerned.

Foreign observers had been quick to grasp the significance of what was happening. "The results which may follow the immediate emancipation of slaves in the West Indies", the New York *Commercial Advertiser* had stated in 1833, "may afford us the lesson of wisdom without the cost of experience."[7] What occurred under apprenticeship was not, of course, a fair test since the vast majority of Negroes were still living under conditions very similar to slavery. But this did not prevent exaggerated claims being made for and against the experiment. J. A. Thome and J. H. Kimball, two emissaries of the American Anti-Slavery Society who toured

5. BFASS, *Annual Reports*, 1840–70.
6. William S. Jenkins, *Proslavery Thought in the Old South* (Chapel Hill, 1935), p. 63.
7. 30 March 1833.

the colonies in 1837, pronounced it a great success.[8] They contrasted the "erect forms, the active movements, and the sprightly countenances", of the freedmen with the dispirited air of the slaves they had seen in the South. Most striking of all was the equable relationship which they found between the races. Even those who had originally opposed emancipation, they claimed, were now persuaded of its benefits. The planters were satisfied because it had relieved them of a tiresome form of property; the poor whites liked it because it "freed them from the yoke of civil oppression"; but most of all the Negroes welcomed it because it had brought them freedom. Only in Jamaica did they encounter conditions of which they really disapproved, though even there they found abundant signs that things were changing for the better. All this was very much in contrast to the accounts of Scoble, Lloyd, Sturge and Harvey who visited the West Indies at the same time and who, writing of course for British audiences, were concerned principally with stressing the defects of the system. All agreed, however, that the Negro had behaved remarkably well and that such shortcomings as were evident were the fault of "that crazy and criminal system of expiring despotism" as Charles Stuart characterized apprenticeship.[9]

Whatever its merits or demerits apprenticeship had meant that Negroes were obliged to work, with the result that sugar production had declined only slightly—from 3·9 to 3·5 million hundredweight.[10] The real test of emancipation came in 1838 when, except in the three colonies of Bermuda, Antigua and Montserrat, where the apprenticeship system had either not been adopted at all or had been ended prematurely, labourers were for the first time free to seek employment or not as they wished. It had been the assumption of most members of Parliament that they would choose not to work. In practice, however, their behaviour varied very much from colony to colony, depending largely on geographic and economic conditions. In the case of those smaller islands where the planters held an effective land monopoly and where all or most of the land was already in use, production continued much as before. In Barbados the annual sugar output actually increased. But in the larger colonies of Jamaica, Trinidad and British Guiana, where large tracts of mountainous and uncultivated land existed, there was a general tendency for Negroes to drift away from the plantations and to set up communities of their own

8. J. A. Thome and J. H. Kimball, *Emancipation in the West Indies: A Six Months Tour of Antigua, Barbados and Jamaica in 1837* (New York, 1838), p. 17.
9. Stuart to Weld, 10 Oct. 1839, in Gilbert H. Barnes and Dwight L. Dumond, eds., *Letters of Theodore Dwight Weld, Angeline Grimké Weld and Sarah Grimké, 1822–1844* (2 vols, New York, 1934), 2, 805.
10. W. L. Burn, *The British West Indies* (London, 1951), pp. 117, 127.

based on a subsistence type of agriculture.[11] Those who remained were erratic in their working habits, often failing to turn up when expected and quitting when it suited them. For want of labour, many estates had to be either abandoned or operated on a much reduced scale. In Jamaica, where the situation was exacerbated by long-standing feuds between the Negroes and their employers, production was halved, and in a number of other colonies the situation was little better. Taking the West Indies as a whole the annual sugar production between the years 1824–33 and 1839–46 declined by 36 per cent and its average value, in terms of the prices offered on the London market, by 21 per cent.[12]

These figures were damaging to the abolitionists. As good liberal progressives they believed that free labour was the best form of labour and had predicted that production would rise. Its failure to do so they at first dismissed as a passing phase—due in the first instance to bad weather conditions. There was some truth in this: 1840 had certainly been a bad year. But when production failed to show any marked improvement the following year they had no alternative but to put the best face on the matter. In the first place, they pointed out, the Negroes had previously been grossly overworked. As a result of emancipation, women and children no longer toiled in the fields and sugar mills for fourteen or sixteen hours a day; it was plainly inhumane for the planters or anyone else to expect them to do so. If employers, instead of adopting new techniques and labour methods, continued using freedmen in the same wasteful fashion in which they had previously used their slaves they had no one but themselves to blame for the results. In any case, the success or failure of emancipation was not to be judged solely in terms of exports. The Negroes had behaved admirably, showing that they were prepared for freedom; the number of marriages among them had increased; wives and husbands were now living together; the number of schools had grown and so had church attendance; societies for mutual relief had been established and were flourishing; crime had diminished. In short, the West Indies, for the first time in their history, were beginning to show some signs of social progress.[13]

There was much truth in these observations. The economic decline

11. H. Paget, "The free village system in Jamaica", *Jamaican Historical Review*, I (1945), 31–48.
12. P. D. Curtin, "Sugar prices and West Indian prosperity", *Journal of Economic History*, *14* (1954), 161. For general accounts of the effects of emancipation in the West Indies see Mathieson, *British Slave Emancipation;* Anton V. Long, *Jamaica and the New Order* (Jamaica, 1956), and Curtin, *Two Jamaicas*.
13. BFASS *Reporter*, 6 April 1842; 20 Aug., 3 Sept. 1845. See also Alexander to Scoble, 8 March 1845, BFASS Papers, C 12/56.

of the West Indies was no new phenomenon resulting from emancipation, but something that had been going on for a long time due to soil exhaustion, outdated techniques and competition from elsewhere. All that the freeing of the slaves had done was to speed up a process which was occurring anyway. It is also true, at least in the case of Jamaica, and presumably in that of other colonies also, that the falling off of sugar production was offset by economic growth in other areas, most notably in mixed agriculture as the Negroes withdrew from the plantations and established settlements and markets of their own. Even those who remained on the plantations were able to play a more active role in the economic life of their communities if only as consumers of local produce.[14]

But well founded though the abolitionists' case was—and in some respects it was probably better founded than they themselves realized—it was hard to convince anyone accustomed to regarding sugar production as the natural index of West Indian prosperity that the situation was not as bad as the planters said it was. Unlike trade figures, greater personal freedom and improved living conditions, real though they were to those who experienced them, were not susceptible to quantitative measurement. It would have helped the abolitionists' case had they been able to quote figures for those other types of production which had increased. But since these consisted mainly of providing produce for home consumption or for small local markets no such figures were available. Who then could say with certainty, without having actually been to the West Indies, that the picture given by the planters was false? It was only too easy for people to imagine the freedmen, as Carlyle did, "sitting yonder with their beautiful muzzles up to the ears in pumpkins, imbibing sweet pulps and juices . . . while the sugar crops rot round them uncut".[15] In the debate over the results of emancipation, which lasted throughout the forties and fifties, it was always the critics who appeared the realists, the abolitionists who seemed to be covering up.

The decline in sugar production gave foreign critics, noticeably silent since it had become evident that the bloodshed and rapine they had prophesied were failing to materialize, the opportunity they had been waiting for to return to the attack. Just as, a generation earlier, many people had attributed the material backwardness of the West Indies to slavery, so now proslavery writers united in attributing it to emancipation. William Crump, writing to John C. Calhoun in 1845 from Kingston, Jamaica, stated that,

14. For a detailed discussion of these developments see Curtin, *Two Jamaicas*.
15. Thomas Carlyle, "Occasional discourse on the Nigger Question", *Fraser's Magazine*, *40*, Dec. 1849, pp. 670–9.

I have been informed by all the more intelligent gentlemen here with whom I have conversed on the subject, that the present prostrated condition of this rich and productive Isle is owing entirely to the emancipation of slavery. The streets and public highways are constantly filled with fine looking men and women, ragged and half starved, with a bit of sugar cane in their hands as food, perhaps the only time they have eaten anything for days past. I wish old Mr Adams, Giddings and their associates could see the condition of these once happy but now miserable people.[16]

In article after article over the next decade Southern journals drummed home the message that British emancipation had failed. The *Southern Quarterly Review*[17] in a piece entitled "British and American slavery" described the disastrous economic repercussions of freedom. Ever since the slaves had been emancipated the value of the West Indies to the mother country had steadily declined. Free to indulge their well-known instinct for sluggishness, the Negroes had withdrawn from the estates and now presented a picture of indolence and inactivity as revolting as in Haiti. Property had declined in value. The various measures by which the governments of the colonies had sought to stimulate the Negro to activity had successively failed. The Charleston *Mercury* treated its readers to a long description of "the atmosphere of barbarism and dereliction that now pervades those once prosperous islands".[18] The sympathies of the Southern planters were especially aroused by descriptions of the plight of their brethren in Britain's colonies. "It is enough to state", lamented one West Indian writing to the *Southern Quarterly Review*, "that of *forty* to *fifty* sugar and coffee estates in St George, I could name about three or four only which are going on vigorously at the moment . . . whilst by far the largest number are totally abandoned, with buildings in ruin and fields in jungle."[19] To the Southerner's way of thinking Parliament's treatment of the planters was a blatant act of robbery. "So much", concluded *De Bow's Review* after describing their predicament, "for the act of a Parliament that makes the taking of a pocket handkerchief 'at home' punishable by death."[20] Such anti-British bias characterized much of the writing on this subject, particularly during the early 1840s when the Texas question was uppermost in the minds of many Southerners.[21]

16. Crump to Calhoun, 16 Jan. 1845, in C. S. Butcher and R. P. Brooks, eds, "Correspondence addressed to John C. Calhoun, 1837–1849", *Annual Report of the American Historical Association, 1929* (Washington, D.C., 1930), pp. 278–9.
17. Oct. 1853, pp. 401–3.
18. 4 June 1853.
19. "Emancipation in the British West Indies", *Southern Quarterly Review*, April 1853, p. 432.
20. "The Practical Effects of Emancipation", *De Bow's Review*, *18* (1855), p. 487.
21. See Chapter 10 below.

Thus, to the South, West Indian emancipation became a symbol and a warning: a symbol of the futility of all schemes designed to elevate the Negro to the level of the white: a warning of what would happen if ever such a thing were attempted there. The most detailed exposition of the Southern case appeared in a pamphlet, published anonymously in 1862, under the title *Free Negroism: or the results of emancipation in the North and West Indian Islands: with statistics of her decay of commerce, the idleness of the Negro, his return to savagism and the effect of emancipation in the farming, mechanical and labouring classes.* But the essentials of the argument had been made familiar to readers of the Southern press long before. In 1844 Calhoun summed them up when he told his fellow Southern Democrat, William R. King of Alabama, that Britain had

failed in all her objects. The labor of the Negroes has proved far less productive, without affording the consolation of having improved their condition. . . . While this costly scheme has had such ruinous effects on the tropical production of Great Britain, it has given a powerful stimulus, followed by a corresponding increase of products, to those countries which have had the good sense to shun her example.[22]

Four years later, a committee of Southern members of Congress issued a manifesto which stated that, blighting though the British experiment had been, it furnished only a faint picture of the effects which a similar measure would have on the United States. At least the British had not been moved by wild fanaticism. They had given the owners some, although scarcely enough, compensation and had made provision for preserving law and order. But such was the nature of American abolitionists that they opposed giving any compensation at all. They would undoubtedly use the blacks to terrorize the whites. The inevitable consequence of emancipation in America would be to create a political alliance between the Negroes and the North, aimed at wresting all control out of the hands of the white Southerners who would be left with no alternative but to abandon their country to their former slaves "to become the permanent abode of disorder, anarchy, poverty, misery and wretchedness".[23]

Countering such arguments was not easy although the London Committee laboured to do so.[24] Foreign visitors to the two World Anti-Slavery

22. Calhoun to King, 12 Aug. 1844 in R. C. Crallé, ed., *The Works of John C. Calhoun* (6 vols, New York, 1854), 6, 385–6.
23. In T. H. Benton, *Thirty Years View, or a History of the Working of the American Government . . . 1820–1850* (2 vols, New York, 1857), 2, 734–5.
24. The consternation felt by some American abolitionists at these claims is shown by the following letter received by the Committee from a correspondent in the Midwest: "But light is needed. We want correct information as to the condition of things in the West Indies. . . . Is it in your power to transmit to me statistics, official or if unofficial, accurate, of the exports and imports of the British West

Conventions were carefully briefed on recent developments and on how best to counter proslavery claims. Lewis Tappan, returning from the 1843 Convention, was able to announce that Clarkson had told him that he had "full proof that the United States Consul at Kingston, Jamaica, was in the habit of sending to the United States fabricated and false information concerning the working of emancipation in the British West Indies".[25] When the opportunity offered, the Committee itself took the initiative. In June 1839, learning that a French agent, Commissioner Jules Lechevalier, had recently visited St Lucia and had been so impressed by what he had seen that he intended to recommend a similar measure to the French authorities, the Committee wrote to the British abolitionist, W. T. Blair, then in Paris, instructing him to give whatever support he could to the Commissioner.[26] Six months later when Isambert, the Secretary of the French Anti-Slavery Society, wrote to Tredgold requesting full information regarding the state of the emancipated colonies he was supplied with a complete set of parliamentary papers on the subject along with copies of a number of tracts.[27] Not all foreign abolitionists, however, felt in need of such close guidance and some were conspicuously dishonest. William Lloyd Garrison, speaking at a 1st of August celebration in Abingdon, Massachusetts, quoted figures on the sugar production of Barbados—one of the two islands whose output had not actually diminished since 1833—from which he concluded that emancipation had universally proven a great economic success.[28] Ralph Waldo Emerson, speaking on a similar occasion in Concord, Massachusetts, in 1844, described the unparalleled increase in prosperity that had come to the West Indies since emancipation. Like many Northern observers he saw emancipation in terms of the contrast between North and South in his own day. Before emancipation, the West Indies, like the South, had stood for economic lethargy and social backwardness, but since emancipation

Indies from 1830 up to the present time? I can easily believe that the production of one or two great staples may have fallen off—but has labor been directed into other channels? Has the totality of production increased? Ample information on these points would be of vast, or incalculable benefit just at this time, in the present state of the [slavery] question in Kentucky and other parts of the South." G. Bailey Jr to J. Scoble, Cincinnati, 19 Jan. 1845, in A. H. Abel and F. J. Klingberg, *A Side-Light on Anglo-American Relations Furnished by the Correspondence of Lewis Tappan and Others with the British and Foreign Anti-Slavery Society* (Lancaster, Pa., 1927), pp. 203–4.

25. *Anti-Slavery Almanac*, 1844, p. 18.

26. BFASS Minute Books, 3 June 1839.

27. BFASS Minute Books, 4 Jan. 1840. This was on the eve of a debate in the National Assembly on the subject of the abolition of slavery in the French colonies.

28. W. L. Garrison, *West Indian Emancipation: A speech delivered at Abingdon, Massachusetts, on the First Day of August, 1854* (Boston, 1854), p. 40.

they had begun, in his mind, to resemble the North. It would not be long, he implied, before the throb of the factory, the whistle of the railroad and the cry of the newspaper vendor would be heard throughout the islands.[29]

While the abolitionists' policy with respect to foreign audiences was to show developments in the West Indies in the best possible light, their policy with respect to British audiences was quite the opposite. Here they stressed the failures rather than the successes, always making plain, of course, that these were the fault of the masters and not the Negroes. Their principal concern was seeing that the freedmen's privileges were respected. For this reason they set their faces against any legislation which singled out the Negro for special attention. As Scoble told a Parliamentary committee of enquiry in 1842, freeing the slaves meant making them subject to the same regulations as everyone else. If the freedmen were, as the planters claimed, reluctant to work it was because they were not paid enough. He knew from experience that no one was more industrious than the West Indian Negro providing he was given fair treatment. The troubles of the West Indies were entirely the fault of the "master class" which "not yet thoroughly weaned from long protracted and inveterate corruption", still imagined that it could behave under the new regime as it had under the old. If only employers were prepared to treat the freedmen in the same way that they would have treated British labourers they would have nothing to fear.[30]

These arguments failed to impress the planters. On the specific issue of wages they pointed out that already in many of the colonies Negroes were being paid so much that some worked only six or seven hours a day and only three or four days a week. To pay them more would make things worse rather than better: those who worked merely in order to satisfy their immediate needs would work shorter hours while those who laboured conscientiously would soon amass enough money to purchase land of their own. In either event the planters would be the losers. Moreover, because of the shortage of labour and the cut-throat competition among employers, wages were already higher than the economy could stand and estates were being run at a loss. Ralph Bernal, MP, informed the same committee in 1842 that he had received no income from his Jamaican estates during the previous three years and had actually been compelled to pay out three thousand pounds from other sources to keep

29. R. W. Emerson, *Address Delivered in the Court House in Concord, Massachusetts, on the 1st August, 1844, on the Anniversary of the Emancipation of the Negroes in the British West Indies* (Boston, 1844).
30. "Report from the Select Committee on the West Indian Colonies", PP 1842, *13*, 295–6.

them running. Even so, he had cane rotting in the fields for want of labour. R. H. Church of Trinidad, who was in a similar position, told the committee that in his opinion no amount of money, however substantial, would persuade the Negroes to work more than a limited number of hours a day.[31]

Convinced that the Negroes would not succumb to the offer of material rewards the planters turned to coercion as an alternative. In Jamaica a series of laws was passed which would prevent the freedmen from wandering off the estates and at the same time enable the planters to recoup in rent a large part of what they paid out in wages. "These crafty ordinances", as one abolitionist described them,[32] meant that a free labourer who disagreed with his employer over some exorbitant and quite arbitrary scale of rents could have his belongings confiscated and be consigned to prison for a short period. Once driven from his home, he could then be arrested almost at will for vagrancy and sent to work with the penal gang for sixty days. Having served one such term, he was in no better position than before and might be arrested again on the same charge immediately upon his release.[33] In Barbados, where similar laws prevailed, the planters sought to establish additional control over their labour force by forbidding emigration to other islands.[34] In British Guiana, Trinidad and many other colonies, devices were adopted to discourage labour mobility and to augment the power of white employers.[35]

Throughout the 1840s, the London Committee busied itself bringing such regulations to the notice of the Colonial Office. Sometimes this was done by correspondence or through the agency of a prominent MP, on other occasions by arranging an interview with the Minister himself. The British government had learned by experience to be wary of laws emanating from the West Indian legislatures and was certainly not prepared to countenance any deliberate attempt to reimpose slavery. The Committee's protests, therefore, did not pass unnoticed. Many of the offending laws, including parts of the Jamaican and Barbados penal codes, against which the Society spoke out vehemently, were disallowed.[36] On the other hand, the government did not want to offend the West Indian planters, who admittedly were in a difficult position, any more than

31. *Ibid*, 93–115, 451–6.
32. Thomas Brewin to Scoble, 11 June 1847, BFASS Papers, C 14/40.
33. BFASS, *Proceedings of the General Anti-Slavery Convention of 1840*, p. 373.
34. *Ibid*, p. 527. "Resolution of the Barbados Auxiliary British and Foreign Anti-Slavery Society, 24 March 1840", in BFASS *Reporter*, 1 July 1840, p. 159.
35. BFASS *Reporter*, 1 July 1848, pp. 110–11.
36. *Ibid*, 2 June 1841, p. 122. See also BFASS Minute Books, 2, 17, 18, 25 June and 6, 14 July 1840.

was absolutely necessary. For this reason it was seldom prepared to go as far as the Society would have liked. For example, Sturge and his colleagues were much distressed that official sanction should be given to the conciliatory policies inaugurated by Sir Charles Metcalfe, the Governor of Jamaica, who, they believed, had gone much further than he need in his desire to placate the planters. They especially resented his having turned against the Baptist missionaries, whom he had rather accurately described as a "political party".[37] They also suspected his motives for having ordered the stipendiary magistrates to discontinue the practice of submitting monthly reports on conditions in the areas under their jurisdiction. These reports and the investigations necessary for their preparation had aroused much resentment in the Colony, and Metcalfe evidently hoped that stopping them would be interpreted by the planters as a gesture of good will.[38] The abolitionists, however, had been in the habit of using them as a basis for their own statements on emancipation and it seemed to them as though the Governor was trying to suppress information. They took the matter up with the Colonial Secretary, Lord John Russell, with the result that the reports were, shortly afterwards, resumed, although on a half-yearly basis only.[39] When, a few years later, the office of stipendiary magistrate was abolished altogether, a deputation waited upon the new colonial minister, W. E. Gladstone, to explain that, in its view, the ordinary magistrates were quite unfitted to assume the duties now assigned to them. Gladstone promised to look into the matter, but the decision was allowed to stand.[40]

Soon after its formation, the British and Foreign Anti-Slavery Society had established a special subsidiary organization—the Jamaica Persecution Fund—to defray the legal expenses of victims of judicial oppression.[41] Samuel Gurney was appointed Treasurer and within a few months subscriptions amounted to well over a thousand pounds.[42] Typical of the cases to engage its attention was that of Dr Palmer, of Kingston, Jamaica, who was imprisoned for making observations offensive to the Jamaican Assembly.[43] Another case was that of the Rev. Thomas Ward, of Falmouth, Jamaica, who was arrested for obstructing the police when they attempted

37. BFASS *Reporter*, 1 July 1840, pp. 152–4; 30 Dec. 1840, pp. 324–5.
38. Long, p. 50.
39. BFASS Minute Books, 14, 18 Feb., 30 March, 7 Dec. 1840; BFASS *Reporter*, 4 Nov. 1840, p. 280. The Committee later attempted to have the practice of submitting monthly reports reinstituted, but without success. *Ibid*, 2 Dec. 1840, p. 309.
40. BFASS Minute Books, 26 Dec. 1845; 27 Feb. 1846.
41. *Ibid*, 27 Sept. 1839.
42. In January 1841, they amounted to £1,312 and by May had increased to £1,466. BFASS *Reporter*, 15 Jan., 20 May 1840, pp. 8, 112.
43. BFASS Minute Books, 31 Jan. 1840; BFASS *Reporter*, 1840, pp. 4, 12, 21.

to break up a gathering of his parishioners.[44] The Fund was liquidated in 1846 when its remaining assets, amounting to just over £230, were transferred to the account of the parent body.[45]

Because of the delays involved in obtaining information from the colonies, abolitionists found themselves working at a constant disadvantage. By the time a case reached their notice it was often too late to intervene. Before a law could be disallowed, a year or more might elapse, and even then there was always the possibility that the colonial legislature would pass another almost the same and so yet another year would elapse before it, too, was disallowed. More effective, therefore, than legal aid or appeals to the government was the policy of providing the Negroes from the plantations with settlements of their own. Much of the early trouble between the planters and the freedmen had arisen over the confusion of wages with rents—the latter sometimes exceeding the former.[46] Once in a home of his own the Negro was free not only from excessive rents and the fear of ejection, but also from petty debt acts, vagrancy acts and most of the other legislative devices by means of which the planters attempted to maintain control over him.[47] Although the London Committee was not directly involved in this undertaking, many of its members were. Early in 1839, Joseph Sturge founded the West Indian Land Investment Company aimed at raising £100,000 to be devoted to the establishment of free and independent Negro villages. A substantial sum had already been collected when it was discovered that the enterprise contravened rules laid down by the Board of Trade.[48] The scheme had, therefore, to be abandoned, but Sturge himself subsequently advanced various sums to the missionaries for the purchase of land. (One of the settlements thus established was named after him. There was also a Clarksonville, a Buxton and a Wilberforce.[48]) Partly as a result of these efforts the number of freeholds in Jamaica more than quadrupled within a very few years.[50] By moving off the estates the Negroes did not necessarily cease to be wage-earners since the income derived from their own lands was seldom sufficient to give them a livelihood. They were, however, free to offer their labour on the open market and to sell their services to the highest bidder.

44. BFASS Minute Books, 25 Sept. 1840; BFASS *Reporter*, 1840, pp. 184, 215, 232.
45. BFASS Minute Books, 30 Jan. 1846.
46. Long, p. 27.
47. BFASS, *Proceedings of the General Anti-Slavery Convention of 1840*, p. 370.
48. The Board of Trade objected to the undertaking on the grounds that it violated regulations designed to prevent the accumulation of land in mortmain: Richard, *Memoirs of Joseph Sturge*, pp. 196–8.
49. Sturge to Rev. John Clark, February 1839; and Clark to Sturge, 18 March 1841, in *ibid*, pp. 199–200, 196–7.
50. Paget, *Jamaican Historical Review*, I (1945), 42.

Sturge was also responsible for the founding of the Jamaican Education Society, through which sums were raised for many years, principally by Quakers, and sent to the Baptist missionaries for the support of schools on the island.[51] Female antislavery organizations were particularly active in this type of work and for many it became their principal field of activity.[52]

Balked in their efforts to establish control over the freedmen by legal devices, the planters turned to what seemed the only remaining solution to their problems—importing labourers from abroad. Schemes of this kind had already been attempted. As early as 1834 the Mauritian planters, anticipating that the Emancipation Act would deprive them of a part of their existing labour force, had begun importing coolies from India, and by 1838 more than 25,000 Indian labourers were working on the island.[53] In 1836 John Gladstone, the father of the statesman, began making inquiries about the possibility of obtaining coolies to work on his West Indian estates. Finding that there were no legal obstacles so long as the emigrants were not forced to go against their will and that return passages were guaranteed at the end of five years, he joined a group of other planters in contracting with a firm of Liverpool merchants to supply two shiploads of coolies. These vessels, the *Whitby* and the *Hesperus*, sailed from Calcutta on 13 January 1838 and arrived in British Guiana on 6 May.[54]

Meanwhile, the Indian Government had become alarmed at the extent of the traffic and the number of reports of fraud and ill-treatment reaching its attention. In 1837 an attempt was made to stop abuses by placing all embarkations under the supervision of government agents. Care was to be taken to see that emigrants were provided with adequate facilities for the voyage and guarantees were to be exacted to ensure that they received free passages home at the end of their five-year indentures. These regulations evidently failed to produce the desired effect, for the following year the Indian authorities felt obliged to appoint a committee to inquire into the circumstances under which coolies were recruited and embarked. At the same time, the Governor of Mauritius, acting on the suggestion of the Governor-General of India, undertook to investigate the treatment

51. Richard, pp. 201–2. Sturge himself was in the habit of subscribing £50 annually.
52. The Birmingham Ladies Negroes Friends Society, for example, contributed a large proportion of its funds to benevolent organizations in the West Indies. Minute Book of the Birmingham Ladies Negroes Friends Society, 1825–52, and Cash Book, 1825–51, Birmingham Public Library.
53. The actual figure given was 25,468, in F. H. Hitchins, *The Colonial Land and Emigration Commission* (Philadelphia, 1931), p. 235.
54. Edgar L. Erickson, "East Indian coolies in the West Indies," *Journal of Modern History*, 4 (1934), 127–46.

of Indian labourers in that colony. The evidence brought to light was more than enough to convince both that the traffic could no longer be tolerated and in May 1839 the Indian Government banned emigration altogether.[55]

Although British abolitionists could claim no credit for this, they had not allowed the traffic in coolies to pass unnoticed. In June 1838, the *British Emancipator* published an account from a correspondent in India describing in detail how coolies were "inveigled to Calcutta, sold, resold, and shipped off to countries they have never heard of".[56] Another correspondent, who had actually visited the *Hesperus* shortly before it set sail for the West Indies, told the Emancipation Committee that the emigrants had had to be driven on board and forced below decks where, according to his account, at least one of them had suffocated.[57] Descriptions of the treatment afforded these emigrants upon their arrival in British Guiana were even more disturbing. At Bellevue, an estate belonging to Andrew Colville to which eighty-two of them had been sent, ten deaths occurred within the first eight months. The remainder, according to one visitor, went about half naked and seemed to be on the verge of starvation.[58] In an attempt to disprove these allegations, the attorney in charge of the estates, James Matthews, invited the Governor of the colony to appoint a commission to inquire into the matter, evidently anticipating that any irregularities that had occurred could be easily glossed over. Unfortunately for Matthews, the committee's proceedings happened to coincide with the visit of John Scoble, then touring the West Indies on behalf of the Central Emancipation Committee. Hearing what was afoot, Scoble arranged to be present during the investigations with the result that several cases of gross mistreatment were brought to light. The manager of the estate, the overseer in charge of the coolies and the estate's doctor—a relative of Mr Gladstone's—were subsequently indicted before the Inferior Criminal Court of British Guiana, and either fined or imprisoned.[59] Similar cases of maltreatment by overseers were subsequently reported from several of the other estates where coolies were employed. At Vreed-en-Hoop, one of Mr Gladstone's plantations, it was evidently a common practice for coolies to be tied up, flogged with a cat-o'-nine-tails and to have salt pickle rubbed into their wounds. Nine

55. G. R. Mellor, *British Imperial Trusteeship 1783–1850* (London, 1951), pp. 185–6.
56. *British Emancipator*, 27 June 1838, p. 121.
57. *Ibid*, 13 June 1838, p. 118.
58. *Ibid*, 9 Jan. 1839, p. 196.
59. BFASS, *Hill Coolies: a brief exposure of the deplorable condition of the hill coolies in British Guiana and Mauritius* (London, 1840), p. 12.

of the original sixty-five emigrants on that estate had died within eighteen months of their arrival and many others were subsequently found to be in serious need of medical attention.[60]

Despite these developments and the outspoken terms in which they denounced the "Gladstone slave trade", British abolitionists were not, in principle, opposed to emigration. What could be more desirable, John Sturge reminded the First World Anti-Slavery Convention, than that a steady stream of labourers should flow into the colonies? Sugar would be raised in almost unlimited quantitities and at a price low enough to undersell the "bloodstained produce" of other nations; the economies of Brazil and Cuba would founder; the slave trade would fade away, and the British experiment, pure and unsullied, would emerge triumphant.[61] Not many abolitionists shared these empyrean visions. All the same there was much to be said for an indenture scheme if it could be made to work effectively. The first problem was how to obtain the necessary emigrants. According to the London Committee—and about this it was adamant— emigration had to be truly voluntary. This meant, that emigrants should not only be free from physical coercion but that, before committing themselves, they should be made fully aware of the nature of their undertaking and agree to accept the conditions laid down. In the past, many of them had been under a misapprehension about what would be required and, in some cases, had been deliberately misinformed. That sort of thing would have to cease. There was also the question of transportation. Eighteen of the 438 coolies shipped to the West Indies had died during the voyage.[62] Here, too, effective safeguards would have to be introduced. Finally there was the problem of protecting the interests of the coolies after their arrival. Clearly, precautions would have to be taken to prevent a recurrence of incidents such as those in British Guiana. Abolitionists also stressed the need for preserving a balance between the sexes. Less than one per cent of the coolies who had so far left India were women. This disparity it was noted had led to "the most horrible and revolting depravity and demoralization" and, it was suspected, had also had a bad influence upon the Negroes with whom the coolies came into contact. The appalling mortality rate among emigrants, especially during their first year, would also have to be reduced. In Mauritius, it was officially estimated, between eight and eleven per cent of the immigrants died an-

60. H. E. F. Young, Secretary to the Government of British Guiana, to James Stuart, attorney in charge of the Vreed-en-Hoop estate, 2 May 1839, ibid, pp. 15-17. See also p. 19.
61. BFASS, Proceedings of the General Anti-Slavery Convention of 1840, p. 361. John Sturge was a younger brother of Joseph Sturge.
62. BFASS, Hill Coolies, A Brief Exposure, p. 8.

nually.[63] It was, the Committee argued, the duty of the British government and of the colonial authorities to see that labourers received adequate medical care, were properly housed and that their welfare was looked after by "an intelligent, active and truly independent magistracy". Unless these requirements were met and every possible precaution taken against fraud, coercion, maltreatment and sickness, emigration should remain banned.[64]

To the Mauritian and West Indian planters, these requirements seemed quite impractical. Labourers were sorely needed. To provide safeguards against a revival of the slave trade was reasonable enough, but to impose conditions of the kind the abolitionists demanded was out of the question. After all, the lot of the Indian coolie, even at the best of times, was an unenviable one. Why should his welfare upon leaving India become the object of so much concern? Was it not enough that he be paid wages, given food and provided with a return passage at the end of five years? It was mainly around this question of safeguards—which were and which were not considered adequate—that the subsequent debate revolved.

Early in February 1840, Lord John Russell announced in Parliament that his Cabinet was considering lifting the ban imposed by the Indian Government to the extent of allowing the reopening of the coolie traffic to Mauritius.[65] Alarmed, the London Committee drafted a vigorous protest to the Commons reminding it of the previous record of the Mauritian planters as shown by their "daring violation of the Laws, disloyalty to the Crown and . . . opposition to the humane measures intended for the benefit of the lately enslaved population". The protest went on:

Your petitioners respectfully submit that the Mauritians are least of all fit to be entrusted with the practical working of a scheme of the kind proposed . . . and are fully and strongly convinced that the . . . measure, being an unwise and unjust expedient for procuring a supply of labour, will have the effect of opening an unlimited field for a New Slave Trade which no enactments in this country, however humanely intended, can prevent or even control.[66]

The following month, a deputation, led by John Scoble, Sir Eardley Wilmot and Charles Lushington, waited on the Colonial Secretary.

63. In BFASS, *Emigration from India: The Export of Hill Coolies and Other Labourers to Mauritius* (London, 1842), figures are cited from various official documents on the subject.
64. "Petition to the House of Commons," *ibid*, p. 73.
65. *Hansard*, 51 (4, 6 Feb. 1840), 1247–50, 1310–11.
66. BFASS Minute Books .18 Feb. 1840.

Russell received them courteously, explained the nature of his scheme and reaffirmed the Government's intention of going ahead with it.[67] Disappointed, the Committee resolved to make an appeal to the country. Advertisements explaining its point of view were inserted in *The Times* and other leading newspapers and a specially printed circular sent to all MPs.[68]

When, on 4 June, the proposal came up for discussion in the House, Sir Eardley Wilmot expressed the Committee's reservations. It did not, he said, mind the importation of coolies into Mauritius providing "restrictions and provisions could be devised to ensure their good treatment and their safe return to their native country when they should desire it". Without these necessary precautions, he feared that "all the past horrors would again take place". Replying for the Government, Lord John Russell said that he entirely agreed with Wilmot's point of view and that it was his intention, by placing recruitment under the supervision of the Indian authorities and by restricting contracts to a period of one year only, to prevent abuses of the sort that had previously occurred. "With restrictions of this kind, backed as they would be by Orders in Council, by instructions to the Board of Control, and to the Governor General of India . . . the immigration might be allowed, and . . . instead of its inflicting manifold miseries upon the coolies it might be made to confer a great benefit to those persons who sought a remunerative price for their services." What could be more foolish than, under the guise of humanity, to refuse men who were unable to obtain a livelihood in their own country the opportunity of earning one elsewhere? Daniel O'Connell, Stephen Lushington and several other members promptly rose to argue that if the Government really wanted to prevent abuses its plan was manifestly inadequate for the purpose. "If any scheme for promoting the emigration of the Indian population were to be adopted", O'Connell maintained, "it ought to be clearly and distinctly defined, so that no mistakes might arise—no frauds be practised—no injustices done—no cruelty perpetrated—no tyranny established—no slavery revived". In this respect the Government's plan fell short of expectation and should be resolutely opposed.[69] Three weeks later, on a motion by Stephen Lushington, the ministerial plan was defeated by 158 votes to 109, much to the satisfaction of the London Committee.[70]

Meanwhile, the West Indies had turned to Europe as a possible source of labour. The fate of those recruited, a curious assortment of Portuguese,

67. *Ibid*, 28 Feb., 13 March 1840.
68. *Ibid*, 27 March, 27 May, 5 June 1840.
69. A full account of the debate is given in *Hansard*, *54* (4 June 1840), 930–47.
70. *Ibid*, *54* (22 June 1840), 1407.

Germans, Irish and English[71] was followed by British abolitionists with melancholy interest. "Of all the misery I ever beheld or heard of," William Knibb later told a Parliamentary Committee, "I have known nothing that has equalled the atrocious system of European emigration".[72] Unused, in many cases, to hard physical labour and exposed to an unfamiliar diet, many fell victim to disease, others became demoralized and took to drink or deserted in vain attempts to secure passages home. Harrowing accounts of their sufferings appeared in almost every issue of the *Reporter*. The Committee became especially concerned when, in 1841, it was discovered that the Jamaicans were making efforts to recruit British labourers. In an attempt to forestall this, a short pamphlet was published under the title *Emigration to Jamaica: Why should not Englishmen, Irishmen and Scotchmen go to Jamaica?* The laws of that colony, it stated, were bad and offered no security whatever to the emigrant. The claims made by recruiting agents in England were "in the highest degree delusive and fallacious . . . calculated only to seduce the credulous and unwary to their ruin". British people should be on their guard and on no account accept at face value the promises and blandishments of West Indian representatives. In 1841, 1,333 British emigrants were landed in Jamaica, but thereafter the traffic dwindled away to almost nothing.[73]

It was quickly apparent that European immigration, meagre in numbers and poor in quality, was no answer to the planters' problems. Expectations were aroused, therefore, when in 1840 and 1841 the Government used its executive prerogative to grant permission to the three major West Indian colonies of Trinidad, British Guiana and Jamaica to import labourers from Sierra Leone. Recruiting agents were duly appointed and ships dispatched. Learning of this the London Committee promptly wrote to the Colonial Secretary, repeating the arguments about safeguards already used with respect to the coolie traffic. If the Government's action, the Committee added, did not in itself constitute a revival of the slave trade, it would certainly be interpreted as such by other nations. France, Holland and other countries with which Britain had treaties, would now feel at liberty, under the guise of importing free labourers, to add to their existing slave populations.[74] Russell, having apparently

---

71. White immigrants introduced into the British West Indies, 1834–50: from Madeira (Portuguese), 20,530; from Great Britain, 2,763; from Germany, 1,067; from France, 31: Mellor, *British Imperial Trusteeship*, Appendix 6.
72. In Mathieson, *British Slave Emancipation*. p. 118; see also Hinton, pp. 409–14.
73. Only 32 British labourers migrated to Jamaica between 1842 and 1845 and there were apparently none at all between 1845 and 1850. PP, 1847/8, *23*, 383; 1850, *39*, 283–4.
74. BFASS *Reporter*, 24 Feb. 1841, pp. 45–6.

misunderstood the Committee's letter, replied with a curt statement to the effect that immigrants were more likely to be free in Britain's own colonies than in those of countries still maintaining slavery.[75] Feeling that further intervention would be useless, the Committee did not pursue the matter except to draw attention, from time to time, to particular cases of ill treatment.[76] From the point of view of the planters, the results of this traffic too were something of a disappointment, though, on an average, rather more than a thousand Negroes were imported annually during the course of the next ten years.[77] The great majority of these were refugees from captured slave ships and were said to be good workers. In 1851 the trade ceased completely owing to a lack of recruits.[78]

The position of the Mauritian planters was meanwhile becoming desperate. The defeat of Russell's scheme had meant not only that they would be unable to obtain more coolies but that, as indentures ran out, they would lose the services of those they already had. Appreciating these difficulties, the Peel Ministry, early in 1842, resolved to give way. There was now not much that the abolitionists could do. As one correspondent put it: "I doubt whether it would be of any use to oppose the proposition. The Government is too strong to give any reasonable prospect of defeating them on any measure that they might propose, but I think that regulations sufficiently stringent may be framed, so as to prevent the possibility of the emigration being any other than voluntary."[79] This was, in fact, all the Committee could hope to achieve. The tactics adopted, however, were essentially the same as those used two years earlier: a deputation waited on Lord Stanley, the Colonial Secretary, to explain the Society's views on the subject; auxiliaries were called on to mobilize public opinion; a petition was presented to Parliament and copies of a special pamphlet— a seventy-six page affair composed largely of articles which had previously appeared in the *Reporter*—were sent to all MPs[80] What the Committee particularly feared was that the Government might attempt to implement the measures without allowing opportunity for debate. Benjamin Hawes, an old friend of the Society—who had already spoken out against the

---

75. R. V. Smith (on behalf of Lord John Russell) to the Committee, 11 Feb. 1841, *ibid.*
76. See, for example, BFASS, *The Treatment of African Immigrants to Jamaica* (London, 1848).
77. *Immigration from Sierra Leone:*

	1841–45	*1846–50*
To Jamaica	1566	1553
To British Guiana	2605	1918
To Trinidad	1826	1331

PP, 1850, *39*, 283–4; 1851, *40*, 409.
78. Though it was revived on a small scale during the 1860s: Hitchins, p. 249.
79. R. D. Alexander to Tredgold, 12 March 1842, BFASS Papers C 4/26.
80. BFASS Minute Books, 11 Feb–13 April 1842; BFASS, *Emigration from India.*

measure[81]—was asked to intervene on the Committee's behalf and to make sure that the question was fully discussed.[82] The Government responded to Hawes's queries with impatience. The importance of the matter, Stanley declared, "appeared to be overrated". The Ministry's intention was simply to give the Governor-General of India, by an act of British legislation, authority to do something which he might already do by an act of colonial legislation.[83] Not in the least daunted by the implication that the Government might go ahead with its scheme whether Parliament approved or not, Hawes persisted and, on the fifth attempt, Stanley agreed to set aside time for debate.[84]

Hawes's objection to the reopening of the traffic—and the Committee's also—arose once again from a conviction that the safeguards would prove ineffectual. He reminded the Commons that the Governor-General of India himself had said that "no strictness of regulation and no vigilance on the part of authorities would immediately prevent the infliction of grievous oppressions and deceits upon large numbers of persons, helpless from their poverty and from their utter ignorance and inexperience."[85] Even if Lord Auckland were proved wrong, how could mortality during the voyage be prevented or justice secured on arrival in Mauritius? Replying to these points, Stanley explained that the Government intended (1) to finance immigration by means of a grant from the Mauritian Assembly and to place responsibility entirely in the hands of Government agents, thus cutting out the private speculators who had been responsible for most abuses in the past; (2) to impose a strict limit, according to tonnage, on the number of immigrants embarked in each ship; (3) to allow immigrants to take with them their wives and children, free of charge; (4) to permit them, upon arrival in the colony, to choose their own employers (5) to limit contracts to periods of not more than one year; (6) to allow immigrants to earn the same wages as free labourers; (7) to provide free return passages at the end of five years; (8) to permit those who wished to leave the colony at an earlier date to travel home at their own expense.[86] This was clearly a much more thoroughly thought-out scheme than any previously put forward. Satisfied that all reasonable precautions were being taken, the House voted its approval of Stanley's proposals by an overwhelming majority.[87]

81. *Hansard*, *60* (28 Feb. 1842), 1179–80; *61* (11 March 1842), 420.
82. BFASS Minute Books, 13 April 1842.
83. *Hansard*, *63* (20 May 1842), 582.　　　84. *Ibid*, *64* (5 July 1842), 984–5.
85. *Ibid*, *60* (1 March 1842), 1324.　　　86. *Ibid*, 1329–45.
87. *Ibid*, *65* (26 July 1842), 660–7. The vote was 118 to 24. Benjamin Hawes, Daniel O'Connell, William Ewart, Charles Villiers and Sir R. H. Inglis voted with the minority.

Once the Mauritian branch of the traffic had been opened, the Government could hardly refuse a similar concession to the West Indies. In November 1843 Lord Stanley sent instructions to India which resulted in Act XXI of 1844 by which the same privileges already granted to Mauritius were extended to Jamaica, Trinidad and British Guiana.[88] Caught off its guard, Broad Street had little opportunity to protest. Indeed, if the Government remained true to its word, there was not much to protest about. However, it followed the ensuing developments with keen interest determined to bring every irregularity to the attention of the authorities and the public.

During the first fifteen months after the lifting of the embargo no less than forty thousand coolies were introduced into Mauritius, of whom about twelve per cent were women.[89] Unable to cope with such an influx, the Mauritian authorities were compelled, in 1844, to decree that the number would thereafter be limited to 6,000 a year.[90] The traffic to the West Indies was considerably less, amounting to approximately 8,000 annually in 1846–48 after which it ceased entirely for two years owing to lack of funds.[91]

The regulations outlined by Lord Stanley were, as soon became apparent, much too restrictive to meet the needs of the planters. A five years system which limited contracts to periods of one year was economically viable only so long as the coolies agreed to re-engage at the end of each contract, and this, in many cases, they were unwilling to do.[92] The planters, seeing their coolies disappearing in the same way that their Negroes had disappeared, sought to maintain control by imposing monthly taxes on those who left the plantations and by other similar devices. The London Committee objected, but to no effect for on this issue the Government was on the side of the planters.[93] Britain, it was now plain, was committed to the immigrant labour system and so to the imposition of whatever restrictions were necessary for making it work. The abolitionists, of course, continued to draw attention to what they considered unduly discriminatory laws. In 1844 they objected when British Guiana adopted an ordinance providing that all future immigration be conducted at the public expense.

88. Erickson, *Journal of Modern History*, 6 (1934), 134–5.
89. Coolie immigration to Mauritius, 1 Jan. 1843 to 31 March 1844: Male coolies, 35,177; Female coolies, 4,530; Children, 1,449; Total, 41,156: BFASS *Reporter*, 28 May 1845, p. 94.
90. Mathieson, *British Slave Emancipation*, p. 228.
91. Hitchins, *The Colonial Land and Emigration Commission*, p. 253. It began again in 1850 with the help of a grant from Parliament.
92. Mathieson, *British Slave Emancipation*, p. 228.
93. BFASS Minute Books, 14 March 1845; 26 Sept. 1846; 15 Jan. 1847; BFASS *Reporter*, 1 Feb. 1847.

It was quite unjust, they argued, to expect the body of the colonists, including the freedmen, to defray the cost of providing cheap labour for the benefit of the planters. The Prime Minister, Sir Robert Peel, agreed with them and the ordinance was disallowed.[94] Two years later, Major Fagan, the Superintendent of Coolies in Trinidad, instituted a particularly harsh system for restricting the mobility of indentured workers in that colony by means of leave tickets. The London Committee drew the matter to the attention of the Colonial Secretary on whose instructions the system was shortly afterwards abolished.[95] Broad Street also continued to be concerned over the relatively small number of women among the immigrants. In 1846 its protests led the Colonial Office to enquire into the coolies' sexual behaviour. A sizeable body of evidence was collected which the Committee was invited to examine. Suspecting that the Government's intention was to smear the immigrants, the Committee refused. The Colonial Office thereupon washed its hands of the matter.[96]

One scheme which caused the Committee particular anxiety was that introduced by Earl Grey in 1847 for obtaining labourers from Africa. The West Indian planters had long regarded West Africa as a potentially rich field for recruitment. Abolitionists, on the other hand, had argued that any such traffic, however closely regulated and supervised, would inevitably give rise to slave trading in the interior.[97] Hitherto the British government had shared their view. (Sierra Leone, being a British colony, was a special case.) But in 1847, at Grey's instigation, it relaxed its stand to the extent of allowing labourers to be recruited on the Kroo Coast where the natives were said to be free from slavery and perfectly willing to emigrate if offered fair terms. The Committee did everything in its power to forestall this plan, sending petitions to Parliament, publishing pamphlets, stirring up sentiment in the country at large and in the West Indies, but all to no avail.[98] The actual number of emigrants obtained from this source was small—less than six hundred—and several of the ships which visited the coast had to return empty. In 1853 the trade was abandoned abruptly when it was discovered, as had been predicted, that a war

94. BFASS Minute Books, 28 June, 12 July, 12 Dec. 1844.
95. *Ibid*, 26 Sept. 1846; BFASS *Reporter*, 1 Sept. 1846, p. 137, 1 Oct. 1846, p. 163; Mathieson, *British Slave Emancipation*, p. 163.
96. Committee to Gladstone, n.d., 1846, in BFASS *Reporter*, 2 March 1846; *ibid*, 1 Dec. 1846, 1 March 1848; BFASS Minute Books, 18 Dec. 1846.
97. See the review of Burnley's *Observations on the Present Condition of the Island of Trinidad*, in BFASS *Reporter*, 26 Jan. 1842.
98. BFASS Minute Books, 26 March, 15 April, 26 June, 27 Aug., 19 Nov., 10 Dec. 1847; 14, 28 Jan., 31 March, 14, 28 April, 11, 25 Aug. 1848.

had broken out among the natives to obtain slaves to sell to British vessels.[99]

In criticizing emigration, abolitionists stressed the "pernicious example" which Great Britain was setting foreign countries and the harmful effect that it would have upon the world antislavery cause. These schemes certainly aroused hostile comment abroad, especially in those countries already antagonized by Britain's suppression policies. The West Indies, observed the Spanish Foreign Minister in a letter to the British ambassador in Madrid, presented a lamentable example of misguided policy:

The slaves emancipated refuse to work . . . and matters have arrived at such a state that Her Britannic Majesty's Government, the same that demand [sic] the absolute emancipation in Cuba since 1820,[100] have . . . authorized Mr Barclay . . . to convey thither from Sierra Leone thousands of Negroes, who . . . under the denomination of forced labourers . . . will be real slaves, torn from their native country and carried to work in slavery . . . and in consequence of the authorization the Royal Navy . . . has already begun to convey Negroes to Jamaica for a slavery which, though temporary, is contrary to existing treaties. So it appears from this that England retrogrades [sic] to slavery for the advantage of her colonies . . . the only path she has found for remedying the evils which emancipation has produced.[101]

Duff Green, the American pro-slavery apologist, cited the system of free labour immigration as proof that Britain's true purpose was not to improve the lot of the Negro but to increase her commerce and extend her power. If, as Britain claimed, indentured labour was cheaper than slave labour, that was only because it was less humane. West Indian emancipation, he asserted, was nothing more than an elaborate subterfuge designed to persuade the United States, France, Spain and Brazil to free their slaves and thereby ruin their economies while the British themselves cynically continued to stock their colonies with so-called free labourers.[102] We have already noted that Southerners were quick to seize on the fact that Negroes liberated from slave ships were not sent back to their own homes but were, in some cases at least, transferred to the West Indies as apprentices, as evidence of Britain's double-dealing.[103] In view of the

99. BFASS *Reporter*, 1 June 1847, p. 88; 1 Sept. 1852, pp. 130–2; 1 Sept. 1853, pp. 209–10; also Hitchins, p. 248.
100. What the Spanish Minister intended to say was "the emancipation of all slaves introduced into Cuba since 1820". By a treaty of 1817 Spain had undertaken to abolish the trade in 1820. Thus, according to Great Britain, all slaves introduced after that date were legally free: Mathieson, *Great Britain and the Slave Trade*, p. 12.
101. Gonzalez to Aston, 20 Dec. 1841, PP, 1843, *34*, 15–16.
102. Sioussat, *Proceedings of the American Antiquarian Society, 40* (1835) 238–40.
103. This arrangement applied initially only to those Negroes captured on the Western side of the Atlantic. Those captured off the African coast (i.e. the great majority) were sent to Sierra Leone. From 1844 onwards, however, these too were put under some pressure to emigrate to the West Indies: Mathieson, *Great Britain and the Slave Trade*, pp. 29, 124–5.

problems that would have been involved in sending them back to their tribes—in which case many would simply have been resold to the traders—this seemed not only the most convenient solution but the most desirable from the point of view of the Negroes themselves. It was only to be expected, however, that Southerners should leap to the conclusion that Britain was merely stealing other people's slaves.[104]

All this was embarrassing to the abolitionists, although possibly less so than the continuing decline in sugar production. As will be evident by this time, the West Indies did not present a clear cut case for emancipation, or, for that matter, against it. What happened there was largely governed by circumstances peculiar to the colonies themselves. It certainly offered no general guidance as to the feasibility or otherwise of emancipation elsewhere. A few of the more acute foreign observers admitted this.[105] But for the most part they were concerned only with finding support for their own partisan arguments. Used in this way it provided ammunition as readily to one side as to another. To that fanatical Southerner, Edmund Ruffin, it was a piece of unmitigated folly.[106] Southerners in general saw it as a cautionary example, differing from that of Santo Domingo only to the extent that the Negro's natural inclination to savagery had been held in check. In the North, on the other hand, the anniversary of British emancipation remained the most important date on the abolitionists' calendar and was an occasion for speeches and sermons. (Since the ending of American slavery had no proper anniversary, having occurred in a piecemeal fashion, it too came to be celebrated on the 1st of August. The anniversary of British emancipation was thus still being celebrated in the United States as late as the 1880s.[107]) William Ellery Channing, speaking on one such occasion declared that British emancipation was an achievement comparable in importance to the landing of the Pilgrim Fathers.[108] Emerson described it as "a day of reason, of the clear

104. Abel and Klingberg, p. 29; S. F. Bemis, ed., *The American Secretaries of State and their Diplomacy* (10 vols, New York, 1927–29), 5, 138–9.

105. Gurley, *Mission to England*, pp. 321–2; see also Richard Hildreth, "*The 'Ruin' of Jamaica*" (New York, 1855). Although Hildreth's aim was partisan his pamphlet is remarkable for its sharp reasoning and historical perspective. He shows that Jamaica's "ruin" was an ancient and chronic complaint which predated the abolition of slavery. Her inability to compete with Cuba, he claimed, was comparable to the failure of Virginia, which had enjoyed a similar prosperity during the 1750s and 1760s, to compete with newer slave states.

106. Avery Craven, *Edmund Ruffin, Southerner* (New York, 1932), pp. 113–14.

107. See Frederick Douglass's speech to the coloured people of Elmira, New York, on 1 Aug. 1880, in *Life and Times of Frederick Douglass* (Collier Books edn., New York, 1962), pp. 493–508.

108. William Ellery Channing, *Address Delivered at Lenox on the First of August, 1842, the Anniversary of Emancipation of the British West Indies* (Lenox, 1842), p. 5.

light".[109] and John Quincy Adams as "an event at which, if the whole human race could have been concentrated in one person, the heart of that person would have leaped for joy".[110] French abolitionists were, on the whole, less extravagant in their use of language since their appeals were directed to the French Assembly rather than to the general public. Nevertheless, to them too, British emancipation became a symbol. To the Duc de Broglie, President of the French Anti-Slavery Society, it was "a victory of the religious spirit"; to the Comte de Montalembert, "a peaceful and sublime memory".[111] Having evoked this symbol, foreign abolitionists never failed to draw from it the appropriate conclusion. The West Indian planters, too, had opposed reform, yet the government *had* intervened and slavery *was* abolished. The British people had refused to be intimidated. They had "responded to the reasonings, pleadings, rebukes of Christian philanthropy as a nation never did before. . . . Once, at least, a great nation was swayed by high and disinterested principles."[112]

These tributes were highly flattering both to Britain and to British abolitionists. They themselves were aware that the experiment was not the unmitigated success that it might have been and that their foreign colleagues were now claiming it was. This failure they put down, initially, to the opposition of reactionary elements, chief among them the planters and their supporters in Britain. This opposition had been expected and even allowed for. What had not been either expected or allowed for was the opposition they encountered from within their own liberal, progressive ranks and which, as the next two chapters will show, gave rise to the bitterest struggle of the post-emancipation period.

109. Ralph Waldo Emerson, *Address delivered in the Court House in Concord, Massachusetts, on the 1st of August, 1844, on the Anniversary of the Emancipation of the Negroes in the British West Indies* (Boston, 1844).
110. Adams to Anne Quincy Thaxter, 29 July 1844, in Abel and Klingberg, p. 13.
111. In Augustin Cochin, *The Results of Emancipation*, translated by M. L. Booth (Boston, 1863), pp. 385–8. The statement by Broglie was made in 1842; that by Montalembert in 1847–8.
112. Channing, *Address Delivered in the Court House in Concord*, p. 26.

The struggle over the sugar duties 1839–1841

It had always been the assumption of the British abolitionists that liberal-minded men would support the antislavery cause. This was the basis for their many and confident predictions of victory. More than any other factor, it accounted for their optimism as, in the months following the ending of apprenticeship, they set about drawing up their plans. If they believed in anything they believed in Progress. Progressive ideas were in the ascendant. Better education, increasing wealth, improved methods of production, easier communication between the different parts of the globe, the growing influence of the industrially advanced nations, and, above all, the increasing power within those nations of an enlightened middle class, all militated, they believed, against the continuance of an institution which clearly belonged to the past. Slavery was a relic left over from an earlier age and as such destined for destruction. They saw themselves as the agents of Progress, exposing evil, sweeping away hypocrisy, preparing the way for the future. The question, as the *Reporter* summed it up, had "become one of time rather than of victory".[1]

Past experience offered substantial support for this view. In the course of the struggles over West Indian slavery and apprenticeship, the great majority of liberal-minded Englishmen had instinctively sided with the abolitionists. Indeed, given the terms in which these issues were generally presented, they could hardly have done otherwise. Anyone who sided with the planters and rejected the appeals of the abolitionists was, by definition, not a liberal. For those who regarded themselves as liberals, these were clearcut issues. This fact was commented on by *The Spectator* on 31 March 1838, in a shrewd article entitled "Sources of English Zeal for the Blacks" in which it observed that British concern for the welfare of the Negro arose from the fact that, unlike most problems, the slavery issue could be reduced to a simple conflict between good and evil. "Ordinary home questions", it concluded, "are as dull as lectures and sermons but slavery has the excitement of a tragedy."

It should be further noted that in so far as economic factors had played a part in the struggle, they had hitherto operated mainly to the advantage of the abolitionists. One historian has even gone so far as to claim that economic changes *required* the abolition of slavery.[2] This is questionable but there is no doubt that they helped to make it possible. In particular, the economic decline of the West Indies had significantly weakened the opposition with which the opponents of slavery had had to contend. Historically, the rise of industrial capitalism and the spread of antislavery principles had coincided. Many regarded them as the same thing or at the very least as different facets of the same thing. Both reflected a belief in the superiority of voluntary as opposed to coercive methods, to the effectiveness of which the buoyancy and expansiveness of the British economy were impressive testimony. Individual freedom and the Dismal Science went hand in hand. That there might be any conflict between them was a matter to which abolitionists at least gave little thought. The last thing they expected was that an economic issue would arise which would not only divide them from the main body of British liberals but lead them into cooperation with their old enemies, the West Indian planters.

Such an issue, however, was already in the making. While production in the West Indies had declined, that in other countries had risen. In 1815 Cuba had produced 42,000 tons of sugar, only slightly more than

1. BFASS *Reporter*, 15 Jan. 1840.
2. Williams, *Capitalism and Slavery*, pp. 135–6, 149–50. For a critique of Williams's views see Appendix C below.

half the total of Jamaica; twenty-five years later it was producing 60 per cent more than all of Britain's West Indian colonies combined. This rapid increase was the result of two factors: the bringing into cultivation of huge tracts of virgin land, mostly old cattle ranges, and the growing number of Negro slaves brought in from Africa, a traffic which as we have seen was encouraged by the Cuban authorities despite Spain's long-standing agreements with Britain. In Brazil, much larger and potentially much richer than Cuba, similar processes were occurring. Thus by 1841 Cuba was exporting 160,000 tons of sugar annually, Puerto Rico 36,000 and Brazil 80,000 as compared with the 100,000 exported by the British West Indies.[3]

But it was not only in terms of the volume of production that British planters were lagging behind. In price, too, the West Indian producers were failing to keep up with their foreign rivals. Had these differences been merely marginal they might not have mattered, but they were much more than that and became more marked still when, after 1838, the value of wages had to be added to the overall costs of production. G. R. Porter in his influential work, *The Progress of the Nation* (3 vols, London, 1836–43) showed that, excluding duties, the cost to the country of the sugar imported into Britain in 1841 was just over £9 million whereas an equivalent quantity of foreign sugar of the same quality, purchased on the world market, would have cost a mere £4 million.[4] For colonial producers to be able to go on asking such high prices was possible only because of the monopoly of the British market they enjoyed, thanks to tariff arrangements. The West Indies had always been given preferential treatment in this respect and in 1825 and 1836, similar privileges had been extended to Mauritius and the British East Indies. The duty charged on British-produced sugars varied somewhat according to their quality and the country's need for revenue but was normally around 24s per hundredweight as compared with 63s per hundredweight for foreign sugars. As the average cost of West Indian sugar on the home market, after duties had been paid, was only about 65s this was more than enough to keep foreign sugars out.[5] In foreign markets, of course, British sugar would not have been able to compete, but since Britain was able, after 1838, to consume all that her colonies produced, this was a purely theoretical consideration.[6]

As might be expected, the high price of sugar was a source of some

3. Noel Deerr, *The History of Sugar* (2 vols, London, 1949–50) *I*, pp. 112, 126, 131, 193–204.
4. *3*, 40–41.
5. "Cheap sugar by free labour", *The Spectator*, Supplement, 15 April 1842, p. 2.
6. Mathieson, *British Slave Emancipation*, p. 143.

grievance. Consumers were not easily reconciled to the need to pay sevenpence halfpenny a pound for sugar of an inferior quality while just across the Channel it was possible to obtain a superior product for fourpence halfpenny. Sugar was already a standard ingredient in the diet of all classes, although working people sometimes made do with substitutes such as treacle. Even for these they had to pay more than was paid on the Continent for the genuine article. Such differences might have been easier to bear had they arisen out of the government's legitimate need for revenue. But this was not the case. As William Ewart explained to the House in 1840, it would have been perfectly feasible, by adjusting tariffs, to lower retail prices, increase consumption, and at the same time benefit the exchequer by as much as £1 million a year.[7] The issue was not taxation but monopoly. It was the planters, not the British government that benefited. The sugar duties, like the corn laws, with which they inevitably became associated in the popular mind, presented a clearcut case of legislation designed to benefit one segment of the community at the expense of the community as a whole.

The abolitionists were perfectly familiar with this aspect of the question. As we have seen, they came from that rising middle class which supported so many of the reform movements of this period, including, of course, the free trade movement. Indeed, up to 1840 the two largely overlapped. Bright and Cobden had been among the leading spokesmen for abolition and Joseph Sturge was probably better known in the country at large as an advocate of free trade than as an opponent of slavery. He had been a founding member of the Anti-Corn Law League and over the years had remained one of its most generous patrons.[8] Certainly, there is nothing to indicate that abolitionists as a body were either unaware of or indifferent to conditions within Britain itself. They belonged, as has been shown, to a vastly extended network of organizations the aim of which, in most cases, was to relieve domestic hardship. As members of this reform establishment, they could not but be sympathetic to any measure that would, in however small a degree, relieve men from the pressures of poverty at home. No one was more conscious of his responsiblities in this respect than Sturge, who reacted to the economic distress of 1839–42, by joining the Chartists, which most free-traders regarded as going altogether too far.[9]

7. *Hansard*, 55 (25 June 1840), 78. See also the evidence given by John McGregor, P. Martineau and G. Warner, "Report from the Select Committee on Import Duties", PP, 1840, 5, 44–50, 150–5.
8. He was in the habit of giving £100 a year to the League's funds. Cobden to Sturge, 20 Feb. 1841, in Richard, *Memoirs of Joseph Sturge*, p. 277.
9. Norman McCord, *The Anti-Corn Law League* (London, 1958), pp. 113–16.

Thus it may be assumed that had the issue of the sugar duties been as straightforward as that of the corn laws, the great majority of abolitionists would have supported their amendment wholeheartedly. What made them hesitate was the intimate connection between sugar and slavery. If reducing the duties on foreign sugars meant throwing open the British market to slave grown produce—as clearly it did in the minds of most of those who advocated it—then its effects on the antislavery cause would need to be weighed carefully. Many abolitionists, including almost all the members of the London Committee, were convinced that they would be adverse. What divided these abolitionists from the free-traders, and from those abolitionists who sided with the free-traders, as many were to do, was a disagreement over how seriously adverse these effects would be and whether, on balance, they would outweigh the very real benefits which all agreed a reduction in the duties would produce at home. In a sense, then, it was a disagreement between those who believed that primary consideration should be given to Britain's world responsibilities, and those who placed her domestic needs first, although in practice this distinction was often lost sight of, or specifically denied, by the protagonists themselves.

As the London Committee saw it, the issue involved much more than matters of principle. It was not simply a question of whether or not British people should consume "blood-stained" produce, objectionable though that might be. What was really at stake were the practical effects which a lowering of the duties would have, first, on the slave trade, second, on the emancipated colonies, and third, on the credibility of Britain's opposition to slavery abroad. Of these three, the first was for most abolitionists the overriding consideration. If slavery was bad, the slave trade was worse. This was a point which those free-traders who argued that there was no distinction between slave-grown sugar and slave-grown cotton and that Britain might as well accept the one as the other persistently failed to grasp. The United States, from which most of Britain's cotton came, had officially outlawed the slave trade in 1807 and since then had ceased to be a major importer of slaves. The case of Cuba and Brazil was quite different. There the trade flourished on a wide scale and with the active assistance of the local authorities. It was true that Britain was seeking to suppress this trade by means of her African blockade but these efforts had so far proved largely ineffectual and, as will be shown in a later chapter, were disparaged by the Committee mainly for that reason. The only limiting factor that they recognized was an economic one—the world demand for slave produce, and, in particular, sugar. When the demand for sugar increased, prices rose, the need for labourers grew and the trade expanded; when demand lagged, prices fell, the need for labour declined and the trade slackened. Thus by opening her ports to Brazilian and Cuban sugar Britain would be widening the world sugar market, increasing the demand for slaves and so giving a "fearful impulse" to the trade. Such a policy was both inhumane and in direct conflict to Britain's own much publicized schemes for suppressing the traffic, in pursuit of which she had expended millions of pounds and the lives of hundreds of her sailors. Furthermore, they contended, by accepting Brazilian or Cuban sugar, Britain would be delaying emancipation in those countries by "at least fifteen years", while, at the same time, "the condition of the wretched and degraded slaves would be rendered more intolerable than ever".[10] Just as Britain had strengthened the position of the Southern planters, by providing a market for United States cotton, so now, by accepting slave-grown sugar, she would be helping to uphold the regimes of their Cuban and Brazilian counterparts.

Initially at least, concern over the effects which a reduction of the duties might be expected to have upon the economy of the West Indies appears to have played a lesser part in the Committee's thinking. This was partly because its members were still uncertain about what actually was happening in the colonies. In 1839 and 1840, it will be remembered, they were looking forward to the rise in production which the change over from a coercive to a voluntary system was expected to produce. They were also much intrigued by the appearance of small peasant proprietors and spent a good deal of time speculating about the economic effects this would have. One speaker at the First World Anti-Slavery Convention even went so far as to say that it might be no bad thing economically if the old plantations were swept away and replaced by small holdings given over to mixed agriculture.[11] Nothing would have pleased the abolitionists more than to see this power of their old enemies broken in this way. It was thus far from clear in 1839 and 1840 how far, if at all, the welfare of the freedmen was bound up with the prosperity of their employers. In any case, to have placed too much emphasis on the economic distress which free trade would bring to the colonies would have invited comparisons between the conditions of the colonists and that of the British unemployed. In stressing the horrors of the slave trade, they were on considerably safer ground. Nevertheless, by 1841 their ideas were beginning to change. They still looked forward to a rise in production but at a more distant date. By 1842 some were arguing openly that it was incumbent on Britain to give her colonies all the support she could while they grappled with the difficult problems of adjustment. Even if this did mean having to pay above the

10. BFASS Minute Books, 5 May 1841.
11. BFASS, *Proceedings of the General Anti-Slavery Convention of 1840*, pp. 61–2.

going market rate for sugar, it was not an excessively heavy burden for the British people to bear.[12] By slow stages they were coming around to the view that the success of Britain's own experiment in emancipation too depended on maintaining the colonial sugar monopoly. Their statements on the subject, however, were never entirely consistent. As late as 1843 John Scoble was able to tell the Second World Anti-Slavery Convention that this was not part of the antislavery case.[13]

The task of mobilizing antislavery opinion against the free-traders naturally fell to Broad Street. It could not, of course, claim to represent all abolitionists or, for that matter, all antislavery organizations. The Glasgow, Edinburgh, Bristol and Dublin bodies still cherished their independent status. But these groups, although they paid lip service to the idea of a world crusade, were in practice concerned almost exclusively with the struggle in the United States. To them, sugar was essentially a marginal issue. It is significant that in their many letters to their American friends it passed virtually unmentioned although they commented at length on almost every other issue of the day.[14] We know from the Glasgow Committee's minute books that opinion there was divided. In 1841 Glasgow came out in favour of free trade, largely it would seem as a means of emphasizing its independence of Broad Street, but later reversed its position.[15] In neither case is there anything to suggest that its views, or those of any of the other independent organizations, carried much weight with abolitionists generally, most of whom, as we shall see, looked elsewhere for leadership.

The London Committee first gave its attention to the sugar question in July 1839. The previous month William Ewart, MP for Wigan and as it happened an old friend of the abolitionists, had suggested to the House the possibility of relaxing the duties as a way of alleviating the hardships caused by the current economic crisis in Britain. The rejection of this proposal was a foregone conclusion, but since it had a bearing on the slavery issue and was the kind of question which seemed likely to recur, Broad Street felt obliged to comment on it. What course the discussion took on this occasion, or on subsequent occasions for that matter, the Committee's minute books do not reveal, but the result was a plan which seemed to offer a sensible compromise between the interests of free-traders and those of abolitionists. This was to recommend that the exist-

12. BFASS *Reporter*, 7 April 1841.
13. BFASS, *Proceedings of the World Anti-Slavery Convention of 1843* (London, 1843), p. 150.
14. See the letters from these organizations in the Garrison and Weston Collections, Boston Public Library.
15. GES Minute Books, 24 May, 18 June 1841; 1 Aug. 1843; 11, 12 April 1844.

ing tariff barrier be maintained with respect to foreign slave-grown sugar but that foreign free-grown sugar be admitted at colonial rates.[16] In this way the price of sugar on the home market would be lowered while foreign producers would be offered a lucrative inducement to free their slaves. Altogether it seemed a remarkably neat solution.

Unfortunately, like most simple answers to complex problems, this one had its drawbacks. In the first place there was very little free-grown sugar on the world market, certainly not enough to make any immediate difference to consumer prices. If the British public were to wait until the free producers, most of whom were in South East Asia, increased their output, or until Brazil and Cuba got around to abolishing slavery, they would have to wait a very long time. Secondly, implementing such a policy would involve the British government in having to distinguish between free and slave-grown produce, a difficult task particularly when, as often happened, cargoes were transhipped in foreign ports. Finally, the effect of taking any sugar, slave or free, from the world market would be to send world prices upward and so set in motion the train of events which abolitionists were trying to prevent. It is doubtful whether, at this early stage, they appreciated these difficulties or indeed anything beyond the plan's obvious advantages, not the least of which was that it dissociated them from the protectionist diehards who would not countenance free trade on any terms. A statement containing these proposals was sent to Joseph Pease, MP for Darlington, with the request that he bring them to the attention of the Commons at the first opportunity. But as the issue was not raised again that year the matter was allowed to drop.

So far the Society had acted with commendable celerity. That it still had not grasped the significance of the issue, however, is suggested by the fact that although sugar was again debated in 1840 it had remarkably little to say on the matter, although it was not entirely inactive. In April it delegated Sturge to explain its proposals to Ewart, and later the same month sent a petition to the Commons.[17] On 22 June the World Anti-Slavery Convention agreed unanimously and virtually without discussion to a resolution introduced by George Stacey affirming that "the British Government shall on no account allow the introduction of slave-grown sugar into the British market".[18] This would have been an excellent opportunity to make known the Committee's views in detail and in parti-cular to drum up support for its compromise solution. The result of this negligence became apparent when three days later, on 25 June,

16. BFASS Minute Books, 9 July 1839.
17. *Ibid*, 10, 24 April 1840.
18. BFASS, *Proceedings of the General Anti-Slavery Convention of 1840*, pp. 519–20.

Ewart renewed his request to Parliament. On this occasion his proposal was in the form of a specific motion for a reduction of the duties on all foreign sugars to 34s per hundredweight. The arguments used in support of it were the classic free trade ones: that greater freedom meant greater prosperity, that monopoly was the bane of trade and that Britain owed no debt of gratitude to the West Indians. Although no one spoke up for the Committee's solution, several speakers, including Daniel O'Connell and Stephen Lushington, drew attention to the effects which the measure would have on slavery. If Parliament supported Ewart's motion, Lushington declared, then she should at the same time scrap all of her treaties for the suppression of the slave trade and withdraw her cruisers from Africa. "That hour when foreign sugar should come into competition with sugar grown by free labour—in that hour would the future of Africa be sealed." In that same hour, he concluded, slavery would also be perpetuated in Cuba, Brazil and in every other country where it prevailed.[19]

There was never any doubt that Ewart's proposal would be rejected, as it duly was by 122 votes to 27. These were simply ranging shots fired by the two sides as they prepared for the major battle that was bound to occur sooner or later. Already the disposition of the opposing forces was becoming clear. The free-traders were in the ascendant. The colonial producers were united in support of their interests. But the abolitionists were already showing signs of disarray. In this respect it is worth noting that the two leading advocates of tariff reform, William Ewart and C. P. Villiers, as well as their two leading opponents, O'Connell and Lushington, had all been members of the World Anti-Slavery Convention whose meetings had ended that very week. But although divisions were evident among the movement's parliamentary leaders, they had not so far spread to the movement as a whole. Outside of London, antislavery sympathizers remained ignorant of what was afoot and the London Committee did nothing by way of alerting them. It published an abbreviated version of the debate in the *Reporter* but without comment and without drawing attention to its own views.[20] This may have been because it feared the divisive nature of the issues involved or, alternatively, because it had not itself yet woken up to the full significance of what was happening. But whatever the reasons, it is clear that its failure to make public its opposition at this early stage and to publicize its own solution was a serious error.

The status of the sugar question changed abruptly when, in January 1841, stories began circulating that the Melbourne Government was considering abolishing the colonial monopoly. The London Committee

19. *Hansard*, 55 (25 June 1840), 94.
20. BFASS *Reporter*, 1 July 1840.

reacted by sending a strongly worded petition-to Parliament and appointing a deputation, led by E. N. Buxton and Samuel Gurney, to see the Prime Minister. Since all there was to go on at that time was rumour not much was to be learned.[21] However, the Government's intentions were clarified on 30 April when the Chancellor of the Exchequer, Sir T. F. Baring, announced in the course of his budget speech that he intended to reduce the duties on all foreign sugars from 63s to 36s per hundredweight.[22] This was still 12s more than colonial producers paid but not enough to keep foreign sugar out. Broad Street now had no alternative but to make its views generally known. Acting, as it later admitted, in the utmost haste, it sent out circulars to all auxiliaries stating its intention of opposing the Government and listing its reasons for doing so. At the same time it arranged for its resolutions on the subject to be advertised in the papers.[23] It then settled down to await the response.

One of the earliest expressions of dissent came from within the Committee's own ranks. George Bennet was an abolitionist of long standing; he had been on the Committee of the Central Negro Emancipation Society and was one of the original Broad Street members. He had been present at most of the meetings at which the sugar issue had been discussed and had also been one of those delegated to wait on the Prime Minister in March. Although he disagreed with the Committee's decision he had so far shown himself willing to abide by the majority view. It came, therefore, as a surprise to his colleagues when a letter bearing his signature appeared in the London *Patriot* of 20 May deploring the "false position" into which the abolitionists had got themselves. The letter concluded:

I beg to assure you, and through you the British public, that many of the Anti-Slavery Committee, and all rightly judging persons (as I sincerely believe) throughout the Kingdom, quite approve of the magnanimous measure of Government for ... cheap sugar and against monopoly and heartily wish them success and trust they will have it.

On the day following the publication of this letter a special meeting of the Committee was held.[24] That evening the Treasurer and the editor of the *Reporter* called at Bennet's house and demanded a public retraction. When he refused, he was summoned to appear at 27 New Broad Street the following day. The interview that followed was very much like a court martial. The letter was read aloud and Bennet asked to retract what

21. BFASS Minute Books, 15 Jan., 5 Feb., 26 March 1841; BFASS *Reporter*, 10 Feb., 7 April 1841.
22. *Hansard*, 57 (30 April 1841), 1305–6.
23. BFASS Minute Books, 5 May 1841; BFASS *Reporter*, 19 May 1841.
24. BFASS Minute Books, 21 May 1841.

he had written. When he again refused, the Committee drafted an official denial, which appeared in the *Patriot* on 24 May, saying that the version of its views given in the earlier letter was "altogether erroneous".[25] Bennet now returned to the attack with a second letter which repeated his earlier charges and went on to state that on this issue "the vast majority" of British abolitionists shared his own views.[26] This letter was not printed, probably as a result of pressure put on the editor by the Committee. By opposing its policies in public he had discredited himself in the eyes of its members and at the next annual meeting he was not re-elected.

Meanwhile, the responses of the auxiliaries had begun to pour in. The Committee's circulars had evidently taken most of them by surprise. Some were prepared to support London from the outset, others wrote requesting further information and a few were quite frankly opposed. Typical of the latter response was a letter from Richard Caton, one of the secretaries of the Bradford Anti-Slavery Society. Bradford, it is worth noting, was one of the towns where economic distress was particularly acute at this time.

The views of the majority (2 to 1) of the acting secretaries are very divided on the Brazilian sugar question and I do very sincerely regret that they do not all accord with the recorded sentiments of the Central Anti-Slavery Committee.

In those sentiments a principle is adopted (I speak as an individual) which *cannot* be carried out to affect the use of all slave grown produce— at the same time that the adoption of it in the instance of sugar—puts sugar, almost or quite a necessity of life, nearly beyond the reach of our actually *famishing* population at *home* where our charity should begin. It is partial in its application and in its results (with other prohibitory laws) *destructive* of the lives of our labouring fellow countrymen. The extension of our trade with the Brazils will open wide the field for the legitimate exercise of the moral influence of British Anti-Slavery principles at the same time that it will afford employment to some portion of our unwillingly idle population at home not one of whom ought to be sacrificed to the lingering tortures of hunger with expectation of benefiting the Negro race when the benefit may be accomplished by other means.[27]

Other correspondents pointed out that London's stand betrayed a want of confidence in the cheapness and efficiency of free labour and so would tend to retard rather than to promote world emancipation.[28] R. F. Forester of Derbyshire argued that London's stand was inconsistent since Brazilian sugar was, in fact, already brought into England in large

25. *Ibid*, 22 May 1841.
26. Bennet to the Editor of the *Patriot*, 24 May 1841, BFASS Papers, C 5/16.
27. Caton to Tredgold, 19 June 1841, *ibid*, C 5/141.
28. See, for example, Richard Evans to Tredgold, 18 May 1841, *ibid*, C 6/64.

quantities where it was refined under bond and re-exported to Europe.[29] Thomas Doyle of the Bristol Anti-Slavery Society also drew attention to this practice, adding that as Britain was already fully engaged in supplying the Continent with cheap foreign sugar the only expansion in the world market likely to result from the Government's measure would be that caused by increased consumption in Britain itself. Since this would continue "only until the supply of free labour sugar, by its greater cheapness, should drive that which was raised by slave labour out of the British market" it was not worth making an issue over.[30]

This faith in the superior efficiency of free as opposed to slave labour was evident in many of the letters received by the Society and was the basis of much of the opposition. As we have seen, the Committee had hitherto been a leading exponent of this view, which had suited its case so long as the main objects of attack had been the slave trade and West Indian slavery. Under the barrage of letters it slowly began to dawn on members that this was not, as they had assumed, a law of nature, universally applicable. It was true that British workmen were rather better than African slaves at operating machines but it evidently did not hold true of free versus slave labour in sugar production, at least not when the many possible variations in soil and climate were taken into account. Explaining this to provincial supporters who still clung to the old doctrines was not always easy. The explanation generally given was that free labour remained the most efficient form but that its advantages might be offset by other circumstances, as in the case of the West Indies where bad managerial policies and worn out lands were the principal causes of economic decline.[31]

Broad Street was also embarrassed by the use its opponents made of its own more extravagant claims regarding the success of emancipation. Some of these, it now became clear, had given an entirely false impression of how the freedmen actually lived. Thus John Candler, returning from a visit to Jamaica in 1840, had treated readers of the *Reporter* to a rhapsodic account of his impressions of life there.

Where else, in the whole wide world, is there a peasantry that with so little toil had such a command over the good things of this life? These people keep poultry.... They keep goats.... They do not work very hard, they live well, they dress handsomely, they send their children to school ... build chapels at their own expense and support entirely many of the missionaries.[32]

29. Forester to Tredgold, 14 May 1841, *ibid*, C 7/15.
30. Doyle to Tredgold, 14 June 1841, *ibid*, C 6/92.
31. "Memorial to the Members of the Birmingham Anti-Slavery Society", BFASS *Reporter*, 15 Dec. 1841, pp. 261–2.
32. *Ibid*, 9 Sept. 1840.

This and other similar passages were now cited by critics as evidence that the freedmen did not need protection. Lord John Russell, speaking as Secretary of the Colonies in the debate following Baring's announcement, turned the tables on his opponents by quoting from their own works. What greater contrast could there be, he demanded, than that between the "extreme comfort" and "happy prospects" of the inhabitants of the West Indies and the condition of workers in Britain's northern cities who could not afford sugar for their coffee, if indeed they could afford coffee? It was absurd for Britain to go on supporting West Indian Negroes in luxury and idleness by paying them what amounted to a bounty of several million pounds a year while her own population was on the verge of starvation.[33] C. P. Villiers had earlier summed up the Government's case neatly by stating that the abolitionists "had at last persuaded themselves that a black man was better than a white one".[34] Thus hoist with its own petard the Committee's only recourse was to avoid such comparisons whenever possible, although this was not always easy when their opponents were constantly making them. Many charged it with being socially reactionary. In May 1841 its annual general meeting was broken up by a group of Chartist hecklers.[35] Its position would have been easier had it been possible to make a clear distinction between those statements which were intended to impress foreign audiences, for whom it was still important to present conditions in the West Indies in the best possible light, and those intended for home consumption, to which other considerations now applied. But in practice the two became muddled, adding yet further to the confusion of the antislavery position.

The sugar debates of 1841 began on 7 May and lasted eight days. They were conducted in an atmosphere of growing excitement. The position of the Melbourne Government had for some time been precarious and had recently become critical as had been shown by four successive Whig defeats in by-elections. Besides the specific issues involved, therefore, these debates were a trial of strength between the Whig administration on one side and a coalition of factions, led by Peel and the Tories on the other. This fact is important for it explains among other things why O'Connell and his Irish followers, who had opposed tariff reductions the previous year, now rallied to the Government's support.

Given this situation, it may seem surprising that appeals to antislavery principles should have featured as prominently as they did in the arguments of both sides. Although the actual issue under discussion was the

33. *Hansard, 58* (7 May 1841), 16–42; see also the speech by H. G. Ward, *ibid*, p. 211.
34. *Ibid, 57* (5 April 1841), 920.   35. BFASS *Reporter*, 19 May 1841.

ministerial measure for reducing the tariff to 36s the debate mainly revolved around a motion by Viscount Sandon, couched in antislavery terms, which deplored the effect that measure would have on the slave trade. It was also noticeable that many who now came forward in support of Sandon and his motion had previously shown no inclination to side with the abolitionists and in some cases had been among their most forthright opponents. The reason however is clear: the abolitionists provided the only respectable arguments for opposing the government's motion. The alternative would have been to appeal to self-interest, in this case a particularly narrow self-interest. Thus those with ulterior grounds for opposing the Government hastened to proclaim themselves good anti-slavery men at heart. This singular transformation, which added a bizarre dimension to the debate, was greeted with derision by the ministerial supporters who dismissed the humanitarian zeal of their opponents as no more than a pretext for overthrowing the Government and protecting monopolistic interests—as in many cases it was.[36] To confuse matters still further, several members with genuine antislavery credentials such as Daniel O'Connell, William Evans and Sir George Strickland supported the Government and so were placed in the ironical position of having to listen to their former opponents reminding them of Britain's obligation to the blacks.

Because of this peculiar combination of circumstances the opinions of abolitionists outside of Parliament became a matter of genuine interest on both sides of the House. Thus the speech by Dr Lushington, who came forward as the acknowledged spokesman of Broad Street, was listened to with particular care. He opposed the measure, he said,

First . . . because it gives a stimulus to the slave trade; secondly, because it will augment the horrors of the existing state of slavery; thirdly, because it is unjust to the West Indies; fourthly, because it is deleterious to the happiness of the emancipated population; fifthly, because it is not just to the capitalists, who have engaged in the cultivation of sugar in the East Indies; and lastly, because I believe there exists no necessity whatever for taking the present course in order to supply the people of England with sugar.[37]

Speakers on the Government side countered by claiming that the London Committee did not represent the views of abolitionists generally. Joseph Brotherton, MP for Manchester and Salford, informed the House that the views of the Manchester Anti-Slavery Society did not concur with those of the London Committee,[38] a statement which Mark Philips, another Lancashire MP, later confirmed by observing that only two

36. See the speeches of Viscount Howick and Joseph Hume, *Hansard, 58* (12, 14 May 1841), 278, 385–6.
37. *Ibid* (13 May 1841), 352.   38. *Ibid* (17 May 1841), 532.

individuals connected with that organization had so far failed to come forward in support of the Ministry. On the fifth day of the debate, Joseph Hume, the well-known radical, told the Commons that he had received letters from no less than five antislavery societies assuring him that they disapproved of Lushington's stand, though which societies these were he did not reveal.[39] Replying to these statements, the Government's opponents quoted J. J. Gurney and Buxton to the effect that any relaxation in the duties would, in Gurney's words, give "a vast new impulse . . . to slave labour and therefore to the slave trade and would increase both the numbers and the energy of those who delight to prey on the vitals of Africa". Others pointed out that the existing supply of sugar was quite sufficient for Britain's needs and ridiculed what Disraeli termed the "picturesque descriptions of the misery of the population for want of it" given by Government spokesmen.[40]

When at last put to the House, Sandon's motion was approved by a vote of 317 to 281, thereby defeating the ministerial measure. Somewhat to everyone's surprise, the Government did not resign immediately, but lingered on for another two weeks until it was defeated on a motion of no confidence. It is also interesting to notice that Lushington, who had voted against the Government over the sugar issue, supported it on this subsequent occasion. No similar shift was observed on the part of the West Indian interest.[41]

In the relative calm that followed the parliamentary debates, Broad Street was at last able to take stock of its position. For the time being its cause had emerged triumphant. On the other hand, it was plain that its stand had cost it much goodwill. In nothern cities such as Manchester, Liverpool, Bolton and Bradford, which in the past had been centres of antislavery activity, opinion was hostile and the local auxiliaries in open revolt. As a first step towards bringing these bodies into line and mollifying liberal opinion generally, London set about removing some of the misconceptions that had arisen. Replying to a letter which appeared in the London *Globe*, J. H. Hinton, the Society's Secretary, dismissed the charge that "sinister influences" had led it to put forward "the *consistent* bread-taxer Lord Sandon, as its champion". Sandon, he explained, was not and never had been a member of the Society. It was pure coincidence that London's policy had happened to coincide with that of others less creditably motivated.[42] The Committee was also at pains to show that

39. *Ibid* (13 May 1841), 383–4.
40. *Ibid* (14, 18 May 1841), 455, 578–9.
41. *Ibid* (4 June 1841), 1241–6.
42. BFASS *Reporter*, 19 May 1841.

although it had temporarily found itself acting on the side of the monopolists it was in general opposed to monopoly. On 4 June it issued a statement urging the removal of all restrictions on foreign grain. This was a proposal to which it was particularly happy to give its approval because, as it pointed out, not only would it ameliorate conditions in Britain but it would also, by encouraging the development of the American grain producing states, help shift the sectional balance in favour of the North and so promote the antislavery cause there.[43]

The Committee had hopes of winning over its disaffected auxiliaries by discussing matters with provincial antislavery leaders. A national convention was called for 29 May to which all auxiliaries were urged to send delegates. Stephen Lushington, John Scoble, J. J. Gurney and Sir George Stephen (who had retired from antislavery work but was summoned back on this occasion) addressed the gathering, but to little effect. Few of the delegates, it turned out, were prepared to be persuaded. As one of them observed in his diary, "all failed to convince us country people that the Committee in London had not taken a very injudicious step".[44]

One auxiliary did fall, or rather was forced back, into line. The Birmingham Anti-Slavery Society had been slow to commit itself, but on 2 June, immediately after the national convention, its committee passed a formal resolution dissociating itself from London's policy—a fact which suggests that the convention may actually have hardened opposition. Joseph Sturge, still secretary of this society, was at that time away in the United States and so unable to intervene. Immediately upon his return, however, he taxed the committee with its action. Finding it not prepared to budge, he sent a circular to all members explaining that by its action the committee had contravened its own constitution, the constitution of the British and Foreign Anti-Slavery Society and the resolutions of the World Anti-Slavery Convention and had, besides, failed in its duty to forward the cause of universal emancipation. At the next annual meeting, held on 24 November, the committee's statement was rescinded and a new one adopted expressing wholehearted approval of the London policy.[45]

But not everyone could be thus easily bludgeoned into supporting the official line, nor was it possible to change the general liberal view that by opposing the free-traders and ranging themselves on the side of the monopolists the London Committee had made a serious blunder.

43. BFASS Minute Books, 4 June 1841.
44. G. E. Bryant and G. P. Baker, eds, *A Quaker Journal, Being the Diary and Reminiscences of William Lucas of Hitchin, 1804–1861* (2 vols, London, 1934), *I*, 242.
45. BFASS *Reporter*, 15 Dec. 1841.

The abolitionists and the sugar duties 1841–1852

The defeat of the Melbourne Government offered a respite from the excitement of the spring and early summer. It was clear, however, that nothing had actually been decided: the sugar duties remained; industrial unrest continued; the free-traders prepared to renew their assault whenever the opportunity offered; the abolitionists still argued among themselves; and the colonial producers looked around for new ways of strengthening their position. Nevertheless, from the protectionist standpoint, the immediate future looked bright, certainly much brighter than it had recently appeared. Peel and the Tories had just won a resounding victory at the hustings on a platform pledging support of the existing tariff system, and had a clear majority of almost a hundred. Whatever the free-traders might do, it looked as though colonial sugar would be safe for some time to come.

Discussion of the sugar question was now conducted in a lower key. The free-traders, for their part, contented themselves by point-

ing out some of the inconsistencies in the Broad Street argument. The greatest weakness of the antislavery position, it was commonly agreed, was that
it was based on a total ignorance of international trade. The decision to
make an issue of sugar was purely arbitrary—they could just as well have
chosen American cotton, Brazilian iron or Cuban tobacco, all equally
the products of slave labour. Britain was already selling cotton goods to
Brazil on a large scale and these were being paid for by the export of Brazilian sugar to Europe, some of which actually passed through British refiner-
ies. These cottons, in turn, were often used for the purchase of slaves.
In fact the whole system of trade was so complex and its different parts
so closely interlocking that there was virtually nothing Britain could do
that could not in some way be construed as giving encouragement to
slavery—short, that is, of withdrawing from trade entirely, in which case
some other country would take her place. Petty scruples over this or that
detail of the system were absurd. Either she accepted the system as a
whole or she did not, and since it was impossible not to accept it she
should not go on vexing her conscience over imaginary responsibilities.
As Richard Cobden, appearing before the Second World Anti-Slavery
Convention in 1843 as a delegate of the Manchester Anti-Slavery Society,
observed the plan of the London Committee was "utterly impractical".

Commerce cannot be bound and cramped in the way you propose. You
must do more than you have proposed to have a shadow of a chance of
accomplishing your object. If you shut out all communication with Brazil,
what avail will this be ? You cannot prevent yourselves, as a commercial people,
ministering to the indirect increase of the trade of Brazil and of every other
country, so long as you encourage any foreign trade at all.[1]

Far better, the free-traders concluded, to emulate the example of the
Great Propounder by mixing with mankind rather than deliberately
drawing away into a position of artificial isolation.

Making it appear as though the abolitionists should either attempt
more or nothing at all had the effect of clouding the issue. The London
Committee in response strove to focus attention on the particular points in
dispute. All systems, Scoble explained to the 1843 Convention, had their
limits and exceptions. This was the case with free trade, to whose general
principles he, like the other members of the London Committee, was as
attached as Cobden. But the issue at stake was not free trade; it was
whether slave products should, in this instance, be allowed access to a
new and lucrative market. It was already generally agreed that free trade
in human beings was wrong. It followed that any action on Britain's
part which would encourage that trade was also wrong. As for the view

1. BFASS, *Proceedings of the World Anti-Slavery Convention of 1843*, p. 146.

that increased trade with Brazil would encourage enlightened principles among the planters there, it was, Scoble pointed out, a mere sophistry, as was immediately apparent if one looked at the lack of enlightenment among American slaveholders.[2] The free-traders' case so far as sugar was concerned, Sir Robert Peel observed on one occasion, was to pretend that they were "labouring to extinguish slavery by increasing the consumption of slave-grown products".[3] The claim that because Britain already imported some slave products she might as well accept others was equally spurious. It was equivalent to saying, O'Connell wrote, that "because I cannot prevent two existing crimes I should consent to the commission of a third".[4]

Judged simply as debating performances the two sides were well matched. Nevertheless, on two points the free traders emerged with a marginal advantage. First, no one seriously doubted that by reducing the tariffs cheaper sugar would be obtained but whether this would produce the effects the abolitionists claimed was less evident. Lord Palmerston, who had done as much as anyone to promote the suppression of the trade, was prepared to say that it would not, and on this issue free-traders were happy to accept his word.[5] Despite the windy generalities of Cobden and others about commerce being the great emancipator, which no one who gave the matter a moment's thought could believe, their arguments had a decidedly down-to-earth quality, at least when they related to Britain and British interests. The arguments of the abolitionists being more dependent on remote contingencies—and, more important perhaps, concerned with remote peoples—were less inclined to impress the popular mind. Secondly, there was a widespread suspicion that anyone who spoke up for the existing duties, irrespective of the arguments used, was in some way influenced by personal economic motives. In Parliament, as we have seen, this was often the case but in the country at large it was less generally so. West Indian organizations existed in London, Liverpool, Glasgow, Dublin and other large cities and from time to time these sent deputations to Whitehall or wrote letters to the press. But their influence was much less than in the past and they made no serious attempt to appeal for public sympathy,[6] which they presumably knew would not be forth-

2. *Ibid*, pp. 147–50.
3. In Mathieson, *Great Britain and the Slave Trade*, p. 82.
4. O'Connell to Sturge, 27 March 1844, in Richard, *Memoirs of Joseph Sturge*, p. 280.
5. *Hansard*, 58 (10 May 1841), 160.
6. For an account of the activities of these bodies see Elsie I. Pilgrim, "Antislavery sentiment in Great Britain, 1841–1854; its nature and decline, with special reference to its influence upon British policy towards the former slave colonies" (unpublished, PhD thesis, Cambridge University, 1957), 71ff.

coming. This reflected more clearly perhaps than anything that had happened so far the sad state into which their affairs had fallen. The truth was that, apart from the arguments provided for them by the abolitionists, they had no case worth presenting. In this respect they were in the same position as their spokesmen in Parliament, with the important difference that while it was relatively easy for an individual to take an antislavery position it was much harder for a West Indian organization to do the same, particularly in areas where the recognized antislavery bodies were free-trade, as was the case in most large industrial cities. It was thus on the abolitionists, or rather on those abolitionists who remained loyal to London, that the task of maintaining a public opposition to the free-traders largely devolved. To this extent the opponents of tariff reduction would seem to have been *less* influenced by personal economic motives than the free-traders, who simply wanted cheap sugar.

Because of the ascendancy of the Tories, 1842 passed off uneventfully. But within the abolitionists' own ranks the sugar issue continued to rankle. This did not prevent them from cooperating on other matters. When, in 1844, John Bright told the House that a number of auxiliaries had broken with London over this question, Joseph Sturge was able to reassure Peel that no "society in its collective capacity ever actually seceded on this ground".[7] All the same, the threat to the solidarity of the movement was very real as became evident during the Second World Anti-Slavery Convention. This assembly, which met in London on 13 June 1843, was much like its predecessor except that the Garrisonians, who had never forgiven Broad Street for its opposition over the woman question, were now conspicuously absent. The leading dissidents on this occasion were the free-traders, who attended in force. Nevertheless, the first three days passed off quietly with reports on the general progress of the cause since 1840. But on the morning of the fourth day the impending storm broke with the introduction of a motion by the Rev. Thomas Spencer of Bath reversing the stand taken by the previous Convention on the tariff issue. The motion ran:

In the judgment of this Convention the introduction of the slave-grown produce of Cuba and Brazil into competition with the free-grown produce of the British West Indian colonies and British India is rendered necessary as an act of justice to the people of this country, and is in consistency with the principles on which this Convention is constituted.[8]

The debate that followed was long and rancorous and touched on practically every aspect of the question. The critics of the London Committee

7. Sturge to Peel, 12 March 1844, Peel Papers, British Museum Add. MSS 40541, ff. 164–6.
8. BFASS, *Proceedings of the World Anti-Slavery Convention of 1843*, p. 128.

claimed that it had departed from proper humanitarian principles and, in particular, had ignored its own teachings respecting the competitive advantages of free labour. Spokesmen for the Committee replied that it had remained true to its original purpose and to the principles laid down by the 1840 Convention. It was not the London Committee but its opponents who had changed their stand. As speech followed speech, feelings ran high. Amendments and counteramendments were bandied back and forth and the audience cheered and booed. Little was said, however, that was not already familiar to most of those present and by the evening it was becoming clear that no useful purpose was being served. It was also evident that the members were fairly equally divided on the subject so that whichever way the decision went it would not carry much weight. So with the concurrence of those present it was agreed not to put the issue to the vote.[9]

The debate in the Convention, inconclusive though it had been, produced one new development. This was the decision of a group of dissident abolitionists, led by Thomas Spencer, G. W. Anstie and W. T. Blair, to establish a new antislavery organization dedicated to achieving the otherthrow of slavery by means of policies consistent with free trade principles. The inauguration of this body, which went under the rather awkward title of The Provisional Committee Appointed by the Members of the Convention of 1843 Favourable to the Motion of the Reverend Thomas Spencer, was held in Freemasons Hall on 22 June, two days after the Convention dissolved. Most, though not all, of its members had attended the Convention. What exactly it could hope to do, apart from criticizing Broad Street, is not evident. Since the leaders came from widely dispersed areas it is hard to see how they expected to establish themselves as a rival body, though that this was what some of them had in mind is shown by a letter which Anstie wrote to Scoble. "We aim", he said, "at the same object, but by means so completely opposed that I do not flatter myself with a hope of union." However, if the British and Foreign Anti-Slavery Society would agree to give up all attempts to combat slavery by means of commercial restrictions his organization would be willing to consider joint action.[10] The London Committee, needless to say, had no intention of capitulating, nor did the subsequent activities of the Provisional Committee give it cause for doing so. In fact nothing more was heard of that organization until March 1844, when a circular appeared through the mails urging auxiliaries of the British and Foreign Anti-Slavery Society to repudiate Broad Street's leadership. Sturge

9. *Ibid*, pp. 127–73.
10. Anstie to Scobie, 29 July 1843, BFASS Papers C 12/114.

promptly responded with a circular of his own defending London's stand.[11] How individual bodies reacted to these two circulars can only be guessed but that some of those whose allegiance had been in doubt now rallied to the defence of the national organization is shown by the letters which subsequently appeared in the *Reporter*.[12] Even W. T. Blair, one of the signatories of the original circular, came over to the London view.[13]

Gratifying though it was to see these signs of wavering on the part of its critics, the existence of a group of acknowledged dissidents within the movement was a source of embarrassment, particularly when it became known that George Thompson had joined them. Thompson, unlike Spencer and Anstie, enjoyed a national reputation. His friendship with Garrison had already placed him at odds with Broad Street. In recent years he had largely given up antislavery work for East Indian affairs, and had in fact only recently returned from an extended visit to India.[14] He remained, however, the one abolitionist capable of challenging Broad Street's leadership and his reappearance on the antislavery scene as one of the dissidents added significantly to the effectiveness of an opposition which had so far lacked a national figurehead.

The strength of this opposition was revealed at the fifth annual meeting of the British and Foreign Anti-Slavery Society held in Exeter Hall on 17 May. These gatherings traditionally took the form of national rallies and were open to members and non-members. On this occasion there were estimated to be more than 4,000 present. Whether, as was later claimed, the assembly was deliberately packed by free-traders and if so what hand Thompson and the Provisional Committee had in it is unclear, although there is no doubt that they had planned in advance to make sugar the major issue.[15] What is clear is that the supporters of Broad Street found themselves for the first time in their experience outnumbered. As was usual on such occasions, everyone present was allowed to vote, a practice which in the past had enabled the Society to claim massive support for its resolutions but which on this occasion worked to its disadvantage. The proceedings opened quietly enough with the reading of messages from Clarkson and others but were soon interrupted by George Thompson who began a lengthy speech on behalf of the many abolitionists

11. The Provisional Committee's circular and Sturge's reply were reprinted in BFASS *Reporter*, 3 April 1844.
12. *Ibid*, 3, 17 April 1844.
13. *Ibid*, 1 May 1844.
14. William Farmer, "Sketch of the life of George Thompson" in *The Liberator*, 34 (1864), 25–49; Stanton, *Sketches of Reforms and Reformers*, pp. 242–3.
15. Thompson to Scoble, 15 May 1844, BFASS Papers, C 22/58.

in the country who, he said, did not share London's views. Specifically he declared, he wished to submit a resolution to the assembly calling on the Committee to refrain from acting on that part of the Society's constitution which pledged the use of "fiscal regulations in favour of free labour" until a special meeting had been held to reconsider the articles of the Society. At times his words were drowned in hoots and cheers and the chairman of the meeting, Samuel Gurney, was obliged to intervene to restore order. The gist of his argument was that Broad Street had committed a serious error in opposing the free-traders and that it was now the duty of the assembly to see that it was rectified. The Committee's own plan for allowing free trade in free-grown sugar was plainly no solution for "consume as much free-grown sugar as you will you do but withdraw it from another market, and the vacancy you occasion is immediately filled up from Brazil".[16] Either the Committee accepted free trade or it did not; there was no halfway solution. By this time the meeting was in complete confusion. Many who sympathized with Thompson's point of view had been antagonized by his manner.[17] This helped the moderates who at last succeeded in making themselves heard and even managed to persuade Thompson to withdraw his motion on condition that the Committee agreed to consult with its auxiliaries. But no sooner had this been settled than Samuel Gurney, feeling that Broad Street should now be given an opportunity to state its case, which had so far scarcely been heard, reopened the subject. Thompson was immediately on his feet in a state of great excitement and demanded that his motion be put to the vote. Several members, including O'Connell and Bright, attempted to mediate but he was in no mood for compromise. The motion was therefore put to the assembly and carried by a small majority.[18]

Broad Street now had no alternative but to call a special general meeting to review the whole question. Care was taken this time to restrict attendance to *bona fide* members of the Society and to ensure a good turn-out of supporters. Some 900 invitations were sent out and resulted in the appearance of 130 delegates in Exeter Hall on 3 June. It was immediately evident that the free-traders were in the minority. Whom, demanded Bright, was the meeting supposed to represent, the London Committee, the British and Foreign Anti-Slavery Society or simply those who happened to be present? There was no denying, however, that it was precisely what it claimed to be, a meeting of the members of the Society, and so fully able to rule on the issue in hand. After some hours of debate a resolution

16. BFASS *Reporter*, 29 May 1844.
17. Richard D. Webb to Elizabeth Pease, 26 May 1844, Garrison Papers.
18. BFASS *Reporter*, 29 May 1844.

was approved endorsing London's policy. "So far as concerns the British and Foreign Anti-Slavery Society", the *Reporter* asserted, "the question of fiscal regulation in favour of free labour must now be considered as finally set at rest."[19] Rather surprisingly, this proved to be the case. Although many abolitionists remained opposed to Broad Street on this issue there were no further attempts to override its authority and nothing more was heard of the Provisional Committee.

The principal reason for this was a change which had occurred in Government policy. For while the abolitionists had been wrangling, the Government had announced its intention of admitting free-grown sugar at preferential rates. In future, the duty charged on sugar from Java, Manila and Indo-China (Siam was included later) would be 36s instead of 66s, or in other words would be reduced to a level only 11s above that at which colonial sugar was admitted.[20] This was not quite what the London Committee had been urging, which was for all free-grown sugars, regardless of origin, to be admitted on an equal footing, but it was much better than nothing.

The results, when they came, proved disappointing. Eighteen forty-five happened to be a poor year for sugar production. Bad weather conditions in Cuba had led to a reduction in exports and to a corresponding rise in European prices. As a result, only a small amount of free-grown sugar actually found its way into the British market—where it accounted for less than three per cent of total sugar imports.[21] Broad Street, of course, was quick to point out the exceptional factors which had led to this result. It also attached some blame to the Government, which had not gone far enough. It was still too much under the influence of monopolists and had failed to take account of the legitimate need of the people of Britain for cheap produce.[22] Thus, through an odd twist of circumstance, they now found themselves using the arguments of the free-traders, although always with the proviso that what they said applied only to the free-grown article. They were still doing so when, in June 1846, the Peel Government, hopelessly divided over the repeal of the corn laws, resigned from office.

Events now moved quickly. On 2 July Lord John Russell took office at the head of a Whig cabinet and on 20 July he put forward a plan for admitting all foreign sugars, regardless of origin, at a uniform rate of 23s 4d. This duty would then be reduced by annual stages until, in 1851,

19. *Ibid*, 12 June, 1844.
20. "Rates of duty on sugar, 1800–1852", PP, 1852/3, 99 (461), 4.
21. In 1845 sugar imports totalled 5,811, 281 cwt. of which 168,180 cwt consisted of foreign free-labour sugar: BFASS *Reporter*, 2 March 1846, p. 42.
22. *Ibid*, 5 March 1845; 2 March 1846.

all sugars would be admitted at the new colonial rate of 14s.[23] From the London Committee's standpoint, this scheme was more objectionable than any so far proposed. In one respect in particular it was a great deal worse than the one they had assisted in throwing out in 1841. On that occasion allowance had at least been made for maintaining a 12s differential in favour of colonial imports. Under the new scheme, even this was to be eliminated.

Russell's announcement had not taken the Committee altogether by surprise. On 11 July, Scoble, anticipating that something of the sort was in the offing, had summoned an emergency meeting to draw up plans of action. As a preliminary measure it had been decided to publish a full statement of its views in the press and to send copies to Peel, Russell and other leading MPs.[24] But once the actual announcement had been made it seemed paralysed. Sturge, true to form, wrote a number of spirited letters to The Times.[25] But no appeals to auxiliary societies were issued,[26] no public rallies held, no deputations appointed. Quite plainly it had given up hope. So also had the Tories. Peel himself was convinced of the futility of further resistance.[27] The corn laws had gone; the sugar duties would surely follow. Even the West Indians, seeing that defeat was inevitable, were prepared to settle for what they could get in the way of unrestricted trade with the United States and the promise of more indentured labourers from Sierra Leone.[28]

In the Commons, opposition to the Government was thus left in the hands of Lord George Bentinck and a group of diehard protectionists and in the Lords to Brougham, Denman, Bishop Wilberforce and a handful of other staunch abolitionist peers. In neither case was it at all effective with the result that, on 18 August Russell's measure passed into law. "The blow", declared the Reporter, "has been struck.... The slave masters and the slave traffickers of Brazil have won a triumph which will fill their hearts with joy."[29]

When the news reached Havana, the town is said to have been illumina-

23. The previous year, as a relief measure, Peel had reduced the duty on colonial sugar from 25s 2d to 14s and on foreign free-grown sugar from 35s 8d to 23s 4d. The duty on slave-grown sugar was reduced from 66s 2d to 63s. "Rates of duty on sugar, 1800–1852", PP, 1852/3, 99 (461), 4.
24. BFASS Minute Books, 11 July 1846; BFASS Reporter, 1 Aug. 1846, pp. 113–14.
25. The Times, 20, 24, 27 July 1846.
26. On 21 July, Scoble was instructed "to draft an appeal to the country", but on 31 July the order was rescinded: BFASS Minute Books, 21, 31 July 1846.
27. Hansard, 88 (27 July 1846), 93–103.
28. Ibid, 87 (20 July, 1846), 1315–16; 88 (27 July 1846), 87–91.
29. BFASS Reporter, 1 Aug. 1846.

ted.[30] Property values rose and the price of slaves was reported to have leaped at least fifteen per cent.[31] Sugar exports boomed. "The production of 1847," one Havana firm later commented in its trade circular, "far exceeded that of any previous year, and the prices obtained by the planters have been so highly remunerative that they are enabled to adopt every means for the further extension of their crops."[32] Sugar exports from Cuba and Brazil, in fact, rose by twenty per cent, approximately ten per cent of the total now being sent to Great Britain.[33] The general economic effects of the new measure were, on the whole, pretty much what its opponents had predicted. Despite a bumper crop, Cuban sugar prices rose slightly in 1847. Meanwhile the prices obtained for West Indian sugar fell steadily from 34s 5d in 1846 to 28s 3d in 1847 to 23s 3d the following year, this last being the lowest price ever recorded.[34]

The effects of this on the West Indies were sadly chronicled by correspondents on the spot. George Blyth, a West Indian Missionary, writing to Scoble in 1847, described the effect on the freedmen.

The estates are now on the verge of ruin and if the proposed equalization of slave and free grown sugar be carried into full effect there is no prospect of any favourable change. . . . Self-interest will of course stimulate the West Indian body to exertion in the present crisis. And I hope the Anti-Slavery Friends will continue to advocate the cause of the Emancipated class. If the present state of things continues they will sink, as certainly as a sailor goes down with his foundered vessel. The grand experiment which has blessed these colonies with freedom must fail and the whole mass of the population will be involved in difficulties as distressing as those which lately desolated Ireland.[35]

30. *Ibid*, 2 Nov. 1946, p. 186; Mathieson, *British Slave Emancipation*, p. 157.
31. Evidence of Commander H. J. Matson in PP, 1847/8, *22*, 104, 116.
32. "Trade circular of Drake Brothers and Co.", 8 Jan. 1848, in BFASS Minute Books, 25 Feb. 1848.
33. "Returns showing the quantities of sugar imported into the United Kingdom", PP (461), 1852/3, *99*, 2-3. Except for a brief rise in the late fifties, the average price of raw sugar on the London Market remained at around 23s until the 1880s when it declined to approximately 11s 6d: Noel Deerr, *History of Sugar*, 2, 531.
34. Market prices of Cuban and West Indian Sugar:

	West Indian Sugar	Havana Sugar
1846	34s 5d	24s 6d
1847	28s 3d	25s 10d
1848	23s 3d	21s 4d
1849	25s 4d	22s 8d
1850	26s 1d	21s 2d

"Returns showing the quantities of sugar imported into the United Kingdom", PP, 1852/3, *99* (461), 2-3.
35. George Blyth to Scoble, 20 Oct. 1847, BFASS Papers, C 13/158.

Despite these gloomy predictions, the total volume of colonial production actually rose in the years after 1846. Expansion was most marked in the case of Mauritius, where the continuing influx of coolie labourers enabled large tracts of virgin land to be brought under cultivation. Between 1846 and 1850 exports rose by a fifth, reaching a level approximately double that of the pre-emancipation era. In the case of the West Indies, the increase was more gradual, and, even in 1852, production was still well below the level which had been reached under the old slave regime, while in certain individual colonies—Jamaica being the outstanding example— it continued to decline depressingly.[36] Taking Britain's colonies as a whole, sugar exports to the mother country rose from 3,901,374 hundredweight in 1841–42 to 6,144,754 hundredweight in 1851–52.[37] The amount of sugar consumed *per capita* in Britain had meanwhile increased from 15 lb. in 1840 to 25 lb. in 1850,[38] so that even this rate of expansion was too slow to keep pace with home demand. The deficit was made up by imports from elsewhere. In 1847, approximately a fifth of the sugar consumed in Britain was of foreign origin—the bulk of it from Brazil and Cuba—and by 1851 this proportion had increased to roughly a quarter.[39]

These developments merely confirmed the London Committee in its view that Russell's measure had been a disastrous blunder. By far the most damning piece of evidence, however, was the way in which the Brazilian slave trade now began to expand. Since the mid-thirties, this trade had fluctuated, sometimes rising as high as 30,000 a year, sometimes dropping as low as 14,000. Now the numbers abruptly shot up to 52,600 in 1846, rising to 57,800 in 1847 and to 60,000 the following year.[40] For the sake of historical accuracy it should perhaps be pointed out that these figures were only estimates and furthermore that, even supposing them accurate, the correlation between them and the British demand for Brazilian sugar could not have been quite as straightforward as the Government's critics assumed. After all, Russell's Bill was not introduced until 20 July and did not pass its third reading until the latter part of August. Since this left too little time for it to have had any appreciable effect on slave imports that year, we must look for some other cause. Professor W. L. Mathieson in his *British Slave Emancipation* has suggested that the initial impulse was the result of Peel's decision in 1844 to open British markets

36. Full statistics on colonial production will be found in PP, 1852/3, *99* (461), 2–11.
37. *Ibid*, pp. 8–9.
38. G. R. Porter, *The Progress of the Nation* (new edn, ed. F. W. Hirst, London, 1912), p. 433.
39. PP, 1852/3, *99* (522), 2–3; *ibid* (461), 8–9.
40. See Appendix A below.

to free-grown sugar. This explanation would be more plausible were it not that the actual quantity of free-grown sugar—only 168,000 hundred-weight in 1845[41] was so small. A much more probable explanation would seem to be that the expansion of the traffic which occurred in 1846 was the result of two factors: the temporary restraints placed on slave imports by the Cuban authorities (Captain-General Valdez, 1840–43, seems genuinely to have wished to see the trade suppressed while his successor, Captain-General O'Donnell, 1843–48, was so anxious to make a profit out of it that he almost taxed it out of existence[42]), and the sharp increase in world sugar prices which followed the disastrous failure of the Cuban crop in 1845.[43] But even when all allowances have been made it is hard not to conclude that the Whig policy was responsible for the continuing high level of Brazilian slave imports in the years after 1846. Britain, after all, was now consuming a sizeable slice of the Brazilian sugar crop—seventeen per cent in 1847–48[44]—as well as a good proportion of the Cuban crop, but for which, production would have been a good deal less profitable than it was. Certainly, in the minds of those Englishmen most concerned with this sudden influx of Negroes into Brazil, the members of the London Committee and the naval personnel responsible for implementing the suppression policy, there was no doubt that this development was a direct result of the Government's action.[45] Even Russell himself, when interviewed by an antislavery deputation in 1848, did not deny that his policy had had an influence on the slave trade, but pointed out that if guilt were to be assigned they themselves must bear part of it for having failed to support the more moderate measure put forward by the Whigs in 1841.[46]

Abolitionists saw their predictions further borne out by the European

41. BFASS *Reporter*, 2 March 1846; Mathieson, *British Slave Emancipation*, p. 157.
42. Mathieson, *Great Britain and the Slave Trade*, p. 141.
43. Owing to draught and hurricane, the crop was said to have been reduced from 200,000 to 80,000 tons. BFASS *Reporter*, 1 Aug. 1846.
44. Comparison between Brazilian sugar exports and the consumption of Brazilian sugar in Britain, 1846–8:

Year	Brazilian sugar exports	Year	Brazilian sugar consumed in Britain
1846–47	2,052,327 cwt	1847	202,268 cwt
1847–48	2,336,226 cwt	1848	351,833 cwt

For Brazilian sugar exports see: William Scully, *Brazil: its Provinces and Chief Cities . . . with Agricultural, Commercial and other Statistics* (London, 1866), p. 24. The above figures are based on the assumption that 1 Brazilian arroba = 32.38 lb. For British consumption see PP, 1852/3, 99 (522), 2–3.
45. See evidence of Matson, Denman and Butterfield, "First Report of the Select Committee on the Slave Trade", PP, 1847/8, 22, 33, 51, 104–17.
46. BFASS Minute Books, 17 March 1848.

response to Britain's actions. On a visit to Holland in 1847 Scoble was assured by M. Oudermeulan, President of the Amsterdam Chamber of Commerce, that had Britain continued to discriminate against slave-grown sugar the abolition of slavery in the Dutch colonies would already have been decided. This information added to the gloom of their deliberations.[47]

After 1846 the sugar issue became linked to the more general question of how to bring about the suppression of the slave trade, and so may best be dealt with in the next chapter. One effect of Russell's measure which ought, however, to be mentioned at this point was the increased prominence which the British and Foreign Anti-Slavery Society henceforward gave to the article in its constitution which called on all members to refrain from using slave produce. This was by no means a new idea. As early as 1795 the Society for the Abolition of the Slave Trade had recommended boycotting slave produced articles, as some individual abolitionists had been doing ever since the 1730s.[48] Sturge himself, like other members of the Committee, had long been scrupulous in this respect, a practice which was commented on with approval by Harriet Beecher Stowe when she visited him in 1853.[49] Nevertheless, compared with their American colleagues, British abolitionists had placed relatively little stress on this aspect of their doctrine. Now they turned to it as a last resort, a gesture more designed, perhaps, to salve their own consciences than to provide an effective check on slave production.[50] For now that the tariff barrier had been removed there was absolutely nothing that they could do to limit the consumption of slave-grown sugar. All the same, a flood of pamphlets and articles appeared, exhorting the public to abstain from slave produce.[51] In practice this was not always easy, since some retailers were dishonest and many were genuinely ignorant of the origin of their goods. During the early 1850s, these difficulties were partially solved by the establishment of special free-produce stores in London and Man-

---

47. *Ibid*, 1 Oct. 1847.
48. Williams, *Capitalism and Slavery*, p. 183. That early abolitionist eccentric, Benjamin Lay, made his own clothes so as to be sure of avoiding materials produced by slave labour. D. B. Davis, *The Problem of Slavery in Western Culture* (Ithaca, New York, 1966), p. 323.
49. Charles E. Stowe, *Life of Harriet Beecher Stowe* (Cambridge, Mass., 1889), p. 224.
50. There was a significant lack of optimism in the Committee's statements with regard to the practical effects anticipated from this policy. See, for example, the letter from G. W. Alexander, BFASS *Reporter*, 2 Nov. 1846, pp. 186–7; also *ibid*, 2 May 1853, pp. 109–11.
51. See the memorials on the disuse of slave produce in BFASS *Reporter*, 1 Jan. 1 Nov. 1847, pp. 1, 161.

chester.[52] In 1847 Sturge contributed five hundred dollars to the Philadelphia Free Produce Association and later the same year, largely at his instigation, Samuel Rhoads visited England to acquaint British sympathizers with the techniques used in the United States.[53] The help of other American visitors, including Elihu Burritt and Frederick Douglass, was also enlisted.[54] By 1851, there were twenty-six free-produce societies in Britain, some independent, others auxiliaries of the British and Foreign Anti-Slavery Society.[55]

As a corollary of these policies, abolitionists again began stressing the importance of East Indian production. Despite India's continuing backwardness, the hope had persisted that, providing the government could be prevailed on to offer the necessary economic inducements, it might do what the West Indies had so embarrassingly failed to do and provide the world with an abundant supply of free labour produce. Former supporters of the now defunct British India Society offered encouragement. "Every fresh mile of road, or railway, or canal," wrote one, "every new steam boat plying on the rivers of India, every fresh court of justice there, is another nail driven into the coffin of American slavery."[56] This was a matter on which free-traders and abolitionists could cooperate. John Bright shared the concern of many cotton manufacturers over Britain's almost total dependence on the United States for raw materials. Writing to Sturge in 1853 about the possibility of increasing the Indian supply he observed: "I fully believe that a wise and economical Government could so free the industry of that country, and so open its communications, that we might have cotton in great quantity from it so as materially to affect our position with regard to the States."[57] But the figures remained disappointing. East Indian sugar producers, deprived of their tariff protection, found increasing difficulty in competing and exports fell off accordingly. In 1866 they were less than a third of what they had been twenty years earlier.[58] Cotton fared better, but progress remained slow up to the American Civil War when, thanks to the cutting off of the Ameri-

52. Ruth A. Nuermberger, *The Free Produce Movement: a Quaker protest against slavery* (Durham, North Carolina, 1942), p. 71.
53. BFASS Minute Books, 17 Sept. 1847; BFASS *Reporter*, 1 Oct. 1847, p. 155.
54. BFASS Minute Books, 27 Nov. 1846; Frederick Douglass, *Report of a Public Meeting Held in Finsbury Chapel, Moorfields, May 22, 1846, to Hear an Address by Frederick Douglass* (London, 1846), p. 11.
55. Nuermberger, p. 58.
56. John Cropper to Wilson Armistead, 1854, quoted in Armistead to Chamerovzow 27 Nov. 1854, BFASS Papers, C 27/62A.
57. Bright to Sturge, 1853, in Hobhouse, *Joseph Sturge*, p. 109.
58. For example, the sugar exports to Great Britain fell from 1,432,274 cwt in 1846 to 1,230,429 cwt in 1856 declining to a mere 396,537 cwt in 1866: PP, 1867, *64*, 953.

can supply, exports suddenly trebled. Thereafter India remained a formidable rival in the world market.[59]

These later issues did little to erase the memory of the bitter defeat over the sugar duties. There was no disguising the fact that by opposing the free-traders the London Committee had made itself and the national organization it represented unpopular. It was no coincidence that popular support for the antislavery cause declined after 1846. On the other hand, it is uncertain whether by taking a different stand it would have fared any better. To have supported the Whigs or remained neutral would not only have meant going against the Society's declared principles— which were quite specific on this point—but would probably have split the antislavery body no less effectively. In fact *whatever* it had decided many sincere abolitionists would have disagreed with it. Lushington, Brougham, Buxton and many others—perhaps the majority, although it is difficult to tell—opposed the free-traders not just because London told them to but because that was what their consciences dictated. Moreover, had the Committee not taken the stand it did, what it feared might well have occurred five years sooner. In 1841, as we have seen, the protectionists took their arguments almost entirely from Broad Street. Without these arguments and without the support of the national organization their case would have been weakened, and very little weakening would have been required—a swing of nineteen votes would have been enough— to decide the issue in favour of the free-traders. It is true that the 1841 measure would have been more moderate than the one finally adopted, but there was no guaranteeing that it would have been kept to. The free-traders would certainly have pressed for its amendment and it is hard to see how they could have been resisted. The result would have been that more slaves would have been carried to Brazil and Cuba. The members of the London Committee never expressed any regrets over the policy they had pursued. Subsequent events, they believed, vindicated their cause so completely that for many years they even continued to hope that Parliament might be persuaded to reverse its decision. They were, of course, disappointed. Preferential tariffs for colonial sugar were reintroduced early in the twentieth century, but by that time the issues of the 1840s had long been forgotten.

59. Imports of cotton into Great Britain:

	From the U.S.	From British India
1860	9,963,309	1,822,689
1864	126,322	4,522,566
1869	4,083,562	4,298,012

"Commissioners Reports, 1870", PP, 1870, *20*, 36.

9

The abolitionists and the slave trade 1839–1853

The problems posed by the slave trade were in some ways even more baffling than those raised by the sugar duties. Enough has been said already to acquaint the reader with the general background to this struggle. Since 1808, when Britain withdrew from the trade, successive governments had striven to secure its suppression by means of agreements with other powers and the use of naval patrols. This was, or rather became, essentially a government policy. Abolitionists who in the early days had been responsible for launching the government on its course, had, by the mid-twenties, turned their attention to other matters. But the government had persevered, and by 1839 had concluded treaties with all save one of the major maritime powers—the United States. This exception was an important one for it made the system as a whole almost unworkable. Much of the trade that was now carried on was, in fact, conducted under the American flag. Very few of the slaves were taken to the United States, since the trade there had been officially banned and anyone caught participating in it was, at least in theory, liable to the death penalty. Nor were the ships used, in most cases, American vessels, although a few were. It was common practice, however, for ships of various origins to carry duplicate sets of American papers to be used in the event of trouble. These could easily be bought in Havana or elsewhere, and wise slavers would make sure, before setting out on a voyage, that they were appropriately provided. This, of course, was illegal and any slaver caught by the United States navy, flying the American flag, was liable to seizure. But few United States naval vessels were to be found in the areas where the trade was conducted so this was unlikely to happen and in any case captains usually took care to see what vessel was approaching before deciding which flag to run up. By this juggling with flags and alternative sets of papers they were able to go on plying their trade. Some were caught, but not until the 1860s, when the United States belatedly began to cooperate, enough to make the trade as a whole unprofitable. As a result upwards of 600,000 Negroes were carried westward from Africa to the New World between 1839 and 1863, most of them to Cuba and Brazil.[1]

This, then, was the situation which confronted abolitionists in the months following the ending of apprenticeship. Buxton's response has already been noted. *The Slave Trade and its Remedy*, was the first detailed treatment of the issue by an abolitionist for many years and the most damning attack so far made by anyone on the official policy. Other abolitionists did not question his assessment of the extent of the problem. Many, as we shall see, rejected his solution, but all shared in varying degrees his sense of outrage and urgency. If such things were still allowed to happen in spite of all Britain's efforts, then the time had clearly come to look more closely at the methods she was using. And the closer they looked the more appalled they became. Buxton had been critical of the suppression policy. Others went much further. Not only, it seemed to them, was Britain failing to check the traffic; she was actually making it worse. Left to their own devices, these critics pointed out, it was reasonable to suppose that the slave traders would have employed seaworthy vessels and taken some care, if only for economic reasons, to keep mortality to a minimum. But because of the African blockade and the certain knowledge that some vessels would be captured, many traders had taken to using only the oldest and most expendable craft they could find. Others, hoping to evade capture altogether, were using vessels which sacrificed accommodation for speed. There was also evidence to suggest that the equipment clauses, which enabled vessels to be seized, even when there were no slaves on board,

1. Curtin, *Atlantic Slave Trade*, p. 234.

were inducing traders to dispense with adequate supplies of water and other provisions on the principle that it was better to lose a percentage of the cargo than to run the risk of losing the whole vessel. Thus many came to believe that to the extent that Britain had striven to make her policy effective she had augmented its horrors. Had there been any prospect that her policy would eventually lead to total suppression this could have been tolerated. But there was no evidence that this was happening. She seemed merely to be compounding the crime without deterring the criminals. The facts spoke for themselves: Britain was, to all appearances, as far away from achieving her object as ever; millions of pounds had been spent on securing treaties and on maintaining an African squadron; the lives of hundreds of her sailors had been lost; and still the trade flourished on a wider scale than ever. All that Britain had done was to bring about a change in the flags under which it was conducted.[2] Clearly a new approach was needed.

Lack of results was not the only reason for objecting to the government's policy. The Quakers and other pacifist elements in the movement had another equally strong motive. For the achievement of its aims the government relied on the use of naval forces to blockade Africa and to patrol along the shores of the New World. In practice, slavers were usually captured without loss of life. Nevertheless, fighting did sometimes occur and even when it did not, the threat of force was usually the deciding factor. To ardent pacifists like Sturge, physical coercion of any kind was repugnant, even when used against those who did not hesitate to use force themselves. At the time of the formation of the British and Foreign Anti-Slavery Society he made plain that it was not his intention to endorse "the methods hitherto pursued to put down the slave trade" because they involved "the violation of the Christian principle in regard to war". It was incumbent on abolitionists to use only "such means as a moral and religious influence may properly afford".[3] A clause to this effect—clause four—was therefore inserted into the Society's draft constitution and later incorporated into the final version.[4] Not everyone was happy with this arrangement. Buxton himself had specifically rejected the pacifist argument.[5] Others wrote expressing dissatisfaction at what they regarded as the introduction of a test. R. K. Greville of the Edinburgh Anti-Slavery

2. Buxton, *The Slave Trade and its Remedy*, pp. 159–60, 175, 205–9. These arguments were repeated in innumerable articles which appeared in the BFASS *Reporter* and in other abolitionist publications; see BFASS, *Proceedings of the General Anti-Slavery Convention of 1843*, pp. 238–44.
3. Joseph Sturge to the Editor of the *British Emancipator*, 23 Jan. 1839, pp. 202–3.
4. BFASS Minute Books, 13 March, 19 April 1839.
5. Buxton, *The Slave Trade and its Remedy*, preface to "The Remedy", pp. ii–v.

Society stated that the members of that organization could not agree to cooperate on such a basis, for "While we are exercising our peaceable influence, is nothing to be done for the hundreds of thousands of poor creatures who are actually *being conveyed* into slavery? If a cargo of slaves is met with on the high seas, and if the captain refuses to listen to moral and religious arguments, is he to be allowed to carry them into port to sell them?"[6] This issue was also discussed at the Society's inaugural meeting. Sturge argued that it was essential to be explicit from the first and so leave no room for future disagreement. The majority of those present were evidently prepared to accept his views since clause four was ratified. Commenting on this step, Stephen Lushington stated that it was his understanding that he would not now be at liberty to recommend, either in committee or at any public meeting of the Society, any measures involving the use of force. The question of what attitude the Society should adopt towards the use of force by the government appears to have been left over. At least, there is nothing in the records to show, as Sir George Stephen later contended, that it undertook to remain neutral on this issue.[7] The Edinburgh Society remained independent, but it is doubtful whether its objections to pacifism were the deciding factor. Glasgow, which also remained independent, agreed with Broad Street on this issue.[8] It is also perhaps worth noting that in later years when rival organizations challenged London's leadership this was not one of the points in dispute. For better or worse, the majority of British anti-slavery organizations were prepared to endorse Quaker principles, or at least to pay them lip service.

They were thus left with the task of finding an alternative policy more in accord with their own strict standards. One obvious possibility was the one proposed by Buxton. Besides Buxton himself, three members of the Broad Street committee, William Allen, Samuel Gurney and Stephen Lushington, held seats on the committee of the African Civilization Society. Most Sturgites, however, opposed this venture, partly on the grounds that it contravened their pacifist principles but mainly because they believed it impractical. Like the government's own measures, its success would depend on armed intervention and treaty-making, applied this time within Africa. It seemed unlikely to them that these would be any more effective on land than at sea or that native chiefs would be any more amenable or trustworthy than the governments with which Britain had

6. Greville to Tredgold, 12 April 1839, BFASS Papers, C 7/70.
7. *British Emancipator*, 1 May 1839.
8. See "Petition of the members and friends of the Glasgow Emancipation Society" in "Second Report of the Select Committee on the Slave Trade", PP, 1847–48, *22*, 172–3.

customarily dealt. Previous experience of dealings in Africa were not encouraging. And even if other forms of commerce did replace slaving, what would prevent Africans from using slavery as a means of production? "We know", wrote John Sturge in a pamphlet attacking the project, "that this is not what Mr Buxton means when he proposes to demonstrate . . . 'the superior value of man as a labourer on the soil to man as an object of merchandise' but we think that this is the way in which alone the African will understand and act on the suggestion."[9] The strongest argument against the scheme, however, was that it had already been tried and had failed. As the secretary of the Bury St Edmunds auxiliary wrote to Tredgold, the African Civilization Society was "but the ghost of the defunct African Institution—which after twenty years of existence despairingly concluded their efforts by declaring that while slavery exists the slave trade will never cease".[10] All the same, Broad Street was reluctant to make a public issue of the matter and deliberately concealed its views until after the first World Convention in order, it later confessed, "to avoid any appearance of dissension".[11] This was a wise as well as a tactful course, for once the government had declared its intention of supporting the Niger expedition there was nothing to be done but to await the outcome.

The results, when they came, confirmed the view, already expressed by Sturge at the time of the founding of the British and Foreign Anti-Slavery Society, that the solution, if any, would be found, not in Africa or on the seas, but within the importing countries. "For my own part", he had written, "I am strongly persuaded of the correctness of the conclusion which Granville Sharp so early arrived at that *to destroy slavery is the only means to extinguish the slave trade.*"[12] This was a view which had much to commend it. It certainly summed up better than most the lessons of past failures. The trouble was that it offered no effective basis for action. As everyone knew, abolition in Cuba and Brazil could not be expected for many years. It was all very well to talk of "laying the axe to the root", but so far abolitionists had found no way of getting at the root. Were they to wait until the "moral and humanitarian influences", on which Sturge had pinned his faith, penetrated into these countries, which would plainly take a long time, or should they devise some more direct form of action? The London Committee aspired to this latter approach

9. John Sturge, *Remarks on the Society for the Extinction of the Slave Trade and the Civilization of Africa and on "The Slave Trade and Its Remedy"* (London, 1841), p. 11.
10. Samuel Fennell to Tredgold, 9 Dec. 1840, BFASS Papers, C 6/151.
11. John Sturge, p. 4. See also the comments by Joseph Sturge, *ibid*, p. 3.
12. Joseph Sturge to the Editor of the *British Emancipator*, 23 Jan, 1839.

although what it would be—and even whether, given their presuppositions, it was possible—remained a continuing source of perplexity.

The search lasted throughout the 1840s and 50s. During the early 1840s the Committee's immediate concern was preventing the trade from expanding, as shown by the valiant stand it took over the sugar question. This does not mean, however, that the search for a more direct way of attacking the trade was halfhearted. On the contrary, the Society was continually active, examining first one proposal, then another, but always failing to find satisfaction and falling back on its basic but essentially negative contention that universal emancipation offered the only effective remedy.

Among the earliest proposals to engage its attention was one put forward by David Turnbull. Turnbull had visited Cuba in 1838 and 1839 and had subsequently published an account of his experiences under the title *Travels in the West*. This work, which appeared early in 1840, quickly aroused interest in Whitehall and led to his appointment later that same year to the combined offices of British Consul and Superintendent of Liberated Africans in Havana. (He was removed from these offices in 1842 at the request of the Spanish authorities who accused him, probably justifiably, of attempting to organize a Negro rebellion.[13]) His plan, which he originally outlined in his *Travels* and later presented to the First World Anti-Slavery Convention, was to widen the jurisdiction of Mixed Commission Courts at Havana and Rio—hitherto concerned solely with cases involving slaves captured at sea—by allowing them to liberate slaves already landed. Newly arrived Negroes, he argued, could be detected at a glance. In any case it would be a relatively easy matter to establish registers of legally held slaves after which the burden of proof could be thrown on to the owners. If Spain and Brazil could be persuaded to negotiate new treaties incorporating these provisions—or add supplementary articles to existing ones—security in the possession of illicitly imported Negroes would cease and the trade would soon be abandoned.[14]

So far as it went, Turnbull's reasoning was impeccable. The fallacy, as Justice Jeremie and others were quick to point out,[15] was that Spain and Brazil would never agree to such arrangements if they included, as they necessarily would, surrendering a measure of their sovereignty. After all, they allowed the trade to continue. Why should they now agree to assign to a partially foreign body an authority which they themselves declined to exercise? For these reasons Sturge himself had little faith in

13. *The Times*, 4 April 1842; BFASS *Reporter*, 6 April 1842.
14. BFASS, *Proceedings of the General Anti-Slavery Convention of 1840*, pp. 251–6.
15. *Ibid*, pp. 256–8; *Westminster Review*, June–Sept. 1840, pp. 150–2.

the plan. On the other hand, nothing would be lost, and something might conceivably be gained, by adopting it. At the very least, it would be better than having no policy at all. It was therefore endorsed by the Society and became for a time part of its official programme. In July 1840 a deputation visited the Foreign Secretary, Lord Palmerston, and urged him to intercede with the Brazilian and Spanish governments. Palmerston, who was already familiar with the plan, undertook to see what could be done.[16] But nothing came of it and within a few years the scheme was forgotten.

The Society cherished hopes that the rulers of North Africa might prove more amenable to British influence. Before 1840 very little was known about the North African branch of the slave trade except that it was said to involve the sale of some 50,000 Negroes annually and was marked by some particularly horrifying features not met with in the West. But during the next few years a good deal more was learned, mainly through the explorations of James Richardson. The Society contributed a total of £55 towards the cost of these expeditions.[17] This was a small sum but since he travelled alone and virtually without equipment his expenses were negligible. By following the main caravan routes leading across the Sahara, he was able to show how the slave trains reached their destinations. In his articles for the *Reporter*, and later in his books, his style is matter-of-fact. Unlike many other travellers, both before and since, he had no romantic illusions about the bedouin. For those Negroes who fell into their hands, crossing the desert was even more of an ordeal than crossing the Atlantic; fewer died of disease but many more from exhaustion, thirst, or to gratify the whims of their captors. Like the carcases of oxen along the Oregon Trail, their skeletons lined the routes that led northward across the desert.[18]

To combat this traffic the Society looked to the intervention of the British consuls in North Africa, some of whom were known to have strong antislavery sympathies.[19] The first such attempt succeeded with amazing promptitude. In April 1841 Sir Thomas Reade, the consul at Tunis, broached the subject with the Bey, who responded by agreeing not only to ban the traffic but to abolish slavery altogether. Learning of the Bey's promise and, further, that orders had been given for the slave market to be torn down—as it duly was—the Society took heart and addresses

16. BFASS Minute Books, 31 July 1840.
17. *Ibid*, 20 Oct., 24 Nov., 8 Dec. 1843; 20 Jan. 1844; 17 Oct. 1845. Richardson died near Lake Chad on 4 March 1851.
18. James Richardson, *Travels in the Great Desert of Sahara in the Years of 1845 and 1846* (2 vols, London, 1848); see also BFASS *Reporter*, 1841–46, esp. 1846, pp. 133, 154, 180, 181.
19. See letters from Richardson to Scoble, BFASS Papers, C 21/32–40.

were dispatched thanking the Bey for his action and expressing the appreciation of the British people.[20] In the wake of this achievement—a perfectly genuine one as it turned out—an auxiliary society was established in Malta under the presidency of the Governor and with James Richardson as secretary. This society acquired an Arabic printing press and began printing and distributing pamphlets.[21] How long the organization lasted is uncertain, but it would appear to have lapsed soon after Richardson's return to England in September 1843. Although a number of other Arab rulers were approached at this time, they proved less accommodating.[22]

The Society had meanwhile been pursuing yet another course of action. Many had long suspected that British merchants were among those engaged in supplying goods and capital to slave traders, though precisely how this was done and to what extent deliberate connivance was involved remained a mystery.[23] Further evidence was needed, and this the Society set itself to obtain through its network of auxiliaries. The results were on the whole unilluminating, which suggests that perhaps British merchants were less guilty than had been claimed. Nevertheless, there was one case which seemed to bear out their contention.[24] In 1840 Pedro de Zulueta, a wealthy London merchant of Spanish origin, had been engaged by the Havana firm of Pedro Montez and Co. to act as an agent in the purchasing and outfitting of a vessel for a trading voyage to the coast of Africa. This vessel was subsequently seized near Cape Palmas by a British cruiser, taken to Sierra Leone and there condemned as a slaver. On being brought to trial—mainly at the instigation of Sir George Stephen—Zulueta claimed to have acted simply as an agent and denied all knowledge of the purposes for which the ship was used, though he admitted many previous dealings with firms engaged in the trade. He was acquitted, though many of the problems arising out of the affair remained unresolved. That he was as

20. *Ibid*, BFASS, *Proceedings of the General Anti-Slavery Convention of 1843*, pp. 4, 213–16, 312–13; BFASS Minute Books, 7 Jan. 1842; BFASS *Reporter*, 23 March 1842, p. 45.
21. BFASS *Reporter*, 1842, pp. 134, 137, 144, 161, 178, 202; Richardson to Tredgold, April, May 1842, BFASS Papers C 9/127–9.
22. BFASS Minute Books, 12 April 1844; Richardson to Scoble, 27 Nov. 1842, 9 March 1843; BFASS Papers, C 21/35, C 21/41. For correspondence between the Foreign Office and British Consuls on this subject see BFASS *Reporter*, 1 Sept. 1847.
23. See "Report on the Employment of British Capital in the Slave Trade", in BFASS, *Proceedings of the General Anti-Slavery Convention of 1840*, pp. 265, 515–18.
24. This was not the only case to receive the Society's attention. See, for example, the case of the *Mary*, BFASS Minute Books, 9 Sept., 4, 25 Nov. 1842; and of the *Caroline*, *ibid*, 5, 26 Dec. 1845, 2, 30 Jan., 27 Feb., 27 March, 3 July, 30 Oct. 1846; BFASS *Reporter*, 1845, pp. 226, 233–6; 1846, pp. 14, 27–8.

ignorant of his employer's business as he claimed may be doubted. On the other hand, it seems unlikely that he was as deeply implicated as abolitionists contended. Probably, like most international financiers, he was prepared to do as his clients asked without enquiring too closely into their affairs.[25]

Finding itself frustrated at every turn, the London Committee now took to actively attacking the government's blockade policy. In a strongly worded petition, signed by Thomas Clarkson and presented to the Commons in February, 1845, the Committee declared

That your Petitioners rejoice in the rapidly spreading conviction, that so long as slavery exists there is no reasonable hope of the annihilation of the slave trade; and that it is felt, not only by those who object upon principle to the use of an armed force, but by the public generally, to be impractical to suppress it by such means.

That a review of the experience of the last twenty-five years renders it obvious that some deeply afflicting evils have resulted from the application of coercive means for the extinction of the slave trade; among which may be enumerated a dreadful aggravation of the sufferings and horrors of the middle passage, a fearful increase in the rate of mortality on the number of unhappy victims shipped for the slave markets, and, on the part of Great Britain, a lamentable sacrifice of life and the expenditure of an enormous amount of treasure in vain.

Your Petitioners respectfully, yet urgently entreat your Honourable House to confine its exertions in future to the employment of such means as are of a pacific character and to concentrate all its efforts on the universal abolition of slavery, as the most effectual mode of extinguishing the nefarious traffic in human beings.[26]

The fact that Clarkson, the only surviving hero of the early struggles against the trade and its leading chronicler, was prepared to support such an attack lent it authority. All the same, the government would have had no difficulty in shrugging it off had it not happened to coincide with another of a much more formidable nature. The architect and leader of this new assault was William Hutt, member of Parliament for Gateshead. Like most of his followers, Hutt was not interested in suppression or—despite his assertions to the contrary—the Negro. His real concern was with economics. He belonged, in fact, to that class of doctrinaire free-trader who regarded all government interference in matters of international trade as an unwarranted meddling with a naturally ordained system.

25. BFASS, *The Trial of Pedro de Zulueta in the Central Criminal Court of the City of London* (London, 1844). An account of this trial, in Spanish, was also published by the Society. See also Minute Books, 25 Aug., 8 Dec. 1843; BFASS *Reporter*, 1843, pp 165–6, 192, 213, 220, 225; 1844, pp. 4, 9, 20, 28, 36, 94; 1845, pp. 120, 122–3.
26. In BFASS *Reporter*, 19 Feb. 1845, p. 28.

Above all, it was a waste of the taxpayer's money. *Laissez-faire* and the utmost economy in matters of public expenditure, he believed, were the cardinal virtues so far as government was concerned. The effect of such principles applied to the suppression policy can readily be imagined. Britain was interfering in a matter which in no way concerned her. Such knight-errantry, admirable in novels, was out of place in the field of international relations. How would Britain feel if, on some equally slender pretext, "British vessels, engaged in smuggling, had been chased, burnt, sunk or run ashore by American or Russian ships of war, fitted out to suppress their illicit operations with France?" Actions of this kind merely aroused national hatreds and jeopardized the position of legitimate traders. If Britain wanted objects on which to lavish her attention, there were plenty to be found at home. Since 1815, he calculated, she had spent no less than £21 million on suppressing the trade; during the same period the needs of her poor had been almost entirely neglected. No wonder foreign nations suspected her of sinister designs. They simply could not believe that she would be so foolish. The answer, therefore, was to withdraw the Squadron and "leave the trade to itself". If it expanded, so much the better, for then it would all the sooner be abandoned. The laws of supply and demand applied to it no less than to other forms of commerce. Once the demand had been satisfied, which would not take very long if the traders were given a free hand, the supply would cease. Already there were signs that the governments of Brazil and Cuba were becoming alarmed at the numerical disproportion between their white and Negro populations. Was it likely, ignorant though they were, that they would fail to see the danger of their situation? Some might think that his policy was inhumane. The truth was that it was much more humane than the present one. In fact, one might say that Britain, by seeking to interrupt the normal working of economic laws, had merely succeeded in prolonging the trade beyond the period of its natural duration. "It was our own blundering and ignorant humanity", he concluded, "which alone sustained the slave trade. To extinguish it, we should leave it alone."[27]

Hutt hoped that his arguments would appeal to humanitarians as well as economic realists. But it was the free-traders outside of Parliament who were most zealous in elaborating this aspect of the case. This they did by pointing first to the barbarous condition of Africa itself. So far, the *Economist* informed its readers, the slave trade was the only means of communication between Africa and the rest of the world. To seal it off would be doing the Africans a disservice. The obvious and humane answer

27. *Hansard, 81* (24 June 1845), 1156–72; see also his comments in *ibid, 96* (22 Feb. 1848), 1101.

was to establish, by means of properly negotiated treaties, a regulated slave traffic along the lines of the present unregulated one, with strong safeguards to prevent overcrowding on vessels and other unnecessary hardships. By pressing for such a policy Britain would be performing a service of great benefit to humanity, and not least to the native Africans themselves.[28]

The London Committee was understandably appalled. The idea of a legalized slave trade conducted under Britain's benevolent auspices contradicted everything they stood for.[29] Ironically enough, most of the evidence produced in support of the plan came from the abolitionists' own writings, a fact which Hutt happily cited as proof of his philanthropic intentions.[30] The most ironical twist of all, however, was the way free-traders now took over the arguments used against themselves during the sugar duties debates. So we find Hutt, supported by W. E. Gladstone, Milnes and others, all of whom had staunchly supported equalization, endorsing a resolution to the effect that the extent of the trade had so far "been mainly governed by the demand for the products of slave labour in the Markets of Europe" and quoting statistics to prove it.[31] The *Economist* which, in 1846, had dismissed as ill-founded the argument that a relaxation of the duties would lead to an increase in the slave trade,[32] was readily admitting two years later, that the "extension of the slave trade in 1847 was the immediate consequence of the abolition of the differential duties".[33] It was H. J. Baillie who carried this line of argument to its logical conclusion when in 1850 he told the Commons that by adopting equalization it had tacitly renounced all responsibility for suppressing

28. *Economist*, 26 Feb. 1848.
29. BFASS Minute Books, 11 Aug. 1848.
30. *Hansard*, 81 (24 June 1845), 1160.
31. *Comparative statement of the extent of the slave trade . . . and the prices of ordinary Havana sugar*

Date	Average price of sugar per cwt s	d	Rise (%)	Fall (%)	Amount of slaves exported	Increase in slave trade (%)	Decrease in slave trade (%)
1820–25	31	0			103,000		
1825–30	34	6	9		125,000	21	
1830–35	24	8		29	78,000		37
1835–40	29	3	19		135,000	73	
1840	25	4		13	64,114		53
1841–44	21	1		17	45,665		29
1845–47	25	7	18		65,743	44	

"Fourth Report from the Select Committee on the Slave Trade", PP, 1847/8, 22, 4.
32. *Economist*, 25 July 1846, p. 957.
33. *Ibid*, 14 Oct. 1848, p. 1161.

the trade. "By the Sugar Bill of 1846", he stated, "it had been boldly declared by the Government of this country that they had paid enough for their philanthropy."[34] It was absurd to encourage the trade with one hand while trying to suppress it with the other. His words were an almost exact paraphrase of the statement made by Lushington nine years before when the free-traders themselves had been under attack.

Despite their annoyance at the free-traders' blatant opportunism and alarm at the character of some of their proposals, the response of the Sturgites was not entirely hostile. It was plain that their newly proclaimed allies were not concerned with assisting the antislavery cause. They were using Broad Street's arguments in much the same way and for much the same reasons that the West Indians had previously used them—because it suited their immediate purpose to do so. There had been no change of heart. On the other hand, they did seem, on this occasion at least, to be on the right side. So for a time the London Committee gave Hutt its qualified support, though only with respect to removing the Squadron. In 1845 we find it "concurring to a certain extent with Mr Hutt in his view of the facts" but differing from him "as to the animus and intent of his motion".[35] There were much better reasons for opposing the present policy than because it raised the level of taxes. As the Committee saw it, there would be nothing wrong with levying such taxes if they were spent efficaciously, as for example on encouraging free labour production in India.[36] As Hutt's position became more radical, however, references to him became more guarded. In its annual report for 1848 it stated that while it was prepared to go along with the free-traders "to a point", it "dare not balance in the same scales the profits of merchants and manu- facturers against the liberty, the civilization and the happiness of their fellow men".[37]

Anyone who reads through the statements put out by the London Committee will see that at no point were its views identical with Hutt's. At the same time it is easy to see why many, who did not go to that trouble, should have supposed that they were. This certainly was the impression which Hutt himself laboured to give; it was also the impression conveyed in the newspapers which reported his speeches. To casual observers— which in practice meant most observers—it looked as though the national antislavery body had got itself into the incongruous position of supporting a group with proslavery designs. Nor was this view confined to outsiders.

34. *Hansard, 109* (19 March 1850), 1111.
35. BFASS *Reporter*, 9 July 1845.
36. "Memorial to Sir Robert Peel", *ibid*, 6 Aug. 1845.
37. *Ibid*, 1 June 1848.

Some of those who had supported the Society most staunchly over the sugar duties, such as Buxton's son, E. N. Buxton, and the editor of the *Patriot*, Josiah Conder, publicly dissociated themselves from its present course.[38] But the bitterest attack came from that other old abolitionist, Sir George Stephen. According to Stephen, a "distinct understanding" had been reached at the Society's inaugural meeting, that on the issue of the government's suppression policy "strict neutrality would be observed". By breaking this pledge, the Committee had finally forfeited the allegiance of all true abolitionists. "The Broad Street Committee", he concluded, "are a simple minority and their anti-coercion doctrines are a mere exception to the views of that great party which we hope yet to see reorganized."[39]

Actually, Stephen was more than a year behind the times, for when his article was published, in November 1849, the Society was already embarked on a new policy quite distinct from that which Hutt advocated. This involved threatening, and if necessary using, economic sanctions against countries which failed to live up to their treaty obligations. As it pointed out in a petition to the Commons, the potential effectiveness of this kind of approach had been greatly enhanced since the settlement of the sugar issue. Brazil and Cuba now had sizeable stakes in the British market and over the years could expect their trade with Britain to increase. Thus if Britain now confronted them with an ultimatum which showed that she was willing not only to reimpose the duties but, in the event of continued non-compliance, to place embargoes on other products too, the authorities there would be hard-pressed not to capitulate.[40]

This idea was an ingenious one. Not least among its advantages was the promise it held of healing the divisions in the movement's own ranks. After almost a decade of frustration and indecision here was a policy on which all might agree: no force would be required, no great expenditure necessary, and backed up by a determined government there were good reasons for supposing that it would succeed. Among those customarily associated with the cause it met with general approval. Even E. N. Buxton, who only a short time before had been berating the Society for its anti-coercionist doctrines, rallied to its support. A special publicity fund was established to which he and others contributed generously.[41] The task of consolidating the movement's ranks was further helped by the Society's

38. BFASS Minute Books, 30 Oct. 1846; BFASS *Reporter*, 1 Dec. 1849.
39. *Ibid*, 1 Dec. 1849; see also Sir George Stephen, *The Negro Trade Considered in Connection with the African Blockade* (London, 1849) and *Anti-Slavery Recollections*, p. 210.
40. BFASS *Reporter*, 1 Feb. 1849.
41. BFASS Minute Books, 10, 23 Feb. 1849. Buxton undertook to contribute £200, Samuel Gurney £100, and Sturge, Alexander and Josiah Eaton £50 each.

critical attitude towards Hutt. This may have been dictated partly by considerations of political expediency. The principal reason, however, was its belated realization that his attack on the treaty system was as subversive from its standpoint as from the government's. Economic coercion no less than physical coercion depended on maintaining the view that other powers had obligations which they were pledged to honour.[42]

Between 1848 and 1852 Broad Street waged a vigorous campaign on behalf of this policy. All the techniques used in the past were brought into play: petitions were circulated, ministers interviewed, advertisements put in the newspapers, lecture tours organized. Two pamphlets were published by the Society, *The Slave Trade and Its Remedy* (London, 1848) and *Slavery and The Slave Trade* (London, 1849) setting forth its views in detail. But to no avail. The public remained unconvinced that the government would go back on its sugar policy, still less that it would put itself in a position where it might be forced to adopt even more draconian measures. Within Parliament the campaign had even less impact. There the lines were clearly drawn between the coercionists and the anti-coercionists. To the former, the Society's pacifist sympathies and long history of opposition to the Squadron made its present position suspect, while to the latter the notion of interfering with the natural workings of the economy by introducing a system of embargoes was anathema. In consequence the Sturgites found themselves ignored by both.

The history of this parliamentary struggle is already so well known it may be passed over briefly.[43] During the years 1845–52, successive committees representing both Houses carried out elaborate enquiries into suppression in the course of which they interviewed practically everyone—ministers, Foreign Office officials, naval personnel, judges of courts of arbitration, ex-consuls, abolitionists—whose experience or views seemed remotely relevant. The result was a mass of evidence which threw much light on how the trade was being conducted and what practical steps had so far been taken to combat it.[44] The crucial questions, however, remained unanswered: was Britain's policy proving effective or was it, as many now believed, merely adding to the horrors? Above all, was it worth Britain's while to persevere? On these issues, the government and its critics remained as divided as ever. The climax of the struggle came in March 1850, as a result of a motion by Hutt calling on Britain to open negotiation with the United States and France with a view to obtaining

42. *Ibid*, 22, 27 Feb. 1850; BFASS *Reporter*, 1 March 1850.
43. See the works by Mathieson and Lloyd cited above.
44. This evidence and the Committee's conclusions will be found in PP, 1847/8, *22*; 1849, *19*; 1850, *9*; 1852/3, *39*.

her release from her obligation to maintain an African Squadron. (Neither of these countries really cared whether Britain kept the Squadron, which she had agreed to do simply as a *quid pro quo*, and would have been pleased to see their own obligations in this respect ended.) Both sides interpreted this motion as a test of confidence. Support for it came from the free-traders, led as usual by Bright and Cobden, and from W. E. Gladstone, a recent convert and the most formidable figure so far to have joined the anti-coercionist ranks. Both Russell and Palmerston gave notice of their intention to resign should it be approved. Their firmness carried the day; after a long debate, which rehearsed all the familiar arguments, it was defeated by 232 votes to 154.[45] Although the issue continued to smoulder for a year or two longer Hutt was never again able to fan it into flames.

What finally decided the issue, and destroyed the free-traders' case, was not parliamentary argument but the suppression of the Brazilian trade. Ever since 1846, when that branch of the traffic had so abruptly begun to expand, rumours had been reaching Britain of growing hostility to the traders within Brazil itself. As with much of the early opposition to the trade in North America, humanitarianism was not the principal or even a very important factor. Many were alarmed at the increasing imbalance between the races. Those who already had all the slaves they wanted did not wish others to have them. Opponents of the Government resented the political influence of the traders, a wealthy group more Portuguese than Brazilian, and one which displayed a marked indifference to the country's problems. There was also a widespread belief that the recent influx of Negroes had caused the outbreaks of yellow fever which had recently been sweeping through Brazilian cities. These rumours, combined with the needling of critics in Britain and the government's recent triumph over them, encouraged Palmerston to take a bolder line. Up to this time Britain's cruisers had punctiliously observed the letter of the law. He now instructed them to pursue slavers into Brazil's territorial waters. With no refuge to go to, those vessels were helpless. British cruisers not only went into Brazilian harbours after their prey, but destroyed barracoons along the coast and even sent expeditions into the interior. Individual traders were reported to have had their entire fleets wiped out. These events, as might be expected, caused a sensation in Rio, whose own harbour was invaded on more than one occasion. Protests were sent to the British ambassador and a number of British nationals were mobbed. But in general Brazilians remained remarkably unperturbed by this invasion of their territory. Britain's actions also received a surprising amount of support in the Brazilian legislature which, in September 1850, finally

45. *Hansard, 109* (19–20 March 1850), 1093–1186.

got around to ratifying the article in the Anglo-Brazilian treaty of 1826 declaring the slave trade to be piracy.[46] The end now came quickly. In 1850 some 23,000 slaves were imported, mainly during the first half of the year; in 1851 the number dropped to 3,000; in 1852 to 800; and in 1853 importations ceased altogether. In August that same year a Commons' Committee for the first time unanimously endorsed the suppression policy.

While the supporters of the Anti-Slavery Society could hardly disapprove of these results they could not bring themselves to endorse the methods used. Like the free-traders, they found the ground cut away beneath them. Their campaign for the adoption of economic sanctions was abandoned in October 1852.[47] The one principle to which they had consistently adhered, the futility of seeking to put down the traffic by means of coercion, had been discredited. In fairness to them it should be remembered that the policy which finally triumphed (although patently non-pacifist) was not the traditional blockade policy, and that but for changes in Brazil it might never have been attempted, or, if it had been, would very likely have failed. It is worth noting that similar steps were not taken against Cuba. It was thus possible to see what had happened as primarily a Brazilian achievement. This at least was how the London Committee chose to interpret it. Letters of congratulation were sent to the Archbishop of Bahia and to Dr Leite, President of the recently established Brazilian Society for the Suppression of the Slave Trade, urging them to turn their attention to the abolition of slavery itself.[48] The replies received were encouraging and further exchanges followed. Here they could feel that they were doing something useful. But with respect to what was left of the slave trade—the Cuban branch—they no longer had a policy. All they could do was to wait and see what happened.

46. Mathieson, *Great Britain and the Slave Trade*, pp. 128–35; Leslie Bethell, *The Abolition of the Brazilian Slave Trade: Britain, Brazil, and the slave trade question, 1807–1869* (Cambridge, 1970), pp. 267 ff.
47. BFASS Minute Books, 1 Oct. 1852.
48. BFASS Minute Books 2 April, 10 May, 6 Aug. 1852; 7 Feb., April 1853. A copy of the letter addressed to the Archbishop will be found in BFASS *Reporter*, 1 Dec. 1852.

10

Relations with abolitionists in Europe and America 1840–1850

Working with foreign abolitionists, the British soon discovered, was not an easy task. Initially hopes were high. "The French, the Dutch, the Dane, the Spaniard, the Brazilian and the American", declared the *Reporter*, "have felt the influence of the extinction of slavery in the British Colonies on their respective systems as the shock of an earthquake is felt in distant regions. . . . They look on us as conquerors; they have read their destiny."[1] Native reformers, it was assumed, would now hurry forward to continue the work which Britain had begun. Already there was substantial evidence that this was happening in France and America. Elsewhere the first signs had yet to appear but few doubted that they would.[2] It was also taken for granted that these foreign abolitionists would look to

1. BFASS *Reporter*, 15 Jan. 1840.
2. BFASS, *Proceedings of the World Anti-Slavery Convention of 1840*, pp. 100–2, 148–88.

Britain for guidance and support. That some might be reluctant to do so or that assistance when given might actually prove a liability was something that simply did not occur to most British abolitionists, although Buxton and Suffield, as we have seen, had warned that this might happen. There was, however, nothing in the history of Britain's own struggle to prepare for the intense hostility felt by foreigners at any suggestion of outside interference in their domestic affairs. Foreign abolitionists were more aware of the danger. "They see everywhere", wrote C. A. Bissette of his fellow countrymen, "the influence of England and the absurd idea paralyses the efforts of men of faith."[3] Bissette was a Frenchman, but he could equally well have been a Dutchman, a Spaniard, a Brazilian or an American.

But in the late thirties these difficulties were not yet apparent. British abolitionists regarded the movements developing elsewhere as simple extensions of their own and what they saw gave them confidence. At this time their highest hopes were pinned on France. Guizot, whose acquaintance they had made not long before when he had attended an antislavery rally in Exeter Hall, now led the Government. It was also known that he had sent a personal note to Thomas Clarkson assuring him that it was his country's intention to abolish slavery in the very near future—probably within a year.[4] Similar assurances came from the members of the French delegation to the 1840 Convention. M. Isambert who led the delegation told the Convention that there were some 265,000 slaves held in France's colonies. Because of domestic political factors the Government had been obliged to discourage public agitation. Nevertheless it was, with the help of various commissions, looking into ways of securing emancipation. At that very moment the French Assembly had before it reports from two such bodies, both strongly in favour of giving the slaves their freedom. His British friends, he concluded, could consider the issue already decided.

In fact the position in France at this time was very like that in Britain during the late 1820s.[5] Politicians had agreed that emancipation was desirable but few were prepared to press for its accomplishment. Louis-

3. Bissette to Scoble, Paris, 19 April 1844, BFASS Papers, C 13/117.
4. Benjamin Robert Haydon, *The Autobiography and Memoirs of Benjamin Robert Haydon, 1786–1846* (ed. Tom Taylor with an introduction by Aldous Huxley, new edn, 2 vols, London, 1926) *2*, 694–5; see also the comments by Joseph Sturge in Frederick Douglass, *Report of a Public Meeting to Receive Frederick Douglass*, p. 3.
5. The nature of the French situation at this time is described in Victor Schoelcher's *Histoire de l'Esclavage Pendant les Deux Derniers Années* (Paris, 1847); Augustin Cochin's *The Results of Emancipation* (English translation by M. L. Booth, 3rd edn, Boston, 1863), and Gaston Martin's *L'Abolition de l'Esclavage, 27 Avril 1848* (Paris, 1948). These works deal mainly with events at the government level.

Philippe explained his own views to Tredgold, Madden and another British abolitionist, the Reverend Dr Wright, in an audience which he gave them in May 1840. Before embarking on emancipation, he believed, attention should be paid to ameliorating slavery. Once that had been done, France could begin considering how the slaves might best be set at liberty. He himself favoured a two stage process not unlike that adopted by Britain.[6] At the time, little importance was attached to these remarks. Probably British abolitionists did not realize how far he was the real head of his own government. Only later, when it became clear that these were also the views of the French Ministry, did their significance sink in.[7]

The first real indication that all was not well with the French movement came two years later. Early in March 1842 a delegation of twenty-two British abolitionists visited Paris to confer with their French colleagues, only to find upon arrival that the anticipated public meetings had been cancelled by decree of the Minister of the Interior.[8] Sturge, who was among the delegates, expressed his indignation by turning down an invitation to dine with Guizot and returned to England in high dudgeon.[9] Thereafter, the reports from Paris spoke of a steadily worsening situation. "The position in France", wrote Isambert in July 1843, "is very bad and on the question of the abolition of slavery and on all other questions of liberty things were much more liberal during the last years of the Restoration."[10] Another correspondent assured Scoble that the intention behind Guizot's promises now stood revealed: it had been to lull the abolitionists into a sense of complacency while arrangements were being made to suppress all forms of protest by force.[11] These views were confirmed by British abolitionists who visited Paris. "I cannot speak very cheeringly of the prospect here", wrote G. W. Alexander in March 1844. "Scoble is more hopeful. I do not, however, despair. We must work in faith when we do not see very bright prospects."[12] What particularly galled both British and French observers was the fact that the Government's delays seemed to be the result not of pro-slavery conviction, but of simple lack of resolution. As the Duc de Broglie, President of the *Société pour*

6. BFASS *Reporter*, 20 May 1840.
7. See, for example, Sturge's comments on the King's attitude in Frederick Douglass, *Report of a Public Meeting to Receive Frederick Douglass*, p. 3.
8. BFASS *Reporter*, 23 March, 6 April 1842.
9. Richard, *Memoirs of Joseph Sturge*, p. 346.
10. Isambert to Madden, Paris, 8 July 1843, in T. M. Madden, ed., *The Memoirs, Chiefly Autobiographical, from 1798 to 1866, of R. R. Madden* (London, 1891), p. 206.
11. C. A. Bissette to Scoble, Paris, 25 July 1843, BFASS Papers, C 13/116.
12. G. W. Alexander to the British and Foreign Anti-Slavery Society, Paris, 14 March 1844, *ibid*, C 12/51.

l'Abolition de l'Esclavage observed: "To wait is wise on condition we wait for something; but to wait for the sake of waiting, to wait through pure carelessness or pure irresolution, for lack of possessing enough good sense and enough courage to set to work, is the worst of all resolves and the most certain of all dangers."[13]

Fifteen years earlier, finding themselves in a similar position, British abolitionists had turned to public agitation. They now urged the French to do the same. The response was not encouraging. In the first place, French abolitionists were much less well prepared for such an undertaking than the British had been. There was, in fact, only one antislavery organization in France at this time, the highly aristocratic *Société pour l'Abolition de l'Esclavage*. This body, founded in 1834, possessed no auxiliaries and, as its Secretary readily admitted, exerted little influence outside the capital. In the second place, considerable doubt existed as to whether the Government would tolerate public agitation on so sensitive an issue.[14] Not easily deterred, Broad Street itself took the initiative by presenting the Paris organization, in the autumn of 1844, with two thousand copies of a pamphlet—a fifty-five page affair specially written for the occasion by G. W. Alexander and John Scoble and printed in Paris—entitled *Liberté Immédiate et Absolue ou Esclavage*.[15] Not content with this, it began subsidizing a new periodical put out by the Paris organization, the *Abolitioniste Française*. After the first few numbers had appeared, Scoble was able to report that it "could now stand alone" and the subsidies were discontinued.[16]

Nevertheless, Broad Street remained dissatisfied with the way in which the Paris organization was running things. Much more, it felt, might be done, especially in the provinces. Like Buxton's old Anti-Slavery Society, de Broglie's organization appeared too wishy-washy in its demands— immediatism was not one of its principles—and too bound up in the events of the capital. What France needed, the Sturgites believed, was something along the lines of the old Agency Committee. Might it not be possible, they began to wonder, to bypass Paris entirely and to appeal directly to the French people?

A preliminary investigation of antislavery sentiment in the French provinces was made by William Forster in the summer of 1845. He found much ignorance on the question, although he was encouraged by the interest and sympathy of some of the people with whom he had talked.

13. In Cochin, p. 85.
14. BFASS *Reporter*, 1 Sept. 1847; BFASS, *Proceedings of the General Anti-Slavery Convention of 1840*, p. 163.
15. BFASS Minute Books, 4 Oct. 1844.
16. *Ibid*, 3 Jan., 13 June, 17 Oct. 1845.

Further antislavery efforts in these areas, he reported, would be well repaid.[17] In October Scoble made a more extensive tour, which took him to Toulouse, Bordeaux and Nantes as well as to several smaller towns along the way. He told the Committee on his return that he had made many useful contacts and drawn up a preliminary plan of campaign. Especially valuable, he believed, would be the support of Professor de Félice of Montauban who had agreed to prepare a pamphlet on the essential sinfulness of slavery.

The plan proposed is first to publish M. de Félice's pamphlet, then to organize, and afterwards to move the Protestant Consistories and Conseils Genereaux throughout France to petition the Chambers, and then, by a succession of well-written and judicious pamphlets, to awaken every portion of society to take an interest in the question, to accomplish which the Friends of the Anti-Slavery Cause in France will require the cordial sympathy and general support of Abolitionists in Great Britain.[18]

Professor de Félice's pamphlet was published in April 1846. He had, he told Scoble, addressed it to the abolitionists of France and particularly to those whom he called "temporizing abolitionists" because they were prepared to put off abolition until some future time. His principal object was to show that the hope of mitigating conditions while retaining slavery was illusory.[19]

Over the next two years de Félice continued to report progress. No new antislavery societies were established, but he was pressing on with his petition campaign assisted by C. A. Bissette, the Negro editor of the *Revue des Colonies*, who was handling the Paris side of things. Bissette, who had already been in touch with the London Committee on a number of occasions, also sent encouraging reports. In Paris alone he had succeeded in collecting 6,000 signatures on behalf of one petition. He had also arranged for the Comte de Montalembert to present his petitions to the Assembly. He was sorry to say, however, that the *Société pour l'Abolition de l'Esclavage* had given him no support and seemed generally hostile to his and de Félice's efforts. For this reason they had decided to publish a new periodical, the *Revue Abolitioniste* as a rival to the conservative *Abolitioniste Française*. In it they intended to promulgate the general principles adopted by the British and to lay particular stress on immediatism.[20] Pleased to find that some Frenchmen shared its views,

17. *Ibid*, 4 July, 1 Aug. 1845.   18. *Ibid*, 17 Oct. 1845.
19. de Félice to Scoble, 11 April 1846, in BFASS *Reporter*, 1 May 1846; Guillaume de Félice, *Emancipation Immédiate et Complète des Esclaves: Appel aux Abolitionistes* (Paris, 1846).
20. Bissette to Scoble, Paris, 19 Jan. 1847, BFASS Papers, C 13/19; BFASS Minute Books, 22 Jan., 12 Feb. 1847.

the Committee began sending various small sums to Bissette to help with his petition campaign and also undertook to subsidize the *Revue Abolitioniste* by providing a monthly subsidy of 300 francs.[21] The first number appeared in March 1847 and was read with much approval in London.[22]

The Society's relations with the Paris organization had meanwhile become tenuous. Feeling that something might still be achieved in that quarter, Scoble, in January 1847, wrote to the Duc de Broglie urging a more positive policy.[23] The reply was a long time in coming and when it arrived turned out to be not from the Duc but from M. de Passy, the Society's vice-president. The contents, neverthless, were pleasing. "After too long hesitation", he wrote, "our Society has become convinced that, in simplifying its task and confining itself to demanding the immediate and complete emancipation of the Negroes, that task will advance more rapidly. . . . It gives us great pleasure . . . that on this fundamental point we now entirely agree with your Society."[24] Coupled with the reports from Bissette and de Félice, this produced a sense of cautious optimism in London. The *Reporter*, in January 1848, reviewing the previous year's events, observed that French abolitionists had never been more active, although it warned its readers that there were many obstacles yet to be overcome.[25]

The February Revolution of 1848 and the sudden elevation of several well-known liberals to office took British abolitionists, like everyone else, by surprise. So did the speed of the ensuing events. On 4 March the new Government established a commission to prepare a plan of emancipation "with the least possible delay". An Act decreeing complete freedom was promulgated on 27 April and took effect two months' later.[26] Broad Street regarded these events as a unique stroke of good fortune. Although it could claim no credit for them, it could claim that its principles had been vindicated. It was especially pleased to note that no compensation was to be paid to the slave owners.[27]

In September the following year Scoble visited Paris and talked to de Passy and de Tocqueville, now ministers of Finance and Foreign Affairs respectively, and also M. Isambert. Bearing in mind Britain's experiences, he urged Isambert in particular not to let the *Société pour l'Abolition de*

21. *Ibid*, 22 Jan., 27 Aug. 1847. Additional sums were contributed privately by Josiah Forster who also subsidized the printing of a tract by Bissette entitled *Martyrologie Coloniale* (Paris, 1847); *ibid*, 14 Jan. 1848.
22. BFASS *Reporter*, 1 April 1847.
23. Scoble to de Broglie, 23 Jan. 1847, *ibid*, 1 Nov. 1847.
24. Passy to Scoble, 16 Sept. 1847, *ibid*.
25. *Ibid*, 1 Jan. 1840.   26. Cochin, pp. 87–97.
27. See the letters of congratulation sent to France, BFASS Minute Books, 28 April 1848.

l'Esclavage lapse, as its services would very likely be needed in "preventing retrograde legislation".[28] Isambert promised to see what could be done but two months later wrote saying that this would not be possible because of "practical difficulties". The same purpose, he assured them, would be served by a newly established government commission to which he himself, de Passy and several other former members of the Paris organization had been appointed.[29] Broad Street did not trust government bodies whatever their composition. All the same, the information it received from the French colonies remained encouraging until the mid-fifties, when disquieting facts began to emerge about the way in which the freedmen were being treated and about the opening up of a new "immigrant slave trade" to the French colonies. There was nothing to suggest, however, that the behaviour of the Negroes was other than creditable and British abolitionists continued to cite the French experience as proof of their own contention that immediate emancipation was the right policy and that Negroes found little difficulty in adapting to freedom.[30]

Two other European countries also abolished slavery about this time, Sweden on the island of St Bartholomew in October 1847[31] and Denmark throughout her Caribbean possessions on 3 July 1848.[32] Slavery in the Dutch colonies was not abolished until 1863.[33] British abolitionists could claim no direct responsibility for any of these developments although they were active in promoting antislavery efforts in all these countries. Delegations from Broad Street had visited Sweden in 1843, Denmark in 1839, 1843 and 1847, and Holland on no less than eight occasions between 1840 and 1858.[34] They had also carried on an extensive correspondence with European sympathizers, plying them with addresses to their respective governments,[35] pamphlets[36] and, in the case of the Dutch movement, small subsidies.[37]

What effect all this had is problematical. There is no doubt, however, that on one occasion intervention proved decisive. In September 1842

28. *Ibid*, 28 Sept. 1849.
29. *Ibid*, 30 Nov. 1849.
30. *Ibid*, 26 Jan. 1849; BFASS *Reporter*, 1 June 1850, 1 Aug. 1851. For a discouraging account of the situation in the colonies see Victor Schoelcher, "The results of emancipation in the French West Indian colonies", *Anti-Slavery Advocate*, May 1855.
31. BFASS *Reporter*, 1 Dec. 1847.   32. *Ibid*, 1 June 1849.
33. BFASS Minute Books, 5 Sept. 1862.
34. Details of these visits will be found in the BFASS Minute Books and *Reporter*.
35. BFASS Minute Books, 27 Dec. 1839; 9, 27 Nov. 1840; 29 Jan. 1841; 9 Aug., 22 Nov. 1844; 1 Feb. 1856; 11 May 1859.
36. *Ibid*, 13 July 1849; 7 March 1851; 1 Dec. 1854; 1 Feb. 1856.
37. The Society, for instance, agreed to finance a tour of Holland by J. S. Mollet of Amsterdam. The sum granted is not mentioned: *Ibid*, 10 Aug. 1849.

Broad Street was shocked to learn that slaves were being held by the Moravian missionaries in the Dutch and Danish West Indies.[38] Protests were promptly sent to the leaders of the Moravian Missionary Society in Denmark and Holland.[39] Since the Moravians relied heavily upon the British for financial support their position was vulnerable. If Broad Street made a public issue of the fact that they were slaveholders, or, as it later threatened, circularized their British subscribers, they would find themselves in difficult financial straits.[40] Orders were therefore sent to the colonies instructing the missionaries to emancipate their slaves forthwith. In its *Annual Report* for 1846, the London Committee was able to report that these slaves had been freed.[41]

National jealousies proved on the whole less of an issue in Europe than in America, mainly because slavery itself was less of an issue. But as Bissette's comments show, it was a factor there also. In the spring of 1854, for example, the Dutch antislavery society turned down an offer by L. A. Chamerovzow, who had recently succeeded Scoble as Secretary of the British and Foreign Anti-Slavery Society, to visit Holland, giving as its reason the need for the Dutch movement to maintain a strictly national character. Chamerovzow did visit Holland later that year but refrained from holding public meetings.[42] In 1855 the Committee began corresponding with a new Dutch organization, the Amsterdam Young Men's Anti-Slavery Society. This body was anxious for British support and several visits by members of the London Committee were subsequently arranged.[43]

But encouraging though these European developments were, they were inevitably overshadowed by what was happening across the Atlantic. What most impressed British abolitionists about this American struggle was its sheer magnitude. Up to 1830 the American antislavery movement had been a small affair, committed to gradualist methods and drawing much of its support from the South. Most antislavery societies were allied in one way or another with the American Colonization Society whose programme was generally accepted as the best way of ridding the country of slavery. The new movement, which sprang up in the early thirties, was very different. It was essentially Northern—mainly, in fact, New England—

38. Knibb to Sturge, 20 July 1842, BFASS *Reporter*, 7 Sept. 1842; BFASS Minute Books, 17 April 1842.
39. BFASS Minute Books, 28 April, 28 July, 27 Oct., 24 Nov. 1843; 22 Nov., 6 Dec. 1844.
40. *Ibid*, 24 April 1846.   41. BFASS *Reporter*, 1 June 1846.
42. BFASS Minute Books, 3 March, 4 Aug. 1854; 15 June 1855.
43. *Ibid*, 19 Feb., 15 June 1855; 4 July, 3 Oct. 1856; 2 July, 3 Sept. 1858.

in membership, scornful of colonization and other gradualist methods, which were patently not working, and uncompromising in its view of slavery as a "sin". The parallels with the British movement are striking. The principal differences were in the problems to be overcome, which in the American case were altogether more formidable, and in the scale of the operations undertaken. The number of antislavery societies active in Britain at any one time, except possibly during the months immediately preceding the passage of the 1833 Act, had never exceeded 80 and their total membership 5,000;[44] the American Anti-Slavery Society in 1838 was able to claim 1,346 auxiliaries with a membership of 100,000.[45] At its height the British movement had supported six full-time paid agents;[46] as early as 1836 Weld and Stanton were claiming seventy. Even allowing for some exaggeration on the American side, it was plain that agitation was being conducted on a scale which made all previous efforts, including Britain's own, appear puny. Transatlantic observers were also impressed by the violence of the American reaction to these efforts. There had been nothing in Britain, or elsewhere, to compare with the anti-abolitionist mobs which in the 1830s roamed American cities, destroying printing presses and burning meeting halls. The accounts which appeared in the newspapers, and in the writings of George Thompson and Harriet Martineau, substantially increased the stature of the American abolitionists in the estimation of observers sympathetic to the cause. "The United States", declared Miss Martineau, "are the birth place of a far nobler abolition spirit than we have ever yet had to boast of." In quiet British rectories and country houses imaginations were stirred by tales of the abolitionists' heroism. To some they became almost legendary figures as to the young Irish visitor to the 1840 World Convention who noted in her diary, "Long life to these American abolitionists. They are a glorious crew. William Lloyd Garrison is one of God's nobility. I don't think I ever saw such an angelic, holy-looking face. . . . Wendell Phillips is delightful too, they are strong and fine and firm—they are American

44. These are probably overestimates. The British and Foreign Anti-Slavery Society would seem to have been more successful at organizing support at the local level than any of its predecessors, with the possible exception of the Agency Society whose records have not survived. Between 1839 and 1870 it received support from 85 provincial societies. Allowing for those which did not contribute, one arrives at a figure of around 100. Probably not more than half of these were active at any given time and many consisted of only a handful of members. Sir George Stephen's claim that there were 1,200 societies active at the end of 1832 (*Anti-Slavery Recollections*, p. 161) was made twenty years after the event, is otherwise unsubstantiated, and should therefore be treated with caution.
45. Dwight L. Dumond, *Antislavery, The Crusade for Freedom in America* (Ann Arbor, 1961) p. 258 and footnote.
46. *Ibid*, pp. 183–9; Stephen, *Anti-Slavery Recollections*, p. 143.

abolitionists, a new race of beings." This idolization of the American antislavery leaders—although less fulsomely expressed—played an important part in the formation of British antislavery attitudes and, as we shall see, resulted in one section of the British movement becoming little more than an extension of the American.[47]

Such responses were encouraged by the full and flattering tributes which American antislavery leaders paid to their British colleagues. "British Christians", Wendell Phillips told George Thompson in 1839, "are the sheet anchor of our cause."[48] The impressive attendance of American delegates at the World Convention of 1840 was formidable testimony to the importance which they still attached to their British connection. Given the position of abolitionists in America at the time, their attitude is readily understandable. Britain was the home of the most ambitious and successful antislavery experiment of the day. British abolitionists had achieved a status and respectability which they still lacked. Wilberforce, after all, had been given a state funeral in Westminster Abbey. More important, perhaps, was the fact that, despite wars and political differences, Britain was still the source of much that Americans looked up to and admired. As Emerson, in a speech commemorating British emancipation, once put it: "Our civility, England determines the style of, insomuch as England is the strongest of the family of existing nations, and as we are the extension of that people".[49] If therefore Britain could be united in its condemnation of American slaveholding, the American public could hardly fail to be moved. This was a view which American abolitionists continually stressed in their messages to their British allies. As usual, it was most pungently put by the *Liberator:*

Let the general mind of England become thoroughly possessed of the facts of American slavery . . . and the hand of destiny will have written the words of doom upon the walls of our Babylon.——When public sentiment is such in the British Islands, that no slaveholder can be received into any pulpit or at any communion table . . . when it is the avowed resolution of the nation that no slaveholder can be received at court, in a public capacity, when the force of enlightened public opinion is brought to bear not only on slavery, but on pro-slavery, in all the relations of public and private life, of the court, the church and the dinner table; then the circle of fire which has already been kindled around the scorpion will grow hotter and hotter, and close nearer and nearer, until it will be compelled to bury its sting in its own brain, and rid the world, by a blessed suicide, of its monstrous existence.[50]

47. Martineau, *Martyr Age of the United States*, p. 15; comments by Maria Waring, June 1840, Webb MSS, Garrison Papers.
48. Phillips to Thompson, 29 July 1839, Garrison Papers.
49. Emerson, *Address Delivered in the Court House in Concord on the First of August, 1844*, p. 18.
50. *Liberator*, 18 Sept. 1846, p. 146.

Garrison's premise, like that of innumerable other American antislavery leaders who expressed themselves on the subject, was that Britain had the power, if only she could be persuaded to use it, to destroy American slavery. She must therefore be urged to give American abolitionists all the support she could. "How great, how awful is her responsibility", wrote one, "if she does not exert this moral power without delay."[51]

These appeals were hardly necessary. Once British abolitionists turned from British slavery to slavery in the world at large, their attention inevitably focused on America. Thomas Clarkson described to the painter Benjamin Robert Haydon, to whom he sat for the official portrait of the 1840 Convention, how this happened in his case. It had occurred shortly after the ending of apprenticeship. He had, he said, been sleeping one night when he was awakened by a voice saying "You have not done all your work. There is America". The room was empty. He sat up in bed and at that moment there occurred to him the idea of writing a pamphlet against American slavery. He began writing the following morning and worked eight hours a day until he was finished.[52] This pamphlet was later published under the title *A Letter to the Clergy of Various Denominations* (London, 1841). Since Clarkson was not a man given to visions, the story is the more revealing.

Other British abolitionists, although in less dramatic fashion, underwent similar conversions at this time.[53] What particularly aroused them was the sheer inconsistency of the American position. How could a country, which more than any other boasted of its freedom and democracy, justify its status as the largest single slaveholding power in the western hemisphere? This, of course, was precisely what the American abolitionists themselves were saying. In Britain the most virulent attacks often came from those who, like Sturge, felt most attracted to the United States. "So long as slavery and the distinction of colour exist", he wrote after his visit there in 1841, "America will always be pointed at with the finger of scorn for her flagrant violation of all truth and consistency."[54] Daniel O'Connell, whose admiration for American ideals was equally strong, expressed himself even more bitterly, observing on one occasion that "of all men living an American citizen who is the owner of slaves is the most despicable".[55] His speeches at the time of the ending of apprentice-

51. E. M. Davis to Elizabeth Pease, Philadelphia, 11 Dec. 1839, Garrison Papers.
52. Haydon, 2, 694–5.
53. See *Slavery in America* (Nos. 1–14, London, July 1836—Aug. 1837).
54. Joseph Sturge, *A Visit to the United States in 1841*, p. 176.
55. Daniel O'Connell, *The Irish Patriot: Daniel O'Connell's Legacy to Irish Americans* (Philadelphia, 1863), p. 8.

ship and at the first World Convention are memorable chiefly as pieces of anti-American invective.[56]

Seeing eye to eye on so many issues meant that relations between the two movements became remarkably close. The British, of course, were concerned mainly with arousing public opinion in Britain and the Americans with arousing public opinion in the free states. But the methods were much the same in both cases. So also, to a surprising extent, were the people. Over the years, many British abolitionists visited America— George Thompson in 1834–35, 1850–51 and 1863–67, R. R. Madden in 1835, J. J. Gurney in 1837–40, John Scoble in 1839 and 1851, Joseph Sturge and John Candler in 1841 and G. W. Alexander in 1851.[57] Charles Stuart spent more time in the United States than in England.[58] Visits by American abolitionists to Britain were even more numerous. Between 1839 and 1860, practically all the leading American antislavery figures made pilgrimages across the Atlantic, some on more than one occasion. The two World Conventions were responsible for drawing many of them over, but others came at other times and some, like Henry C. Wright and Frederick Douglass, stayed for long periods.[59] These visits usually meant, whether they were intended to or not, lecture tours. In 1840 James G. Birney and Henry Stanton were taken by Scoble on a tour that resulted in their addressing meetings in twenty-six towns.[60] Garrison's visits in 1840 and 1846 were equally strenuous.[61] The leaders of the two movements also corresponded, often at great length, about affairs in their respective countries.[62] It was common practice to exchange periodicals and to reprint articles of particular interest. Pieces taken from American

56. These are reported in, respectively, *British Emancipator*, 22 Aug. 1838, and BFASS *Reporter*, 17 June 1840.
57. W. P. and F. J. Garrison, *William Lloyd Garrison*, *1*, 434; *2*, 58; *3*, 304, 333; Madden, *Memoirs*, p. 96 ff; J. J. Gurney, *Memoirs of Joseph Gurney*, ed., J. B. Braithwaite (2 vols, Norwich, 1854), *2*, 82–154; Sturge, *A Visit to the United States in 1841;* Abel and Klingberg, *A Side-Light on Anglo-American Relations*, pp. 80, 255, 313–19.
58. As a retired East Indian official with a pension of around $800 a year he was free to move back and forth across the Atlantic. See the references to him in Barnes, *Antislavery Impulse* and in Barnes and Dumond, *Weld-Grimké Letters*. There is also a certain amount of material on Stuart in the Estlin Papers, Dr Williams's Library, London; the Anti-Slavery Papers, Rhodes House, Oxford, and in the Boston Public Library antislavery collections. In 1838 he visited the West Indies in company with Scoble and from 1840–1843 spent a good deal of time in England. He died in Canada in 1865.
59. Wright was in Britain almost constantly from 1841 to 1847, Douglass from the autumn of 1845 until the spring of 1847.
60. Abel and Klingberg, p. 71, note 37.
61. W. P. and F. J. Garrison, *2*, 366–420, *3*, 150–86.
62. See the Abel and Klingberg volume cited above. The originals of these letters and much other relevant material will be found in the Anti-Slavery Collection,

publications appeared in almost every issue of the *Reporter* and its own were widely reprinted in the United States.

Efforts were made to pass this information on to the general public by means of tracts and lectures. During its early years the British and Foreign Anti-Slavery Society published three pamphlets on America: *Slavery and the Internal Slave Trade in the United States of North America* (London, 1841), *An Epitome of Anti-Slavery Information* (London, 1843) and *American Slavery* (London, 1846). The second World Anti-Slavery Convention, its name notwithstanding, was virtually a conference on American slavery. Abolitionists also sought to enlist the cooperation of the various denominational bodies. Several of these had, in fact, already raised their voices against American slaveholding. In 1833 British Baptist leaders had urged the American Baptist Convention to support antislavery efforts and the English representatives at the 1836 Methodist General Conference in Cincinnati had also called for an antislavery stand.[63] Many British churchmen, however, had mixed feelings about such tactics fearing that indiscriminate agitation would destroy good relations between the churches of the two countries. The Rev. F. A. Cox and the Rev. J. Hoby, who attended the 1835 Baptist Triennial Convention in Richmond, Virginia, adopted a neutral position on the grounds that they were guests in a foreign country and that to have done otherwise would have wrecked the convention.[64] Most abolitionists roundly condemned their pusillanimity, the more so because Dr Cox happened to be on the committee of the Universal Abolition Society. There is no doubt, however, that the churches were peculiarly sensitive to the moral dilemmas raised by slavery. The abolitionists addressed many of their appeals specifically to churchmen; both of Thomas Clarkson's pamphlets on American slavery, *A Letter to the Clergy of Various Denominations*, already mentioned, and *A Letter to Such Professing Christians in the Northern States of America as have No Practical Concern with Slave-Holding* (London, 1844) were directed at this audience, as was also the London Committee's *American Slavery*.

As regards more direct forms of action, British abolitionists laboured under obvious disabilities. In this respect, however, their position was not

Rhodes House, Oxford. There are many letters reflecting the Garrisonian connections in the Garrison, Weston and May Papers, Boston Public Library, and in the Estlin collection, Dr Williams Library, London.

63. Lorman Ratner, *Powder Keg: Northern opposition to the antislavery movement, 1831–1840* (New York, 1968) pp. 107, 110.

64. F. A. Cox and J. Hoby, *Baptists in America: a narrative of the deputation from the Baptist Union in England to the United States and Canada* (London, 1836), pp. 67–73.

essentially different from that of the American abolitionists themselves. Because of the peculiar structure of the Federal Government and the way slavery existed under the protection of state law within the individual states there was no way of attacking it directly. To this extent the citizen of Manchester and the citizen of Boston were almost equally powerless. What they could do—and it was towards this that abolitionists directed their efforts—was to oppose the slaveholding interests on a number of marginal issues. Some of these, like the citizen's right to petition Congress and to transmit antislavery material through the mails, were matters of academic interest outside the United States. But there were others which concerned the British almost as much as the Americans.

The most important of these questions was Texas. The Texan Revolution of 1836 had provoked a wide variety of responses around the world. Mexicans still claimed Texas as part of Mexico. Southern planters were attracted by the possibilities offered for agrarian expansion and wished to see her absorbed into the United States. The Texans, fearing reconquest by Mexico, would have been delighted to have this happen. But although Texas was a tempting prize, the American government was reluctant to take the necessary steps, partly because of the opposition of Northern Whigs who did not wish to see the balance between the sections altered to their disadvantage, but mainly because it did not want the country to become embroiled in a war with Mexico. Britain, for her part, was anxious for Texas to remain independent, hoping that she would serve as a check on the growing might of the United States and also provide a base from which to extend her own trade and influence in the Americas.[65]

American and British abolitionists were naturally reluctant to allow Southerners their way. It was already well known that cotton used up land so rapidly that the South needed to expand in order to survive. Their plans were somewhat complicated, however, by the fact that the Texans held slaves. Although technically abolished by the Mexican Congress in 1830, slavery had continued to exist and had been recognized by the new constitution. Thousands of small planters from the Southern states had already begun moving across the border and there were rumours of an expanding slave trade with Cuba.[66] The attitude which British abolitionists should adopt towards these developments was outlined by O'Connell in a letter to Sturge as early as August 1839. The aim, he explained, should be twofold: to keep Texas independent and to get rid of slavery so that, like Canada, she would provide "an asylum for people

65. R. A. Billington, *Westward Expansion, The History of the American Frontier* (second edn, New York, 1960), pp. 501–2.
66. DuBois, *Suppression of the African Slave Trade to the United States*, pp. 165–6.

of colour".[67] As a first step Britain should make plain that recognition of Texas would be conditional upon emancipation. A pamphlet by John Scoble setting forth these objectives was issued in December under the title *Texas, its Claims to be Recognized as an Independent Power by Great Britain*. Since he had only just returned from a visit to the United States, Scoble was also able to incorporate the views then current among American abolitionists. He thus set out to show that the Texan revolution was the result of a deliberate conspiracy on the part of American slaveholders. Their aim had been to wrest this large and valuable territory from Mexico in order legally to reinstitute slavery, to provide themselves with new lands and a market for their surplus slaves, and ultimately, through annexation, to swing the balance of power within the nation to their own advantage. The Texans themselves were a group of unprincipled ruffians. By affording them recognition without making emancipation a precondition, Britain would be jeopardizing her own position as the leading advocate of freedom in the world and at the same time losing a valuable opportunity for striking a blow against slavery and the American slave system. A deputation from the Society formally communicated these views to the Melbourne Government.[68]

The Texans were already sharply conscious of the way in which the slavery issue had interfered with their plans for obtaining British recognition. As early as July 1838 J. P. Henderson, the Texan agent in London, had written that "the British Ministry are convinced that Texas is entitled to recognition, but they dare not recognize for fear of offending the O'Connell abolition party who now in fact control that Government".[69] Henderson's failure and subsequent recall were noted with satisfaction by the *Reporter* in March 1840, which also quoted from an article in an American newspaper which attributed both developments to those "two meddlesome fellows, Sturge and Scoble".[70] But this triumph was short-lived. Britain's desire for an independent Texas meant that she could not delay too long in offering recognition, particularly once Texas had been recognized by the United States. Thus in November it was announced that a series of treaties had been concluded with the new republic. The London Committee, unaware even that negotiations had been going on, responded with indignation and a protest was promptly dispatched to

67. 26 Aug. 1839, in *British Emancipator*, 4 Sept. 1839.
68. BFASS Minute Books, 28 Sept., 29 Oct. 1839.
69. Henderson to Secretary of State, 26 July 1839, in G. P. Garrison, ed., *Diplomatic Correspondence of the Republic of Texas* (in 3 pts, Am. Hist. Assn. Annual Reports for 1907–9), *3*, 1261.
70. In BFASS *Reporter*, 25 March 1840, p. 56. The name of the American newspaper is not given.

the Foreign Secretary.[71] Palmerston replied that he had acted to uphold Britain's true interests and that in any case the treaties had no bearing on the issue of Texan slavery.[72]

American abolitionists had meanwhile been urging the British to use their influence to persuade their government to offer economic inducements to the Texans to give up slavery. The architect and leading exponent of this policy was Stephen Pearl Andrews of Massachusetts. His plan, he stated, was for Britain to "buy up" Texas. She should "lavish money upon the undertaking, for she can never take a step so directly tending to the extinction of slavery and the slave trade throughout the world".[73] Although the idea appealed, nothing much was done about it until the summer of 1843, when the American delegation to the second World Convention arrived in England. Texas naturally came in for a good deal of discussion on the convention floor and resolutions on the subject were proposed and approved.[74] These resolutions, along with a memorial from Broad Street, were presented by a deputation to Lord Aberdeen, the new Foreign Secretary, on 12 July.[75] Both the resolutions and the memorial were somewhat vague, merely calling on Britain to use her influence to obtain Texan abolition, but failing to specify the means to be used. This deficiency, however, was made up for by Lewis Tappan, leader of the American delegation, who, acting as spokesman for the group, expounded at length—as he had done earlier to the Convention—upon the expediency of Britain's granting a loan to Texas on condition that the Texan government would agree to undertake emancipation. Aberdeen told Tappan that this was a matter he was already looking into. Gratified at this news the deputation departed.[76]

The Texan government had long been aware that the best way of achieving annexation was to play on America's suspicions of Britain. These events, therefore, were watched with a keen eye by Ashbel Smith, Texan chargé d'affaires at Paris and London. Smith was a shrewd diplomatist. As early as the previous January he had sought to arouse Southern fears by outlining in a letter to Isaac Van Zandt, the Texan chargé d'affaires in Washington, the dangerous position in which the South would find itself in the event of Texas becoming a free-soil republic under British protection.

71. BFASS Minute Books, 2 Dec. 1840.
72. Foreign Office to BFASS, 14 Dec. 1840, BFASS Papers, C 161/17.
73. Andrews to Tappan, 15 Oct. 1839, in Tappan to Sturge, 19 Oct. 1839, in Abel and Klingberg, p. 60.
74. BFASS, *Proceedings of the General Anti-Slavery Convention of 1843*, pp. 296–307.
75. BFASS *Reporter*, 26 July 1843.
76. *Ibid*, BFASS Minute Books, 28 July 1843.

The independence of Texas and the existence of Slavery in Texas is a question of life and death to the slave holding states of the American Union. Hemmed in between the free states on their northern border and a free Anglo-Saxon State on their southern border and sustained by England, their history would soon be written. *The establishment of a free state in the territory of Texas is a darling wish of England for which scarcely any price would be regarded as too great. The bargain once struck, what remedy remains to the South?*

The British abolitionists, he added, were a ruthless group of men who would stop at nothing in their efforts to gain control over Texas. It was already well known that they had helped finance the construction of the two Mexican cruisers then blockading the Texan coast, the *Guadalupe* and the *Montezuma*, by purchasing Mexican bonds.[77] These facts, he told Van Zandt in a private note, should at once be brought to the attention of Calhoun and other Southern leaders.[78]

Much of this was pure invention. At the time of writing, the British government had not indicated that Texan emancipation was one of its official aims nor were the British abolitionists at that time agitating the issue. Whether they were, as alleged, holders of Mexican bonds is not revealed, but considering their pacifist views it seems unlikely. The events of the summer, however, gave Smith the material he needed. He attended the World Convention, mixed with the delegates, and quizzed Aberdeen on his interview with the Tappan deputation.[79] The results of these investigations he relayed to Washington in a series of dispatches deliberately designed to arouse Southern apprehensions. On 19 June, for example, he wrote directly to Calhoun that he had it on good evidence that Britain's purpose was "to make Texas a refuge for runaway slaves from the United States, and eventually a negro nation, a sort of Hayti on the continent, to be more or less . . . under the protection of the British Government".[80] These claims were backed up by General Duff Green of Kentucky who happened at that time to be passing through London. Green, as we have seen, was an outspoken critic of British antislavery policies and had influence in American government circles. In July, he wrote to Secretary of State Upshur that he had been "authorized by the Texan minister to say to you that Lord Aberdeen has agreed that the British Government will guarantee interest (upon a loan) upon condition that the Texan

77. Smith to Van Zandt, 25 Jan. 1843, in Garrison, *Diplomatic Correspondence*, 3, 1106–8.
78. Smith to Van Zandt, 26 Jan. 1843, in Harriet Smither, "English abolitionism and the annexation of Texas", *Southwestern Historical Quarterly*, 32 (1928–29), 199.
79. *Ibid*, pp. 195–6; Smith to Jones, 31 July 1843, in Garrison, *Diplomatic Correspondence*, 3, 1116–19.
80. In Smither, *Southwestern Historical Quarterly*, 32 (1928–29), 200.

Government will abolish slavery".[81] Whether this was Green's exaggeration or Smith's is uncertain. Smith's own account of the Aberdeen interview, as relayed to the Texan Secretary of State, Anson Jones, indicates that he, personally, did not believe any such promises to have been made.[82] Nevertheless, Green's letter was enough to alarm Upshur who, without waiting for further confirmation, wrote to Van Zandt suggesting that negotiations for a treaty of annexation be reopened immediately.[83]

Meanwhile, oblivious to what was happening, the London Committee was pressing ahead with its plans. On 6 October it issued two memorials, one addressed to Sam Houston, President of Texas, urging him to give his support to immediate abolition,[84] the other to Santa Anna, President of Mexico, calling upon him to make emancipation a necessary condition of any agreement with Texas.[85] Both were promptly cited by Smith as further evidence of Britain's intentions.[86]

The abolitionists had fallen into a trap. In seeking to influence the British government they had helped to bring about the very thing they had been intent on avoiding. They were slow to see the danger. Aberdeen, however, quickly grasped what was happening and set about trying to reassure the Americans. On December 26, writing to Calhoun, Upshur's successor at the State Department, he explained that Britain favoured emancipation in Texas in much the same way as she supported emancipation in other parts of the world, but had never dreamed of acting secretly or underhandedly in the matter.[87] Calhoun was not to be won over. Britain, he stated, was free to do as she pleased with slavery in her own colonies, but when she went beyond and made it "her settled policy, and the object of her constant exertion to abolish it throughout the world, she makes it the duty of all other countries, whose safety or prosperity may be endangered by her policy, to adopt such measures as they may deem necessary for their protection".[88] Among these measures was the annexation of Texas.

There was now little abolitionists could do to stay the course of events. The debates in Congress over the annexation treaty were fully covered

81. Green to Upshur, July 1843, in J. S. Reeves, *American Diplomacy under Tyler and Polk* (Baltimore, 1907), p. 129.
82. Smith to Jones, 31 July 1843, in Garrison, *Diplomatic Correspondence*, 3, 1116–19.
83. Reeves, pp. 132–4.
84. Clarkson to Houston, 6 Oct. 1843, BFASS *Reporter*, 27 Dec. 1843.
85. Clarkson to Santa Anna, 6 Oct. 1843, *ibid*, 29 Nov. 1843.
86. Smith to Jones, 29 Jan. 1844 in Garrison, *Diplomatic Correspondence*, 3, 1479.
87. Aberdeen to Calhoun, 26 Dec. 1843, in E. D. Adams, *British Interests and Activities in Texas, 1838–1846* (Baltimore, 1910), p. 162.
88. *Ibid*, p. 163.

in the *Reporter*.[89] A momentary glint of hope appeared when the annexationists failed to muster the necessary two-thirds majority in the Senate, but it did not last. The American abolitionists had meanwhile compounded their error by entering their own candidate, James G. Birney, in the 1844 presidential contest, which had the effect of throwing New York to the Democrats and thus assuring the victory of the more resolutely expansionist of the two major party nominees, James K. Polk. The subsequent annexation of Texas by joint resolution of both houses of Congress came as a bitter blow to the opponents of slavery on both sides of the Atlantic.

Two other issues which engaged the attention of British abolitionists during these years were the imprisonment of British coloured seamen by the Southern state authorities and the protection of American fugitive slaves who sought asylum on British soil.

Ever since the 1820s it had been a common practice in Southern states to "quarantine" coloured seamen when their vessels docked at Southern ports. South Carolina's Negro Seamen's Laws were especially notorious, but similar regulations were to be found in the statute books of North Carolina, Georgia, Florida, Alabama and Louisiana. These provided that all coloured seamen, and in some cases coloured passengers also, were to be automatically seized and lodged in the nearest gaol, at the captain's expense, for the duration of a ship's stay in port. Most of these detainees were Americans, a fact which naturally gave rise to protests from Northern States whose citizens, innocent of any crime, regularly found themselves the inmates of Southern prisons. But foreigners were not immune, as was shown by the fact that at one point in 1843 no less than fifteen British subjects were being held in accordance with these regulations in Charleston gaol alone.[90] There were well-authenticated cases of British subjects being mistreated as detainees and one of a free Negro from Nassau, whose captain had failed to redeem him, being actually sold into slavery.[91] Over the years the British government had protested repeatedly to the American authorities and had been assured in response that these laws were state matters and that the Federal Government was therefore powerless to intervene. Secretary of State Buchanan informed Ambassador Pakenham on one occasion that any attempt by the administration in Washington to annul these laws would jeopardize the Union.[92] In 1843 Broad Street began pressing the Foreign

89. BFASS *Reporter*, 1844, pp. 16, 40, 72, 90–5, 118, 131, 144, 152.
90. Philip M. Hamer, "Great Britain, the United States, and the Negro Seamen Acts, 1822–1848", *Journal of Southern History*, I (1935), 3–28.
91. *Ibid*, pp. 18–19.
92. *Ibid*, p. 25.

Office to take a stronger stand.[93] Aberdeen believed in proceeding cautiously. Palmerston, who succeeded him in 1846, tried taking a firmer line but this, much to the disappointment of the abolitionists who had urged him on, achieved no better results.[94] In 1850 the attention of the British public was drawn to the issue as a result of a court action by a coloured steward against his ship's captain for wages for the period he had spent in Charleston prison.[95] Up to this time few MPs had been aware of what had been happening. On learning of it they responded with surprise and indignation. As it was now abundantly clear that the Federal authorities had no power to override the Southerners, Palmerston determined on the highly unorthodox policy of asking the British consuls in the South to begin independent negotiations with the individual state governments. Surprisingly, these efforts bore fruit. North Carolina, Florida and Alabama, although they kept the laws on their books, agreed not to enforce them. Louisiana exempted British subjects from its quarantine restrictions in 1852 and Georgia followed suit in 1854. Negotiations with South Carolina, the most uncompromising of the Southern states, dragged on longer but in 1857 it too agreed to exempt British nationals providing they agreed to remain on board their vessels. So matters rested until the Civil War swept away slavery and with it what remained of the Negro Seamen Acts.[96]

Protecting fugitive slaves seeking asylum on British territory became an issue in the early forties. Increasing numbers of these fugitives had been fleeing to Canada, where it was assumed they would be beyond the reach of pursuing masters.[97] It thus came as a shock when, in September 1842, it was learned that under Article 10 of the new Anglo-American treaty then awaiting ratification, Britain might be obliged to return some of these fugitives. It was Charles Stuart who first drew the London Committee's attention to this possibility. He pointed out that under this article provision was made for extraditing criminals. It would be only too easy for the United States to trump up charges against fugitives, many of

---

93. BFASS Minute Books, 24 Nov. 1843.
94. *Ibid*, 27 Feb., 24 April, 28 Aug. 1846; 22 Jan. 1847; 25 Aug. 1848; BFASS *Reporter*, 1 May 1846.
95. *Ibid*, 1 May 1850.
96. Philip M. Hamer, "British consuls and the Negro Seamen Acts, 1850–1860", *Journal of Southern History*, *I* (1935), 138–168; BFASS Minute Books, 1 Nov. 1850; 7 March 1851; 2 March, 6 July, 5 Oct., 2 Nov. 1855; 4 Jan. 1856; 2 Jan., 6 Feb. 1857.
97. Canadian slavery had been abolished by the 1833 Act, but in most areas it had already been eroded by local action. See Robin W. Winks, "A sacred animosity: abolitionism in Canada", *The Antislavery Vanguard*, ed. Martin Duberman, pp. 303–4.

whom had been obliged to commit what could be construed as criminal
acts in order to make their escape. The existing treaties between the United
States and Britain specifically exempted fugitive slaves from extradition.
Would not the new treaty, for want of such provisions, be open to mis-
construction?[98] Anxious for reassurance, Broad Street took the matter
up first with Stephen Lushington, then with Lord Ashburton who had
been responsible for negotiating the treaty, and finally with the Foreign
Secretary, Lord Aberdeen.[99] All attempted to set the minds of the
Committee at rest, but, as Aberdeen explained, since the United States
had agreed to the treaty, altering its wording would now be a cumbersome
business. Still not satisfied, and urged on by Lewis Tappan, who wrote
confirming that many Americans were under the impression that ratification would mean the surrender of fugitives from Canada,[100] the Committee
decided to have the matter raised in Parliament.[101] On 30 June, when the
treaty came up for its second reading in the Lords, Lord Brougham
spoke up on their behalf and proposed that Article 10 be modified along
the lines suggested by Broad Street. Aberdeen was unwilling to accept
this suggestion but repeated his assurances about the care with which
the Government would watch over its operation.[102] Two months later,
when the treaty came up for discussion in the Commons, Benjamin Hawes
and Vernon Smith again put forward the Committee's case, receiving
valuable support from Lord Palmerston and T. B. Macaulay. But a
motion by Hawes to limit the operation of the article to freemen was
defeated by fifty-nine votes to twenty-five.[103]

Still suspicious, the abolitionists decided to await a test case. One
arose almost immediately. Seven Florida Negroes fleeing to the Bahamas
killed a white man in the process and it was quickly learned that the
United States was about to apply, under the provisions of the new treaty,
for their extradition. On 24 December, a U.S. Marshal appeared in
Nassau and requested their surrender. The Bahaman authorities, dissatisfied with the evidence submitted, ordered the case dismissed. This
news was greeted with relief by abolitionists on both sides of the Atlantic,
who had been following the case with keen interest.[104] "This decision",

98. BFASS Minute Books, 30 Sept. 1842.
99. *Ibid*, 7, 28 Oct., 25 Nov. 1842; 27 Jan., 8, 24 Feb. 1843; BFASS *Reporter*,
8 Feb., 8 March 1843.
100. Tappan to Scoble, 27 Dec. 1842, in Abel and Klingberg, p. 109.
101. BFASS Minute Books, 13 March 1843.
102. *Hansard*, 70 (30 June 1843), 472–9.
103. *Ibid*, 71 (11 Aug. 1843), 564–86.
104. This case is reported in detail in BFASS *Reporter*, 10 Jan., 21 Feb., 17 April
1844, which also gives the correspondence between the Marshal and the Bahaman
authorities.

stated the New York *Evangelist*, "will have an important bearing, and discloses, more fully than any other decision that has yet occurred, the determination of Great Britain with regard to our fugitive slaves."[105] Anxiety over the wording of the extradition article subsided, although abolitionists continued to keep a watchful eye on developments. No fugitive was ever actually surrendered, but the possibility that one might be remained a source of uneasiness right up to the Civil War.[106]

Within the United States, nativist hostility to the abolitionists was as marked in the 1840s as in the 1830s. The two World Conventions, the agitation of the Texas question, and the attitudes commonly expressed by European visitors and in the foreign press, strengthened the belief that abolitionism was a foreign and, in particular, a British import. This was a widely held view in all sections. Southerners, of course, had obvious reasons for opposing the abolitionists, but Northerners too felt threatened. Some, although probably a minority, held that slavery was justified, or, at the very least, that it constituted the best means so far devised for controlling the Negro. But even among those who rejected these views there were grave doubts about the capacity of white society to absorb large numbers of free Negroes. Above all, there was the fear that the slavery issue, if taken up and pressed far enough, would tear the Union apart.[107] Attributing any challenge to the stability of their national institutions to sinister foreign influences was already a familiar American trait. Despite the prestige of her culture, Britain was America's traditional enemy and at times during the early 1840s the two countries were close to war. It thus came naturally enough to Northerners as well as Southerners to see in this new threat to their national life evidence of British plotting. Britain, wrote Francis P. Blair to Andrew Jackson in 1840, "sends her missionaries and her money to our shores and her old Federal allies are now joined in strict alliance with the abolition proselytes whom she has successfully encouraged in the North".[108] The Philadelphia *Sentinel*

105. In *ibid*, 17 April 1844.
106. In 1861 the case of John Anderson, a Missouri slave who slew his master while escaping, became a *cause célèbre* when an Upper Canada court ruled that he should be handed over to the United States authorities. The London Committee, prompted by Thomas Henning, Secretary of the Toronto Anti-Slavery Society, and John Scoble, took up his case and obtained a writ of *habeas corpus* on his behalf. The writ was not served as by the time it arrived in Canada Anderson had already been released, on a technicality, by another Canadian court: BFASS Minute Books, 4 Jan. to 3 May 1861; BFASS *Reporter*, 1861, pp. 60–2, 90–3, 133–5, 215; BFASS *Annual Report for 1861*, p. 14. For a fuller account of this incident see Robin W. Winks, *The Blacks in Canada: A History* (New Haven, 1971), pp. 175–6.
107. Ratner, p. 1 ff.
108. Blair to Jackson, 10 Sept. 1840, in John Spencer Bassett, ed., *The Correspondence of Andrew Jackson* (7 vols, Washington D.C., 1926–35), 6, 76.

commenting on the plans of American abolitionists to attend the second
World Convention observed that "these *philanthropic* Americans have
told our most deadly foe that we have three millions of enemies burning
for revolt in our very midst".[109] If the American abolitionists were not
actually hired by the British, it was at least plausible to suppose that they
were in league with them and were continually prompted and sustained
from abroad.

To a degree, of course, this was true. As was to be expected, however,
the anti-abolitionists, like the exponents of other conspiracy theories before
and since, made their enemies seem more ruthless and formidable than
they actually were. This was partly intentional. Foreign enemies, whether
they were Jacobins, Bavarian Illuminati, Freemasons, or British abolitionists, were politically useful. There were already numerous examples
in American history of the way in which such myths had been deliberately
fostered and exploited.[110] One would be underestimating American politicians to suppose all their cries of alarm genuine. Yet here, as in other
instances, a very little enquiry would have shown that the facts were not
as these alarmists claimed.

In the first place, the claim that the American movement was paid for
by British gold was grossly exaggerated. American agents visited Britain
in the hopes of raising money for their various causes and in some cases
were handsomely rewarded. John Keep and William Dawes, who toured
Britain in 1839–40 on behalf of Oberlin College, succeeded in collecting
no less than 30,000 dollars. This was probably the largest single sum
collected by antislavery agents in Britain prior to the Civil War, although
Harriet Beecher Stowe in the 1850s did almost as well. Others experienced
disappointment. The proceeds of John A. Collins's tour of Britain in
1840–41 were a mere 1,000 dollars. During the early fifties, the British
gave generously to the support of Canadian antislavery efforts and in
particular to the settlement of American fugitives in Canada. They also
contributed to antislavery bazaars in the United States by sending goods
and, on occasion, money. The American and Foreign Anti-Slavery
Society showed its awareness of public sensitivity by refusing to accept
funds raised in this way, but both Garrison and Douglass, as we will see,
came to rely on British benevolence. Nevertheless, in relation to the total
extent of American antislavery efforts, the amounts contributed remained
small and certainly did not play the decisive role which the abolitionists'
enemies claimed. Such rumours as the one that Garrison had received

---

109. Leavitt to [Scoble?], 1 May 1843, in Abel and Klingberg, p. 135.
110. Richard Hofstadter, *The Paranoid Style in American Politics* (New York, 1965),
pp. 3–40.

£6,000 from London and had been promised £50,000 more were, as he regretfully pointed out, entirely unfounded.[111]

Equally absurd was the claim that the American antislavery campaign was part of a unified conspiracy. Even the most cursory survey would have revealed that the movement was far from united. Between 1834 and 1838 it had been temporarily dominated by a central organization, the American Anti-Slavery Society. It was this body, modelled on the British Agency Anti-Slavery Society, that had employed Stanton, Weld and their "seventy" to evangelize the country. (Whether the number of agents ever reached this total is open to doubt although the actual number could not have been much short of it.) Although the Americans had undoubtedly learned much from the British it cannot be claimed that they took their methods entirely from them. Many American abolitionists had served their apprenticeship in the religious revivals of the 1820s and so were already familiar with the techniques of itinerant lecturing. They also soon learned that a centralized system, admirably suited to a small country like Britain, was not well adapted to the needs of the United States. By the late thirties initiative had largely passed to the state bodies which, in many cases, it had helped to create. These were autonomous organizations, each having its own periodical and network of auxiliaries. Some of them, like those in New York, Pennsylvania and Ohio, had memberships running into tens of thousands. These state bodies carried on the evangelical work in their own areas, circulating petitions, distributing literature, assisting fugitives and, above all, putting pressure on the local political organizations.

This devolution of power from the national to the state organizations gave the movement a structure more in accordance with the political structure of the country. And by the late thirties abolitionists were turning increasingly to political action. The leaders of the national organization, Leavitt, Stanton, Birney, Weld, Whittier and the Tappan brothers, viewed these changes without regret. They had been among the first to realize that the American Anti-Slavery Society had served its purpose. Their personal contribution to the new political activism was the establishment, in 1840, of the Liberty Party which was later to merge with the Free Soil Party and which, in turn, became the nucleus of the new Republican Party of the 1850s. These political structures were henceforward to be the central focus of antislavery activity, in so far as anything as multifarious and dependent on state and local action can be said to have had a central focus.[112]

At the same time that these developments were occurring the ideological

---

111. Harwood pp. 235–9, 626–7, 666–9; Tappan to Chamerovzow, 14 Feb. 1854, in Abel and Klingberg, p. 337.
112. Barnes, *Antislavery Impulse,* p. 78; Dumond, *Antislavery,* pp. 183–9, 300–4.

split between the main body of the movement and its extremist wing, led by William Lloyd Garrison, was widening. Even more than the British, the Americans had tended to take a fundamentalist line on slavery. Not only was slavery sinful, it was sin incarnate. The Garrisonians were certainly not alone in this view—which was shared by abolitionists of all complexions—but they were remarkable to the extent that they failed to see anything beyond it. Despite Garrison's journalistic brilliance—or perhaps because of it—the leaders of the movement had never entirely trusted him. Their doubts were confirmed by the increasing radicalism he showed as the thirties progressed. They distrusted his way of linking antislavery with extraneous causes—antisabbatarianism, women's rights, pacifism, "no government", and anticlericalism. They too viewed some of these causes sympathetically—women's rights and pacifism in particular—but they believed that associating them with the struggle against slavery to the extent of making them an integral part of the antislavery creed, as Garrison did, merely alienated support and diverted attention from the main issue. His attacks on the clergy and his characterization of the Congregational Church as "a cage of unclean birds" were cases in point. Above all they objected to his rejection of political action, in which they had believed all along and to which they were now actively committed. His denunciation of the American Constitution as a pro-slavery document —an argument which he later carried to its logical conclusion when he burned it in public—and his advocacy of Northern secession from the Union under the slogan "No Union with Slaveholding" struck them as doctrinaire nonsense. How, they demanded, would Northern secession benefit the slave?

Yet Garrisonianism was, in its way, a natural enough response to the frustrations of the American situation. Finding no political solution to the issues with which he was confronted, Garrison had responded by denouncing the entire system. This meant rejecting not only the Constitution and slavery but everything else in society which failed to measure up to his own perfectionist standards. There was thus a logic, if sometimes a rather crazy one, in his argument. It was a logic however which most abolitionists rejected. They were no more able than he to see a political solution to the fundamental problems of slavery in the individual states, but there were other issues, in particular the issue of its expansion into the territories, over which the Federal Government did have authority. Here at least intervention could be effective. This was the view of most abolitionists outside of New England. Even in Garrison's native Massachusetts his followers constituted a minority of the antislavery body. Nevertheless, they were a highly organized and militant minority. In

1839 they came close to taking over the American Anti-Slavery Society by the simple expedient of packing the annual general meeting with their supporters. The following year, as we have seen, they succeeded. The original committee resigned *en bloc* leaving the Garrisonians in undisputed control. What Garrison was left with was actually little more than a name but it was enough to mislead many Englishmen, and many of his own countrymen too, into believing that he spoke for the movement as a whole.[113]

It was ironical that it should have been at the First World Convention, that gathering intended to demonstrate to the world the solidarity of their movement, that British abolitionists first found themselves embroiled in this essentially American dispute. As we have seen, when the first invitations were issued in June 1839, few were even aware that differences of opinion existed among abolitionists on the other side of the Atlantic. Broad Street's American connection had from the first been with the American Anti-Slavery Society. It would therefore seem more than likely, as the Garrisonians later claimed, that it was in response to the promptings of Lewis Tappan or some other member of that body that in February 1840 it issued its second invitation limiting membership of the Convention to *male* delegates. Possibly Scoble, who had just returned from the United States, acted as intermediary. Even so, there is nothing to indicate that the members of the host organization had yet grasped the real issues underlying the dispute. Keeping male and female organizations separate was, it was true, an established British practice although it seems unlikely that, had the Americans been united in calling for its suspension, it would have been insisted on in this instance. The subsequent attempts of the Garrisonians to have their women seated, and Garrison's own refusal to join the delegates on the Convention floor, ended in ruffled feelings on both sides. The issue was as much one of temperament as philosophy. George Thompson's support of his old mentor merely exasperated Sturge. William Lucas, a provincial delegate, who observed them both at the Convention commented in his diary, "George Thompson is certainly a first rate orator but if there is any truth in physiognomy his wild and sullen countenance indicates anything but high principle. How different from the honest humble countenance of Joseph Sturge".[114] Such men simply could not work together, or not for long at any rate. Matters were made worse when, after their return to America, the Garrisonians began denouncing their late hosts with an extravagance customarily reserved

113. *Ibid*, pp. 172–97; Thomas, *The Liberator*, p. 256 ff. For a discussion of the ideological differences between the Garrisonians and anti-Garrisonians see Aileen S. Kraditor, *Means and Ends in American Abolitionism: Garrison and his critics on strategy and tactics, 1834–1850* (New York, 1969).
114. William Lucas, *A Quaker Journal, I*, 201.

for their domestic enemies. The Massachusetts Anti-Slavery Society, Garrison's own organization, accused them of having committed "an act of usurpation upon the rights of the Abolitionists of the world", and, "an assumption of despotic power more worthy of a slavery-ridden American Congress than a solemn assemblage of British philanthropists".[115] By contrast, relations with the main body of American delegates remained entirely amicable. On virtually every issue—including now the need to resist the Garrisonians—they saw eye to eye. After their resignation from the American Anti-Slavery Society the anti-Garrisonians had established a new organization, the American and Foreign Anti-Slavery Society. Since this was simply the old body under a new name the London Committee, which felt that it had seen more than enough of the Garrisonians, had no qualms about switching allegiance. It was this organization which henceforward provided it with information, and to which it turned for advice on American matters.[116]

Among British abolitionists generally, however, there was still much uncertainty about the claims of the rival factions. Few, even among those who attended the Convention, fully understood the issues involved. For most the fact that Sturge and the London Committee supported one group and George Thompson the other proved the deciding factor. In Scotland, where Thompson had long enjoyed a devoted following, support for the Garrisonians was strong from the outset.[117] It was also evident among those already noted for their radical sympathies such as William Smeal of Glasgow and Elizabeth Pease of Darlington or who were already at odds with the London philanthropic establishment, as was the case with Richard D. Webb of Dublin, a lapsing Quaker turning towards Unitarianism. Like the American Garrisonians, these British followers had a ready aptitude for name-calling. After a visit by Scoble to Dublin in company with Birney and Stanton, Webb wrote to Elizabeth Pease: "His unsleeping hostility, his watchful malignity against the old organizationists in general and Garrison in particular is odious beyond measure. . . . The impression he left after him was that of a self-willed, tyrannically-minded, narrow-souled, clever bigot".[118]

115. Massachusetts Anti-Slavery Society to Tredgold, 18 Feb. 1841, BFASS Papers, C 5/143.
116. For letters received by the Committee from the American and Foreign Anti-Slavery Society see Abel and Klingberg.
117. The Glasgow abolitionists had in fact already been made aware of the American quarrels as a result of a speech made there by George Thompson two years earlier; see *Speech of George Thompson, Esq., on the Divisions among American Abolitionists* (Glasgow, 1838); also *Seventh Annual Report of the Glasgow Emancipation Society* (Glasgow, 1841).
118. R. D. Webb to Elizabeth Pease, 4 Nov. 1840, Garrison Papers.

Nevertheless, it took time for lines to harden. In public at least the London Committee declined to embroil itself in the American controversy and allowed the attacks on it by the returning Garrisonians to pass unchallenged. This policy was easily maintained so long as its critics were in the United States. In December 1840, however, John A. Collins, an ardent Garrisonian newly arrived in Britain on a fund-raising mission, wrote to Broad Street soliciting support. He was told that the American Anti-Slavery Society's recent behaviour had led to a loss of confidence and therefore that no assistance would be forthcoming.[119] Undaunted, Collins pressed on with his tour lecturing British audiences on the delinquencies not only of the New Organizationists, as the members of the American and Foreign Anti-Slavery Society were called, but also of their allies on the London Committee. Among British abolitionists, still unfamiliar with the division in the American antislavery body, these accusations produced consternation, and letters were soon pouring into the Broad Street office. Unwisely as it later turned out, two members of the Committee, acting on their own initiative, put into circulation copies of letters from the Rev. Nathaniel Colver of the Massachusetts Abolition Society—the leading anti-Garrison body in that state—warning British abolitionists against Collins. This made the dispute more bitter and placed the London Committee in the awkward position of having to explain away its members' action.[120] In the case of some provincial organizations Collins's visit proved seriously disruptive. The Glasgow Emancipation Society, although much influenced by Thompson, had so far remained neutral to the extent of offering equal hospitality—on separate occasions— to both Old and New Organizationists. But in April 1841, Alexander Harvey wrote to Tredgold: "I am afraid that our Society here will be split into two parts. The majority of the Committee are decidedly opposed to Collins and his party but he has a few friends in it as indiscreet as himself and pushing matters to a crisis."[121] The Glasgow society did subsequently split, the Garrisonian minority, led by Smeal and Murray, taking control with the assistance, at one point, of a group of Chartist agitators who insisted on having their own resolutions read into the minutes.[122] In Edinburgh Collins's visit produced similar turmoil, which

119. BFASS Minute Books, 1 Jan. 1841.
120. Elizabeth Pease to the Committee of the British and Foreign Anti-Slavery Society, 25 March 1841, John Scoble to Elizabeth Pease, 25 April 1841, BFASS Papers; G. W. Alexander to James Houghton, 11 Nov. 1840, Abel and Klingberg, pp. 67–9. A detailed account of the Collins episode, containing most of the relevant correspondence, will be found in *G.E.S. Seventh Annual Report* (Glasgow, 1841).
121. Harvey to Tredgold, 19 April 1841, BFASS Papers.
122. GES Minute Books, 27 April 1841.

resulted in the women's branch turning Garrisonian while the men's branch remained strictly New Organizationist.[123]

It seems likely, although it would be hard to prove, that in Scotland, as in New England, the influence of waning Calvinism contributed to the development of Garrisonian attitudes. There are certainly obvious similarities between the two areas as regards the condition of intellectual life.[124] It is also notable that all the groups which at this time and subsequently went over to the Garrisonians were in regional centres—Glasgow, Edinburgh, Dublin, Bristol and to a lesser extent, Manchester and Leeds—noted for their independent-mindedness. The Scottish Garrisonians set great store by the fact that they represented a *national* movement, unlike their rivals who were the mere representatives of a London based organization. Other Garrisonians could not make this claim although they did derive satisfaction from being the leading British representatives of what, at least in the United States, passed for a national movement. Dislike of the wealthy Broad Street Quakers was also an important factor in determining allegiances as is shown by the frequent sneers at "respectable" and "cautious" abolitionists.[125] At least three of the leading Garrisonians, Smeal, Webb and Elizabeth Pease, were already quarrelling with the London Quakers before Garrisonianism became an issue, and two of them, Webb and Mrs Pease, subsequently quit the Society of Friends. Even more than the Sturgites, the British Garrisonians regarded conscience as the ultimate touchstone. "Thank God!" wrote Garrison during one of his British visits, "it is not policy but principle by which I am to be governed. . . . As Wendell Phillips once finely remarked—'God has not sent me into the world to abolish slavery, but to do my duty.' "[126] It was such attitudes as these, not class or economic differences, which accounted for the general "ultraism" of their branch of the movement. To all outward appearances they were solid, middle-class citizens, indistinguishable from Broad Street supporters. William Smeal was a prosperous Glasgow grocer, John Murray a customs officer, Richard D. Webb a successful printer, and John Bishop Estlin a noted Bristol eye surgeon. As a group they may have been less wealthy than the members of the Broad Street

123. C. Duncan Rice, "The Scottish factor in the fight against American slavery" (unpublished PhD thesis, University of Edinburgh, 1969) pp. 63 ff.
124. This point is made in G. C. Taylor, "Some American reformers and their influence on reform movements in Great Britain, 1830–1860" (unpublished PhD thesis, University of Edinburgh, 1960) pp. 37–40.
125. The Garrisonian case against the London Committee is exhaustively set forth in R. D. Webb, *The National Anti-Slavery Societies of England and the United States* (Dublin, 1852).
126. Garrison to Henry C. Wright, Bristol, 26 Aug. 1846; in W. P. and F. J. Garrison, *William Lloyd Garrison*, 3, 169–71.

Committee but they occupied roughly comparable positions in their respective communities and were similarly engaged in a wide spectrum of benevolent endeavours. They belonged, in short, to the same philanthropic establishment, albeit to provincial and dissenting branches of it.

Family and religious ties were, if anything, more marked in the case of these dissentients. Those who were not Quakers were mostly Unitarians, another closely-knit group. The Unitarian connection is particularly evident in the case of Estlin, who first became interested in American slavery as a result of meeting Samuel May at a Unitarian meeting in 1843 and later through reading works by American Unitarians, and who, with the assistance of his daughter Mary, spent his latter years proselytizing his own brand of Garrisonianism, with marked success, among his co-religionists in the West Country.[127] Among these dissentients, antislavery activity often led to matrimony. In 1840 Smeal's daughter Jane, who was Secretary of the Glasgow female organization, married John Wigham, who was Secretary of the Edinburgh men's society, and promptly took over its female branch. This, as we have seen, she radicalized, much to the chagrin of her husband who remained a New Organizationist. In the fifties, Elizabeth Pease married Professor Nicol of Glasgow and so joined the Smeal circle, while Jane Wigham's stepdaughter, Eliza, married into the family of the Dublin Webbs. Altogether, opposition to Broad Street was very much a family affair.[128]

Thus the British situation, to a remarkable degree, began to resemble the American, with one important difference—the national organization remained firmly in the hands of the anti-Garrisonians. After Collins's departure in the summer of 1841 the controversy died down, though none of those who had engaged in it showed any sign of altering his position. Thompson remained the only figure with a national reputation to have thrown in his lot with the Garrisonians. He, however, had largely given up antislavery work and now divided his time between Anti-Corn Law and East Indian Affairs. In 1843 he went to India where he became caught up in the controversy over the deposed Raja of Sattara whose case he later argued unsuccessfully—but evidently profitably—before the Court

127. Details of these activities will be found in the Estlin Papers, Dr Williams Library, London. For an account of his antislavery career see Samuel May, "Memorial of the Late Mr Estlin", *Liberator*, 16 Nov. 1855, pp. 182 ff.

128. These family and religious connections as well as the economic and social backgrounds of the British Garrisonians are explored in Rice, *passim*. There are also valuable comments on the Garrisonian-Unitarian connection in Louis Billington, "Some connections between British and American reform movements, 1830–1860, with special reference to the Anti-Slavery Movement" (unpublished MA thesis, University of Bristol, 1966), pp. 310–14; and in Taylor, pp. 29–33.

of Directors of the East India Company.[129] The Glasgow, Edinburgh and Dublin groups corresponded regularly with Garrisonians in America. Webb, especially, was an indefatigable correspondent exchanging views on antislavery and other matters, including the barbarity of the Catholic Irish, a subject on which, he was pleased to discover, his views were shared by his Boston correspondents.[130] But so far as British affairs were concerned they were largely inactive. To them, the antislavery movement meant simply the antislavery struggle in America, or, more precisely, the struggle between abolitionists there for control over the movement.[131] The American Garrisonians, with characteristic eclecticism, seemed more interested in criticizing British society than in British views on slavery. The existence of a hereditary monarchy and aristocracy reminded them of the hereditary privileges of Southern planters. Henry C. Wright, who arrived in England shortly after Collins's departure, and spent the next six years there campaigning on behalf of peace, temperance, hydropathy, antislavery and various other causes, noted in his journal that "the aristocracy of England resemble the slaveholders of America exceedingly in their looks. . . . They are fat, pot-bellied and have a sensual appearance—in their temper—impatient of contradiction. They seem to have no fellow feeling with other human beings. They are a savage people".[132]

According to Garrison the British were "crushed beneath an overgrown monarchy and a bloated aristocracy". He advised Miss Pease to "boldly aim for the destruction of these . . . the watchword should be— at the risk of martyrdom, or execution for high treason—Down with the throne!"[133] As the Pease family were among the largest employers of industrial labour in the North of England—they owned practically the whole town of Middlesbrough—they could hardly be expected to take such advice seriously, still less look forward optimistically to the bloody

129. The Raja had been deposed by the British authorities in 1839 on suspicion of having had treasonable dealings with the Portuguese in Goa. George Thompson, *Case of Pertaub Shean, the Raja of Sattara, Dethroned by the East India Company on the Testimony of False Witnesses* (London, 1846). For Thompson's financial circumstances at the time see Thompson to Webb, 12 Aug. 1845, Weston Papers.
130. The membership of Webb's Hibernian Anti-Slavery Society was entirely Protestant and, to judge from Webb's letters to Garrison, strongly anti-Catholic. Webb MSS, Garrison Papers; see also Wendell Phillips to Richard Allen, 30 March 1842, *ibid.*
131. See the Webb, Houghton, Pease, Estlin and Thompson letters, Boston Public Library. Here, as elsewhere, I am greatly indebted to Dr G. C. Taylor of the University College of Wales, Aberystwyth, for having allowed me to make use of her typescript copies of these materials.
132. Wright's Journal, 6 Sept. 1843, in Billington, p. 177.
133. Garrison to Pease, 28 Feb. 1843, Garrison Papers.

revolution which he prophesied as being imminent. Like other British Garrisonians, the Peases declined to send delegates to the second World Convention on the grounds that, once again, women would not be represented. This was a relief to the London Committee, already beset with more than its share of troubles over the sugar issue.

In the summer of 1846 Garrisonianism once again raised its head, this time as a result of a tour of Britain by Garrison himself in the course of which he was joined by Wright, James N. Buffum and the Negro abolitionist Frederick Douglass. This visit, sponsored by the Glasgow organization,[134] aroused a good deal of interest since his name was already well known, although few outside the movement had any clear notion of what he stood for. Douglass too was a great attraction and by his intelligence, courtesy and dignified platform bearing much impressed the British, few of whom had seen an American Negro, still less a fugitive slave. Mary Howitt, wife of the author William Howitt, wrote to her sister,

I am just now deeply interested in the anti-slavery question, the real thorough Abolitionist view which would cut up the crying sin root and branch, and spare none of its participants. Our friend, William Lloyd Garrison, is now in London, with one of the most interesting men I ever saw, a runaway slave, Frederick Douglass. . . . I can talk of nothing but the "dear blacks".[135]

Even such obviously frivolous reactions were galling to Broad Street, which did not, of course, hold to the "real thorough Abolitionist view". Of more immediate moment, however, was the decision of the Garrisonians to set up what they had so far significantly lacked, a national organization.

Plans for this new body were discussed at a meeting between Garrison and his British sympathizers in London on 10 August. An inaugural meeting followed a week later at which a constitution was approved and a committee elected. It was, Garrison proudly claimed, "a real, old-fashioned, old-organized, American antislavery meeting (such, I am quite certain, as was never before held in England)".[136] George Thompson, as befitted his position as the leading British Garrisonian, was made President. A striking feature of the Anti-Slavery League was its close resemblance to the body it was supposed to supplant. It was originally intended that the League would have its own periodical and auxiliary network but these never materialized. Its official statement of objectives closely paralleled

134. *Liberator*, 2 Oct. 1846.
135. Margaret Howitt, ed., *Mary Howitt: An Autobiography* (2 vols, London, 1889) 2, 33–4.
136. Garrison to Webb, 19 Aug. 1846, Garrison Papers. Full accounts of these proceedings are given in *Liberator*, 18 Sept., 2 Oct. 1846. See also W. P. and F. J. Garrison, *3*, 159–60.

that of the older organization.[137] But although the League claimed to support universal emancipation, its real purpose, as its own statements and those of its American sponsors made clear, was to act as a sounding board for Garrison and his supporters in America. Henry C. Wright, who was present throughout these proceedings, informed readers of the *Liberator* that "I am here to get the people of this country to aid in this great and Godlike enterprise . . . the DISSOLUTION OF THE AMERICAN UNION . . . and the people will rally to this work at the call of our ever faithful and potent friend, Wm. L. Garrison."[138] To the Sturgites this was a dangerous heresy which could only bring discredit to the movement. J. H. Hinton, the editor of the *Reporter*, attempted to point this out at the League's inaugural meeting and was voted down.[139] But on this issue the great majority of abolitionists, at least in England, sided with Broad Street.

As might be expected, the Leaguers lost no time in denouncing the British and Foreign Anti-Slavery Society. They accused it of showing insufficient militancy on the American slavery issue and of deliberately misrepresenting the true abolitionists of the United States.[140] According to Wright, it stood in the way of American emancipation by helping to sustain the Liberty Party and thereby that " 'covenant with death and agreement with hell', the American Union".[141] Most abolitionists regarded this as pure nonsense. There was one charge, however, which had some substance. The previous year, a delegation of four London Quakers, two of whom, George Stacey, Clerk of the Yearly Meeting, and Josiah Forster, were Broad Street stalwarts, had visited Indiana on behalf of the British Society of Friends in an attempt to heal a schism which had developed among the Quakers there. In recent years, American Quakers, haunted by memories of the Hicksite separations of the twenties and alarmed at the "ultraism" of the abolitionists and the possibility of the violent break-up of the Union, had become exceedingly cautious about condemning slavery. This attitude was especially marked in Indiana, a border state where popular hostility towards the abolitionists was strong. But in spite of this a number of Quakers had aligned themselves with the abolitionists, and when their Yearly Meeting had attempted to discipline them had broken away and established a rival Yearly Meeting of their own. Other

137. This will be found in *Liberator*, 2 Oct. 1853, p. 153; see also *First Report of the Anti-Slavery League* (London, 1847).
138. Wright to the Editor of the *Liberator*, 5 Aug. 1846, *Liberator*, 18 Sept. 1846, p. 147.
139. *Ibid*, 2 Oct. 1846, p. 153; Garrison to Webb, 19 Aug. 1846, Garrison Papers.
140. BFASS Minute Books, 30 Oct. 1846; BFASS *Reporter*, 2 Nov. 1846, p. 180.
141. *Liberator*, 18 Sept. 1846, p. 147.

matters besides slavery were involved, but that was undoubtedly the chief precipitating factor. The secessionists claimed to be acting not merely out of conscience but in accordance with the instructions of British Quakers, who in recent years had been bombarding them with letters urging them to take a more resolute stand against slavery.[142] Nevertheless, the London delegation had sided with the original body and called on the secessionists to return to their proper allegiance. Josiah Forster, always noted for his stern views on Quaker orthodoxy, was reported to have said—and very probably did say—that "dearly as he loved the Anti-Slavery Cause, he could not, under any circumstances, suffer it to be compared with the union of the Society of Friends".[143] The British Yearly Meeting refused to recognize the secessionists, who remained unrepentant. Whether this proved, as the Garrisonians had all along claimed, that the London Quakers were lukewarm in their attitude to American slavery is open to debate, but it certainly provided their enemies with a stick to beat them with, as they continued to do for the next decade.[144] Broad Street's response to this and other League attacks was to ignore them. This was a wise policy since any reply would have led to countercharges and stirred up a public controversy from which it would have derived no benefit and which would very likely have done it much harm. Although the Leaguers kept up their assault for some months it was entirely a one-sided affair.

The League's most notable achievement was the organization of a monster gathering in Exeter Hall on 28 September 1846, to protest against the decision of the Evangelical Alliance, at that time holding its inaugural meetings in London, to admit slaveholders to membership.[145] The Alliance, an association of evangelical Christians of various denominations, was intended to strengthen the bonds between Protestant groups in different parts of the world. Abolitionists, both in Britain and the United States, hoped to gain publicity for their cause by persuading the Alliance to take a strong stand on slavery. Broad Street, acting through J. H. Hinton,

142. Copies of these are in "Epistles Sent, 1818–47" MSS, Friends' House, London.
143. Walter Edgerton, *A History of the Separation in Indiana Yearly Meeting of Friends which Took Place in the Winter of 1842 and 1843 on the Anti-Slavery Question* (Cincinnati, 1856), p. 334.
144. For fuller accounts of this episode see Drake, *Quakers and Slavery in America*, pp. 164–8; Rufus M. Jones, *The Later Periods of Quakerism* (2 vols, London, 1921), 2, 587–95; Levi Coffin, *Reminiscences* (Cincinnati, 1876), pp. 230 ff; Benjamin Seebohm, *Memoirs of William Forster* (2 vols, London, 1865), 2, 201–6, and Edgerton cited above. For the way in which the Garrisonians subsequently exploited it see Chapter 11 below.
145. There is an account of these proceedings and of the speeches given by Garrison, Thompson and Douglass in BFASS *Reporter*, 1 Oct. 1846.

who was a member of the Provisional Committee of the Alliance, had begun lobbying well in advance of the inaugural meetings and had even published a short pamphlet on the subject.[146] Initially, most British clergymen were prepared to support Hinton; but when it became evident that a section of the American delegates, led by Dr Thomas Smyth of South Carolina, would secede rather than have their practices questioned a shift of opinion took place and Hinton's motion for exclusion was defeated.[147] The Exeter Hall meeting, at which Garrison, Douglass and Thompson were the principal speakers, helped to draw attention to these proceedings. Garrison later described it as falling on the Alliance "like a thunder bolt from heaven", but it would seem to have had no practical effect beyond, possibly, strengthening the resolve of the proslavery delegates.[148]

In Scotland the principal issue taken up by the League was the acceptance by the newly established Free Church of donations from sympathizers, mostly Scottish expatriates, in the Southern states. The actual amount was never disclosed but was probably around nine thousand dollars. The British and Foreign Anti-Slavery Society had already drawn attention to the matter in a pamphlet published the previous spring.[149] The Leaguers threw themselves into the controversy with their usual zeal receiving valuable support from a great variety of church organizations which, for quite other reasons, were antagonistic to the Free Church. The "Send Back the Money" campaign achieved amazing proportions. During the summer and early autumn there were mass gatherings in Edinburgh, Glasgow, Aberdeen and many other Scottish towns. But in spite of all this excitement, the money was never returned.[150]

Garrison's visit, in short, was something of a fiasco. His attacks on

146. BFASS Minute Books, 27 March 1846; BFASS *Reporter*, 1 May 1846, p. 73. The pamphlet consisted mostly of letters which had passed between Broad Street and the London Provisional Committee of the Alliance. Its title is not revealed, but the material contained in it will be found in *ibid*, 1 April 1846, pp. 51–3.
147. A full account of the Alliance's proceedings is given in *ibid*, 1846, pp. 145–208.
148. Garrison to Samuel May, 19 Dec. 1846, Garrison Papers. The position of the proslavery delegates certainly became more uncompromising thereafter. BFASS *Reporter*, 1846, pp. 183–6.
149. BFASS *American Slavery: Address of the Committee of the British and Foreign Anti-Slavery Society to the Moderator, Office Bearers and Members of the General Assembly of the Free Church of Scotland* (London, 1846).
150. Rice, pp. 272–346; George A. Shepperson, "Thomas Chalmers, the Free Church of Scotland and the South", *Journal of Southern History*, 17 (1951), pp. 517–37; GES Minute Books, 21 April–28 Oct. 1846. This campaign caused some embarrassment to the Irish Garrisonians who were at this time receiving famine relief gifts from America, including some from Southern states. Again, the money was not returned, although some Scottish Garrisonians apparently believed that it should be: Eliza Wigham to M. W. Chapman, 1 April 1847, Weston Papers.

the monarchy and sabbath observance and his hobnobbing with radical leaders like Henry Vincent and William Lovett offended middle-class sensibilities. "His great error", in Estlin's view, was "to mix himself up *unnecessarily* with vexed English questions, under some sort of quixotic notion, as it appeared to me, that the more unpopular he made himself with the middle classes of society in the country, the more he should promote the a[nti]s[lavery] cause!!"[151] In fashionable radical circles his ideas were quickly taken up and equally quickly discarded. Frederick Douglass was a good deal more successful in winning the hearts of his British hosts, some of whom joined together before his departure to purchase his freedom and also to put up the money for him to start his newspaper, the *North Star*.[152] Garrison, who was rapidly becoming jealous of Douglass, opposed this venture, as he opposed everything which threatened his own authority. There were signs, too, that Douglass's confidence in his own powers were increasing and that he had begun to feel, quite rightly, that the Garrisonians were lumbering themselves with issues which had no bearing on the cause of the Negro. Their British visit thus marks an important turning-point in the relations between these two men, and, by extension, between the Garrisonians and the rising Negro abolition and civil rights movements in America.[153]

Following Garrison's departure in November, the Anti-Slavery League quickly lost impetus. At its annual meeting in 1847 its income during the previous year was put at £445 (as compared with Broad Street's £1,716) and its liabilities at £128.[154] No further meetings appear to have been held. The fact is that the British Garrisonians lacked the momentum necessary for maintaining a national organization of their own. This is scarcely surprising considering how far Garrison's doctrines were the peculiar product of his own personality and of the frustrations of the American situation. The position in Britain was sufficiently similar for people to respond to his emotional appeal but too different and, above all, too far removed from the American scene of conflict, for his ideas to take

151. Estlin to Samuel May, 1 Oct., 2 Nov. 1846, May Papers. Both Lovett and Vincent were active members of the League which, in Lovett's view, was "an instrument of great good" since slavery was "one link in the great chain of oppression". Garrison wrote glowingly of the support he was receiving from them, concluding enthusiastically, "such men I revere". William Lovett to Garrison, 1 March 1847; Garrison to Helen Garrison, 18 Aug., 3 Sept. 1846; Garrison to Estlin, 19 Aug. 1846, Garrison Papers.
152. Douglass, *Life and Times*, pp. 255–8.
153. *Ibid*, pp. 259–60; Thomas, p. 389; Louis B. Filler, *The Crusade Against Slavery* (New York, 1960), pp. 143, 206; Philip S. Foner, *Frederick Douglass* (New York, 1964), pp. 62–83.
154. *First Report of the Anti-Slavery League* (London, 1847); *Eighth Annual Report of the British and Foreign Anti-Slavery Society* (London, 1847).

firm root. In Scotland, where they had the greatest impact, their success was mainly due to the way in which Garrisonians exploited existing tensions between the provinces and the metropolis and between the rival religious sects. Even there their mass appeal was shortlived and within a year had largely evaporated. British Garrisonianism, as we shall see, survived into the fifties but only as the creed of a small, scattered—but highly vocal—group of Garrison's personal admirers and those abolitionists who, for various reasons, felt disaffected from Broad Street.

11

Antislavery issues
of the 1850s

As the days of Britain's own struggles over
West Indian slavery and apprenticeship
receded, abolitionist activity in Britain
declined. By the mid-fifties a new generation
which had not been exposed to the anti-
slavery campaigns of the twenties and thirties
had reached maturity. This new generation
was inclined to take its opposition to slavery
for granted. It was part of a familiar
process. What had begun as the seemingly
impractical proposals of a few eccentrics had
become the subject of grave legislative
deliberations and had now attained the
status of unquestioned assumptions. As a
consequence, these younger men and women
lacked the personal commitment, the evan-
gelizing zeal, which had characterized so
many of their elders. Those who were of a
benevolent or reforming inclination found
other, more immediate, demands on their
energies. The Crimean War gave a new
urgency to the peace movement. Britain's
own transition from an agricultural to an
industrialized society continued to give rise
to pressing problems. Suffrage reform, poor
relief, care for the sick and aged, improvement of working and living conditions,
temperance, and the redemption of criminals

were the issues which engaged the attention of this new generation. More and more, the energy and enthusiasm which twenty years earlier had found expression in the crusade against slavery was channelled into other types of endeavour.

To the general public, the antislavery struggle had by now come to mean simply the sectional controversy in the United States. The debates in Congress over the Compromise of 1850 and the Kansas question were followed in Britain in much the same way that two decades earlier Americans had followed the struggles over the West Indian emancipation, with the important difference that whereas the Americans had seen in the British contest obvious implications with respect to their own institutions, the British regarded the issue as already settled. John Bright and others warned them against interfering in the affairs of the United States, pointing out that, whatever the morality of such behaviour with respect to a foreign power, the end result would be to do more harm than good.[1] This, of course, abolitionists hotly denied, but most people agreed with Bright and chose either to ignore the contest or to watch from the sidelines. Among those who followed these American developments the conviction grew, as the fifties progressed and successive crises arose and were resolved, that this was a controversy that would go on, if not for ever, at least for a very long time and that, despite the dire predictions of the participants, it constituted no serious threat to the continuance of the Union. Most sympathized with the North on the grounds that it opposed the extension of slavery although there were some who professed to admire the "gentlemanly" qualities of the Southern planters or who took satisfaction in the travails of a country which they were tired of having held up to them as a symbol of democratic achievement. As always, the attitudes which people adopted towards America tended to reflect their views on domestic issues. Some were better informed than others, but on all sides there was a great amount of ignorance as to the nature of the questions involved and the way in which the American governmental system actually worked.[2]

Even to the uninformed, however, the American contest presented a dramatic spectacle. Apart from newspaper accounts and travellers' descriptions, the British were kept informed of developments by a continual stream of transatlantic visitors, who appeared on lecture platforms around the country. In a day before the advent of the cinema and television and when the theatre was frowned on, at least by the religious, as immoral, lectures constituted one of the most popular forms of entertainment. It

1. Abel and Klingberg, *A Side-Light on Anglo-American Relations*, p. 47.
2. Ephraim Douglas Adams, *Great Britain and the American Civil War* (2 vols, New York, 1925), *1*, 26 ff.

was common for these lecturers to visit small towns and even villages as well as major cities. Their statements were commonly reported in the press and many of them also wrote pamphlets describing the causes they represented.

During the early fifties the curiosity of the British was especially piqued by the arrival of a succession of coloured visitors, including several ex-slaves driven to seek asylum abroad by the new Fugitive Slave Act. Some of them made full use of the opportunities offered to enlist support for their causes and to improve their own educations; others, exploiting the burgeoning legend of the underground railroad, became practically entertainers. Henry "Box" Brown travelled from Bradford to Leeds in the box in which he had made his intrepid escape, emerging to the applause of the assembled spectators.[3] William and Ellen Craft, who were of a more serious turn of mind, spent two years under the tutelage of the Misses Lushington in Surrey, after which they were established in a house in London[4] which they used as a base from which to make their antislavery tours. Unlike white abolitionist visitors, some of whom were less than impressed by what they saw of Britain and tactless enough to say so,[5] these Negroes were united in lavishing praise on their host country.

For the first time in my life [wrote one] I can say "I am truly free". My old master may make his appearance here, with the Constitution of the United States in his pocket, the Fugitive Slave Law in one hand and the chains in the other, and claim me as his property, but all will avail him nothing. I can here stand and look the tyrant in the face and tell him that I am his equal! England is, indeed, the "land of the free and the home of the brave".[6]

Three of them subsequently wrote books reaffirming their affection for the country—of which, of course, they had been given a singularly privileged glimpse—in terms most flattering to their hosts.[7] So concerned were the abolitionists for the welfare of these coloured visitors that a

---

3. Larry Gara, *The Liberty Line, the legend of the underground railroad* (Lexington, Kentucky, 1961), p. 121.

4. *Anti-Slavery Advocate*, Oct. 1852, p. 6; Jan. 1854, p. 124.

5. Highest marks for tactlessness must go to the Garrisonians, but they were not the only offenders. Henry Stanton in 1849 offended his British colleagues by observing that just as Miss Pecksniff in *Martin Chuzzlewit*, having been told that her side face was much better looking than her front view, always presented her profile to her admirers, so Britain, in her dealings with other countries, always liked to be viewed as the champion of humanity and liberator of the human race. Stanton, *Sketches of Reforms and Reformers*, p. 199.

6. William Wells Brown, *Three Years in Europe* (London, 1852), p. 9.

7. *Ibid*, William G. Allen, *The American Prejudice Against Colour* (London, 1853); Samuel Ringgold Ward, *Autobiography of A Fugitive Negro* (London, 1855). Another common feature of these works was that the authors were all inveterate name-droppers.

special organization, the Ladies' Society to Aid Fugitives from Slavery, was established to look after their needs.[8] The British public was also prepared to be generous, so much so that in August 1853 the *Anti-Slavery Advocate* felt obliged to warn readers against giving money to vagrants who passed themselves off as American fugitives. George Borrow in his *Wild Wales* records meeting one of these, an Antiguan, in Chester who told him that all a coloured man needed to do to make a living in Britain was to attend religious meetings and speak out against slavery and the United States. That all British people were not equally gullible is shown by the fact that in 1854 a West Indian was jailed for three months for just such an imposture.[9]

The most famous antislavery visitor to tour Britain in the 1850s was Harriet Beecher Stowe whose novel, *Uncle Tom's Cabin*, published in March 1852, had even more readers in Britain than in America. During the first eight months it had broken all records by selling over a million copies in England and was soon being presented on the stage and even set to music.[10] With such remarkable advance publicity her tour could hardly have failed to arouse interest. In fact it soon developed into something very like a triumphal progress. From the moment of her arrival in April 1853 crowds flocked out to see the author of the story which everyone had read or seen performed and over which even the Queen was reported to have shed a tear. In London, where the Duchess of Sutherland became her mentor, the whole of fashionable society turned out to pay her homage. She dined with the Lord Mayor, the Foreign Secretary, the Lord Privy Seal and other members of the cabinet, and was introduced to practically every figure of note in British public life. Even the Archbishop of Canterbury felt obliged to entertain her. Moving in such illustrious circles left her little time for meetings with the metropolitan abolitionists although on her travels she saw something of their provincial colleagues. She did however attend a soirée arranged for her by the British and Foreign Anti-Slavery Society, and she also put in an appearance at its annual meeting in company with the Duchess of Sutherland, who was heard to remark on entering that it looked as if she were in for "one of our genuine Exeter Hall 'brays' ".[11] This meeting was also memorable

8. This body, founded on 4 Nov. 1853, remained active until January 1856. Its minute books and a booklet describing the aims and activities will be found in BFASS Papers, C/84.

9. *Anti-Slavery Advocate*, May 1854.

10. F. J. Klingberg, "Harriet Beecher Stowe and social reform in England", *American Historical Review, 43* (1938), 545.

11. Forrest Wilson, *Crusader in Crinoline: the life of Harriet Beecher Stowe* (London, 1942), p. 229.

for an outburst by her husband against what he considered the ignorant anti-Americanism of British audiences. Calvin Stowe had become increasingly exasperated at what he considered the inordinate fuss which was being made over his wife's visit and the political overtones which it was acquiring. In Edinburgh there had even been rumours that the American flag had been mutilated. Anxious to set the record straight he took it upon himself to remind his audience that they consumed the greater part of America's slave produce and were therefore at least as deeply implicated in the sin of slaveholding as were Northerners.[12] The standard reply to this was that Britain had not subscribed to the Fugitive Slave Law, to which abolitionists added that *they* were opposed to the use, in any form, of slave produce.[13] Professor Stowe's attack would have been better directed had it been aimed not at abolitionists but at aristocrats like his wife's mentor, the Duchess of Sutherland. There was, after all, a significant difference between the anti-Americanism of someone like Sturge, who fundamentally admired America, and of those who despised all it stood for. Certainly the Stowes' association with the Duchess did nothing to enhance their reputations in America,[14] or in Scotland where her part in the Highland Clearances was still vividly remembered. Mrs Stowe's record of her visit, *Sunny Memories of Foreign Lands* (London, 1854), in which she spoke of the clearances as "advancing civilization", drew a well-deserved rebuke from a former inhabitant of Sutherland, Donald McLeod, entitled *Gloomy Memories of the Highlands of Scotland* (Toronto, 1857), which pointed out, among other things, that her fondness for the aristocracy had got her into some very dubious company.[15] Working-class spokesmen also criticized Mrs Stowe for exacerbating the sectional conflict in the United States and so bringing democracy into disrepute. The responses to her visit revealed a deep suspicion in some quarters that she and other abolitionists were out to destroy the reputation of America, the great hope of working-class people around the world.[16]

12. *Ibid*, p. 222; Klingberg, *American Historical Review*, *43* (1938), 544–9.
13. The ensuing correspondence with the BFASS is in BFASS Papers, C 36/123–5.
14. See the address to the Duchess reputedly written by Mrs Tyler, wife of the ex-President, and Lewis Tappan's remarks on it, in Abel and Klingberg, pp. 41–2, 323–4.
15. Rice, "The Scottish factor in the fight against American slavery", pp. 496–501.
16. These suspicions were also voiced when the abolitionists attacked Louis Kossuth during his visit to America for refusing to take sides on the slavery issue. In the view of British political radicals Kossuth pursued the correct course in putting the cause of European democracy before that of the American Negro. *Ibid*, 494–6; L. Billington "Some connections between British and American reform movements", pp. 265–9; Abel and Klingberg, pp. 276–312.

Yet in spite of these controversies the most striking thing about Mrs Stowe's visit was the amount of genuine antislavery feeling it revealed. Her appeal, apart from her reputation as a best-selling author, lay in the fact that she offered a straightforward undenominational brand of anti-slavery sentiment requiring no action beyond a simple affirmation of belief in the wickedness of slaveholding. To a public grown weary of academic disputes between rival antislavery and religious factions this was a welcome change. Throughout her tour she was showered with gifts which, by the time of her departure, totalled over 20,000 dollars.[17] Equally indicative of the popular interest she aroused was the famous "Affec-tionate and Christian Address of many Thousands of the Women of Eng-land to their Sisters, the Women of the United States of America", named, after the Duchess of Sutherland's London residence, the Stafford House Address, which was signed by some half-million British women.

One of the most interesting things about this address is the fact that it was the work of a group, the Stafford House clique, which had no organiza-tional affiliations with the movement. There were at this time still some thirty antislavery bodies in existence, though many of them were barely active. Their condition contrasts sharply with the popular enthusiasm and activity inspired by Mrs Stowe, in which, however, some did partici-pate and were, at least temporarily, brought to life.[18] In England, all were in one way or another affiliated to the British and Foreign Anti-Slavery Society with the exception of the Bristol and Clifton Ladies Anti-Slavery Society which had recently come under the control of the Garrisonians and broken away.[19] In Scotland, slavery remained very much an issue between the warring sects which took the view that "softness" on this question was as good a stick to beat their rivals with as any other. What actually constituted "softness" could be construed as meaning simply support of the wrong group of abolitionists.[20] In Glasgow there were now four antislavery societies, Smeal's Glasgow Emancipation Society and its female branch which, since the divisions of 1841, had remained staunchly Old Organizationist, and their New Organization rivals, the Glasgow New Association for the Abolition of Slavery and its female equivalent, founded as a result of visits to the city by the Negro aboli-

17. What became of this money has never been established; her biographer sup-poses that she probably appropriated it for her personal use: Wilson, p. 225.
18. Some, however, objected to the wording of the Stafford House Address. See BFASS *Reporter*, 1 Jan., 1 Feb. 1853; Klingberg, *American Historical Review*, 43 (1930), 549.
19. See below.
20. L. Billington, p. 188; Rice, p. 5.

tionist J. W. C. Pennington in the early fifties. These anti-Garrisonian bodies were now the more active, the Glasgow Ladies New Association enjoying particular prestige on account of having been the official sponsor of Mrs Stowe's visit. In Edinburgh the movement was still divided along the lines of sex, the female society under the direction of Jane and Eliza Wigham supporting the Garrisonians while the male branch, which was much less active, supported Broad Street.[21] Wales, which had never taken much interest in the cause, now had no antislavery societies at all. Judging from the coverage given to the issue in the Welsh press, slavery impinged on the consciousness of Welshmen principally as an issue affecting specific groups of Welsh settlers in America.[22] The only remaining antislavery society in Ireland was the small but frenetically active Hibernian Anti-Slavery Society in Dublin which under Webb's guidance remained a Garrisonian stronghold.[23]

The principal problem facing all these British antislavery bodies was their simple inability to do anything that would materially affect the American issue. This was no new problem but in the thirties and forties it had at least been plausible to assume that the conscience of America needed to be awakened. Now that it *had* been awakened they were at a loss as to what to do next. Their American correspondents could offer little guidance. To those of them who turned their attention to politics, as many of them did, British support had become less important than before. Increasingly their own time was being taken up with problems of a kind which the British could hardly be expected to understand. Acting through the Free Soil and Republican parties meant that they became involved in the intricacies of local and state issues and were obliged to accommodate themselves to the usual horse-trading of American politics. There were, of course, some who declined to allow their identities to become submerged in these political efforts. Among these, the Garrisonians stood out on account of their steadfast refusal to abandon the high ground of moral principle and their vehement denunciations of all who did. The position of other independent and semi-independent groups is harder to delineate. Lewis Tappan's American and Foreign Anti-Slavery Society continued into the fifties and still communicated regularly with Broad Street,[24] but this was, as the Garrisonians pointed out, little more than a correspondence society. Frederick Douglass, who since his break with Garrison had become a leading figure in his own right, controlled

21. Rice, pp. 383, 390–1.
22. G. E. Owen, "Welsh anti-slavery sentiments, 1790 to 1865, a survey of public opinion" (unpublished MA thesis, University of Wales, 1964).
23. Rice, pp. 236–9.
24. Abel and Klingberg, pp. 238–367.

an organization based on Rochester. Others, such as Gerrit Smith and William Goodell, also in up-state New York, the Cheever brothers in New York City and the so-called Bird Club in Massachusetts, represented particular groupings, though the lines between them were often blurred since they frequently cooperated and were all involved in one way or another in political activity.[25]

Even these American abolitionists, however, had little control over the way events developed. The most that the British could do was to affirm their abhorrence of slavery and their support for those who attacked it. What Mrs Stowe accomplished with ease, native abolitionists laboured to achieve. But although they lacked her flair, the end result was much the same.

The plight of the organized antislavery bodies during the fifties is evident in the case of the British and Foreign Anti-Slavery Society. Although it was still the only organization with national pretensions, its influence had steadily declined. Its London Committee, which had met on an average thirty-two times a year in 1841–45, met only fourteen times a year in 1854–58.[26] During the summer months, when members were away from town, eight or ten weeks would often elapse during which no meetings were held at all. The Committee itself had shrunk to half its original size and the number of those present at meetings had also declined.[27] In terms of occupation and religious affiliation its membership remained much the same. Of the original hard-core members, approximately half had either died or retired.[28] Others, like Hinton, Ball and Alexander, had become irregular in their attendance. Filling the places of these members was difficult. The most active of the new recruits were Robert Alsop, a pharmacist, Thomas Binns, a headmaster, and Samuel Sturge, like his brother Joseph Sturge, a corn merchant. These were not young men; Alsop had been born in 1803, Binns in 1789 and Sturge in 1792. There were also younger recruits, among them Charles Gilpin the well-known publisher and Samuel Gurney Jr, but these would seem to have been less active and were certainly less regular in their attendance at meetings. Although the average age of the Committee as a whole, thanks to these new additions, did not increase significantly, the average age of

25. James M. McPherson, *The Struggle for Equality: Abolitionists and the Negro in the Civil War and Reconstruction* (Princeton, 1964), pp. 3–8.
26. BFASS Minute Books, 1841–45, 1854–58.
27. The number of members in the Committee dropped from 30 in 1840 to 15 in 1857 and the average number present at meetings from 10 to 8. BFASS *Annual Reports*, 1840, 1857; BFASS Minute Books, 1841–43, 1855–57.
28. Temperley, "British and Foreign Anti-Slavery Society", Appendices I and II.

the members of its inner caucus did. In 1855 Joseph Sturge was sixty-two, Josiah Forster seventy-three, George Stacey sixty-eight, Robert Forster sixty-three and Henry Sterry fifty-two. They were also becoming more conservative with the years. Even their own secretary regarded them as a "strait-waistcoated" lot.[29] In terms of its leadership, the Society was an ageing organization.

The Society's decline is also reflected in its financial accounts. Its average yearly income dropped from £2,400 in 1841–44 to £900 in 1851–54.[30] Since it had never depended to any significant extent on popular support, and since the large donors on whom it had relied were still as rich as ever, these figures suggest that even the stalwarts of the antislavery cause were losing faith. Also revealing for the light it throws on the state of the movement in the country at large is the drop in the number and size of subscriptions and donations received from auxiliary organizations. Thus in 1855–56 it received only fourteen contributions (£64) from this source as compared with thirty-three (£489) twelve years earlier.[31] Most significant of all was the decline in the number of male organizations. During the forties more than half the auxiliaries had been male bodies, but in 1852–53 only five out of thirteen, and in 1857–58 only one out of eleven societies contributing to the Society's funds were male.[32] In such towns as Birmingham, Chelmsford, Exeter and Liskeard, where organizations of men and women had formerly existed side by side, the male organizations had by 1852 become inactive leaving the women, with their sewing circles and charity drives, in sole possession of the field.[33]

This decline in the Society's income had a marked effect on its policies. Since an ever increasing proportion of its dwindling resources was now absorbed by rent, salaries and other fixed expenses, relatively little was left for other purposes. Financing publications, which in its early years had taken up around a third of its income, was by the mid-fifties absorbing only a tenth.[34] In 1845 the *Reporter* changed from a fortnightly to a monthly publication and, in 1853, its size was reduced from quarto to octavo. It continued to appear at monthly intervals until 1868 when it became a quarterly. By 1860 its circulation had fallen to 700, of which only eighty copies were sold, the remainder being sent to the Society's subscribers or otherwise distributed free of charge.[35] The cost of its editing

29. Chamerovzow to Brougham, 10 Jan. 1861, Brougham Papers.
30. BFASS *Annual Reports*, 1641–44, 1851–54.
31. *Ibid*, 1843–44, 1855–56.   32. *Ibid*, 1852–3, 1857–8.
33. The predominance of women in the British movement was noted by American visitors: see the comments of J. Miller McKim in *Anti-Slavery Advocate*, Jan. 1854.
34. BFASS *Annual Reports*, 1840–43, 1855–60.
35. BFASS Minute Books, 2 March 1860.

and printing fell from £631 in 1841–42 to £143 in 1853–54, while the total cost of the Committee's publications declined, during the same period, from £1,181 to £169.[36] The output of individual pamphlets on questions of public interest—such as those on slavery in British India and on the recognition of Texas—was reduced during the late 1840s and had practically ceased by 1853. It was resumed again, though only to a limited extent, during the 1860s.

In other respects too there was a marked diminution in the Society's activities. During the 1840s the Secretary had been a busy man, interviewing cabinet ministers, lobbying MPs, drafting memorials, composing pamphlets and corresponding with a host of people in Britain and abroad. By the mid-fifties this was no longer the case. Chamerovzow, who succeeded Scoble in 1852, began his career with a valiant effort to heal the rifts in the movement which, as will be shown presently, ended in failure. Thereafter he continued to perform most of the tasks which his predecessor had performed, but in a mechanical way. The sense of urgency had gone, and for weeks and sometimes months at a time he was left with almost nothing to do. The *Reporter* had become largely a compendium of antislavery information, much of it culled from American magazines and newspapers or from *Parliamentary Papers* and other official publications. The Minute Books and *Annual Reports* still reflected the Committee's wide range of interests. Yet closer scrutiny reveals that the developments described were not, for the most part, developments in which the Society was involved any more than the achievements celebrated were its achievements.

These changes may, in part, be ascribed to its own past failures. It had promised great things of West Indian emancipation and then been obliged to confess that sugar production had declined; had opposed the government on the question of the Indian coolies and been overruled; had agitated against free trade in sugar and been defeated; had sought to enlist British sympathy on behalf of the American abolitionists and been denounced by a highly vocal section of those abolitionists as a hindrance to the cause. Even Lewis Tappan had been led to observe that the best way of getting something done in America was to make it known that British abolitionists were against it. The most striking of Britain's recent achievements, the suppression of the slave trade to Brazil, had been accomplished not with the Society's support but in the face of its strenuous opposition. All told it was not a record to inspire confidence.

Yet to ascribe the Society's decline solely to its past failures is rather

36. BFASS *Annual Reports*, 1842–43, 1854–55.

to miss the point. For its loss of impetus can also be seen as the result of success—not the Society's success, perhaps, but the success of the antislavery cause generally. In opposing the government's suppression policy the Society had erred but the fact remains that, according to Foreign Office estimates, the number of Negroes carried westward annually had dropped from 135,000 in 1835–40 to a mere 7,000 in 1853–56. Although the immigrant labour traffic to Mauritius and the West Indies continued, many of its worst abuses had been removed. Slavery as a legalized institution had been abolished throughout Britain's eastern possessions. Apart from encouraging economic growth in these areas, a policy which the Society continued to advocate, there was little more that could be done. France, Denmark and Sweden had abolished slavery in their possessions. In the United States the abolitionists had succeeded in making slavery the leading political issue of the day and stood in little need of further support or encouragement. In the Dutch legislature, too, slavery was receiving an increasing amount of attention and there were encouraging signs that abolitionist agitation in the country generally was on the increase.[37] Whatever the Society's own failures and successes, its initial aims were well on the way to being achieved.[38]

The fact is that by the mid-fifties most of the issues which had engaged its attention during the forties had been decided and no new ones of importance had arisen to take their place. If the younger generation failed to support the antislavery cause, it was largely because it realized, more clearly apparently than its elders, that the British movement had for the time being achieved all that could reasonably be expected of it. Thus the underlying cause of the Society's decline—and the decline of antislavery activity generally—was not public disapproval, or even public inertia, so much as a genuine lack of issues.

This void was felt with peculiar acuteness during the mid-fifties. In 1853, having lately abandoned its campaign for the economic coercion of Brazil and Cuba, and urged on by its energetic new Secretary, it undertook a general review of its policies. After prolonged discussion and much heart-searching it concluded that "the two most practical points to agitate are: the growth of cotton in India and on the West Coast of Africa; and the position of the American religious bodies on the question of slavery".[39] These were both old chestnuts and it is clear from subsequent developments that it had thought up no new ways of tackling them.

37. BFASS *Reporter*, 2 June 1856, pp. 134–6.
38. As the Society itself was pleased to note. See BFASS *Annual Report*, 1853, pp. 3–4; Chamerovzow to Brougham, 30 July 1858, Brougham Papers.
39. BFASS Minute Books, 5 Oct. 1853.

During the next five years the Society was largely dormant. Meetings, of course, continued to be held, resolutions approved and one or two minor issues taken up. One of these was the question of British nationals owning slaves abroad. In its early years, much agitated about this problem, it had succeeded in persuading Lord Brougham to introduce a Bill making it an offence to hold slaves in foreign countries. This was duly passed[40] but remained entirely a dead letter since the offenders were, and took care to remain, outside British jurisdiction. The only effect of the Act seems to have been to persuade some holders of stock in a Brazilian mining company to present their latest dividends, totalling £75, to the Society. Since it was at that very time agitating against the Free Church for its acceptance of "bloodstained money" the sum was hastily returned to its donors.[41] In the 1850s the issue came up again, this time in relation to a group of British subjects holding slaves in Dutch Guiana who had drawn attention to themselves by petitioning the Dutch legislature against emancipation. After assuring the Dutch that these individuals were, at least in the eyes of their own countrymen, criminals, the Society arranged through the Foreign Secretary for the British Consul at Paramaribo to explain to them that they were liable to prosecution should they ever return to Britain.[42] Another case involved the opposite situation, a foreign slaveholder carrying on his operations on British territory. The individual involved was a Portuguese national, Don Cayatenes, who apparently used a considerable body of slaves to cultivate ground nuts on the British owned island of Bolama off the Guinea coast. The facts were well authenticated but by the time the Colonial Office, prodded by the Society, got around to investigating he had moved his slaves elsewhere.[43]

Various other incidents of this kind engaged the Committee's attention, several involving foreign visitors who brought with them Negro servants who were suspected of being slaves, although this was never proved.[44] Other cases involved issues which were to become more important later in the century, among them the problem of illegal slavery in the Trans-

40. 6 and 7 Victoria, C 98; see also BFASS Minute Books, 13, 20 Aug., 3 Sept. 1841; 7 Jan., 7 Feb., 29 April, 13 June, 29 July 1842; 12 Jan. 1844; Scoble to Brougham, 10 Sept. 1841; 3, 9 Aug. 1842, Brougham Papers; *Spectator*, 15 July 1843.
41. BFASS Minute Books, 12 Jan., 28 June, 31 Aug. 1844; E. S. Abdy to Scoble. 12 July 1844, BFASS Papers, C 12/3.
42. BFASS Minute Books, 1, 6 April, 1 July, 7 Oct. 1859; 6 Sept. 1861.
43. BFASS Minute Books, 13, 28 July, 28 Sept. 1849; 5 July 1850.
44. Since few of these servants could speak English, and all were afraid of their masters, their precise status was almost impossible to determine. See the case of Dr Barth, *ibid*, 4 Jan., 3 Oct., 7 Nov., 5 Dec. 1856.

vaal[45] and "blackbirding" in the Pacific.[46] The Crimean War acquainted some British people with the horrors of Turkish slavery. Prompted by a vigorous letter from Richard Cobden on the subject, the Committee began collecting information on the trade in eunuchs and concubines to Constantinople.[47] Native servitude in Africa also came in for some attention when it was learned from British functionaries on the Gold Coast that slavery was endemic throughout the area. Further investigation showed, however, that Britain's authority over the natives was uncertain and that any attempt to interfere with their tribal practices was likely to be strongly resisted.[48] The Society also became much concerned during 1857 and 1858 over the growth of the French *emigré* system for supplying its Indian Ocean and New World colonies with Negro labourers from the Portuguese colony of Mozambique. In theory these were free labourers, but they were supplied by the same people who had formerly provided slaves, and in much the same way. There were none of the safeguards which, thanks largely to humanitarian protests, had been incorporated into British emigration schemes, and except for a few farcical formalities it amounted to simple slaving. The Society sent an address to Napoleon III and also succeeded in interesting several members of the British government in the matter. But there was nothing Britain could do beyond making her disapproval known. The practice continued until 1864 when Napoleon abolished it by decree.[49]

Apart from America, the question which took up the greatest amount o the Committee's time during the early and mid-fifties was the position of the freedmen in the West Indies. Here the lack of issues was particularly apparent. The crucial years, from the Society's point of view, had been the late thirties and early forties, when there was a real possibility that the planters would succeed in reducing the freedmen to the condition of serfs. Once this danger had passed, as by the mid-forties it had, nothing

45. BFASS Minute Books, 7 Feb., 1 April, 1 July 1853; 3 Feb. 1854; 2 Nov. 1855; 4 Jan., 2 May 1856. The Boers had undertaken, by the Rand River Convention of 1852 and the Bloemfontein Convention of 1853, not to permit slaveholding. In spite of this there is considerable evidence that they continued to do so: see Sir John Harris, *A Century of Emancipation* (London, 1933), p. 117.

46. The first case to reach the Committee's attention was in 1859 and involved the seizure of a group of natives from the Gilbert Islands, who were subsequently sold to planters on the French island of Bourbon off the coast of Mozambique. BFASS Minute Books, 4 Feb., 4 March, 1 April, 7 Oct. 1859.

47. *Ibid*, 2 March 1855; Cobden to Sturge, 28 July 1854; Sturge Papers, British Museum, Add. MSS 43722/29.

48. BFASS Minute Books, 7 Feb., 23 March, 1 April, 1 July 1853; 19 Feb. 1854; 11 April 1855.

49. *Ibid*, 4 Sept., 2 Oct., 6 Nov., 4 Dec. 1857; 1 Jan., 5, 15 Feb., 5 March, 19 April, 7 May 1858; James Duffy, *Portugal in Africa* (London, 1962), p. 97.

remained to be done but to keep a watching brief on developments to see that such attempts were not renewed. On the advice of its West Indian correspondents it continued addressing memorials to the Colonial Office protesting against such measures as the British Guiana licensing and registration ordinances and the Jamaican suffrage regulations. But these were largely ignored, mainly because the measures in question were less oppressive than the Committee had been led to suppose. The British Guiana licensing law, for example, was little more than a law requiring pedlars to have licences and was less stringent than a similar regulation already in force in Britain.[50] For a time in the mid-fifties the Society had high hopes that the colonies' economic difficulties could be solved by improved techniques of production but interest in this declined with the sugar boom of 1857–60 and did not revive thereafter.[51] For the benefit of foreign audiences, it continued to stress its belief that the economic plight of the colonies was the result of mismanagement and not of emancipation. As before, there was much truth in this claim although the underlying causes were more complex than it was prepared to admit, or possibly realized.[52]

Although the mid-fifties were uneventful years for the Society an unexpected series of developments led to some quickening of activity in the closing years of the decade. In 1854, the year of the final equalization of the sugar duties, the world price of sugar stood at 23s 9d per hundredweight, but soon it began to rise and by 1857 reached 38s.[53] To the hardpressed colonial planters this was a boon. The number of Indian labourers taken to Mauritius rose from 12,725 in 1857 to 29,946 in 1858, reaching 44,397 in 1859, and there was a proportionate increase in the traffic to the West Indies.[54] As before, the Society was not opposed to this traffic; what it did demand was that the balance between the sexes be preserved, that care be taken to avoid mortality during the voyage, that the articles of indenture be respected upon arrival and that the cost be borne by the planters and not, as was generally the case, by the public exchequer.[55]

50. Ibid, 2 Aug. 1850; BFASS Reporter, 1 Oct. 1850, pp. 148–9, 157; W. L. Mathieson, The Sugar Colonies and Governor Eyre (London, 1936), p. 79, n. 1.
51. See for example, "Important experiments on cane juice", BFASS Reporter, 31 May 1855, and Chamerovzow's address to the Amsterdam Young Men's Anti-Slavery Society on the same subject in ibid, 1 Sept. 1855.
52. The state of the colonies at this time is admirably described in Mathieson, The Sugar Colonies and Governor Eyre, and Curtin, Two Jamaicas.
53. See Appendix A below.
54. Hitchins, The Colonial Land and Emigration Commission, appendices XI and XII. In the West Indies the effects were felt a year later. The number of labourers introduced was: 1858—4,130; 1859—8,342; 1860—11,484; 1861—11,809; 1862—14,549.
55. BFASS Minute Books, 3 May 1861.

It succeeded in enlisting the support of Brougham and Charles Buxton in its efforts to have a parliamentary committee appointed to review the whole question and a public meeting, presided over by Lord Brougham, was held. The Society had no difficulty in showing that, despite the government's regulations, frauds and abuses continued on a wide scale. The report of the later Sanderson Committee (1910) substantially supports this contention,[56] but at the time the Government was content to brush all criticism aside with the bland assurance that, on the whole, the system was working to everyone's advantage. In spite of the efforts of Brougham, Buxton and the Society no enquiry was instituted and no general changes in the immigration system made.[57]

The demand for labourers to cope with the booming sugar market was not confined to Britain's colonies. The Spanish colonies, too, experienced a need for more hands, only in their case it was slave, not free, labour that was involved. Since the ending of the Brazilian branch of the traffic and the subsequent abandonment of their public campaign for the imposition of economic sanctions the Sturgites had been without a slave trade policy. The nature of their views and of the problems facing the Government is revealed in an account of a long and unusually frank interview they had in 1857 with Lord Clarendon, the Foreign Secretary.[58] Britain's policy on the Cuban question, he explained, needed careful handling. The Government was prepared to do everything in its power to suppress the slave trade but it was keenly aware that any hasty action would, as he put it, "throw the island into the lap of the United States", which was now coveting it in much the same way as a generation earlier she had coveted Texas. For this reason it had to proceed cautiously. When the deputation asked him how he felt about applying economic sanctions against Cuba he replied that he regarded it as entirely impractical on account of British public sentiment on the free-trade issue. Chamerovzow then asked whether it would not be possible for Britain to purchase Cuba in return for the cancellation of Spanish debts. The United States, he pointed out, had offered to buy Cuba for 100 million dollars (actually it was 130 million) whereas Spain's debt to Britain exceeded 250 million. Clarendon conceded the attractiveness of the idea but explained that the Spanish debt was a private debt contracted by bankers who had advanced the money for a consideration and agreed to take all risks. It would be improper for the government to intervene, and in any case an attempt to

56. See the extracts from the *Sanderson Report* in Harris, pp. 65–73.
57. BFASS Minute Books, Feb. 1859–Feb. 1860; Mathieson, *The Sugar Colonies and Governor Eyre*, pp. 133–5.
58. BFASS Minute Books, 6 March 1857.

buy Cuba would inevitably lead to trouble with the United States. Apart
from persevering with the interception policy and issuing remonstrances
to the Spanish government—admittedly an ineffectual business—there
really was not much that Britain could do. The deputation felt flattered
by Clarendon's frankness but chastened by his reasoning.

At this time the Cuban slave trade was relatively small—a mere 7,000 in
1857—but thereafter it grew rapidly, reaching 30,000 in 1859.[59] In the
late fifties this issue replaced American slavery as the Society's major
concern and continued to dominate its affairs until 1862 when, as we shall
see, the possibility of a solution appeared. In the meantime, however,
the Committee displayed something of its old crusading spirit. Three
pamphlets, The Slave Trade As It Is (London, 1860), An Address to
Esparto (London, 1861) and The African Slave Trade to Cuba (London,
1862) were distributed[60] and over a thousand large placards depicting
the interior of a slave ship were put on public display.[61] These activities
were almost entirely confined to the London area. An attempt to broaden
the protest by enlisting the support of people outside the metropolis
was abandoned after much fruitless travelling by the Secretary when
it became clear that almost everyone formerly connected with the Society
was either dead or "incapacitated by age or infirmities from taking any
active part in a public movement".[62] Even if they had not been, it is hard
to see how their support would have helped to solve the problem. As so
often in the past, the means adopted bore little relation to the object sought.
There were, however, some significant changes. No voices were raised
on this occasion against Britain's suppression policies. More surprisingly,
the Society began pressing the Government to employ the same drastic
measures towards Cuba that it had previously used with such salutary
effect toward Brazil. This was politically impossible for the reasons
Clarendon had given.[63] What accounted for this change in the Committee's
attitude is not clear, but it seems unlikely that so drastic a departure could
have occurred had it not been for Sturge's death in 1859.[64]

None of these issues (except, of course, American slavery) was of much

59. See Appendix A below.
60. In all, some 25,000 copies of these pamphlets were sold. A fourth pamphlet,
The Slave Traders of Liverpool (London, 1862) concerned the case of the Nightingale,
an American vessel which shortly after being outfitted in Liverpool was captured
off the African coast with 500 slaves on board. For details see BFASS Minute
Books, 6 Jan. 1862.
61. Ibid, Feb–June 1862.   62. Ibid, 7 March 1862.
63. Brougham was obliged to explain to the Society that Parliament would never
agree to this proposal: Ibid, 14 June 1861.
64. Sturge, who was elected President of the Peace Society in 1858, retained his
pacifist principles until his death: Richard, Memoirs of Joseph Sturge, pp. 565–7.

concern to the general public. Nor did any of them enter to any significant extent into the thinking of the Garrisonian branch of the movement. So far as it was concerned, these were red herrings introduced by the Broad Street Quakers to divert attention from the real purpose of the movement, which was to mobilize British support on behalf of the one true spokesman of the antislavery cause in America, William Lloyd Garrison.

Even at the best of times the amount of public support given to the Garrisonians had been small. Only in Scotland had they been able to attract a large following and then only because of their success in exploiting existing religious feuds. By 1850 even this following had largely dropped away. The once influential Glasgow Emancipation Society had been reduced to the Smeals and Murrays and a small circle of their friends.[65] Financially it had never recovered from the debts incurred in the "Send Back the Money" campaign.[66] Its total receipts and expenditures, which had amounted to over £500 in the two years 1845–47 totalled only £50 a year during the next four years, after which records cease.[67] The Hibernian Anti-Slavery Society now consisted simply of the members of the Webb and Houghton families.[68] To a large extent, indeed, British Garrisonianism had become a family affair, run by the Smeals, Murrays, Webbs, Houghtons, Wighams (female), and Estlins. To this list must be added various Unitarian friends of the Estlins, such as the Rev. S. A. Steinthal of Bridgwater, the Rev. Francis Bishop of Liverpool and the Bristol and Clifton Ladies whom Mary Estlin succeeded in enticing away from Broad Street. Even more than in the forties the rank-and-file support for the Garrisonians—in so far as they had a rank-and-file—came from Unitarians.[69]

The only significant figures connected with this branch of the movement not so far mentioned are Wilson Armistead, a Quaker philanthropist who was responsible for initiating various antislavery projects in the Leeds area and who gave his somewhat equivocal support to the Garrisonians;[70] George Thompson's son-in-law, F. W. Chesson, who helped to reorganize the Manchester Anti-Slavery Union in the early fifties and who later became secretary of the Aborigines Protection Society; and, of course, George Thompson himself. Thompson remained the only figure of national

65. Rice, pp. 479–80.
66. William Smeal to W. W. Brown, 12 Dec. 1850, Weston Papers.
67. Receipts for the period 1 Feb. 1847 to 1 Feb. 1851 amounted to £174.10s 2d, expenditures to £207.10s, of which only some £60 would appear to have been new expenditures. GES *Annual Reports*, 1845–51.
68. Rice p. 479.
69. *Ibid*, pp. 346–7; 421–7; L. Billington, pp. 310–14.
70. For an account of these see Armistead to Chamerovzow, 7 April, 10 Aug., 24 Sept. 1853, BFASS Papers, C 27/49, 53, 55.

stature with avowed Garrisonian principles, although his actual contribution to the cause in the fifties was minimal. Thanks to his association with the Raja of Sattara he had managed to set himself up comfortably in Chelsea and in the general election of 1847 had been elected to Parliament by Lushington's old constituency of Tower Hamlets with, so it was said, the largest popular majority of any member of the new House.[71] Although a good stump speaker he was less effective in the give-and-take of parliamentary debate. What antagonized his constituents, however, was his continual involvement in what they considered irrelevant outside activities and in particular a prolonged absence in the United States from November 1850 until June 1851. As he himself admitted, the reason for this visit—a lecture tour arranged for him by the American Anti-Slavery Society—was largely financial. The Raja's money was now running out and he hoped to collect enough in lecture fees to carry him through the next session.[72] The tour itself was undoubtedly a success. It contrasted markedly with the reception given him on his previous visit, showing what changes fifteen years of antislavery agitation had wrought. He travelled from Maine to Pennsylvania and as far West as the Great Lakes and Upper Canada, being greeted everywhere, according to Wendell Phillips, as "a universal idol".[73] The daily accounts of his doings which he sent to Miss Anne Warren Weston, a Massachusetts admirer to whom he had formed an attachment, showed that he was enjoying himself immensely.[74] But in Britain the response was hostile, and became progressively more so as the date of his return was postponed. Even Garrisonian sympathizers had doubted the propriety of a British MP collecting fees as an antislavery lecturer in America.[75] Radicals who had previously supported him, even though they had doubts about the antislavery cause, entirely lost patience. The *Friend of the People* declared that he should "look at home, and stay at home, to reform the slavery disgracing his native land". His chances of re-election, it added, were "infinitesimally small".[76] This proved to be the case. On his return he was given a stormy reception by his constituents and in the general election of 1852 he was obliged to stand down.[77] The next seven years were a bleak period in

71. Stanton, p. 244.   72. Thompson to Garrison, 3 Oct. 1850, Garrison Papers.
73. Phillips to Elizabeth Pease, 9 March 1851, Garrison Papers.
74. Thompson to A. W. Weston, Jan.–March 1851, Weston Papers.
75. J. B. Estlin to A. W. Weston, 31 Oct. 1850, Weston Papers.
76. No. 24, 24 May 1851.
77. Thompson to [?] 15 Aug. 1851, Thompson Papers, Boston Public Library; Thompson to Garrison, 7 June 1852, Garrison Papers. Accounts of his lecturing activities in Britain will be found in *Anti-Slavery Advocate*. For example, in April, 1853, it reported that he had lectured in Basingstoke, Romsey, Rochester and London.

Thompson's life. There was not enough antislavery work in Britain to keep him in pocket money, though he still appeared quite often on anti-slavery platforms. Most of the other causes with which he had been associated were now dead and in any case he had usually ended by quarrel-ling with his colleagues, who in consequence were not disposed to come to his rescue now.[78] In 1853 he tried, with the assistance of Miss Weston, to find employment with the American Anti-Slavery Society, but even it was doubtful about employing an Englishman to preach disunion on a full-time basis.[79] For a while he worked for an insurance company and then, with the help of his son-in-law, as editor of a reform magazine, the *Empire*.[80] After this collapsed in 1856 he made a second trip to India, this time on behalf of a textile company, and there fell ill with a "bilious fever". His employers having meanwhile gone bankrupt, he returned to England penniless, partially paralysed, and with no prospects of employ-ment. A collection got up on his behalf helped to tide him over for the time being, but as the decade closed it looked very much as though his career was at an end.[81]

Although small in numbers and without an effective national organiza-tion or leader the Garrisonian branch of the movement nevertheless remained highly vocal. Its mouthpiece, the *Anti-Slavery Advocate*, financed by Estlin and Armistead, edited by Estlin and Webb, and printed by Webb in Dublin, continued to appear throughout the fifties, providing its readers with rather livelier fare than the staid *Reporter*.[82] The Garrison-ians were also active pamphleteers. Webb's *The National Anti-Slavery Societies of England and the United States* (Dublin, 1852) was one of the ablest statements of the Garrisonian case to appear on either side of the Atlantic, and Estlin, Armistead, Chesson, and the Bristol and Clifton Ladies also revealed themselves talented in this line.[83] Altogether they

78. Webb to Edmund Quincy, 22 July 1853, Webb-Quincy Correspondence, Boston Public Library.
79. Ellis Gray Loring to A. W. Weston, 9 Sept. 1853, and Lucretia Mott to A. W. Weston, 18 Nov. 1853, Weston Papers.
80. Thompson to A. W. Weston, 4 March 1853, and R. D. Webb to Edmund Quincy, 21 Aug. 1854, Webb-Quincy Correspondence, Boston Public Library; *Anti-Slavery Advocate*, Feb., May, June, 1855.
81. Rice, p. 464; Chamerovzow to Brougham, 22 Dec. 1860, 6 Jan. 1861, Brougham Papers.
82. It was originally intended that this would be the organ of a body to be known as the Anglo-American Anti-Slavery Association, but as with so many other Garrison-ian attempts to establish a national organization to act as a counterweight to the BFASS, this one failed: *Anti-Slavery Advocate*, 1 Oct. 1852, p. 1; 1 July 1856, p. 380; Estlin to Garrison, 7 June 1852, Garrison Papers.
83. John Bishop Estlin, *Slavery in America* (Bristol, 1846); Wilson Armistead, *A Tribute for the Negro: Being a Vindication of the Moral, Intellectual and Religious Capabilities of the Coloured Portion of Mankind* (Manchester, 1848), *Five Hundred*

succeeded in trumpeting their leader's praises-in such a way as to mislead a great many people as to the amount of influence he had in America, which by this time was very little indeed.[84]

Committed though they were, they could hardly have sustained these efforts without continued encouragement and visits from American Garrisonian representatives. The amount of attention which American Garrisonians paid to Britain, and which contrasted with the behaviour of most other groups of American abolitionists, stemmed in part from their reliance on the British to help eke out their meagre budgets. The value of this support is hard to estimate since most of it was in the form of articles to be sold at the annual Boston Bazaar. After 1858, when the Bazaar was discontinued and a "subscription anniversary" substituted, British contributions accounted for approximately a third of the total receipts.[85] It is also clear that, having eschewed political involvement, Garrisonians were as happy denouncing slavery and the New Organizationists in Britain as they would have been anywhere else. Throughout the fifties they strove to make their British allies feel as though they were active participants in the American struggle. American abolitionists, Parker Pillsbury assured a group of middle class ladies,

value your aid above all price. It is the vitality of our annual bazaar, and the bazaar is the chief instrumentality, I might say our chief reliance, for pecuniary aid, "the sinews of war".... And besides your moral influence against the awful iniquity is the voice of seven thunders in the ear of the oppressor. A slaveholder said in congress not long ago that the South and slaveholders stood with slavery *at bay against the world.* It is true. Let the world's stern rebuke pursue them.[86]

Besides Pillsbury, the most notable Garrisonians to visit Britain in the 'fifties were James Miller McKim, Sarah Pugh, Samuel May and Mrs

Thousand Strokes for Freedom (London, 1853); F. W. Chesson, "A brief sketch of the anti-slavery movement in America", in H. G. Adams, ed., *God's Image in Ebony* (London 1854); Bristol and Clifton Ladies' Anti-Slavery Society, *Special Report of the Bristol and Clifton Ladies' Anti-Slavery Society ... January 1851 to June 1852, with a Statement of the Reasons for its Separation from the British and Foreign Anti-Slavery Society* (London, 1852).

84. Even in America, old style abolitionism had become something of an anachronism. Garrison now interested his fellow countrymen principally for the way in which he *responded* to events. As the grand old man of radical antislavery he was accorded a grudging recognition, but his personal influence steadily declined: Thomas, *The Liberator*, pp. 367 ff.

85. Of the 6,095 dollars raised in 1859–60, 2,367 dollars came from foreign, mostly British, sources. Many of those who contributed would appear to have been well-wishers rather than active abolitionists. Harwood, "Great Britain and American Antislavery", p. 636.

86. Pillsbury to Mrs Tribe, President of the Bristol and Clifton Ladies Anti-Slavery Society, 1 May 1854, in *Anti-Slavery Advocate*, June 1854, pp. 163–4.

Maria W. Chapman who, in her Paris exile, continued to keep a watchful eye on British developments.[87] Like Collins, Wright and Garrison himself in the forties, they kept the fires of discord well stoked and effectively forestalled all attempts to reunify the movement. Their principal coup, engineered by Mary Estlin and Mrs Chapman, was the conversion of the Bristol and Clifton Ladies Anti-Slavery Society. Originally founded in 1840 as an auxiliary of the British and Foreign Anti-Slavery Society this somewhat somnolent body had hitherto limited its operations to collecting money on behalf of Broad Street.[88] Now, moved to furious action, it published a series of vicious attacks on the national organization accusing it, among other things, of having "grievously retarded the Anti-Slavery Cause throughout the world".[89] The London Committee did not itself reply but Lewis Tappan took up its cause with his *Reply to Charges Brought Against the American and Foreign Anti-Slavery Society* (London, 1852) to which John Scoble contributed an introduction. In this he accused the Garrisonians of having, by abandoning politics, abandoned the cause of the Negro and went on to state that their criticisms of the churches had been pressed to the point of undermining all organized religion, thus laying the movement open to charges of infidelity. It was now the turn of the American Garrisonians to reply. This they did with a pamphlet by Edmund Quincy entitled *An Examination of the Charges of Mr John Scoble and Mr Lewis Tappan Against the American Anti-Slavery Society* (London, 1852) which surpassed its predecessors in the violence of its language. It was a melancholy sight, it stated, to see a body such as the London Committee, which had "done such noble work in its day, sink into a malicious dotage, only saved from the pity which its anile feebleness might excite by the contempt aroused by its impotent malignity". Webb too joined in the fray with his *National Anti-Slavery Societies* which contrasted the situations of abolitionists in the two countries. What right had the wealthy Broad Street Quakers to rail against the hard-

87. Details of their comings and goings will be found in GES Minute Books; in Webb's correspondence, Garrison and May Papers, and in the Minute Books of the Bristol and Clifton Ladies Anti-Slavery Society, Dr Williams' Library, London—henceforward referred to as BCLASS Minute Books.
88. BCLASS Minute Books, 17 Sept. 1840 to 11 Sept. 1851. That this body may already have had radical leanings is suggested by the fact that during the controversies arising out of Garrison's visit in 1846 it was not sure which side to support. It wrote to Thompson asking for information about the Anti-Slavery League but when he failed to reply the matter was dropped. In 1848, its members were surprised to learn that the *Reporter* would not accept an advertisement on behalf of the Boston Anti-Slavery Bazaar, but again the matter was not pursued: *ibid*, 5 Nov. 1846; 4 Feb. 1847; 3 Feb. 1848; F. Armstrong to Garrison, 3 Sept. 1846, Garrison Papers.
89. *Bristol Examiner*, 23, 30 Aug., 6, 13, 27 Sept. 1851.

working, zealous and much-maligned agents of the American Anti-Slavery Society? It was simply another case of the rich and respectable turning their backs on the poor and deserving.

As with political groups out of power and with no prospect of attaining it, the sheer impotence of the abolitionists encouraged that manic fringe of the movement whose posturings and denunciations bore only a tenuous relation to their supposed object, the liberation of the American Negro. This particular dispute would doubtless have dragged on longer had not Scoble, against whom the Garrisonians' bitterest shafts had been aimed,[90] announced in the summer of 1852 his intention of resigning in order to take up a position as resident superintendent of the Dawn Institute, a settlement for fugitive American Negroes in Upper Canada. This would appear to have been an entirely voluntary decision but there is no doubt that his departure relieved the Committee, which had sought to remain aloof from these controversies, of an embarrassment.[91] His successor, Chamerovzow, made genuine efforts to win over the dissidents, and but for the American Garrisonians might have succeeded. He opened the pages of the *Reporter* to accounts of their meetings, wrote conciliatory letters, begged their advice, and made elaborate plans for a World Anti-slavery Convention to which all factions would be invited.[92] British Garrisonians noted these efforts with approval. Webb thought Chamerov-zow "an honest, straightforward, well disposed man—most desirous to help the cause"; Smeal wrote congratulating him on the "improved tone" of the *Reporter;* the Bristol and Clifton ladies expressed satisfaction at the "enlarged and liberal policy" adopted by Broad Street, and Estlin even went so far as to send a small donation.[93] On all sides there were expressions of willingness to work together for the reunification of the movement.

All the same, it remained an uneasy alliance. Old antagonisms were not easily laid to rest and had an uncomfortable habit of resurfacing at the smallest provocation. This tendency was embarrassingly evident in the

90. Webb, p. 9, accuses him of being a back-stairs operator who was afraid to face the Garrisonians in public but who delighted in slandering them in private.
91. Scoble's propensity for feuding subsequently helped produce similar rifts in the ranks of the Canadian abolitionists. For an account of his later career see Winks, *Blacks in Canada*, pp. 201–4.
92. The idea was first mooted at a meeting between members of the Broad Street Committee and the Edinburgh New Anti-Slavery Association held in Edinburgh Music Hall on 15 Oct. 1853; *Anti-Slavery Watchman*, Nov. 1833, p. 25.
93. Webb to Samuel May, 3 June 1833, May Papers; Smeal to Chamerovzow, 16 April 1852, BFASS Papers C 36/526; BCLASS Minute Books, 18 March 1853; BFASS Minute Books, 6 May 1853; Samuel May "Memorial to the Late Mr Estlin", *Liberator*, 14 Dec. 1855, p. 199.

case of the first serious attempt at joint action, the launching of the Manchester Anti-Slavery Union. The leading spirit behind this enterprise was Frederick William Chesson, an enthusiastic young protégé—he was only twenty—of George Thompson's.[94] Like Thompson, Chesson was an avowed Garrisonian, but in the improved atmosphere created by Chamerovzow he showed himself not simply willing but positively anxious to work with the Sturgites. During the course of the autumn he discussed his plans with Chamerovzow and in the first number of his new periodical, the *Anti-Slavery Watchman*, which was to be the official organ of the Union, spoke glowingly of the opportunities for cooperation.[95] The Union's inaugural meeting, held on 24 November, went off well, with speeches by Chamerovzow, Chesson, Thompson and Sturge—the first time Thompson and Sturge had appeared together on a platform for almost a decade.[96] Within a month, however, the Union's committee found itself hopelessly divided over whether to appoint the Rev. F. W. Hemming, who claimed to be on a fund-raising mission on behalf of the American and Foreign Anti-Slavery Society,[97] as its agent. Chesson and Thompson strenuously opposed his appointment on the grounds that his ties with the New Organizationists made him an unsuitable person to represent a non-sectarian body like the Union. Hemming himself made matters worse by accusing his critics of "malignant motives" and describing Garrison as the leader of the "infidel party". When the majority continued to support him, Chesson and Thompson resigned and set about establishing a rival body, the North of England Anti-Slavery and India Reform League. These events were sadly recorded in the third and final issue of the *Watchman*.[98] Little was heard of either body thereafter, although the League did succeed in holding a general convention on 1 August, 1854, run this time on strictly Garrisonian lines.[99]

Despite this setback, Chamerovzow's efforts might still have accomplished something had it not been for the intervention of the American

94. Chesson had met Thompson when he attended the Manchester Peace Conference which Chesson had organized in the summer of 1853. He later married Thompson's second daughter: for an account of his career see *Aborigines' Friend*, March, 1889, pp. 513–23.
95. *Anti-Slavery Watchman*, Nov. 1853, p. 17.
96. *Ibid*, Dec. 1853; *Anti-Slavery Advocate*, Jan. 1854, p. 122.
97. The American and Foreign Anti-Slavery Society had actually disowned him although this was not known at the time. Tappan to Chamerovzow, 19 Nov. 1853, in Abel and Klingberg, pp. 333–4.
98. See also BFASS *Reporter*, 1 March 1854, and Chesson to M. W. Chapman, 17 Jan. 1854, Weston Papers.
99. The main delegates were all Garrisonians and it passed resolutions fully endorsing the policies of the American Anti-Slavery Society. *Anti-Slavery Advocate* Sept. 1854, pp. 189–200.

Garrisonians. In reply to Webb's eulogistic comments on Chamerovzow's character, May declared himself "totally distrustful" of Broad Street's policies which he interpreted as having been undertaken "with the hope of obtaining the control of the newly-awakened anti-slavery feeling which the long labours of the faithful abolitionists and Mrs Stowe's book have been instrumental in producing".[100] As he and other American Garrisonians saw it, Chamerovzow's "entente cordiale" was simply a cunning attempt, all the more so because it traded on feelings of generosity and good-fellowship, to undermine the loyalty of their British supporters. They resolved therefore, to see that it was stopped.[101] At Chamerovzow's so-called World Convention, held in London on November 29–30, 1854, they succeeded. Parker Pillsbury, who had been enlisting support against Chamerovzow since his arrival in Britain the previous spring and who was regarded as something of a fanatic even by Wendell Phillips, blew the meeting apart with a vitriolic attack on the national organization and on the London Quakers for the part they had played in the Indiana schism. He concluded with a demand for an unconditional endorsement of the policies of the American Anti-Slavery Society. This left the Sturgites no alternative but to vote the proposal down. The meeting broke up in disarray, effectively ending all hopes of reconciliation for the remainder of the decade.[102]

Thereafter the movement, if it can still so be called, became progressively more fragmented. Broad Street, although it maintained its connection with the Tappanites,[103] devoted less and less time to American issues. The Garrisonians, after their disruptive intervention, maintained a hostile silence. The Glasgow Emancipation Society met only two or three times a year, usually to greet some visiting American celebrity.[104] The Bristol and Clifton Ladies, while remaining independent, returned to their accustomed somnolence.[105] Even Webb's epistolary labours showed signs of slackening. Other groups came and went. In Scotland the United Presbyterian Church, stung by Garrisonian attacks on the allegedly racist policies of its missionaries in Africa, established in 1855 the New Edinburgh Anti-Slavery Association, but this never amounted to much and

100. May to Webb, 25 Oct. 1854, May Papers.
101. See Chapman to Garrison, Oct. 1854, and Pillsbury to May, 2 Feb. 1855, in Rice, pp. 458–61.
102. *Anti-Slavery Advocate*, Jan. 1855, pp. 225–32; BCLASS Minute Books, 7 Dec. 1854; GES Minute Books, 4 April 1855; Estlin to Chamerovzow, 21 May 1855, BFASS Papers, C 157/37; May, "Memorial to the Late Mr Estlin", *Liberator*, 21 Dec. 1855, p. 202.
103. See Abel and Klingberg, pp. 236–367.
104. GES Minute Books, 4 April 1854 to 10 Oct. 1859.
105. BCLASS Minute Books, 11 Feb. 1854 to 29 Nov. 1861.

by 1856 had disappeared.[106] Wilson Armistead's Leeds Anti-Slavery Society, founded in 1853, was remarkable as the only British antislavery body to apply Garrisonian principles to its own structure by establishing a single committee consisting of both women and men. The equality of the sexes was further emphasized in its emblem, a variant of the traditional Wedgwood plaque, showing two figures, one male and one female, with the words 'AM I NOT A WOMAN AND A SISTER' subscribed under the usual 'AM I NOT A MAN AND A BROTHER'. Despite these radical features, it sought to steer a middle course between the Thompson–Garrison and Sturge–Tappan wings of the movement; but following the debacle of the 1854 World Convention it broke off relations with the London Committee, after which little was heard of it.[107] In 1857 its place was taken by the Leeds Young Men's Anti-Slavery Society which leaned towards the Garrisonian position although this did not prevent it offering its hospitality to visitors with New Organizationist affiliations.[108] Another group which tried to follow an independent course, although in this case leaning towards the Broad Street position, was that centred around the Quaker family of Henry and Anna Richardson of Newcastle. Their main American connection was with Frederick Douglass, whose acquaintance they had made when he visited England in the forties, and with an even older friend, Miss Julia Griffiths, an English woman to whom they had introduced him and who had followed Douglass to America where she had become his constant companion. In 1855 Miss Griffiths returned to England and with the assistance of the Richardsons travelled about collecting funds on his behalf. In 1858 she married a clergyman in Halifax but this does not seem to have interfered with her fund-raising activities.[109] The Richardsons were also responsible for publishing *The Slave*, a penny news-sheet devoted to disseminating free-produce information. After the Richardsons gave it up in 1854 it was for a time edited by the American free-produce leader, Elihu Burritt. It ceased publication in 1856.[110]

106. Interestingly enough, these were the same people who in 1845 had supported the Garrisonians, whose principles they loathed, in their attacks on the Free Church, Rice, pp. 5, 380.
107. Armistead to Chamerovzow, 7 April, 10 Aug., 24 Sept. 1853; 27 Nov. 1854, BFASS Papers, C 27/49, 53, 55, 62.
108. As it did in the case of Mrs Sarah Remond, sister of the Negro abolitionist Charles Remond, who visited Britain in 1859–60: BFASS *Reporter*, 2 Jan. 1860.
109. Foner, pp. 87–92, 132–50.
110. L. Billington, appendix, pp. xi–xxiv; *The Slave: His Wrongs and Their Remedy* (numbers 1–48 new series, 1–24, Newcastle, 1851–56). The Garrisonians disapproved of the Richardsons' efforts, partly because they had never forgiven Frederick Douglass for his apostasy, but mainly because they believed that the free-produce movement threatened their own leadership: see the attack on *The Slave* in *Anti-Slavery Advocate*, Feb. 1854, p. 131.

These were all marginal activities. Indeed, the whole British antislavery movement had become, by the mid-'fifties, very much a marginal affair, with more than its share of cranks, visionaries and habitual schismatics. Had the British public taken any interest in the matter it would have been hard pressed to distinguish one group from another let alone judge the respective merits of the foreign organizations to which they were affiliated. Those few who did were understandably baffled. In Scotland, where rival factions existed side by side and were simultaneously competing for articles to send to Mrs Chapman's Boston Anti-Slavery Bazaar, Frederick Douglass's Rochester Bazaar and the New York Vigilance Committee's Bazaar, the situation was particularly confusing.[111] All people could do, apart from ignoring these appeals, as most did, was to judge the causes by their sponsors, which usually meant siding with (or against) a particular church group. In England the situation was different to the extent that particular groups enjoyed monopolies in their own areas, as did Armistead in Leeds, the Richardsons in Newcastle and the Estlins in Bristol, while the metropolitan society concentrated increasingly on other and, so it believed, potentially more rewarding areas of endeavour.

There was, however, one type of activity on the importance of which all factions agreed. This was persuading the churches to take a more positive stand against American slavery and, in particular, refusing fellowship to slaveholders. Here organized abolition undoubtedly had some impact, though by the fifties there were other reasons why the churches' attitudes should have begun to change. Since most American denominations had already split over this issue,[112] and since British connections were mainly with their Northern branches, which had themselves become outspoken critics of the institution, there was nothing to be lost and conceivably something to be gained by following suit. All the same, the abolitionists, who may have exercised little influence on the general community but were often individually influential in their church organizations, helped matters along and were always ready to denounce any visiting American suspected of slaveholding or even of proslavery sympathies.[113] The most notably successful campaign of this kind was that waged by both the British and Foreign Anti-Slavery Society and the Garrisonians

111. Rice, 397–477. See also Smeal to Garrison, 4 March 1853, Garrison Papers; Smeal to Chamerovzow, 16 April 1853, BFASS Papers, C 36/52. A list of British organizations contributing to the Boston Bazaar will be found in *Anti-Slavery Advocate*, March 1853, p. 46.
112. For an account of these schisms see Filler, *Crusade Against Slavery*, pp. 123–6.
113. See the cases of Dr Chickering and Dr Belcher in Abel and Klingberg, pp. 38–9, 263–95, and of the Rev. Bishop Simpson and the Rev. Dr McClintock in GES Minute Books, 27 July 1857.

at the time of the Great Exhibition of 1851 to have Southern clerical representatives, whom Estlin described as "entitled to no more respect than Borneo Pirates or professional thieves", ostracized by the British religious community.[114] Abolitionists took much satisfaction from the fact that the British branch of the Evangelical Alliance, meeting in conjunction with the Exhibition, reversed its 1846 stand by excluding foreign slave-holding delegates.[115] As a result of these and other efforts it became virtually impossible for any minister sympathetic to slavery to enter a British pulpit.

As the fifties closed there were some signs that the bitter divisions of the early years of the decade were beginning to heal. American visitors such as Sarah Remond and George Cheever were welcomed on to platforms without being denounced by one or other antislavery party, although this could still happen as was shown by George Thompson's attack on Frederick Douglass during his visit to Scotland in 1860.[116] Whether this altered attitude reflected a genuine reconciliation or the general feebleness of the movement it is hard to say. What is clear is that organized antislavery had pretty much run itself into the ground.

114. BFASS Minute Books, April–June, 1851; Samuel May, "Memorial of the Late Mr Estlin", *Liberator*, Nov. 1855, p. 190.
115. This campaign and the Garrisonians' subsequent campaigns to reform the churches are admirably described in Rice, pp. 364–9.
116. R. Botsford, "Scotland and the American Civil War" (unpublished PhD thesis, University of Edinburgh, 1956), pp. 53–87.

12

Antislavery issues of the 1860s

The outbreak of the American Civil War in April 1861 brought a quickening of interest in the slavery issue. The firing on Fort Sumter and Lincoln's call to arms took most British people by surprise. Although the press had given extensive coverage to the 1860 elections and to the ensuing declarations of the states of the deep South of their intention to secede, these developments had not been taken very seriously by the British. The sectional contest had been going on so long that the notion that something out of the ordinary might now be happening was hard to accept. Since this was also a view generally held by Americans, or at all events by Northerners,[1] it indicates no particular obtuseness on the part of the British, who for the most part were merely repeating what the American press told them.

Nevertheless, when war actually did break out the government responded with commendable speed by declaring that it was Britain's intention to remain strictly neutral. "We have not been involved in any way in that contest", Lord Russell, the Foreign Secretary, told the Commons, "and for

1. David M. Potter, *Lincoln and His Party in the Secession Crisis* (New Haven, 1942).

God's sake, let us, if possible keep out of it."[2] British subjects were forbidden to enlist on either side; port authorities were instructed not to build or equip vessels of war for use by the belligerents; and British traders were told that if they went on trading with America they must do so on the clear understanding that normal maritime practices respecting blockade and contraband in time of war would apply. Apart from recognizing the South's belligerent status—as did the Union—no official recognition was extended to what the British Government, following correct diplomatic usage, referred to as "those states styling themselves the Confederate States of America".[3]

Once these decisions had been made—and it is difficult to see what other decisions could have been made in the circumstances—no further action was needed except to keep a watchful eye on developments. There was no significant body of opinion in the country which felt that the Government should have behaved in any other way. Thus the British found themselves in the agreeable position of being able to indulge in a prolonged debate as to what the struggle was, or might conceivably be, about and what attitudes it was appropriate for them to adopt towards it. How seriously this debate should be taken is hard to say. Much that was said throws more light on British than on American issues. The fact that John Bright was a firm supporter of the Union persuaded many that there must be something to be said for the Confederacy, while the professed admiration of the aristocracy for the chivalrous and "gentlemanly" qualities of the Southerners swayed others in the opposite direction. Since only attitudes were required the debate was largely free-wheeling, although from time to time American facts and events obtruded. Liberal free-traders, who had assumed that the Republicans were transatlantic versions of themselves, were shocked by the introduction of the Morrill Tariff; the Trent incident, involving the seizure of two Confederate diplomats from a British vessel on the high seas, revealed an unexpected belligerency on the part of the British public; and, of course, individual battles and campaigns were mulled over and their significance discussed.

One notable feature of this debate was that virtually no one was prepared to defend slavery. Everyone—at least everyone who mattered—agreed that slavery was wrong. But even a deeply felt abhorrence of slavery did not necessarily predispose people to side with the Union. For the first seventeen months of the war it was a demonstrable fact that abolition was not one of the North's war aims. Even after it became one, many

2. Adams, *Great Britain and the American Civil War*, *1*, 90.
3. *Ibid*, *1*, 94–5.

continued to believe that, however misguided Southerners might be in their choice of domestic institutions, they were quite justified in exercising their democratic right to self-determination. More important in determining British attitudes was the widespread assumption, encouraged during the early part of the war by the military reversals suffered by the Northern armies and later by the biased reporting of *The Times* and other newspapers, that, irrespective of rights and wrongs, the Union was doomed. From this it followed that the whole Northern war effort was misguided. Hence the hostile reception given by the supposedly antislavery British press to Lincoln's emancipation proclamation which, since most assumed that the North would never be in a position to implement it, was construed as an invitation to Southern Negroes to begin a servile insurrection. The fear of a reign of terror in the South, which had haunted imaginations since Sumter, reached a climax in the latter months of 1862. *The Times* conjured up images of "horrible massacres of white women and children, to be followed by the extermination of the black race in the South" and wondered if Lincoln would ultimately "be classed among that catalogue of monsters, the wholesale assassins and butchers of mankind".[4] Only gradually did these fears recede and not until Lincoln's assassination was there anything like unanimity in the expressions of approval over the course he had pursued.

It is, of course, easy to be critical of the British press. In the light of modern historical knowledge it is clear that there was much prejudice and a good deal of plain ignorance. But in these respects it was not very different from the American press, the reactions of which to the Emancipation Proclamation were almost equally hostile. It would have been surprising if the press of a neutral nation had shown itself less critical than the journals of the North, many of which remained highly biased in their treatment of the Lincoln administration. Even so, it is curious how few British newspapers and periodicals were consistently sympathetic in their attitudes to the North. The *Spectator*, the *Morning Star*—the organ of the Bright faction—and the *Daily News* were among the few that were. Others, like the *Economist* and the *Edinburgh Review*, reflected the prevailing confusion in public sentiments. *The Times*, the most powerful journal in the country, was on the whole antagonistic towards the North and in the closing stages of the war became definitely pro-Southern. Similar divisions are to be found in the working-class press. Old Chartists

4. *The Times*, 22 Oct. 1862. For a full account of British responses to Lincoln's announcement of his intention to issue the Emancipation Proclamation see Adams 2, 75–115. In April 1865 *The Times* paid a generous tribute to Lincoln, *ibid*, pp. 259–61.

sternly refused to identify themselves with capitalists either in Britain or America. George Troup, editor of the *Bee Hive* and perhaps the most influential radical journalist of the period, happened to be a devout member of the Free Church of Scotland, which, he felt, had given him more than enough insight into abolitionist methods. In his columns he fulminated against Northern tariffs and antislavery fanatics alike. How far the readers of these publications agreed with the statements they read is a matter of conjecture. But it is reasonable to assume that the wide variety of views appearing in the press indicates that, at all levels of society, opinion was sharply divided.[5]

Given the intensity of public interest in the American struggle one might have supposed that the nation's antislavery bodies would have hastened to offer enlightenment. In fact, for the first eighteen months of the war, very little was heard from them. Various explanations can be advanced: the enfeebled condition into which by the time of the outbreak of war they had sunk, the fact that the morality of slavery was no longer really an issue, their ignorance of military matters, and the reluctance of the Lincoln administration to embrace emancipation as a war aim. Even so, it is unlikely that their voices would have gone unheard had they had anything of importance to say. Their real problem was that now, as in the past, they found themselves seriously encumbered by their ideological assumptions.

The firing on Fort Sumter placed the Garrisonians in an especially difficult predicament. For years they had preached the need for the dissolution of the Union. They believed, quite sincerely, that this would lead to the emancipation of the slaves although quite how this would work in practice was not entirely clear. It was pointed out, however, that the North, once independent, would no longer be obliged to return runaways and that the United States Army could not be called on to put down slave insurrections. Uprisings would thus occur. The South would suffer as it deserved. More important, in the border states, increasing numbers of slaves would begin running away. In order to keep control over their labour force, planters would begin programmes of emancipation. Neighbouring states would be obliged to follow suit and in due course the whole system would be rolled up. At least this was the theory, but since disunion had never been seen as an imminent possibility the matter had not been subjected to the close scrutiny it deserved. What really weighed with the Garrisonians was the desirability of the North's dissociating itself from the "sin" of slaveholding, after which the South, morally and politically

5. Adams, *passim;* Royden Harrison, *Before the Socialists: studies in labour and politics, 1861–1881* (London, 1965), pp. 40–77.

isolated, could safely be left to face the awful retribution which surely awaited it. During the secession winter of 1860–61 their chief concern had been to see that nothing was done to dissuade the Southerners from their chosen course. Garrison himself rejoiced that "at last 'the covenant with death' is annulled and 'the agreement with hell' broken".[6] Except that it was the South that was separating from the North rather than vice versa the Garrisonian plan was being realized. The idea that the North would fight rather than see the Union dissolved had not been taken seriously. In the past it had always backed down and presumably would do so again. When fighting did break out, Garrison and his followers fell silent. To have insisted on the South's right to secede would have placed them on the side of the Confederacy, and would have required an adherence to principle which even they found daunting. Wendell Phillips, who appealed to a close Boston friend for advice, was bluntly told that unless he changed his position he would never be listened to again. This was the simple truth and there was no avoiding it. After passing through an agony of indecision they came out strongly and unequivocally for the Union. "For the first time in my antislavery life," Phillips told a cheering audience in Boston Music Hall, "I speak under the stars and stripes and welcome the tread of Massachusetts men marshalled for war."[7]

Thus, at a stroke, Garrisonianism was stripped of almost all its distinctive features. For the first time in almost two decades the *Liberator* appeared on 26 April without its familiar 'NO UNION WITH SLAVEHOLDERS!'. Along with other abolitionists they turned their attention to making the war into an antislavery crusade.

British Garrisonians, as ever, took their cues from the United States. Most of them, however, were unprepared for the abruptness of Garrison's *volte face*. Their perplexity was revealed in Webb's first editorial in the *Anti-Slavery Advocate* of 1 June. British people, he argued, should feel gratified that the Union "as it existed a few months ago" was "at an end for ever". Either the North would win, in which case a new Union free of slavery would emerge, or it would lose and the South would be left to struggle with its own problems. In either event the results would be salutary. Meanwhile, the British need feel no qualms about welcoming the resort to arms since legalized slavery was itself "a state of warfare" and as such much more productive of misery and degradation than "any short, sharp contest" of a purely military kind. This was putting

---

6. *Liberator*, 4 Jan. 1861. For a fuller account of Garrisonian responses to secession see McPherson, *Struggle for Equality*, pp. 31 ff.

7. In *ibid*, p. 50.

a bold face on the matter. Privately he wrote to his American friends that the British were surprised at the "unreasoned exaltation" and "unqualified gratification" shown at the opening of what promised to be a long and bloody struggle. Plainly he did not understand the war fever that was now sweeping through the North. He added that he and his friends were also extremely puzzled as to why, after hearing for so long "that the Union was one of the chief bulwarks of the slave system", they should be expected to greet with delight a war for its maintenance. Americans should not feel surprised, he concluded, at the continued silence of Exeter Hall.[8] As late as September 1862 the *Advocate* was still in two minds over whether it *wanted* the North to win.[9]

Although most of them eventually got used to their American coadjutors' change of ground, the British Garrisonians remained perplexed by Lincoln's attitude. Were his assertions that he had no intention of interfering with slavery to be taken literally or could he be relied upon to act, as the Constitution empowered him to do in time of war, against the institution? Until this point was cleared up they felt that there was not much that they could do.

The publication of his preliminary emancipation proclamation on 22 September 1862, details of which were sent to them by an ecstatic Samuel May, finally convinced them of the righteousness of the Union cause.[10] Giving practical assistance, however, was another matter since by this time most of the Garrisonian groups were beyond resuscitation. The Bristol and Clifton Ladies had held their last meeting in November 1861.[11] The Glasgow Emancipation Society lingered on long enough to celebrate the Emancipation Proclamation, after which it too ceased operations.[12] The Hibernian Anti-Slavery Society was too small and remote to play any important role, though the indefatigable Webb continued to provide a link with the members of Garrison's Boston Circle.[13] Most significant of all, the *Anti-Slavery Advocate*, for more than a decade the organ of the British Garrisonians, ceased publication in May 1863.

8. Webb to [?], 26 July 1861, Weston Papers. The Garrisonians' confusion was increased when pro-Confederate publications began taking up their old doctrines. Botsford, "Scotland and the American Civil War", p. 389.

9. *Anti-Slavery Advocate*, 1 Sept. 1862, p. 549.

10. "It is a poor *document*, but a mighty *act*. . . . Joy, gratitude, thanksgiving, renewed hope and courage fill my soul": May to Webb, 23 Sept. 1862, in McPherson, p. 119.

11. BCLASS Minute Books, 29 Nov. 1861.

12. GES Minute Books, 10 Jan. 1861–4 Nov. 1863. It began meeting again in 1873 in response to approaches from the British and Foreign Anti-Slavery Society which at that time was worried about slave-trading in Africa and Turkey: *ibid*, 29 Sept. 1873–2 Feb. 1876.

13. See the references to him in McPherson, pp. 60, 84, 103, 119, 229.

"I did not think it right to go on with it at Miss Estlin's expense",
wrote Webb, "besides . . . a great many of the . . . papers are strongly
Northern and there was no use keeping alive our little farthing rush-
light."[14]

There was one organization, however, which became during the latter
part of the war an active and powerful body. This was the London Emancipation Committee, founded in 1859 by Thompson's son-in-law, F. W.
Chesson. Initially it was an insignificant body made up of what Webb,
with his usual acerbity, described as "a most incongruous medley in everything except a mutual friendly feeling towards the cause."[15] Like other
Garrisonian attempts to launch a metropolitan organization this one
would doubtless have foundered very soon had it not been for the war. Even
this failed to produce any immediate response since according to the London
correspondent of the *Liberator* no pro-Northern public meetings were
held in the nation's capital during the first eighteen months of the war.[16]
What finally provoked it to action was the preliminary emancipation
proclamation and, more important, the growing realization of Union
sympathizers in Britain that they needed an organization to oppose the
pro-Confederate groups which by 1862 were beginning to spring up around
the country. In November it issued a prospectus in which it described
its aims as being to counteract Southern sympathies in Britain and to
encourage the United States government in the prosecution of its emancipation policy. On 11 November it held an inaugural meeting at which it
transformed itself into the London Emancipation Society.[17] John Stuart
Mill became a committee member and Bright, Cobden and others gave
their active support. It published a series of pamphlets on the war and its
causes (Southern aggression[18]) and arranged meetings for such visiting
speakers as Henry Ward Beecher and the coloured lecturer William A.
Jackson, whom it billed as "Jefferson Davis's ex-coachman".[19] By the
end of 1863, according to George Thompson, there were similar organizations in every British town and city.[20] One of these, the Manchester Union
and Emancipation Society, is remembered as the sponsor of the famous
letter from the working men of Manchester to President Lincoln to which

14. Webb to May, 30 May 1863, May Papers.
15. Webb to May, 10 March 1859, May Papers.
16. *Liberator*, 5 Dec. 1862, p. 195.
17. London Emancipation Society, *Prospectus* (London, 1862).
18. The *Prospectus* lists seven, e.g. F. W. Newman, *The Good Cause of President
Lincoln*; Edward Laboulaye, *Why the North Cannot Consent to Disunion*, and
George Brown, *The American War and Slavery*.
19. Thompson to Garrison, 5 Dec. 1862; 5 Feb. 1863, in *Liberator* 26 Dec. 1862,
p. 206, 27 Feb. 1863, p. 34.
20. Thompson to Buffum, 10 Dec. 1863, *ibid*, 15 Jan. 1864.

the President gave a characteristically gracious reply.[21] Most of the 114 pro-Union public meetings (by no means a complete catalogue) listed by the American Minister in his dispatches to Secretary of State Seward as having been held in 1862–65 were the work of these bodies.[22] The fact that Adams kept such a list indicates how gratified the American government was by these developments. Lincoln even drafted a resolution as a model for British public meetings to follow. It ran:

Whereas, while *heretofore* States, and Nations, have tolerated slavery, *recently*, for the first time in the world, an attempt has been made to construct a new Nation, upon the basis of, and with the primary, and fundamental object to maintain, enlarge, and perpetuate human slavery, therefore,

Resolved: that no such embryo State should ever be recognized by, or admitted into, the family of Christian and civilized nations; and that all Christian and civilized men everywhere should, by all lawful means, resist to the utmost, such recognition or admission.[23]

Clearly, had the Whig administration shown any inclination to recognize the Confederacy at any time during the latter part of the war such a cry would have gone up that it would have been lucky to remain in office.

One result of these events was to bring about a revival in the fortunes of George Thompson. From the first he and Garrison had seen eye to eye on the causes of the war. His American friends had helped him through his illness but he was still desperately short of money. Early in the war he approached various Americans in London with the suggestion that they employ him as a lecturer, but was turned down. He described to Garrison a number of meetings he had addressed, but the list is sparse and it seems unlikely that they generated much enthusiasm. With the burgeoning of the pro-Union campaign, however, he found himself in his element. He and Chesson were the mainstays of the London Emancipation Society. Provincial societies needed speakers and had funds with which to pay them. (Thomas Bayley Potter, President of the Manchester body, is said to have contributed £5,000 out of his own pocket.[24]) Former enemies spoke eulogistically of his staunch adherence to the cause. At a banquet given in his honour, John Bright went so far as to describe him as the "real liberator of the slaves in the English colonies".[25]

At the end of 1863, feeling that affairs in Britain were developing satis-

21. The text of this letter will be found in B. B. Sideman and L. Friedman, eds, *Europe Looks at the Civil War* (New York, 1960) pp. 166–8; Lincoln's reply is in Roy P. Basler, ed., *The Collected Works of Abraham Lincoln* (8 vols., New Brunswick, New Jersey 1953–55), *6*, 63–5.
22. Adams, *2*, 223.
23. Copy sent by Sumner to Bright, April 1863, in *ibid*, p. 113.
24. W. P. and F. J. Garrison, *William Lloyd Garrison*, *4*, 66.
25. Adams, *2*, 224, n. 1.

factorily, his American friends invited him to the United States where
an even more enthusiastic reception awaited him. On his arrival, he was
officially greeted by the Governor of Massachusetts. In New York and
other cities he was handsomely entertained. The climax to his visit was a
lavish reception given in his honour in the Hall of the US House of
Representatives, presided over by Vice-President Hannibal Hamlin.
Lincoln, who was in the audience, invited him to the White House
where the two men discussed antislavery matters. Thompson repaid
these attentions by campaigning for Lincoln's re-election in the autumn
of 1864. The following April he and Garrison were invited down to
Charleston for the official raising of the Union flag over Fort Sumter.
"I look back", he wrote to a friend, "on the thirty years and six months
which have elapsed since I landed on [these] shores. . . . Then I was
denounced by a slaveholding President for preaching the doctrine of
Universal Liberty. Today I am the guest of an anti-slavery President,
on board a United States Government vessel . . . going to celebrate the
triumph of Garrisonian abolitionism in Charleston."[26]

No less remarkable than the transformation of Garrison and Thompson
into loyal Unionists was the almost total eclipse during these years of the
British and Foreign Anti-Slavery Society. Up to the outbreak of war,
abolitionists of all complexions had claimed to be pacifists. Unlike the
Garrisonians, however, the Broad Street Quakers took their principles
seriously. They were not prepared to accept Webb's sophistry that slavery
was "a state of warfare" since, plainly, it was no such thing. Impeccable
though their reasoning may have been, its conclusion was embarrassing
for it aligned the Society with the South, which would have been happy
to lay down its arms providing the North did the same. As it was obviously
ludicrous for an antislavery society to argue for Southern independence,
an arrangement which these particular abolitionists had always opposed,
they took the easier course of ignoring America altogether. During 1861
and the early part of 1862 they paid more attention to developments in
Russia than to the conflict in the United States. Even after the preliminary
emancipation proclamation they could not bring themselves to express
approval of the course the North was pursuing. Asked to draft a letter of
congratulation to the President, Chamerovzow, who did not share these
pacifist beliefs, spent months working on a text that would meet the objec-

26. Thompson to R. F. Wallcut, 8 April 1865 in W. P. and F. J. Garrison, *4*, 137.
Thompson subsequently settled in Roxbury, Massachusetts, where he lived,
until 1867, as a close neighbour of Garrison. He returned to England in company
with Garrison in May 1867, and died in Leeds in July 1877. Details of his career
from 1861 onwards will be found in *ibid*, pp. 1, 10, 27–9, 65–75, 99–110, 136–7,
190, 281, 290.

tions raised by Committee members. "To persevere in their endeavours to obtain justice for the slave" was struck out and "to persevere in all righteous endeavours to obtain, by moral means, justice for the slave" substituted. The final version was so obscurely worded that it could be read as a plea to Lincoln to send his armies home. Lincoln did not reply to this letter as he did to others sent to him by British organizations at this time.[27]

In the early sixties, the Society's major concern was still the Cuban slave trade. Although it could not endorse Lincoln's war policy, it welcomed wholeheartedly his willingness to negotiate a treaty with Britain for the suppression of this traffic. This treaty, which was concluded in April 1862, allowed British and American ships a mutual right of search and provided for the seizure and trial of suspected vessels. In a small way the Society contributed to the success of this measure by drawing attention to deficiencies in the way in which it had been drafted overlooked by the signatories. In its original form, the treaty had applied only to vessels found within two hundred miles of the African coast or within thirty leagues of Cuba. On looking over its text for an article he was preparing, Chamerovzow was struck by the fact that Puerto Rico was not within the areas specified. He brought this to Brougham's attention, pointing out that unless the treaty were amended Puerto Rico would almost certainly become a centre for the transhipment of slaves, who could then be sent on to Cuba on an intercolonial arrangement. Brougham took the matter up with the Foreign Secretary who confessed that the omission was the result of an oversight and would be rectified. An additional article to the treaty was accordingly negotiated and the right of search extended not only to Puerto Rico but also to Madagascar.[28]

The Treaty of Washington proved a death blow to the Atlantic slave trade. Now that Britain and the United States were working together, blockade running became increasingly difficult and, by 1865, virtually impossible. Although there is no record of when the last slaver sailed from Africa to the New World, by the mid-sixties the traffic was, for all practical purposes, at an end.[29]

At this time the public's attention was again drawn to the West Indies, in particular to Jamaica. Racial tensions there had been rising and in 1865

27. BFASS Minute Books, 7, 17 Nov., 5, 22 Dec. 1862. The text of the address is given in BFASS, *The Crisis in the United States* (London, 1862), p. 4. Lincoln did reply to the London, Manchester and Bradford addresses. C. F. Adams to Chamerovzow, 21 May 1863, in BFASS *Annual Report for 1863*, p. 20.
28. BFASS Minute Books, 6 June 1862, 1 May 1863; BFASS *Reporter*, 1863, p. 109; Lloyd, *The Navy and the Slave Trade*, p. 176.
29. Lloyd, pp. 176–83.

serious disturbances occurred in the parish of St Thomas-in-the-East. These events were the result of a combination of factors: religious enthusiasm, administrative incompetence and economic distress due to the closing of American markets during the war. There is no doubt that the disturbances were a genuine threat to public safety and required prompt and forceful action by the authorities. But it is also clear that the measures adopted—the burning of villages and the almost random slaughter of some four hundred Negroes—were far more drastic than the situation warranted. The British and Foreign Anti-Slavery Society joined in the general storm of protest and took an active part in pressing for the institution of legal proceedings against Governor Eyre. An agent appointed by the Society visited Jamaica in the spring of 1866 and on his return submitted a report condemning the Governor's actions and absolving the Negroes from blame. Proceedings against the Governor were begun but had to be dropped when a London grand jury failed to find a true bill of indictment.[30] Had these events occurred a few years earlier they would undoubtedly have been exploited by proslavery groups abroad. Despite abolitionist apprehensions,[31] they now attracted little attention outside Britain. Since Lincoln's Emancipation Proclamation and the abolition of slavery by the Dutch (who had freed their slaves in 1863) the success or failure of West Indian emancipation had ceased to be an issue.

But the principal concern of abolitionists after 1863, and in a sense the climax to all the humanitarian efforts of the years since West Indian emancipation, was the campaign to help the American freedmen. Some antislavery societies preferred not to engage in this work on the grounds that freedmen's aid and antislavery agitation were two different things. Virtually all their members, however, were actively involved in it. Often it was just a question of name. All the Quaker members of the Broad Street Committee belonged to the Central Committee of the Society of Friends for the Relief of the Emancipated Slaves of North America, including G. W. Alexander who was treasurer of both.[32] Elsewhere, antislavery organizations which had become inactive reappeared as freedmen's aid bodies. In Glasgow, the Freedmen's Aid Society, founded in November 1864, contained all the surviving members of the old Glasgow Emancipation Society, the dominant personality being, once again,

30. Chamerovzow to Brougham, 23 Nov., 7 Dec. 1865, Brougham Papers; Andrews to Chamerovzow, 10 Feb. 1868, BFASS Papers, C 27/12; BFASS Minute Books, 20 Nov. 1865–31 Jan. 1866 and 9 Nov. 1866; BFASS *Reporter*, 1 Sept. 1866; Mathieson, *The Sugar Colonies and Governor Eyre*, pp. 197–240; Burn, *British West Indies*, pp. 136–42; Curtin, *Two Jamaicas*, pp. 195–203.
31. Chamerovzow to Brougham, 23 Nov. 1865, Brougham Papers.
32. BFASS *Reporter*, 1 July 1865.

William Smeal.[33] In other British cities familiar names crop up: in Edinburgh the Wighams; in Darlington the Peases; in Bristol, Mary Estlin; in Dublin, Richard Webb and James Houghton; in Leeds, Wilson Armistead and Thomas Harvey; in Birmingham, Edmund Sturge; in London, L. A. Chamerovzow, F. W. Chesson, Thomas Fowell Buxton Jr, Josiah Forster, Samuel Gurney Jr, and Robert Alsop. Altogether there were in Britain some forty or fifty freedmen's aid societies. At the time of the inauguration of the National Freedmen's Aid Committee, a central body designed to coordinate the activities of these organizations, a handsome tribute was paid to the memory of Joseph Sturge. The dominant figure in the whole British freedmen's aid enterprise was, as it happened, another Birmingham Quaker and a relative of Sturge's, Arthur Albright, who as Secretary of the Midlands branch of the movement, played in the sixties a role very much like that which Sturge himself had played in the thirties and forties.[34]

As in America, freedmen's aid in Britain began as a number of separate organizations, mostly representing particular denominations or groups of local well-wishers. The first of these was the London Freedmen's Aid Society, inaugurated at a meeting on St James's Hill, Piccadilly, on 24 April 1863. Others followed until by 1865 there were some forty or fifty such bodies scattered about the country. In May 1865 an attempt was made to pool resources by establishing the National Committee of British Freedmen's Aid Societies, which gave place a year later to the National Freedmen's Aid Union.[35]

The sums collected by these organizations were impressive. In July 1868 Thomas Phillips, Secretary of the National Freedmen's Aid Union, told General O. O. Howard of the American Freedmen's Bureau that the freedmen's movement in Britain had up to that time produced in money and goods (mainly clothing and agricultural implements) nearly £120,000.[36] Garrison, representing the American Freedmen's Union Commission at the Paris Anti-Slavery Convention of 1867, put the British contribution at £80,000. In all, he estimated, about a fifth of the money so far collected from private individuals on behalf of the American freedmen came from foreign, mostly British, sources.[37] Because of the multiplicity of organiza-

33. Minute Books of the Glasgow Freedmen's Aid Society, Mitchell Library, Glasgow.
34. For a fuller account of British freedmen's aid see Christine Bolt, *The Anti-Slavery Movement and Reconstruction* (London, 1969), pp. 54–140.
35. *Ibid*, p. 59.
36. Phillips to Howard, 7 July 1868, BFASS Papers C 11/125.
37. BFASS, *Special Report of the Anti-Slavery Convention held in Paris. . . . 1867* (London, 1869), p. 37. This was the figure he was authorized to use (400,000 dollars) by the American Freedmen's Aid Commission and, according to Ira V.

tions involved, these figures are impossible to check, but unless they are wildly exaggerated it would appear that the British contributed more to helping American Negroes during the years 1863–68 than they had done to assisting the antislavery cause in all the years since West Indian emancipation.

As usual, most of the principal donors were Quakers. As early as the summer of 1865, the Quaker Central Committee had collected almost £6,000. Levi Coffin, the American Quaker who organized the Western Freedmen's Aid Commission and who spent a year in Britain soliciting funds on its behalf, claimed to have raised 100,000 dollars, most of it from Quakers. In his *Reminiscences* he recalls a gathering held in Leeds after a Friends' Quarterly Meeting at which he collected almost £1,000.[38] Even the small Irish Quaker body was able to contribute around £1,500 a year. In all, the Quakers probably gave £25,000 through their own organizations, besides contributing generously to their local freedmen's bodies and directly to freedmen's aid societies in America. Next to the Quakers, the Congregationalists were the most active religious group and by the summer of 1866 had forwarded to the American Missionary Association sums amounting to £3,000. Other denominations made smaller donations. Among the local organizations, Bristol, which was evidently one of the most active, could claim by the time of its dissolution in 1868 to have collected in excess of £4,000.[39]

This extraordinary burst of generosity represented the culmination of Britain's efforts on behalf of the American Negro. After the frustrations of the forties and fifties, here was an opportunity of giving positive assistance. As a result, the ideological disputes which had plagued abolitionists for so long melted away. Although individual groups did not always see eye to eye, and sometimes sharply disagreed, over practical matters, theoretical issues played almost no part. In their desire to help the freedmen Old and New Organizationists, pacifists and non-pacifists, joined ranks.

As practical men they also showed commendable resourcefulness. One of their most notable achievements was to arrange with the United States Government that all goods sent to America on behalf of the freedmen be allowed entry free of duty. It was estimated that this and the concessions obtained from railroads and shipping agencies saved the

Brown (*Journal of Southern History*, *15*, 1949, 30), it represented the Commission's estimate, based on a careful examination of records, of the total amount, in money and kind, contributed by Britain for freedmen's aid, through both nonsectarian and missionary societies, from February 1862 to July 1867.
38. Coffin, *Reminiscences*, p. 690.
39. Bolt, pp. 83–113.

movement £20,000.[40] A similar practicality is evident in the decision to wind up the enterprise. In July 1868 Phillips wrote to the Freedmen's Bureau explaining that it had never been the intention to provide aid on a permanent basis and that, with the general assent of its members, the National Freedmen's Aid Union was bent on dissolving itself.[41] The corresponding American body, the American Freedmen's Union Commission, finding increasing difficulty in raising funds, had also determined to disband so that the two ceased operations almost simultaneously.[42]

The ending of freedmen's aid marks the end of a chapter of antislavery effort no less decisively than West Indian emancipation. As in the 1830s, abolitionists had achieved their immediate goals. Spain, Portugal and Brazil were now the only Christian nations to acknowledge slavery. The two principal issues which had engaged their attention during the intervening decades, American slavery and the Atlantic slave trade, had ceased to exist. In the United States, the culmination of the antislavery crusade, the adoption of the Fifteenth Amendment in March 1870, which extended the right of voting to all races, was followed by a period during which the freedom extended to the Negro was gradually eroded. In Britain, too, the cause of the freedmen, West Indian as well as American, was largely forgotten.

But as the sixties closed there were signs that the British branch of the movement was far from dead. At the Paris Anti-Slavery Convention of 1867, sponsored by the British and Foreign Anti-Slavery Society, the Comité Français d'Emancipation and the Sociedad Abolicionista Espaniola, a succession of speakers outlined the problems yet to be tackled. The Rev. James Clarke of Jamaica gave instances of the way in which the coolie traffic was being abused; Chamerovzow described Egypt and Turkey's involvement in slavery; others mentioned Cuba, Brazil and the Far East. But what really fascinated the delegates was Africa, in particular the recent revelations of Dr Livingstone respecting the East Coast slave trade and the way in which slave-traders operated in the interior. Some spoke of the opportunities for missionary activity, others of the need for gunboats. The way in which their minds were turning was most clearly summed up by a French delegate, Lieutenant Mage, who pointed out that irrespective of the tactics used, the aim henceforward must be "the creation, in the interior of Africa, of settlements where civilization shall set a good example

40. *Ibid*, p. 61; Coffin, p. 700.
41. Phillips to General Howard, 7 July 1868, BFASS Papers.
42. Bolt, pp. 138–9.

[and] where missionaries shall preach the Holy Word".[43] The time had come, he concluded, when abolitionists could at last carry their mission into the African heartland.

As one chapter was ending, a new one was beginning.

43. BFASS, *Special Report of the Paris Anti-Slavery Convention*, p. 19.

Epilogue

Britain's efforts to combat slavery during the last three decades of the nineteenth century are a separate story and one which can here be touched on only briefly. Its main outlines, however, are familiar enough. From the 1870s onwards Britain, along with other European powers, began extending her authority over vast tracts of African territory. The indigenous peoples could offer little in the way of resistance to these advances and by the end of the century the process was virtually complete. Almost all of Africa south of the Sahara lay under the control of one or another of the European powers.

Except for the forces of nature and their own imperial rivalries, the only significant opposition met with by the Europeans came from the Arabs. Like the Europeans, the Arabs had long regarded tropical Africa as a reservoir of servile black labour. The Islamic slave trade was much older than the European. At least since the eighth century and possibly earlier, Arabs had been trading Negroes northward to their dominions.[1] Only very recently, however—in fact since the 1850s—had they themselves begun penetrating into the African interior in search of human merchandise.[2] It was the accounts of their atrocities, recounted by

1. A. J. Wills, *An Introduction to the History of Central Africa* (2nd edn, London, 1967) pp. 73–82; Bernard Lewis, "Race and colour in Islam", *Encounter, 30* (Aug. 1970), 18–36.
2. Sir Reginald Coupland, *The Exploitation of East Africa, 1856–1890* (London, 1939), pp. 134–51.

Livingstone and other African travellers, which so horrified Europeans in the eighteen-sixties and seventies.

Broadly viewed, the suppression of this traffic may be seen as the result of the substitution of European for Arab rule. Whatever their attitudes towards slavery, it was plainly contrary to the interests of the invaders, intent on establishing territorial control, to permit anarchy within their new possessions. There is no doubt, however, that genuine idealism played a part in this achievement. Publicly at least, all the powers were committed to ending the traffic, and although, in practice, they often found difficulty in working together for this purpose, as became evident at the Berlin (Congo) Conference of 1884–85 and the Brussels Conference of 1889–90,[3] it is plain that their commitment was in large part sincere. Certainly among those British nationals most directly responsible for dealing with the trade—John Kirk in Zanzibar, Harry Johnston in Nyasaland, General Gordon in the Sudan and Frederick Lugard in Nigeria—abolitionist principles provided a powerful stimulus to action.[4] At home, humanitarians who might otherwise have been inclined to look askance at such imperial ventures clamoured for suppression. So too, anxious for the safety of their new flocks, did the missionary societies. In short, the suppression of the trade was one of those issues, rare in politics, on which all interested parties could unite. As a result, the traffic had virtually disappeared by the end of the century, at least from areas under European control.

Dealing with slaveholding proved a much trickier matter. From an early stage it was clear that slavery, or at all events practices analogous to it, existed on a broad scale throughout tropical Africa. The Arabs, of course, practised it both on a domestic level—household servants, retainers, concubines—and as a means of agricultural production. The state of Zanzibar, the principal power in East Africa before the coming of the Europeans and up to the end of the century still a political entity to be reckoned with, was a slave empire in the classic sense. But among the black Africans themselves slavery was widely practised, often as an integral part of tribal life. To interfere with it would undoubtedly arouse hostility, which was the last thing the new colonial powers wished. It was also evident that much that could be represented as slavery was relatively benign, and even when it was not was so interwoven into the social fabric that to attempt to remove it would simply create other problems.

For these reasons Africa's new rulers were disposed to move cautiously.

3. Suzanne Miers, "The Brussels Conference of 1889–1890: the place of the slave trade in the policies of Great Britain and Germany", in Prosser Gifford and W. Roger Louis, eds, *Britain and Germany in Africa: imperial rivalry and colonial rule* (New Haven and London, 1967), pp. 82–118.
4. Coupland, *British Anti-Slavery Movement*, pp. 189–251.

At Berlin and Brussels the powers deliberately limited their discussions to the subject of the slave trade.[5] In the case of the British the commitment to the principle of indirect rule specifically discouraged immediate action. Whatever they may have felt about this policy on moral grounds—in practice most of them appear to have agreed with it and learned to cherish the odd ways of the "natives"—it was plain to Britain's colonial administrators that they lacked the resources to rule otherwise.[6] As the representatives of a power which in the past had led the world in the struggle against slavery they were prepared to act against it whenever the opportunity offered. Sometimes they went quite far. But they were not prepared to jeopardize their own authority in the process. Tact and a light hand were what was needed. Much better, they believed, that abolition should come gradually through the dissemination of enlightened principles among the Africans than by the imposition of decrees by themselves.

There was much to be said for this. Often slavery was better than the alternatives. It was hard to justify interference when the individuals involved lost their means of subsistence thereby and were simply set adrift to starve. Nevertheless, it was an embarrassing fact that since the extension of British rule to Africa, Britons could no longer boast, as they had done earlier in the century, that slavery was forbidden throughout their dominions. This naturally troubled abolitionists at home. More disturbing was the extent to which, in their view, Britain had allowed herself to become involved in actually upholding the institution.

The position of the British and Foreign Anti-Slavery Society as the leading abolitionist organization in the country was no longer disputed. It was, in fact, the only abolitionist body to survive into the seventies, its principal rivals of the sixties having so identified themselves with the American Unionist cause that when the war ended they soon faded away.[7] Auxiliaries no longer played any significant part in its operations. Sympathizers in the provinces either contributed directly to London or supported local branches of various African missionary organizations whose

5. Much to the disappointment of the British and Foreign Anti-Slavery Society whose deputation at Brussels had arrived bearing draft resolutions on the subject of slavery. BFASS *Reporter*, March–April 1890, pp. 30–1.
6. John D. Fage, "British and German colonial rule: a synthesis and summary", in Gifford and Louis, pp. 691–706.
7. The Glasgow Emancipation Society, which had not met since 1863, put in a brief reappearance during the seventies. In November 1873 it sponsored a public meeting to hear a missionary lecture on the subject of slave-trading in east Africa and in 1876 it joined with Broad Street in protesting against an Admiralty circular forbidding British ships' captains from giving refuge to fugitive slaves. Its last recorded meeting was on 2 Feb. 1876: GES Minute Books, 29 Sept. 1873—2 Feb. 1876.

activities it helped sponsor. Financially the Society was in better shape than for almost two decades. Its income averaged around £2,000 a year and thanks to a number of bequests and legacies it had, by the end of the century, succeeded in accumulating a small surplus.[8] With the extension of the popular press in these years and the growing number of contacts by British nationals with slavery, the amount of paper work handled by the Secretary grew prodigiously. But in other respects it remained unchanged. Most of its support still came from Quakers, many of them the sons and grandsons of original members. It continued to reject the use of force as a means of achieving its goals and still maintained that the abolition of slavery was the only effective way of ending the slave trade. It also retained its traditional scepticism towards arguments which sought to judge slavery in pragmatic terms, regardless of whether those who advanced them were slaveholders or, as was now more often the case, British colonial officials.

In the past, the Society had shown no particular fondness for imperialism. It is doubtful if its members could have been brought to approve of it now had the humanitarian prospects been less alluring. What they did, in effect, was to adopt a double standard, deploring new acquisitions when the object was merely political and strategic, but applauding them and even calling for further extensions when some humanitarian object was in view.[9] As always, the Society's interests were far ranging. The struggles for abolition in Brazil and Cuba, slave-trading in Polynesia, and the traffic in indentured labour all round the world received its attention. But its principal and overriding concern was Africa.[10] Throughout the last three decades of the century it sought to maintain a constant pressure on the British government, and through it on foreign governments, to pursue a more active policy against slavery. The major success of these years, for which the Society could claim a measure of credit, was the holding

8. In 1902 this amounted to £5,000: BFASS *Annual Report*, 1902. Among the gifts received by the Society was one of £2,000 from Cardinal Lavigerie as part of a grant given to him by the Papacy to use for antislavery purposes: BFASS *Reporter*, 1889, pp. 2, 52.

9. In 1880, for example, the *Reporter* was simultaneously condemning "distant and costly wars with semi-barbarous nations" and calling for more effective action in Africa against "the slave-trader and his ferocious bands". In January 1882 it hoped that "the year now dawning will not pass over without seeing the English Consular flag raised in more than one place in the Soudan, and on the Red Sea": BFASS *Reporter*, 1 May 1880, p. 38, 1 Jan. 1882, p. 4.

10. BFASS, *A Summary of the Work of the British and Foreign Anti-Slavery Society During the Nineteenth Century* (London, 1900); Joseph Cooper, *The Lost Continent; or, Slavery and the Slave Trade in Africa, 1875, with Observations on the Asiatic Slave-Trade, Carried on under the Name of the Labour Traffic, and Some Other Subjects* (London, 1875).

of the Brussels conference which led to the achievement of the most comprehensive international agreement so far obtained for combating the slave trade.[11] In Parliament the debates revolved mainly round the old question of immediatism versus gradualism, the Society's spokesmen accusing the government of timorousness and delay, while it charged them with being doctrinaire, precipitate and out of touch with the realities of the situation. Each side had a case. There is no doubt that the problems confronting the government were often a good deal more complicated than the Society realized or would admit. To assert in the context of a debate on Zanzibar, as a Society spokesman did on one occasion, that the aim should be "to raise the moral tone of the home life of the Arab population" indicated scant acquaintance with the social structure of that protectorate.[12] On the other hand the Society was consistently successful in shaming the government into removing regulations forbidding the giving of refuge to fugitive slaves by British nationals.[13]

Although these debates continued beyond the end of the century it was becoming plain that indigenous slavery was less of a problem than other forms of exploitation. The Congo scandals of 1897–1906, the disclosure in 1909–10 of forced labour practices by the Amazon Rubber Company, a British registered body, along the Putumayo river in Peru, and the publication in 1910 of the Sanderson Report on indentured labour drew public attention to the seamier aspects of late nineteenth-century imperialism. These revelations were vigorously publicized by the Anti-Slavery Committee.[14] Since the 1890s its attention had been turning from the specific issue of slavery to the more general question of the ill-treatment of native peoples by Europeans. As a result, its work increasingly overlapped with that of the Aborigines Protection Society.[15] In 1909 the two amalgamated to form the Anti-Slavery and Aborigines Protection Society.

11. Greenidge, *Slavery*, pp. 175–6.
12. BFASS *Reporter*, June–July 1899, p. 124.
13. BFASS, *Summary of the Work of the British and Foreign Anti-Slavery Society*, pp. 24–96.
14. Greenidge, pp. 163–6; Harris, *A Century of Emancipation*, pp. 140–215.
15. The APS had been founded in 1838 by the Quaker philanthropist and pioneer ethnologist, Dr Thomas Hodgkin. Hodgkin had earlier been active on the affairs of the ephemeral British African Colonization Society (1834–35) and throughout his life was an outspoken champion of the American Colonization Society. British abolitionists, who had been taught by their American colleagues to regard a colonizationist and a proslavery man as virtually the same thing, viewed both Hodgkin and his organization with suspicion. It was not until American slavery had been abolished that the APS and the BFASS were able to cooperate. The issue which first brought them together was the Jamaican rebellion of 1865. Thomas Hodgkin

This body still exists. Allowing for changes in the value of money its annual budgets are about what they were a century ago. Its list of Committee members still contains a number of Quaker names, although this connection has lately become weaker. Its major concern is now the preservation of primitive peoples and upholding the rights of racial minorities. It has long been active in drawing public attention to discriminatory practices in Southern Rhodesia and is currently much concerned with the position of the Amazonian Indians. It also claims to have been the first body in Britain to have called for public condemnation of South African apartheid.

Although slavery has now been officially abolished almost everywhere, its suppression still remains a problem in certain parts of the world, most notably in the Arabian Peninsula and throughout the countries bordering on the Sahara. Official abolition is, indeed, one of the principal obstacles to effective suppression since it is difficult to hold nations to account for something they have publicly declared non-existent. It would be unjust, however, to hold those states within whose borders it occurs entirely responsible since many of them have been active in instituting measures for its eradication. As the British themselves found, the problems posed by indigenous slavery are always complex and are especially so when, as with the Tuareg in the Sahara, the groups involved are poor and live in areas remote from centres of government.

These facts are acknowledged by the Society. Since the nineteenth century its aggressive moralism has largely disappeared. Dealing with nomadic peoples, or even with the sheikdoms of the Persian Gulf, is obviously quite a different matter from dealing with the United States or France and hardly merits the same feelings of moral outrage. The problem, as the Society sees it, is now principally an economic and social one and as such is best handled by international bodies. Since the 1920s, much of its energy has been directed towards this end. Between the wars it lobbied the League of Nations and was largely responsible for the establishment, in 1932, of a Standing Committee of Experts on Slavery. The United Nations has no such permanent body, although the Society has continually pressed for one. In 1952 the Society was granted consultative status by the UN and this has enabled members to participate in the Economic and Social Council's discussions. What it would like to see, however, is a standing body, similar to the High Commission on Refugees or the Narcotics Control Board, with machinery for collecting information

to Elliott Cresson, 30 Sept. 1840, and Hodgkin to Dr Lovell, 28 March 1841.—Hodgkin Letter Books in the possession of the present Thomas Hodgkin; BFASS Minute Books, 1865–67.

and the authority to recommend emancipation programmes in specific areas.[16]

At present there is little likelihood of this proposal being accepted, mainly, it believes, because of the oversensitive nationalism of the developing nations. The Society is embarrassed that most of its criticisms nowadays are directed against non-European administrations. It points out that this is a historical accident and that the western nations, which did less than they might when they held power, have no cause to feel smug. Nevertheless, slavery remains a touchy subject. In recent years the Society has been described as a tool of the British government, an arm of the Kremlin and an agent of neocolonialism. It is, of course, none of these but a small liberal pressure group with a rather specialized range of interests. In this capacity it has performed, and will no doubt continue to perform, a useful function.

16. Information supplied by the Society's Secretary.

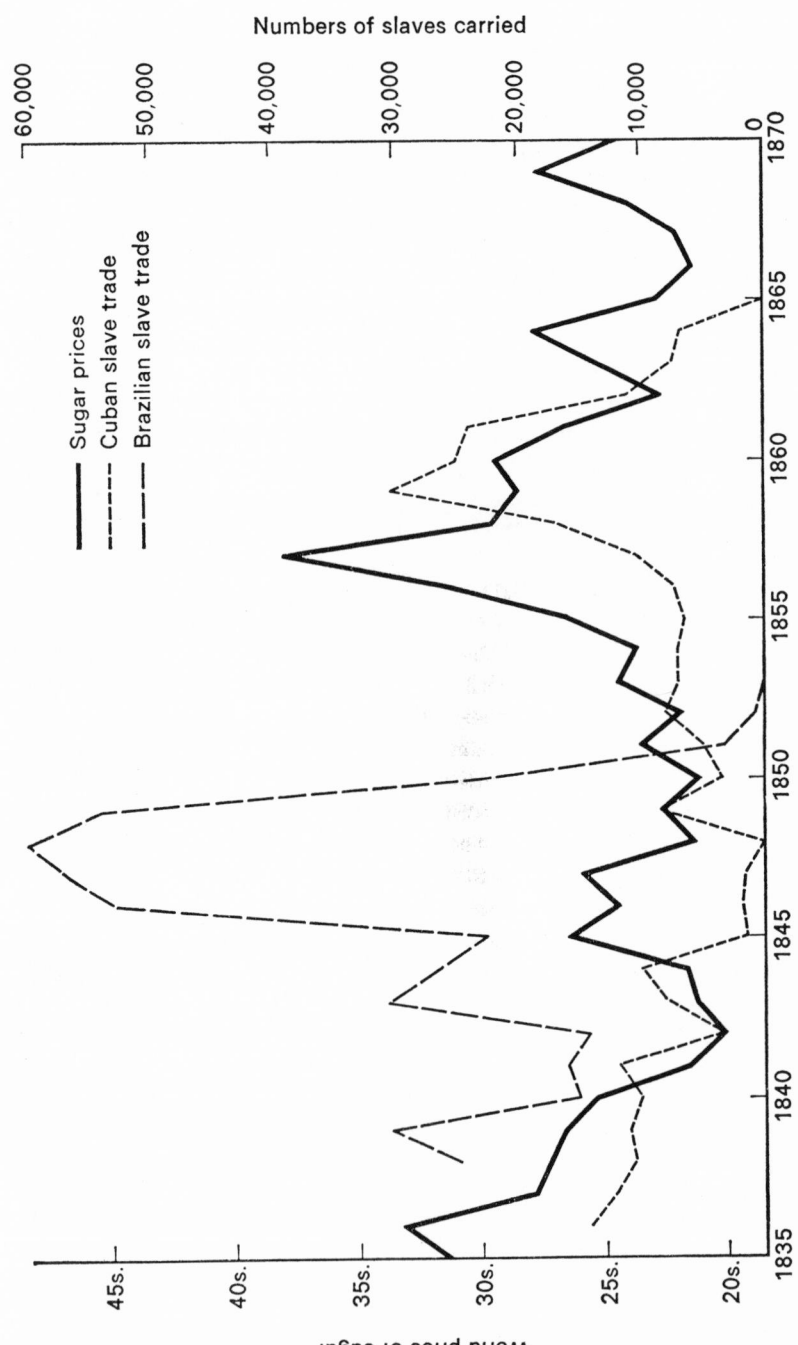

Numbers of slaves carried

60,000   50,000   40,000   30,000   20,000   10,000   0

——— Sugar prices
–·–·– Cuban slave trade
– – – Brazilian slave trade

World price of sugar

45s.   40s.   35s.   30s.   25s.   20s.

1835   1840   1845   1850   1855   1860   1865   1870

Appendix A

See graph on opposite page

SOURCES: *Sugar prices*. Average London prices in shillings per cwt. of Havana sugar (ordinary yellow), exclusive of duty, in P.P., 1852/3, 99, 567; 1867/8, 64, 321; 1868/9, 56, 489; 1870, 61, 559.
Slaves imported, 1836–40. H. J. Matson, *Remarks on the Slave Trade and African Squadron* (London, 1848), p. 7. These figures are taken in preference to the official Foreign Office estimates for these years which, on the basis of other available evidence, appear very much inflated. See Philip D. Curtin, *The Atlantic Slave Trade*, pp. 37–42.
Slaves imported, 1841–64. Compilation of Foreign Office estimates of the numbers of slaves exported westward annually from Africa to Cuba and the Spanish colonies and to Brazil and the Portuguese Colonies, in Christopher Lloyd, *The Navy and the Slave Trade*, Appendix A.

Appendix B

Leading antislavery societies

I. METROPOLITAN ORGANIZATIONS, 1783–1970   PUBLICATIONS

1783–1792	Society of Friends, Meeting for Sufferings Committee on the Slave Trade.*	
1787–1807	Society for the Abolition of the Slave Trade.*	
1807–1827	African Institution.	*Reports* (1807–27)
1823–1839	Society for the Mitigation and Gradual Abolition of Slavery throughout the British Dominions, also known as The Anti-Slavery Society.*	*Reports* (1824–26) *Anti-Slavery Reporter* (1825–36)
1831–183[5?]	Agency Committee of the Anti-Slavery Society; (after 4 July 1832) Agency Anti-Slavery Society; (after 17 Feb, 1834) British and Foreign Society for the Universal Abolition of Negro Slavery and the Slave Trade.	*Report* (1832) *Tourist* (1832–33) *Abolitionist* (1834–35)

* For minute books see Bibliography.

1837–1839	Central Negro Emancipation Committee.	*British Emancipator* (1837–40)
1839–present	British and Foreign Anti-Slavery Society; (after 1909) Anti-Slavery and Aborigines Protection Society; (after 1945) Anti-Slavery Society for the Protection of Human Rights.*	*Reports* (1840–present) *British and Foreign Anti-Slavery Reporter* (title varies, 1840–present)
1839–1843	Society for the Extinction of the Slave Trade and for the Civilization of Africa.	*Friend of Africa* (1841–1843)
1846–1847	Anti-Slavery League.	*Report* (1847)
1859–186[6?]	London Emancipation Committee; (after 11 Nov. 1862) London Emancipation Society.	

2.   INDEPENDENT PROVINCIAL ORGANIZATIONS, 1840–1870

1833–1876	Glasgow Emancipation Society.	*Reports* (1833–51)
1833–186[5?]	Hibernian Anti-Slavery Society (Dublin).	
1833–186[5?]	Edinburgh Ladies' Emancipation Society.	
1840–1861 (Became ind. 1851)	Bristol and Clifton Ladies' Anti-Slavery Society.*	
184[6?]–185[6?]	Newcastle upon Tyne Free Produce Association.	*The Slave* (1851–56)
1853–1854	Manchester Anti-Slavery Union.	*Anti-Slavery Watchman* (1853–54)
1854–1855	North of England Anti-Slavery and India Reform League.	
1853–185[5?]	Leeds Anti-Slavery Society.	
1857–186[5?]	Leeds Young Men's Anti-Slavery Society.	
1862–1866	Manchester Union and Emancipation Society.	

* For minute books see Bibliography.

Appendix C

Eric Williams and slavery

It was the belief of the abolitionists that the success of their movement represented the triumph of high moral principles over the forces of evil. For more than a hundred years, historians agreed. Contemporaries had referred to Wilberforce and his circle, usually derisively, as "the saints". Historians took the term literally. In the canons of Whig history, the abolitionists were securely enshrined.

Then came Eric Williams with his *Capitalism and Slavery* (Chapel Hill, 1944) which baldly asserted that the abolitionists' importance had been "seriously misunderstood and grossly exaggerated" (p. 178) and that abolition was primarily the result of economic forces, in other words of greed, self-interest and the lust for power, the same forces that had built up the slave system: "When British capitalism depended on the West Indies, [the capitalists] ignored slavery or defended it. When British capitalism found the West Indian monopoly a nuisance they destroyed West Indian slavery as the first step in the destruction of West Indian monopoly" (p. 169). The abolitionists' role, in so far as they had one, was in helping this process along. A few of them (he speaks highly of Clarkson) were genuine idealists but they had no clear idea of what they were doing. What really counted were the forces of economic, not moral, change. It was "mercantilism" that created the slave system and "mature capitalism" that destroyed it. He states his case forcefully: "The attack falls into three phases: the attack on the slave trade, the attack on slavery, the attack on the preferential sugar duties. The slave trade was abolished in 1807, slavery in 1833, the sugar preference in 1846. These three events are inseparable" (p. 136).

But in what sense were they inseparable? At first sight the Williams thesis appears strikingly simple—so much so that it achieves the distinction, rare among ambitious works of scholarship, of being aesthetically pleasing. But on closer examination it turns out to be anything but simple. At one level it sets out to show how, from 1783 onwards, the economic and political interests which supported the colonial slave system were gradually weakened and replaced by the emerging forces of industrial capitalism. At another level it purports to prove that these new interests were inherently hostile to British slavery. And at yet other levels it is a statement about the relative importance of economic as opposed to other sorts of motive, and, closely bound up with this, the extent to which selfless idealism, such as that attributed to the abolitionists, contributed.

It says much for the boldness of Williams's conception that it is still the subject of lively debate. In recent years it has come in for a good deal of hostile comment. Few historians today, however, would dissent from his conclusion that the decline of the West Indian interest and the appearance of new interests not bound up with slavery were crucial factors. Plainly, without these changes the ideas and principles proclaimed by the abolition-ists would not have triumphed in the way they did or at the time they did. Similarly, it is doubtful if many would nowadays associate themselves with the view that Britain's actions reflected a singular measure of national virtue or placed her on a different moral plane from other nations—a claim which foreigners have understandably found galling.

The objections to Williams's account have mostly related to his second contention, namely that Britain's economic development in the early nineteenth century not only permitted but in some way required the destruction of slavery. This is a peculiarly difficult matter either to prove or disprove since it necessarily involves making judgments about the motives which were uppermost in the minds of those responsible. Williams's own evidence is sketchy. He is, of course, quite right in his assumption that public statements are not always to be taken at their face value. Expressions of high moral intent are often a cloak for less worthy designs, as can be seen from the way in which the protectionists exploited the moral responsibility case during the sugar duties debate. This, however, is a technique which can equally well be used the other way around, as when the abolitionists argued that emancipation would increase labour efficiency. In these instances the deception is easily recognized, but in other cases, particularly when many conflicting interests were involved, as was true of the debates over the 1807 and 1833 Bills, the overriding motive is harder to identify. What is needed, as Roger Anstey, in a fine critique of Williams,[1] has pointed out, is a clear statement as to what the economic considerations were and a demonstration of how they came to be translated into legislative action.

In Williams's own work this is scarcely atempted. His statement that "overproduction [of sugar] in 1807 demanded abolition; overproduction in 1833 demanded emancipation" (p. 152) amounts to little more than assertion. In the lengthy debates of 1807 the possible diminution in sugar production which might be expected to follow the ending of the slave trade was only twice mentioned and there is no ancillary evidence to suggest that this was a consideration to which contemporaries attached importance.[2]

Similar objections apply to his treatment of the emancipation issue. Here his argument is that the capitalists "destroyed West Indian slavery as a first step in the destruction of West Indian monopoly" (p. 169). The way in which he sees this happening may be best expressed in his own words: "The West Indian situation was aggravated by the fact that production was in excess of home consumption. This surplus, estimated at twenty-five per cent, had to be sold in European markets in competition with cheaper Brazilian or Cuban sugar. This could be done only by subsidies and bounties. The West Indian planters were being paid, in fact, to enable them to com-pete with people who, as we have seen, were some of Britain's best customers.

1. Roger T. Anstey, "*Capitalism and Slavery*: a critique", *Economic History Review, 21* (1968), 307–20.
2. *Ibid*, pp. 313–15. I am also indebted to Professor Anstey for sending me a copy of his forthcoming article, "Towards a Re-Interpretation of the Abolition of the British Slave Trade, 1806–07" which shows that the interplay of economic and idealistic motives among those responsible for framing the 1806 and 1807 Bills was a good deal more complicated than Williams allows.

... To the capitalists this was intolerable" (p. 152). Actually, the bounties to which he refers were simply refunds of taxes paid on sugar brought into Britain which were repaid when, after undergoing manufacture, it was exported to the Continent. It is hard to see why anyone should have objected to this system, or to the new system, introduced in 1833, which allowed all sugar, regardless of origin, to enter Britain free of duty providing it was manufactured in bond and re-exported.[3] This question was not raised by any speaker during the emancipation debates. In fact the whole monopoly issue was hardly touched on. One would be hard pressed to see in this any deep seated designs on the part of the spokesmen of industrial capitalism. The fact is that British consumers, capitalist or otherwise, had little cause for complaint in the early thirties. Sugar prices on the London market were lower than ever before. It is true that had the British been free to import Brazilian sugar they would have been lower still, but the difference seldom amounted to more than six shillings per hundredweight. This was quite a different situation from the one which arose seven years later when the differential widened to twenty-eight shillings.[4]

It could, of course, be argued that the anti-monopolists were being extraordinarily devious and that their aim in carrying through emancipation was to restrict West Indian production so that it would coincide with home demand. In this way they would create a true monopoly, so driving up prices to such an extent that popular sentiment would demand that the system be destroyed. At one point this is what Williams appears to be saying. "This was parliamentary strategy. Every effort was being made to make West Indian cultivation as expensive as possible" (p. 153). Who, one wonders, planned this strategy and did no one point out that having created a true monopoly they might have difficulty in getting rid of it? Until substantiating evidence is produced it makes more sense to assume that monopoly was not a major issue in 1833 and only became one when sugar prices subsequently rose.

When he descends to the level of attributing roles to individuals or small groups, Williams is often equally unconvincing. Joseph Sturge (p. 158) is shown as a representative of the new capitalist class that was turning against the West Indies. Did he have the destruction of the West Indian monopoly in mind? Plainly not. Who would suppose from Williams's account that he led the national antislavery organization into a prolonged struggle for the *retention* of the preferential tariffs. His statement (p. 191) that the likely effect which the equalization of the sugar duties would have on the slave systems of Latin America "aroused not even comment from the abolitionists" could hardly be further from the mark. Equalization was, as we have seen, the principal abolitionist issue of the 1840s. No less misleading are his innuendoes (pp. 186–87) regarding the investments made by individual

3. In 1831–32 exports of sugar amounted to approximately 25 per cent of imports while bounties accounted for £1,124,137 out of a total tax levy of £5,778,413. P.P., 1831/2, *34*, 575–81. For a fuller account of the sugar tariff question see L. J. Ragatz, *The Fall of the Planter Class in the British Caribbean, 1763–1833* (New York, 1928), pp. 353–83.
4. The prices of Brazilian and British colonial sugars are given in P.P., 1841, *26* (290), 281.

abolitionists in the East Indies which, he suggests, influenced their views on West Indian affairs. He fails to note that abolitionists made a point of investing in East Indian enterprises precisely *because* they disapproved of West Indian slavery. These are not isolated examples. After a careful examination of his treatment of Pitt and Palmerston, Professor Anstey concludes that Williams "uses evidence misleadingly, or makes large claims on only partial evidence, or ignores evidence".[5]

This is not the place to attempt an overall assessment of the Williams thesis, which would require much more research, particularly with respect to the abolition of the slave trade, than has so far been undertaken. The present study overlaps Williams's at a few points only. Nevertheless, it is evident that the thesis, as it stands, is in need of substantial modification. If the forces of industrial capitalism were not inherently hostile to British slavery—and Williams patently fails to show that they were—then it follows that the attack on it must have been motivated by other considerations. On present evidence it would appear that these were primarily religious and idealistic in origin. The economic changes described by Williams were important to the extent that they removed obstacles which had stood in the humanitarians' way. British governments were prepared to go along with the attack on slavery so long as they could be assured that they would not have to sacrifice too much in the process. In 1807 and 1833 this was done and they bowed to the humanitarians' demands. In 1846, faced by an enormous discrepancy in price between colonial and foreign sugar and a mounting clamour from all classes for the removal of the preferential tariffs, the Russell administration reversed a long established policy, much to the disgust of the abolitionists who had hoped for better from their government.

5. *Economic History Review, 21* (1968), 318.

Bibliography

As material for this book has been drawn from extremely varied sources, only the more important items are listed here. For a full list of the sources used readers should refer to the footnotes in the text.

1. *Manuscripts*

This study is based in large part on the records of various British antislavery bodies. The most valuable—and voluminous—of these are the British and Foreign Anti-Slavery Society Papers in Rhodes House, Oxford. They include the Minute Books of the London Committee (vol. 1: 1839–42; vol. 2: 1842–47; vol. 3: 1847–60; vol. 4: 1860–72); the Memorials and Petitions of the Society (2 vols, 1839–70); and incoming correspondence filed in sections under the names of recipients (Tredgold, 7 vols; Beaumont, 1 vol.; Scoble, 12 vols; Bolton, 4 vols; Chamerovzow, 12 vols; Sturge, 3 vols; Clarkson, 1 vol.). The Society did not begin keeping a record of outgoing letters until March 1869.

The principal source for the study of the activities of the British Garrisonians is the vast collection of letters to and from British abolitionists in the Garrison, May, Weston, Chapman, Quincy-Webb and Estlin collections in Boston Public Library. These are all well indexed. I was also fortunate in being able to consult a typescript selection of these letters prepared by Dr G. C. Taylor.

The following is a list of the other major collections used and their locations:

Thompson-Clarkson MSS 2/9, Friends' House, London.
Minute Book of the Meeting for Sufferings Committee on the Slave Trade, 1783–92, Friends' House, London.
Minute and Account Books of the Standing Committee of the Meeting for Sufferings Appointed to Aid in Promoting the Total Abolition of the Slave Trade and Slavery, 1820–33, MSS 115–17, Friends' House, London.
Society for the Abolition of the Slave Trade, Committee Minutes, 1787–1807, British Museum.
Society for the Mitigation and Gradual Abolition of Slavery Throughout the British Dominions, Committee Minutes, 1823–1840, Rhodes House, Oxford.
Glasgow Emancipation Society, Committee Minutes, 1833–76, correspondence pamphlets, etc., Mitchell Library, Glasgow.
Bristol and Clifton Ladies' Anti-Slavery Society, Committee Minutes, 1840–61, correspondence, pamphlets, etc., Estlin Collection, Dr. Williams's Library, London.
A certain amount of antislavery material will also be found in the Sturge Papers, British Museum; the Brougham Papers, University College, London; and in the Letter Books of the Society of Friends, Friends' House, London.

2. *Government publications*

In this category the two most important sources are Hansard's *Parliamentary Debates* and House of Commons *Sessional Papers*. The latter proved especially fruitful with respect to the West Indies, the slave trade, India, coolies and the sugar duties question. Following up particular topics is made easy by two comprehensive and accurate indexes: *General Index to the Accounts and Papers, Reports of Commissioners, Estimates, etc., Printed by Order of the House of Commons, 1801–1852* (London, 1853), and *General Alphabetical Index to the Bills, Reports, Estimates, Accounts and Papers, Printed by Order of the House of Commons, 1852–1899* (London, 1909).

3. *Newspapers and periodicals*

For a list of antislavery periodicals and of the organizations publishing them see Appendix B above. In addition to these, use was made of the files of Garrison's *Liberator* (Boston, 1831–65), which contains much material on the activities of British abolitionists. In spite of its editorial bias, the *Liberator* made a practice of reprinting articles on the slavery issue in Britain, many of them from British publications, reflecting a wide variety of viewpoints.

Many of the issues with which the abolitionists were concerned were matters of general public interest—apprenticeship, the slave trade, the sugar duties, etc.—and so received considerable attention in the national papers. Partly for reasons of convenience, I have chosen to describe these mainly in terms of what was said in Parliament, which of course was also where many of the decisions on these issues were made. But the same shades of opinion could equally well have been illustrated from the newspapers of the period.

4. *Miscellaneous antislavery publications*

ADAM, WILLIAM, *The Law and Custom of Slavery in British India: In a Series of Letters to T. F. Buxton Esq.*, London, 1840.

ADAMS, H. G., ed., *God's Image in Ebony*, London, 1854.

ARMISTEAD, WILSON, ed., *Five Hundred Thousand Strokes for Freedom*, London, 1853.

—— *A Tribute to the Negro: Being a Vindication of the Moral, Intellectual and Religious Capabilities of the Coloured Portion of Mankind*, Manchester, 1848.

BRISTOL AND CLIFTON LADIES' ANTI-SLAVERY SOCIETY, *Special Report of the Bristol and Clifton Ladies' Anti-Slavery Society ... January 1851 to June 1852, with a Statement of the Reasons for its Separation from the British and Foreign Anti-Slavery Society*, London, 1852.

BRITISH AND FOREIGN ANTI-SLAVERY SOCIETY, *An Address to Esparto*, London, 1861.

—— *The African Slave Trade to Cuba*, London, 1862.

—— *American Slavery: Address of the Committee of the British and Foreign Anti-Slavery Society to the Moderator, Office Bearers and Members of the General Assembly of the Free Church of Scotland*, London, 1846.

—— *British Aid to the Confederates*, London, 1863.

—— *The Crisis in the United States*, London, 1862.

BRITISH AND FOREIGN ANTI-SLAVERY SOCIETY, *Emigration from India: The Export of Coolies and Other Labourers to Mauritius*, London, 1842.

—— *Hill Coolies: a brief Exposure of the Deplorable Condition of the Hill Coolies in British Guiana and Mauritius*, London, 1840.

—— *Proceedings of the General Anti-Slavery Convention Called by the Committee of the British and Foreign Anti-Slavery Society, June 12 to June 23, 1840*, London, 1841.

—— *Proceedings of the General Anti-Slavery Convention Called by the Committee of the British and Foreign Anti-Slavery Society, June 13th to June 20, 1843*, London, 1843.

—— *Slavery and Internal Slave Trade in the United States of North America*, London, 1841.

—— *Slavery and the Slave Trade in British India*, London, 1841.

—— *The Slave Trade As It Is*, London, 1860.

—— *The Slave Traders of Liverpool*, London, 1862.

—— *Special Report of the Anti-Slavery Convention held in Paris . . . 1867*, London, 1869.

—— *A Summary of the Work of the British and Foreign Anti-Slavery Society During the Nineteenth Century*, London, 1900.

—— *Texas: Its Claims to be Recognised as an Independent Power by Great Britain*, London, 1839.

—— *The Treatment of African Immigrants in Jamaica*, London, 1848.

—— *The Trial of Pedro de Zulueta in the Central Criminal Court of the City of London*, London, 1844.

—— *What the South is Fighting For*, London, 1863.

BUXTON, T. F., *The African Slave Trade and Its Remedy*, 2nd edn, London, 1840.

CLARKSON, THOMAS, *The History of the Rise, Progress and Accomplishment of the Abolition of the African Slave Trade by the British Parliament*, 2 vols, London, 1808.

—— *A Letter to the Clergy of the Various Denominations and to the Slave-holding Planters in the Southern Parts of the United States of America*, London, 1841.

COCHIN, AUGUSTIN, *The Results of Emancipation*, trans. M. L. Booth, 3rd edn, Boston, 1863.

EDGERTON, WALTER, *A History of the Separation in the Indiana Yearly Meeting of Friends: Which Took Place in the Winter of 1842 and 1843 on the Anti-Slavery Question*, Cincinnati, 1856.

ESTLIN, JOHN BISHOP, *A Brief Notice of American Slavery and the Abolition Movement*, Bristol, 1846.

FÉLICE, GUILLAUME DE, *Emancipation Immédiate et Complète des Esclaves: Appel aux Abolitionistes*, Paris, 1846.

GARRISON, WILLIAM LLOYD, *West Indian Emancipation: A Speech Delivered at Abingdon, Massachussetts, on the First Day of August, 1854*, Boston, 1854.

HILDRETH, RICHARD, *The "Ruin" of Jamaica*, New York, 1855.

MARTINEAU, HARRIET, *The Martyr Age of the United States of America*, Newcastle upon Tyne 1840.

QUINCY, EDMUND, *An Examination of the Charges of Mr. John Scoble and Mr. Lewis Tappan Against the American Anti-Slavery Society*, London, 1852.

STEPHEN, SIR GEORGE, *The Niger Trade Considered in Connexion with the African Blockade*, London, 1849.

—— *A Third Letter to the Right Hon. Lord John Russell on the Plans for the Civilization of Africa*, London, 1840.

STUART, CHARLES, *Liberia: Or the American Colonization Scheme Examined and Exposed*, Glasgow, 1833.

STURGE, JOSEPH, and HARVEY, THOMAS, *The West Indies in 1837, being the Journal of a Visit to Antigua and Jamaica . . . For the Purpose of Ascertaining the Actual Condition of the Negro Population*, London, 1838.

TAPPAN, LEWIS, *Reply to Charges Brought Against the American and Foreign Anti-Slavery Society*, London, 1852.

THOME, J. A., and KIMBALL, J. H., *Emancipation in the West Indies. A Six Months' Tour in Antigua, Barbadoes and Jamaica in 1837*, New York, 1838.

THOMPSON, GEORGE, *A Voice to the United States of America from the Metropolis of Scotland, being an Account of Various Meetings held in Edinburgh on the Subject of American Slavery upon the Return of Mr. G. Thompson from his Mission to that Country*, Edinburgh, 1836.

WEBB, RICHARD D., *The National Anti-Slavery Societies of England and the United States*, Dublin, 1852.

5.   *Biographies, letters and other source materials*

ABEL, A. H., and KLINGBERG, F. J., eds., *A Side-light on Anglo-American Relations, 1839–1858, Furnished by the Correspondence of Lewis Tappan and Others with the British and Foreign Anti-Slavery Society*, Lancaster, Pa., 1927.

ALLEN, WILLIAM, and THOMSON, T. R. H., *Narrative of the Expedition Sent by Her Majesty's Government to the River Niger in 1841*, 2 vols, London, 1848.

ALLEN, WILLIAM, G., *The American Prejudice Against Colour*, London, 1853.

BANDINEL, J., *Some Account of the Trade in Slaves from Africa, as Connected with Europe and America, Especially with Reference to the Efforts made by the British Government for its Extinction*, London, 1842.

BARNES, GILBERT H., and DUMOND, DWIGHT L., eds, *Letters of Theodore Dwight Weld, Angeline Grimké Weld and Sarah Grimké, 1822–1844*, 2 vols, New York, 1934.

BELL, JOHN HYSLOP, *British Folk and British India Fifty Years Ago: Joseph Pease and His Contemporaries*, London, 1891.

BROWN, WILLIAM WELLS, *Three Years in Europe*, London, 1852.

BUXTON, CHARLES, *Memoirs of Sir Thomas Fowell Buxton, Bart., with Selections from His Correspondence*, London, 1848.

DOUGLASS, FREDERICK, *Life and Times of Frederick Douglass*, 1892.

GARRISON, W. P., and GARRISON, F. J., *William Lloyd Garrison, 1805–1879, the Story of his Life Told by his Children*, 4 vols, New York, 1885–89.

GURLEY, R. R., *Mission to England on Behalf of the American Colonization Society*, Washington, D.C., 1841.

HINTON, JOHN HOWARD, *Memoir of William Knibb, Missionary to Jamaica*, London, 1847.

HOARE, PRINCE, *Memoirs of Granville Sharp*, London, 1820.

LIVINGSTONE, DAVID, *Missionary Travels and Researches in South Africa*, London, 1855.

—— *Narrative of an Expedition to the Zambezi and its Tributaries*, London, 1865.

LONDON FRIENDS' INSTITUTE, *Biographical Catalogue*, London, 1888.

MADDEN, T. M., ed., *The Memoirs, Chiefly Autobiographical, from 1798 to 1866 of R. R. Madden*, London, 1891.

MASSIE, JAMES WILLIAM, *America: The Origins of her Present Conflict, her Prospects for the Slave and her Claim for Anti-Slavery Sympathy, Illustrated by Incidents of Travel During a Tour in the Summer of 1863*, London, 1864.

MOTT, JAMES, *Three Months in Great Britain*, Philadelphia, 1841.

RICHARD, HENRY, *Memoirs of Joseph Sturge*, London, 1865.

RICHARDSON, JAMES, *Travels in the Great Desert of Sahara in 1845 and 1846*, 2 vols, London, 1848.

STANTON, HENRY B., *Sketches of Reforms and Reformers of Great Britain and Ireland*, New York, 1849.

STEPHEN, SIR GEORGE, *Anti-Slavery Recollections: In a Series of Letters Addressed to Mrs Beecher Stowe*, London, 1854.

STOWE, CHARLES E., *Life of Harriet Beecher Stowe, Compiled from her Letters and Journals*, Cambridge, Mass., 1889.

STOWE, HARRIET BEECHER, *Sunny Memories of Foreign Lands*, London, 1854.

STURGE, JOSEPH, *A Visit to the United States in 1841*, London, 1842.

TOLLES, F. B., ed., *Slavery and "The Woman Question": Lucretia Mott's Diary of her Visit to Great Britain to Attend the World's Anti-Slavery Convention of 1840*, Haverford, Penn., 1952.

WARD, SAMUEL RINGGOLD, *Autobiography of a Fugitive Negro*, London, 1855.

6. *Secondary materials: Books*

ADAMS, EPHRAIM DOUGLAS, *Great Britain and the American Civil War*, 2 vols, New York, 1925.

BANAJI, D. R., *Slavery in British India*, Bombay, 1934.

BARNES, GILBERT H., *The Antislavery Impulse, 1830–1844*, New York, 1933.

BETHELL, LESLIE, *The Abolition of the Brazilian Slave Trade: Britain, Brazil and the Slave Trade Question, 1807–1869*, Cambridge, 1970.

BOLT, CHRISTINE A. *The Anti-Slavery Movement and Reconstruction*, London, 1969.

BURN, W. L., *The British West Indies*, London, 1951.

—— *Emancipation and Apprenticeship in the British West Indies*, London, 1937.

CORWIN, ARTHUR F., *Spain and the Abolition of Slavery in Cuba, 1817–1886*, Austin, Texas, 1967.

COUPLAND, SIR REGINALD, *The British Anti-Slavery Movement*, London, 1933.

CURTIN, PHILIP D., *The Atlantic Slave Trade: A Census*, Madison, Wisconsin, 1969.

CURTIN, PHILIP D., *Image of Africa: British Ideas and Action, 1780–1850*, Madison, Wisconsin, 1964.

—— *Two Jamaicas: The Role of Ideas in a Tropical Colony, 1830–1865*, Cambridge, Mass., 1955.

DAVIS, DAVID B., *The Problem of Slavery in Western Culture*, Ithaca, New York, 1966.

DEERR, NOEL, *The History of Sugar*, 2 vols, London, 1949–1950.

DRAKE, THOMAS E., *Quakers and Slavery in America*, New Haven, 1950.

DUBERMAN, MARTIN, ed., *The Anti-Slavery Vanguard: New Essays on the Abolitionists*, Princeton, 1965.

DUMOND, DWIGHT L., *Antislavery: The Crusade for Freedom in America*, Ann Arbor, 1961.

ELKINS, STANLEY, *Slavery: A Problem in American Institutional and Intellectual Life*, Chicago, 1959.

EMDEN, PAUL H., *Quakers in Commerce: A Record of Business Achievement*, London, 1940.

FILLER, LOUIS B., *The Crusade Against Slavery*, New York, 1960.

FONER, PHILIP S., *Frederick Douglass*, New York, 1964.

FOX, E. L., *The American Colonization Society, 1817–1840*, Baltimore, 1919.

GARA, LARRY, *The Liberty Line, the Legend of the Underground Railroad*, Lexington, Kentucky, 1961.

GREENIDGE, C. W. W., *Slavery*, London, 1958.

GRIGGS, EARL LESLIE, *Thomas Clarkson, Friend of the Slaves*, London, 1936.

HARRIS, SIR JOHN, *A Century of Emancipation*, London, 1933.

HITCHINS, F. H., *The Colonial Land and Immigration Commission*, Philadelphia, 1931.

HOBHOUSE, STEPHEN, *Joseph Sturge: His Life and his Work*, London, 1919.

HOWARD, WARREN S., *American Slavers and the Federal Law, 1837–1862*, Berkeley, 1963.

JENKINS, WILLIAM S., *Proslavery Thought in the Old South*, Chapel Hill, 1935.

JORDAN, DONALDSON, and PRATT, EDWIN J., *Europe and the American Civil War*, Oxford, 1931.

KLINGBERG, F. J., *The Anti-Slavery Movement in England*, New Haven, 1926.

KRADITOR, AILEEN S., *Means and Ends in American Abolitionism: Garrison and His Critics on Strategy and Tactics, 1834–1850*, New York, 1969.

LLOYD, CHRISTOPHER, *The Navy and the Slave Trade: the Suppression of the African Slave Trade in the Nineteenth-Century*, London, 1949.

McPHERSON, JAMES M., *The Struggle for Equality: Abolitionists and the Negro in the Civil War and Reconstruction*, Princeton, 1964.

MARTIN, GASTON, *L'Abolition de l'Esclavage, 27 Avril, 1848*, Paris, 1948.

MATHIESON, WILLIAM LAW, *British Slavery and its Abolition, 1823–1838* London, 1926.

—— *British Slave Emancipation, 1838–1849*, London, 1932.

—— *The Sugar Colonies and Governor Eyre*, London, 1936.

—— *Great Britain and the Slave Trade, 1839–1865*, London, 1929.

MELLOR, G. R., *British Imperial Trusteeship, 1783–1850*, London, 1951.

NUERMBERGER, RUTH A., *The Free Produce Movement: A Quaker Protest Against Slavery*, Durham, North Carolina, 1942.

NYE, RUSSEL B., *William Lloyd Garrison and the Humanitarian Reformers*, Boston, 1955.

PARRY, J. H., and SHERLOCK, P. M., *A Short History of the West Indies*, London, 1963.

QUARLES, BENJAMIN, *Frederick Douglass*, Washington, D.C., 1948.

RICHARDS, LEONARD L., *"Gentlemen of Property and Standing": anti-abolition mobs in Jacksonian America*, New York, 1970.

RATNER, LORMAN, *Powder Keg: Northern Opposition to the Antislavery Movement, 1831–1840*, New York, 1968.

SOULSBY, H. G., *The Right of Search and the Slave Trade in Anglo-American Relations 1813–1862*, Baltimore, 1933.

STAUDENRAUS, PHILIP J., *The African Colonization Movement, 1816–1865*, New York, 1961.

THISTLETHWAITE, FRANK, *The Anglo-American Connection in the Early Nineteenth Century*, Philadelphia and Oxford, 1959.

THOMAS, J. L., *The Liberator: William Lloyd Garrison*, Boston, 1963.

WILLIAMS, ERIC, *Capitalism and Slavery*, Chapel Hill, 1944.

WILLS, A. J., *An Introduction to the History of Central Africa*, 2nd edn, London, 1967.

WILSON, FORREST, *Crusader in Crinoline: the Life of Harriet Beecher Stowe*, London, 1942.

WINKS, ROBIN W., *The Blacks in Canada: A History*, New Haven, 1971.

WYATT-BROWN, BERTRAM, *Lewis Tappan and the Evangelical War Against Slavery*, Cleveland, Ohio, 1969.

7. *Articles*

ANSTEY, ROGER T., *"Capitalism and Slavery*: a critique", *Economic History Review, 21* (1968) 307–20.

CURTIN, PHILIP D., "Sugar prices and West Indian prosperity", *Journal of Economic History, 14* (1954), 157–73.

DAVIS, DAVID B., "The emergence of immediatism in British and American antislavery thought", *Mississippi Valley Historical Review, 49* (1962–63), 209–30.

—— "James Cropper and the British anti-slavery movement, 1821–1823", *Journal of Negro History, 45*, (1960), 241–58.

—— "James Cropper and the British anti-slavery movement, 1823–1833", *Journal of Negro History, 46* (1961), 154–73.

DONALD, DAVID, "Toward a reconsideration of the abolitionists", in D. Donald, *Lincoln Reconsidered: Essays on the Civil War Era* (New York, 1956), pp. 18–36.

ERICKSON, EDGAR L., "East India coolies in the West Indies", *Journal of Modern History, 4* (1934), 127–46.

GALLAGHER, J., "Fowell Buxton and the new African policy, 1838–1842" *Cambridge Historical Journal, 10* (1950–52), 36–58.

HAMER, PHILIP M., "British consuls and the Negro Seamen Acts, 1850–1860", *Journal of Southern History, 1* (1935), 138–68.

—— "Great Britain, the United States and the Negro Seamen Acts, 1822–1848", *Journal of Southern History, 1* (1935), 3–28.

KLINGBERG, F. J., "Harriet Beecher Stowe and social reform in England", *American Historical Review, 43* (1938–39), 542–52.

MIERS, SUZANNE, "The Brussels Conference of 1889–1890: the place of the slave trade in the politics of Great Britain and Germany", in P. Gifford and W. R. Lewis, eds, *Britain and Germany in Africa: Imperial Rivalry and Colonial Rule,* New Haven, 1967, pp. 83–118.

PAGET, H., "The free village system in Jamaica". *Jamaican Historical Review, 1* (1945), 31–48.

RICE, C. DUNCAN, "The anti-slavery mission of George Thompson to the United States, 1834–1835", *Journal of American Studies, 2* (1968), 13–31.

SHEPPERSON, GEORGE A., "Thomas Chalmers, the Free Church of Scotland and the South", *Journal of Southern History, 17* (1951), 517–37.

SIOUSSAT, ST GEORGE L., "Duff Green's 'England and the United States' with an Introductory Study of American Opposition to the Quintuple Treaty of 1841", *Proceedings of the American Antiquarian Society, 40* (1930), 175–276.

SMITHER, HARRIET, "English abolitionism and the annexation of Texas", *Southwestern Historical Quarterly, 32* (1928–29), 193–205.

TEMPERLEY, HOWARD, "British and American abolitionists compared", in M. B. Duberman, ed., *The Antislavery Vanguard,* Princeton, 1965, pp. 343–61.

—— "The O'Connell-Stevenson contretemps: a reflection of the Anglo-American slavery issue", *Journal of Negro History, 47* (1962), 217–33.

WOODS, JOHN, "The correspondence of Benjamin Rush and Granville Sharp, 1773–1809", *Journal of American Studies, 1* (1967), 1–38.

8. Unpublished theses

BILLINGTON, LOUIS, "Some connections between British and American reform movements, 1830–1860, with special reference to the anti-slavery movement", University of Bristol, MA, 1966.

BOTSFORD, R., "Scotland and the American Civil War", University of Edinburgh, PhD, 1956.

HARWOOD, THOMAS F., "Great Britain and American antislavery", University of Texas, PhD, 1959.

HUNT, E. M., "The North of England agitation for the abolition of the slave trade, 1780–1800", University of Manchester, MA, 1959.

LIPSCOMB, PATRICK C. III, "William Pitt and the abolition of the slave trade", University of Texas, PhD, 1960.

OWEN, G. E. "Welsh anti-slavery sentiments, 1790–1865: a survey of public opinion", University of Wales, MA, 1964.

PILGRIM, E. I., "Anti-slavery sentiment in Great Britain, 1841–1854, its nature and decline, with special reference to its influence upon British policy towards the former slave colonies", University of Cambridge, PhD, 1957.

RICE, C. DUNCAN, "The Scottish Factor in the Fight Against American Slavery", University of Edinburgh, PhD, 1969.

TAYLOR, G. C., "Some American Reformers and their Influence on Reform Movements in Great Britain, 1830–1860", University of Edinburgh PhD, 1960.

Index

Index